STRINDBERG: THE PLAYS

VOLUME TWO

THE PLAYS OF STRINDBERG
(1849–1912)
with their dates of composition

PRE-INFERNO

1869   A Birthday Gift (lost)
      The Freethinker
1870   Hermione
      In Rome
1871   The Outlaw
1872–1877   Master Olof
1876–1877   Anno 48
1880   The Secret of the Guild
1882   Lucky Peter's Journey
      Sir Bengt's Wife
1886–1887 The Robbers (The
      Comrades)
1887   The Father
1888   Miss Julie
      Creditors
1888–1889 The Stronger
1889   Pariah
      The People of Hemsö
      Simoom
1892   The Keys of Heaven
      The First Warning
      Debit and Credit
      In the Face of Death
      A Mother's Love
      Playing with Fire
      The Bond

POST-INFERNO

1898   To Damascus, *Part I*
      To Damascus, *Part II*
      Advent
1899   There are Crimes and
      Crimes

      The Saga of the Folkungs
      Gustav Vasa
      Erik the Fourteenth
1900   Gustav Adolf
      Midsummer
      Casper's Shrove Tuesday
      Easter
      The Dance of Death, *Part I*
      The Dance of Death, *Part II*
1901   The Virgin Bride
      Swanwhite
      Charles XII
      To Damascus, *Part III*
      Engelbrekt
      Queen Christina
      A Dream Play
1902   Gustav III
      The Dutchman (fragment)
      The Nightingale of Witten-
      berg
1903   Exodus (Moses)
      Hellas (Socrates)
      The Lamb and the Beast
      (Christ)
1907   Storm
      The Burnt House
      The Ghost Sonata
      Toten-Insel (fragment)
      The Pelican
1908   The Last Knight
      Abu Casem's Slippers
      The Protector
      The Earl of Bjälbo
1909   The Black Glove
      The Great Highway

AUGUST STRINDBERG

THE PLAYS
VOLUME TWO

Introduced and
translated from the Swedish
by MICHAEL MEYER

SECKER & WARBURG
LONDON

THESE TRANSLATIONS
FIRST PUBLISHED IN ENGLAND 1975 BY
MARTIN SECKER & WARBURG LIMITED
14 CARLISLE STREET, LONDON W1V 6NN

SBN 436 50005 1 (HARDCOVER)

TEXT SET IN 11/12 pt IBM BASKERVILLE,
PRINTED BY PHOTOLITHOGRAPHY, AND
BOUND IN GREAT BRITAIN AT THE
PITMAN PRESS, BATH

CONTENTS

To SIBYLLE, with love

FOREWORD

THE EIGHT PLAYS contained in this volume all belong to Strindberg's post-INFERNO period,* those five years of explosive creativity from 1898 to 1903 when he wrote no less than twenty-six plays. Four of them — EASTER, the two parts of THE DANCE OF DEATH, and THE VIRGIN BRIDE — are more or less straightforwardly realistic, though they all explore the supernatural; the other four — the three parts of TO DAMASCUS, and A DREAM PLAY — were an attempt to do something quite new in drama, roughly equivalent to what Picasso was, within the next few years, about to do for painting and James Joyce for the novel. All eight plays were greeted with general incomprehension. THE DANCE OF DEATH had to wait nine years before it was staged in Sweden, A DREAM PLAY and THE VIRGIN BRIDE both five years; and although EASTER and Part I of TO DAMASCUS were both performed fairly soon after publication, neither was adequately staged or enthusiastically received. Thanks to Strindberg's founding of his own Intimate Theatre in 1907, THE DANCE OF DEATH and EASTER achieved some recognition in his lifetime, but neither TO DAMASCUS nor A DREAM PLAY was understood, or regarded as theatrically valid, until long after his death in 1912.

Strindberg is often supposed to have become accepted in his own country in his later years; some at any rate of his plays began to be performed, he was acclaimed by the young, and huge crowds attended his funeral. But this acceptance was very limited. Many of the productions of his plays occurred only at his own theatre (including MISS JULIE, which had had to wait sixteen years for its Swedish première). His historical plays, which he wrote largely as

*See pp. 13–14.

pot-boilers, were performed at the Royal Theatre and
Svenska Teatern in Stockholm and were mostly successes;
but his more ambitious works were either rejected, like
ADVENT and A DREAM PLAY, or, like TO DAMASCUS
and EASTER, poorly performed and received. Had he not
founded his own theatre, several of his best plays would
have remained unstaged at his death, and several of his early
works such as MISS JULIE and THE FATHER would have
remained forgotten. As it was, they too received a very
mixed reception. The reviews of the Intimate Theatre productions show that he was no longer regarded as a force to
reckon with in literature or the theatre. And although the
young acclaimed him, they did so more because he was a
rebel against society than as a playwright. The literary
establishment, meanwhile, treated him like a leper. It is
amazing to reflect that he, of all writers, was never elected
to the Swedish Academy.

Few writers of Strindberg's stature can have been as
scorned by their fellow-authors as Strindberg was. Even
Ibsen's treatment by the Norwegians pales in comparison
with Strindberg's treatment by the Swedes. Ibsen at least
received a civil-list pension for most of his life; Strindberg,
who needed one much more, never did. And Ibsen's genius
was finally, if grudgingly, admitted by his compatriots,
which can scarcely be said of Strindberg. Even the acclaim
which Strindberg received in Germany and France during
his lifetime had little effect in Sweden. The (at best) indiffer-
ence with which the majority of his fellow-writers regarded
him was, in his post-INFERNO period, partly due to his
embracing of religion, or at any rate — since he never adopted
any specific religion, and disapproved of much of the gospel of
Christ — to his acceptance of the existence of a God. During
the 1890s, there had developed in Europe a reaction against
the atheistic naturalism of such writers as Zola, so that
Strindberg, living in Germany and France, was merely
following a fairly general trend among European thinkers
and men of letters. But when he returned to Sweden in
1896, he found that Swedish intellectuals still clung to what
he regarded as an out-of-date and negative attitude, mock-

ing him as a crazed neurotic whose reversion to religion and
mysticism marked him as a pre-Darwinian sentimentalist. In
the mighty struggle between the writer and God which is
the main theme of TO DAMASCUS, they could see nothing
but a private settling of Strindberg's accounts with humanity; the religious element embarrassed them. Similarly, they
seemed blind to the fact that in THE DANCE OF DEATH
he was painting not merely a dreadful marriage but the
awfulness of a world in which people have no belief in God
nor in any future beyond their worldly existence. When, in
1899, Strindberg gave a dinner in Stockholm for his old
friends, he noted sadly that it was "like a farewell dinner
from the eighties".

Nor, in Sweden then, were there the directors to interpret his plays. In this, Strindberg was less lucky than Ibsen:
August Lindberg, an outstanding interpreter of Ibsen, no
longer had his own company by 1898, but was now merely
a distrusted employee of less imaginative managers (he
wanted to direct and act the lead in TO DAMASCUS when
it was first produced, but had to stand by and see both
tasks ill performed). Harald Molander, who had directed
both GUSTAV VASA and ERIK THE FOURTEENTH
brilliantly in 1899, died prematurely in 1900 at the age of
forty-two. Thus, when Strindberg's more demanding plays
were performed, they were done so badly as to confirm the
opinions of those who doubted him. The first production
of TO DAMASCUS in 1900 sadly smoothed the jagged
edges of the play, presenting the protagonist as a sentimen-
tal romantic instead of the Prometheus that Strindberg intended; and the first production of A DREAM PLAY in
1907 was likewise so weak and romanticized that at the
dress rehearsal Strindberg despaired, and wished (apart
from Harriet Bosse's performance) that the play had remained unstaged. Even when he founded his own Intimate
Theatre that year, he was (like Ibsen) too poor a director
to achieve the kind of production that his plays required.
His OPEN LETTERS TO THE INTIMATE THEATRE,
despite their psychological insights, and the reminiscences
of those who worked with him there such as August Falck,

show how curiously old-fashioned his appreciation of staging technique was. (This may have been because he hardly ever went to the theatre, even when abroad.) It was not until after his death that Max Reinhardt in Germany and Olof Molander (the son of Harald Molander) in Sweden revealed the depth and theatrical validity of his symbolical plays — and of many of his best and least appreciated realistic plays too. A DREAM PLAY, indeed, had to wait until Molander's 1935 production in Stockholm before it was fully appreciated.

MICHAEL MEYER

ACKNOWLEDGEMENTS

AS BEFORE, I gladly acknowledge my debt to three pioneers in the field of Strindberg research: the late Professor Martin Lamm, for his STRINDBERGS DRAMER (Stockholm, 1924–26) which had a considerable influence on Olof Molander's early stage productions, and his AUGUST STRINDBERG (Stockholm, 1940–1941, revised edition 1948); Docent Torsten Eklund, whose great edition of Strindberg's letters has now reached its fourteenth volume; and Docent Gunnar Ollén, to whose admirable STRINDBERGS DRAMATIK (Stockholm, 1961, revised edition 1962) I am indebted for much of the factual background information contained in my introductions. Docent Carl-Reinhold Smedmark's definitive edition of Strindberg's dramas has, sadly, not yet extended to the eight plays given here, and I have followed the text of the Bonnier edition of SKRIFTER AV AUGUST STRINDBERG (Vols. X and XI, Stockholm, 1946). I am also grateful to Mrs Mary Sandbach and her publishers for permission to quote from her excellent translations of INFERNO (Hutchinson, 1962) and FROM AN OCCULT DIARY (Secker & Warburg, 1965).

I must thank the British Broadcasting Corporation for commissioning the translations of TO DAMASCUS and THE VIRGIN BRIDE; Sir Peter Daubeny and the Royal Shakespeare Company for commissioning the translation of A DREAM PLAY; and the Pitlochry Festival Theatre for commissioning the translation of EASTER.

M.M.

Introduction to

TO DAMASCUS

STRINDBERG wrote Part I of his trilogy TO DAMAS-
CUS with no thought of a sequel; nor, when he
followed it with Part II, had he any intention of
writing any sequel to that. Thus, Part I can be regarded as
a play in itself (and is often so performed in Sweden); Parts
I and II can also be regarded as an entity, and are sometimes
performed as one, with cuts. Part III is seldom acted, alone
or with the preceding parts; by the time he began it he had
married, and by the time he completed it he had parted
from, Harriet Bosse, his third wife, and he changed the important character of the Lady so as to incorporate certain
traits of her. Yet there are scenes in Part III such as the
trial, the two marriage scenes and the final scene in the
monastery, which show Strindberg at his best, and others,
such as the scenes with the Tempter, which reveal that
Shavian delight in argument and paradox which was so
much a part of Strindberg's character but which is still so
little recognized as such outside Scandinavia.

He began to plan Part I in Paris on 19 January 1898,
three days before his forty-ninth birthday. It was his first
play for nearly six years. In 1892, traumatically divorced
from his first wife Siri, still unrecognized as a dramatist
although he had by then written twenty-five plays including
THE FATHER, MISS JULIE and CREDITORS, impov-
erished, and denounced as a blasphemer and corruptor of
the young, he had left Sweden for Berlin, to dilute his
sorrows in a Bohemian circle of writers and painters which
included Edvard Munch, Knut Hamsun and the Pole, Stani-
slas Przybyszewski, who was to become at the same time his
private enemy and one of his most distinguished disciples.
In May 1893 Strindberg married a young Austrian journa-
list, Frida Uhl; but after a stormy year he left her too, and
moved on to Paris, where for two years, living in a succes-
sion of cheap hotels, he immersed himself in scientific

NB →

experiments, trying to discover the origin of all matter and, especially, to make gold. At times during these years, he walked the brink of insanity; then he found solace in the writings of his countryman Emmanuel Swedenborg, that Blake-like visionary whom Blake himself had so admired. Swedenborg taught Strindberg to believe that life was not a chaos but that he was being punished for his sins by a just God, and that all things were planned in detail by a wise and and merciful Providence. Punishment and suffering he now accepted as a sign of grace, and each new agony as evidence that a further sin had been erased from his book. Through Swedenborg, too, he came to believe in the existence of "powers", disciplinary spirits acting for the Almighty whose principal task was to destroy the sin of pride.

Shortly before he left Paris for Sweden, in the autumn of 1896, Strindberg's plays began to be performed again in his homeland, which eased his financial worries. This, together with his new-found peace of mind, enabled him to turn again to creative writing. In May and June 1897 he wrote (in French, because he believed that no one would publish it in Sweden) INFERNO, an account in diary form of the Purgatory through which he had just passed. That autumn and winter he followed it with two sequels, entitled LEGENDS and JACOB WRESTLES; then, after the turn of the year, he began TO DAMASCUS.

Part I of TO DAMASCUS was an attempt to state in dramatic form what, in Strindberg's opinion, he had failed adequately to describe in JACOB WRESTLES: his strife with God, and his eventual acceptance of God's existence. During the past decade or so he might have been (and often was) described as a confirmed atheist; but he had not always been one, if he was then (which is much debated), and his atheism such as it was had been the defiant and aggressive atheism of a man who is not completely sure of his position. Like Ibsen, Strindberg was never fully able to escape from his religious upbringing; unlike Ibsen, he confessedly returned to a belief in God. But Strindberg's new-found religion was not orthodox Christianity; it was no less defiant and aggressive than his atheism. "The fact was," he wrote in INFERNO, "that a kind of religion had developed in me, though I was quite unable to formulate it. It was a spiritual state rather than an opinion founded upon theories, a hotch-potch of impressions that were far from being condensed into thoughts. . . In my boyhood I had borne the Cross of Jesus Christ, but I had repudiated a God who was content to rule over slaves cringing before their tormentors." As an adult Strindberg had always despised the meekness demanded and demonstrated by Christ, and the idea of having someone else to suffer on one's behalf. He wanted to settle his accounts directly with God, and not through some intermediary to whom he would have to feel a debt of gratitude.

At the same time, Parts I and II of TO DAMASCUS are — as which of Strindberg's plays is not? — a survey of his own married life, in this case his second marriage. When he married Frida, and indeed throughout their brief time together, he was poor and they were supported by her parents; hence the haunting figure of the Beggar whom the Stranger unwillingly recognizes as a mirror of himself, an image which he would like to reject but cannot. The book which the Lady reads against the Stranger's wishes and which turns her against him is A MADMAN'S DEFENCE, Strindberg's bitter account of his first marriage with Siri which, like INFERNO and for the same reason, he had written in French, and which had been savagely attacked on publication. Many of the scenes in Part I are based on episodes from his second marriage. Those by the seashore stem from his honeymoon on Heligoland. The visit to the Lady's parents is a more or less straight account of the visit which Strindberg and Frida paid to her grandparents in the village of Dornach in Austria, when they arrived so destitute that, like the characters in the play, they lacked the money to pay the ferryman. Frida's grandfather had been a noted lawyer who now devoted himself mainly to hunting; her grandmother, once a celebrated beauty, greeted Strindberg with suspicion from the start, and the superstitious locals crossed themselves when they met him on the road along the Danube, which was lined with Calvaries.

The scene in the Abbey of Good Hope was based on
Strindberg's experiences in the Paris Hôpital de St Louis,
where he had spent three weeks suffering from the painful
skin disease of psoriasis, and from consequent blood poisoning. In INFERNO he gives a vivid description of the place:

"The bell sounded for lunch and I found myself among
a company of spectres. Faces like death's-heads, faces of the
dying. A nose missing here, an eye there, a third with a
dangling lip, another with a crumbling cheek. . . . In the
midst . . . moved our kind mother, the Matron. . . . She
taught us to smile at our sufferings, as if they had been so
many joys, for she knew how salutary pain can be."

The origin of the scenes in the gorge is likewise explained
in INFERNO:

"When I took a walk in the outskirts of the village
[Dornach], the little stream led me towards the gorge between the two hills. The truly magnificent entrance to it,
between masses of fallen rocks, lured me on with a strange
and irresistible fascination. The perpendicular side of the
rock, upon which the ruined castle stood, came down right
to the bottom and formed a gateway to the ravine itself at
the spot where the stream became the mill-race. By a freak
of nature the top of the rock looked like the head of a
Turk, so like, that everyone in the district had noticed it.

"Under it, nestling against the wall of rock, was the
miller's wagon shed. On the door handle hung a goat's horn,
containing the grease for lubricating the wagons, and, close
by, leaning against the wall, was a besom.

"In spite of the fact that all this was perfectly natural
and just as it should be, I could not help asking myself what
demon it was who had put those two insignia of witches,
the goat's horn and the besom, just there and right in my
way on this particular morning.

"I walked on along the dark, damp path, feeling
decidedly uneasy, and pulled up sharply before a wooden
building of unusual appearance. It was a low, oblong shed
with six oven doors. Ovens! . . . The image of Dante's Hell
rose up before me, the sinners being baked red hot . . . and
the six oven doors. Was it a nightmare? No, it was a

commonplace reality, that was made perfectly plain by a horrible stink, a stream of mire, and a chorus of grunts coming from the pig-sty. . . .

"The waterfall and the mill-wheel made a noise that was just like the humming in my ears that had been with me ever since those first nights of agitation in Paris. The mill-hands, white as false angels, handled the machinery like executioners, and the great paddle-wheel performed its Sisyphean task of sending the water running down cease-lessly, over and over again.

"Further on was the smithy, with the begrimed, naked smiths armed with fire-tongs, pincers, sledge-hammers, standing in the midst of fire and sparks and glowing iron and melted lead and a din that made my head whirl and my heart thump against my ribs. . . .

"I returned the way I had come, lost in contemplation of a sequence of accidental circumstances which, taken to-gether, formed one great whole, awe-inspiring but by no means supernatural."

TO DAMASCUS also contains, inevitably, several of Strindberg's more or less permanent obsessions: his old sense of guilt at being unable to support the three children of his first marriage, his fear that they might acquire an unsympathetic, even a cruel, stepfather, his lack of recogni-tion as a scientist (which seems to have bothered him much more than his lack of recognition as a writer), his agora-phobia, his fear of darkness (especially now that he was living alone), and his fear of madness. With his new-found religion came doubts about the gospel of permissiveness which he had earlier preached with such effect on the young; the invalids whom the Stranger meets at the sulphur springs in Part III are people who have followed his teach-ing and contracted syphilis — hence his horror at, as he supposes, seeing his own son among them. Strindberg's interest in the occult also left its mark; in Paris he had maintained close contact with the French occultists, and had been much impressed by their experiments in hypnosis, telepathy and black magic. Dreams, as always, fascinated him; as did the idea of the *Doppelgänger*, the dream self that each of us has in addition to our "real" self (hence the character of the Beggar). He noted in INFERNO:

"A stranger . . . was put into the room adjacent to my writing desk. This unknown man never uttered a word; he seemed to be occupied in writing something behind the wooden partition that separated us. All the same, it was odd that he should push back his chair every time I moved mine. He repeated my every movement. . . . When I went to bed the man in the room next to my desk went to bed too."

The occultists confirmed his suspicion that a man has the power to revenge himself on another, even at a distance. In Berlin, he had had an affair with the Norwegian Dagny Juel, famous as one of the models of Edvard Munch. After Strindberg, Dagny (who was later murdered by another lover) had become the wife of Przybyszewski, and in Paris Strindberg became convinced that Przybyszewski (now, according to Munch, in France) was trying to kill him by, among other methods, projecting electricity into him. He kept on hearing the Pole's favourite melody, Schumann's *Aufschwung*, and would hastily change to another hotel, whither it would pursue him. The plays of the Belgian symbolist Maurice Maeterlinck, which Strindberg had read and much admired, may have influenced the method and structure of the drama.

"My play [Part I] creeps beautifully forward," Strindberg wrote to the author Gustaf af Geijerstam on 2 March 1898 from Paris, "and gives me good hopes now that I am over the brow." By 8 March he had finished it. "Here is a play of the value of which I have no idea," he informed Geijerstam that day, enclosing it. "If you find it good, chuck it in at the theatre. If you find it impossible, hide it away." Two days later he wrote a cryptic yet revealing letter to Axel Herrlin, a young academic with whom he had had many conversations about the occult during his stay in Lund the previous year, and who had written to Strindberg describing some Inferno-like experiences that he had recently had:

"Who stages these performances for us, and with what

purpose? Are they real? Is there a hell apart from this? Or is
it to frighten children? My own crisis, which lasted nearly
seven months, has given me no further certainty, except
regarding certain points. I know what is demanded of me
ethically, but the demands seem gradually to be intensified.
Alchemy and occultism, divination and exploring what is
hidden, are absolutely forbidden, but not speculative
chemistry. On the other hand, I seem to have been granted
again the grace of being able to write for the theatre, and
have just completed a big play which I am grateful to have
been permitted to write. But I admit that it is a gift which
can be taken from one if one misuses it." He goes on to
speak of his religion, and of his fear lest he might "be punished with religious fanaticism and led astray. But I'm not
sure whether this is a trial which one must withstand or a
calling which must be obeyed. My earlier fatalism has been
translated into a belief in Providence, and I fully realize
that standing alone I have nothing and can achieve nothing.
But I shall not attain complete humility, for my conscience
will not permit me to commit suicide as an individual."

On 1 April he tried to comfort a newspaper editor,
Waldemar Bülow, who had written to Strindberg that he
felt persecuted. "It is not people who persecute you;
people are too lazy and self-occupied to waste time persecuting others. No, it is someone else, the Invisible One, whom
you have challenged." On 23 April, in Lund, he wrote a
moving letter to another correspondent who suffered from
a conviction that she was persecuted, his sister Elisabeth,
to whom he was deeply attached and who later that year
was to be admitted to a mental home. "As regards your
feelings that you are persecuted, they are like the ones I
had when I was ill; and they lack any foundation; though
not wholly so, since one is said to persecute oneself. If you
have read my book IN FERNO, you can see the causes of
my delusions of persecution, arising mainly from self-
reproach. . . . Whether your case resembles mine I don't
know and have no right to ask or demand; but one piece
of advice I can give you; try to search out the purpose of
Providence in punishing you with these torments." And on

12 May he wrote to Geijerstam: "I wonder where the grass grows where some time I may rest my weary bones; my Colonus, where the wild hunt of my Eumenides will cease!"

On 24 May, in a letter to his three children by Siri, he described Part I of TO DAMASCUS as "the best play I have written, and one which gives me and my friends who have read it, great hopes". On 5 June, still in Lund, he addressed a long letter to the Swedish poet Gustaf Fröding, who suffered so violently from hallucinations that the same month he, like Elisabeth, was admitted to an asylum:

"Don't use the word hallucination (or even delirium) as though it stood for something unreal. Hallucinations and delirium possess a certain kind of reality — or they are phantasmagoria consciously designed by the Invisible One to frighten us. They all have a symbolic meaning. For example, the projections of alcoholic delirium are always the same: flies and rats. The direct progeny of filth. . . . I am sure that your visions are to be found in Swedenborg, and if you could write them down from memory you would do yourself, me and many people a great service. I would interpret them for you; you would see that there is a consistency in them, a meaning and a good intent. When I chanced to find my hallucinations described in Swedenborg, I was freed. Now, when in the night they attack me, I lie and balance these torments against the evil things I have thought and done. I at once think: 'Serve you right! Take note and don't do that again!' And so I regain peace; till I sin again. But don't suppose that I am punished just for wine and women; no, every harsh word I have spoken of others, even if it is true and well known; hubristic thoughts; and much besides, all come under scrutiny. I don't believe in any Hell but this, though I don't know. And Swedenborg's Hell is an exact description of life on earth; I don't think we leave this world until we have had our ration of suffering. But we, we seem to have a task to fulfil, and it is no use throwing oneself like Jonah into the sea to escape one's calling. We must stand forth and prophesy, and risk being disavowed like Jonah. My development is not as absurd as it appears. 'Pull down!' said the Spirit, and I pulled down. 'Now build!' says the Spirit. . . . And now I shall try to build."

In June his eldest daughter, Karin, informed him that she wished to become a Roman Catholic. A few years earlier, Strindberg would have greeted this news with alarm or contempt; now he welcomed it. He was himself attracted by the discipline of Catholicism, though he never went so far as to embrace it.

"Beloved Karin!

I find it difficult to say how happy I am that you have of your own free will decided to adopt a religion. You know that I have always given you full freedom regarding spiritual matters, partly because I myself entertained doubts, partly because I didn't believe I had the right to try to influence you. I am especially happy that you have discovered Catholicism, since I regard it as the only religion for us Westerners, and since I have found Protestantism to be no religion but merely theology, intellectual argument, free-thinking which only results in godlessness and doubt. 'Our fathers' faith', that is Catholicism, and the Protestants now seem to be returning to it in droves. . . . But, Karin, let your religion be a living thing, a guiding rein for your thoughts and actions. Look at my undisciplined and vacillating life, grounded on a lack of religion. . . . And do not believe that He Who decides our destinies is evil. Those seemingly 'evil powers' that torment us when we have done wrong cannot be evil, since they persecute and punish evil with pangs of conscience and the like. Were these powers evil, they would encourage our vices and persecute what is good in us. . . . So, we are ruled by Good. Whether I shall ever bind myself by any formal religion I don't know, but if I did it would be Roman Catholicism."

That summer in Lund — we do not know exactly when — Strindberg began Part II of TO DAMASCUS; but, with characteristic inconsistency, it turned out less forgiving and resigned than Part I. "I have several times ground to a standstill in my new play," he wrote to Emil Kléen on 9 July. "Decided to burn it, as totally worthless, although I'm near the end of Act Four. But I'm going on. It is conceived in

hatred and deals with hateful people. Although it's strongly
constructed and has a number of good things in it, it upsets
me and makes me ill. *Tristis sum!*" But by 3 August he was
able to tell his German translator Emil Schering that it
was finished and would be published in a single volume
with Part I although "I don't want it [Part II] to appear in
German, partly so as not to spoil the effect of Part I, partly
for other reasons". These "other reasons" amounted in fact
to one reason only — a desire, most untypical for Strindberg, to spare the feelings of Frida's relatives, who are much
less sympathetically portrayed than in Part I. (Nor is it clear
why the publication of both parts together in German
should "spoil the effect of Part I" when he was allowing
them to appear under a single cover in Swedish). When the
Swedish edition appeared that autumn, Strindberg asked
Geijerstam to send a copy to Ibsen, who had celebrated
his seventieth birthday the previous spring, an occasion
which had been marked by the appearance of a *Festskrift*
to which Strindberg (who had been hostile towards Ibsen
ever since the publication of a A DOLL'S HOUSE nineteen
years previously) had not contributed. "Just say this," he
commanded Geijerstam, "Strindberg is ashamed that, as a
prominent Swedish author, he did not join in the homage
to the Master, from whom he learned much. But he was in
a state of depression and did not think his homage could
honour or gladden anyone." Fearful lest this might be
taken to imply a modification of his antagonism to Ibsen's
general view of life, he assured Geijerstam that his homage
would have been "to the master of dramatic art, not the
philosopher".

   During the next three years Strindberg, in an extraordinary burst of creative activity, wrote no less than seven-
teen full-length plays, including several of his finest —
ADVENT, THERE ARE CRIMES AND CRIMES, GUSTAV
VASA, ERIK THE FOURTEENTH, EASTER, both parts
of THE DANCE OF DEATH, THE VIRGIN BRIDE and
A DREAM PLAY. Halfway through this period, in the
summer of 1900, two years after he had finished Parts I
and II of TO DAMASCUS, the Royal Theatre in Stockholm

prepared to stage Part I; Strindberg fell in love with the twenty-two-year-old actress Harriet Bosse, whom he had chosen to play the Lady, and, having to consider the play closely again, he began to meditate a third part. He began to write it the following February, naturally in a somewhat different mood from that in which he had composed the first two parts. "I long for cleanness, beauty and harmony," he wrote in his OCCULT DIARY on 11 February. "Act Two of TO DAMASCUS III is influenced by B[osse], who has now entered into my life." On 6 May that year (1901), they married, but after seven weeks, on 26 June, she left him. A week later, on 2 July, they were temporarily re-united, but it was during this week of estrangement that he wrote the bitter scenes of the break-up of the marriage between the Stranger and the Lady and the Stranger's decision to abandon the world and retire into a monastery (though he did not complete the play until the autumn).

Several times during his INFERNO crisis Strindberg had considered becoming a monk; he had even planned with a friend to establish a lay monastery, and in August 1898 had entered a Belgian monastery, Maredsous, but had left after one night because he did not like the food — a five-course dinner with wine, which he found too much — or the other guests. In 1901 he began to think about it afresh. On 16–18 February he wrote to the painter Richard Bergh: "Last night you said something about an Italian monastery where one can stay. 1. Does one have to pay? 2. Where is it? 3. What's it called? 4. Can one write to them? 5. Do they only speak Italian? Couldn't one manage in Latin or French? . . . Even if I didn't stay there for life, I long to go there and get away from here. . . . Now that I have fulfilled the promise of my youth and done my duty to my country, I think it would be becoming of me to disappear, almost think it would be a duty to public modesty to hide my alarming and upsetting self. And let my works speak! By themselves! . . . The loneliness that some unknown compulsion forces me to seek closes around me like darkness. Isolating myself from the banalities of life increases my feeling that I shall soon be unable to endure even being looked at by people. I await a change in my destiny — a great crisis — a complete break with the past. Perhaps an end to the road which now seems to me so dream-like. So I am settling my wordly affairs and preparing for departure." But, unlike the Stranger, Strindberg decided that he could not, after all, annihilate his wordly self. "All that I know, little as that may be," he had written in IN FERNO, "springs from one central point, my Ego. It is not the cult but the cultivation of this which seems to me to be the supreme and final goal of existence. . . . To kill the Ego is to commit suicide."

The story of Father Uriel in the final act of Part III of TO DAMASCUS reflects Strindberg's bitterness at his loss of faith in every ideal that he had successively embraced. Intelligence and flexibility, he complained in IN FERNO, led a man to be condemned as a renegade. As though anticipating his own future development, he had written his first great play, MASTER OLOF (1872—77), about just such a man. Addressing "the Powers", he complained in IN FERNO: "Fantastic, but exactly the vicious circle that I foresaw in my twentieth [sic] year when I wrote my play MASTER OLOF, which I now see as the tragedy of my own life. What is the good of having dragged out a laborious existence for thirty years only to learn by experience what I had already anticipated? In my youth I was a true believer and you made of me a free-thinker. Of the free-thinker you made me an atheist, of the atheist a monk. Inspired by the humanitarians I extolled socialism. Five years later you showed me the absurdity of socialism. You have cut the ground from under all my enthusiasms, and suppose that I now dedicate myself to religion. I know for a certainty that before ten years have passed you will prove to me that religion is false. . . . How can you require that we take seriously something that appears to be no more than a colossal jest?" Parts I and II of TO DAMASCUS are the work of a man who has found a kind of peace. Part III is the bitter lamentation of a man who has been deprived even of that.

TO DAMASCUS

A Trilogy

(1898—1901)

This translation of TO DAMASCUS was commissioned by the British Broadcasting Corporation. Part I was broadcast, in a shortened form, on Radio 3 on 4 July 1971 (and repeated on 10 October 1971) with the following cast:

NARRATOR	Martin Friend
THE STRANGER	Stephen Murray
THE LADY	Zena Walker
THE BEGGAR	Edward Kelsey
A MOURNER	Patrick Tull
A LANDLORD	Antony Higginson
THE DOCTOR	John Rye
THE MADMAN	Brian Hewlett
A HOTEL PORTER	Patrick Tull
THE MOTHER	Eva Stuart
THE GRANDFATHER	John Ruddock
THE ABBESS	Sheila Grant

Special sound and music by Malcolm Clarke of the B.B.C. Radiophonic Workshop.

Directed by Charles Lefeaux

On 3 April 1975, Part I was performed at the Traverse Theatre, Edinburgh. The cast was:

THE STRANGER	Roy Marsden
THE LADY	Katharine Schofield
THE BEGGAR	Christopher Ryan
THE DOCTOR	Christopher Malcolm
THE SISTER } THE ABBESS }	Meg Davies
CAESAR	David Bedard
THE MOTHER	Susan Carpenter
THE OLD MAN	John Young
THE DOMINICAN	Finlay Welsh

Designed by Poppy Mitchell
Directed by Michael Ockrent and David Gothard

PART I
(1898)

CHARACTERS*

THE STRANGER
THE LADY
THE BEGGAR
A LANDLORD
FIRST FUNERAL GUEST
SECOND FUNERAL GUEST
THIRD FUNERAL GUEST
THE DOCTOR
THE SISTER
A MADMAN
A HOTEL PORTER
THE SMITH
THE MILLER'S WIFE
THE OLD MAN
THE LADY'S MOTHER
THE ABBESS
THE CONFESSOR
MINOR CHARACTERS AND SHADOWS

* This is the actual list of characters, and differs considerably from Strindberg's own list as prefaced to the play. He names only the Stranger, the Lady, the Beggar, the Doctor, the Sister, the Old Man, the Mother, the Abbess, the Confessor, and "Minor Characters and Shadows". This is by no means the only instance of Strindberg's "List of Characters" differing from the actual list. (Translator's note)

SCENES

Act 1. At the street corner
           At the Doctor's

Act 2. A hotel room
           By the sea
           On the highway
           At the gorge
           In the kitchen

Act 3. The rose room
           The asylum
           The rose room
           The kitchen

Act 4. At the gorge
           On the highway
           By the sea
           The hotel room

Act 5. At the Doctor's
           The street corner

ACT ONE

Scene 1. At the street corner

*A street corner with a bench beneath a tree. The side-
portals of a small Gothic church, a post-office and a
café with chairs outside. The post-office and the café
are shut.*

*The sound of a funeral march approaches, then fades
into the distance.*

The STRANGER *stands on the edge of the pavement,
seeming to wonder which way to go. A church clock
strikes; first four notes, the quarters, in a highish tone,
then three o'clock, in a lower.*

The LADY *enters, inclines her head to the* STRANGER
is about to pass him, but stops.

STRANGER: So there you are. I thought you would come.

LADY: You called me, then? Yes, I felt it. But why do you
stand here, on the street corner?

STRANGER: I don't know. I must stand somewhere while
I wait.

LADY: What are you waiting for?

STRANGER: If I only knew. For forty years I have been
waiting for something. I believe it is called happiness; or
it may just be the end of sorrow. Listen to that dreadful
music again. Listen! Don't go, please don't go. I shall be
frightened if you go.

LADY: We met yesterday for the first time. And talked
alone for four hours. I felt sorry for you, but that doesn't
mean you may take advantage of my kindness.

29

STRANGER: That's true, I shouldn't. But, I beg you: don't leave me alone. I am in a strange city, I haven't a friend, and the few people I know seem worse than strangers — almost enemies.

LADY: Enemies everywhere, alone everywhere. Why did you leave your wife and child?

STRANGER: If I only knew. If I only knew why I exist, why I stand here, where I must go, what I must do. Do you you think some people are damned before they die?

LADY: No, I don't think that.

STRANGER: Look at me.

LADY: Have you never found any happiness in life?

STRANGER: No. And when I thought I had, it was just a ruse to tempt me to prolong my misery. Whenever the golden fruit fell into my hand, it was always poisoned or rotten.

LADY: What is your religion?

STRANGER: Only this: that when life becomes too much to bear, I shall go my way.

LADY: Where?

STRANGER: Into annihilation. This knowledge that I hold death in my hand gives me an incredible feeling of power —

LADY: Good God, you speak of death like a toy.

STRANGER: Well, life is a toy — to us writers. I was born melancholy, yet I've never been able to take anything seriously, even my own sorrows. And there are moments when I doubt whether life has any more reality than the things I write. [*The funeral march is heard: psalm tunes; De Profundis.*] Here they come again. Why must they march round the streets like this?

LADY: Are you afraid of them?

STRANGER: No. But it irritates me, it's as though it had

happened before. I don't fear death. Only solitude. Because when one's alone there's always someone else. I don't know whether it's myself or someone else, but in solitude one is never alone. The air grows thicker, it begins to sprout, to grow things which you can't see but which are there, and alive.

LADY: You've noticed that?

STRANGER: Yes. I've been noticing everything lately. Not just things and incidents, forms and colours — now I see thoughts and what things signify. Life used to be just a great nonsense. Now it has a meaning, and I see a purpose in it where before I saw only a game of chance. So when I met you yesterday I thought you had been sent, either to save me or to destroy me.

LADY: Why should I destroy you?

STRANGER: Because it was your destiny.

LADY: I don't want to destroy you. I pity you. I've never seen anyone before whose mere appearance made me want to weep. What's on your conscience? Have you done something that hasn't been found out, or punished?

STRANGER: You may well ask that. I've no more crimes on my conscience than many who go free. Yes, one thing. I wasn't willing to be life's fool.

LADY: One must let oneself be betrayed in some degree to be able to live.

STRANGER: It seems almost to be a duty, and one I'd gladly be relieved of. Or there may be some other secret in my life that I don't know about. There's a story in my family that I'm a changeling.

LADY: What's that?

STRANGER: A child the fairies have left in exchange for a human one.

LADY: And you believe that?

STRANGER: No. But there might be something in it. When I was a child I cried continuously and felt I didn't belong to this life. I hated my parents as much as they hated me. I resented discipline and convention. I only longed for the forest and the sea.

LADY: Have you ever seen visions?

STRANGER: Never. But I've often felt that two powers rule my life. One gives me everything I want, while the other stands there and smears every gift with filth, so that it's worthless and I don't want to touch it. I've had everything I wanted in this life, and it has all seemed worthless.

LADY: You have had everything and yet are discontented?

STRANGER: That's what I call being cursed.

LADY: Don't blaspheme! But why didn't you look for something beyond this life, in a place where no dirt is?

STRANGER: Because I've never believed in anything outside it.

LADY: What about those fairies?

STRANGER: Oh, that was just a fantasy. Shall we sit down?

LADY: All right. But what are you waiting for?

STRANGER: Really for the post-office to open. There's a letter waiting for me which keeps on chasing me without ever finding me. [*They sit.*] Tell me a little about yourself.

LADY [*starts knitting*]: There's nothing to tell.

STRANGER: It's strange, but I'd like to think of you as something without a name. I only know your surname. I'd like to name you myself. Let me think. What shall I call you? Yes. I shall call you Eve. [*With a gesture to the wings.*] Trumpets! [*The funeral march is heard.*] That funeral march again! I shall give you an age too, for I don't know how old you are. You are thirty-four — which means you were born in 1864. And a character, because I

don't know what kind of person you are. A good one, I
think; your voice is like my dead mother's. I mean my
idea of a mother — my own mother never kissed me, but
I remember she hit me. I was reared in hatred. Hatred — a
blow for a blow, an eye for an eye. You see this scar on my
forehead? My brother did that with an axe, because I'd
knocked his tooth out with a stone, I didn't go to my
father's funeral, because he had me thrown out from my
sister's wedding. And I was born illegitimate, the son of a
bankrupt, while the family was in mourning for an uncle
who'd committed suicide. Now you know my family. As is
the tree, so is the fruit. I managed with difficulty to
escape fourteen years hard labour, so I suppose I ought
really to be grateful if not exactly happy. To the powers.

LADY: I like to hear you speak, but you mustn't meddle
with the powers. It troubles me. Please.

STRANGER: To be honest I don't believe in them, yet
they keep returning to my thoughts. Don't you think
there are lost souls that have failed to find peace? I think
so. Then I must be one too. Once I thought I would find
peace, through a woman. But that turned out the worst hell
of all.

LADY: You say such strange things. Yes, you are a lost
soul. But you will find peace.

STRANGER: Through the sound of bells and holy water?
I've tried that. But it was like when the Devil sees a crucifix. Let's talk about you.

LADY: There's no need. Have you never been accused of
misusing your talents?

STRANGER: I've been accused of everything. No man was
ever so hated, or so lonely. I went alone, and I came alone.
When I entered a public place, people moved away from
me. When I wanted to rent a room, it was always taken.
The priests cursed me from the pulpits, the scholars from
their lecture platforms, my parents in my home. Once the

church committee tried to take my children from me. Then I raised my fist to heaven and reviled God.

LADY: Why are you so hated?

STRANGER: I don't know. Yes — I couldn't see people suffer. And I said so, and I wrote: "Free yourselves and I will help you!" And I said to the poor: "Don't let the rich exploit you." And to women: "Don't let men crush you." And — which I suppose was the worst — I said to children: "Do not obey your father and mother when they are unjust." The result was, everyone united against me, rich and poor, men and women, parents and children. I became sick, poor, beggared, dishonoured, divorced, denounced, exiled, alone, and now — ! Do you think I am mad?

LADY: No.

STRANGER: You're the only one who doesn't. I like you for that.

LADY [gets up]: I must leave you now.

STRANGER: You too!

LADY: You mustn't stay here.

STRANGER: Where shall I go?

LADY: Home, to work.

STRANGER: I'm not a worker. I'm a writer.

LADY: I didn't mean to hurt you. But writing is a gift which can be taken away. Don't forfeit it.

STRANGER: Where are you going?

LADY: There's something I must do.

STRANGER: Are you religious?

LADY: I am nothing.

STRANGER: All the better, then you can become something. Oh, I wish I was your old blind father, whom you

could lead to the market place to sing, but my tragedy is
that I can't grow old — that's the way with children
who've been left by the fairies, they don't grow old, they
just get enormous heads and scream. I wish I was someone's dog whom I could follow so that I'd never be alone —
a little food now and then, a kick now and then, a pat now
and then, a whipping —

LADY: Now I must go. Goodbye.

STRANGER [*absently*]: Goodbye.

> *She leaves him sitting on the bench. He takes off his
> hat, wipes his forehead. Then he draws with his stick
> in the dust. The* BEGGAR *enters. His appearance is
> very strange. He rummages in the gutter.*

STRANGER: What are you scrabbling for, beggar?

BEGGAR: I don't know what you mean. Anyway, I'm not
a beggar. Have I asked you for anything?

STRANGER: I beg your pardon. One shouldn't judge by
appearances.

BEGGAR: No, you shouldn't. Can you guess who I am?

STRANGER: It doesn't interest me.

BEGGAR: How can one tell in advance? People never get
interested until it's too late. *Virtus post nummos!*

STRANGER: You know Latin?

BEGGAR: You see. You're interested already. *Omne tulit
punctum qui miscuit utile dulci.* I've succeeded in everything I've attempted, because I've never attempted anything. I call myself Polycrates, that fellow with the ring.
I've got everything I wanted in life. But I never really
wanted anything, and, bored with success, I threw my
ring away. Now I'm old I miss it and rummage for it in
the gutters. But if I don't find a gold ring, I don't turn my
nose up at the odd cigar butt.

STRANGER: I'm not sure if that's wisdom or rubbish.

BEGGAR: Neither am I.

STRANGER: Do you know who I am?

BEGGAR: Doesn't interest me.

STRANGER: People never get interested until — no, damn
it, you're turning me into a parrot. It's as bad as picking
up other men's cigar butts. Be off with you!

BEGGAR [*raises his hat*]: And you don't want to pick up
mine?

STRANGER: What's that scar on your forehead?

BEGGAR: I got that from a close relative.

STRANGER: No, now you're frightening me. May I feel
you and see if you're real? [*Touches the* BEGGAR *on the
arm.*] Yes, you're real. Will you condescend, my dear sir,
to accept a small coin in return for a promise to look for
Polycrates' ring in some other suburb? *Post nummos
virtus* — no, there I go again. Be off with you!

BEGGAR: I'll go. But you've given me too much. Here's
three-quarters back. Then it's just a loan between friends.

STRANGER: Am I your friend?

BEGGAR: At least I am yours. And when a man's alone in
the world, he can't be choosy.

STRANGER: Would you be offended if I called that
impertinent?

BEGGAR: Not at all, not at all. When we meet again, I'll
have an epithet for you. [*Goes.*]

STRANGER [*sits and draws with his stick*]: Sunday afternoon. Long, grey, gloomy Sunday afternoon. Everyone
digesting roast beef and cabbage and boiled potatoes. The
old are sleeping, the young smoking and playing chess —
the servants have gone to evensong and the shops are shut.
Oh, this long, murderous afternoon, the day of rest, when
the pulse ceases to beat, when it's as impossible to meet
a friendly face as to get into a pub —

The LADY *enters. She now wears a flower in her bosom.*

STRANGER: Hullo! I can't open my mouth today without being proved a liar.

LADY: Are you still sitting here?

STRANGER: What does it matter whether I draw in the sand here or elsewhere, as long as I draw in the sand?

LADY: What are you writing? Let me look.

STRANGER: I seem to have written: Eve, 1864. No, don't walk on it.

LADY: What would happen?

STRANGER: Bad luck. For you and me.

LADY: You know that?

STRANGER: Yes. And I also know that that rose you are wearing in your breast is a Mandragora. That symbolizes malice and slander, though it used to be used as a medicine to cure madness. Will you give it to me?

LADY [*hesitates*]: As a medicine?

STRANGER: Of course. Have you read my books?

LADY: You know I have. I have you to thank for teaching me freedom and belief in human rights and human dignity.

STRANGER: Then you haven't read my last books.

LADY: No. And if they're different from your first books, I don't want to.

STRANGER: Promise me you will never open any of my books again.

LADY: Let me think first. Yes, I promise.

STRANGER: Good. But don't break that promise. Remember Bluebeard's wife when curiosity tempted her to unlock the forbidden room —

LADY: You're already beginning to talk like a Bluebeard. Have you forgotten that I am married, that my husband is a doctor and that he admires your work, so that his house stands open any time you wish to enter it?

STRANGER: I have done my best to forget it. I've so wiped it from my mind that it has ceased to have any reality for me.

LADY: In that case, will you come home with me?

STRANGER: No. Will you come home with me?

LADY: Where?

STRANGER: Anywhere. I have no home. Money sometimes, but seldom. It's the only thing life didn't jib at giving me, perhaps because I never really wanted it.

LADY: Hm!

STRANGER: What are you thinking?

LADY: I'm surprised I'm not offended by your sense of humour.

STRANGER: Humour and earnestness are the same thing to me. Ah! Now the organ has begun to play, which means the cafés are going to open.

LADY: Is it true that you drink?

STRANGER: A great deal. Wine helps my soul to leave its cell, I escape into space, I see what no man has seen and hear what no man has heard —

LADY: And the day after?

STRANGER: I have beautiful pangs of conscience, a liberating sense of guilt and remorse, a pleasure in the body's torment while the soul hovers like smoke about my brow. It is like a limbo between life and death, when the spirit feels it has stretched its wings and could if it wished take flight.

LADY: Come with me into the church for a moment. You

won't hear a sermon, only the music of evensong.

STRANGER: No, not the church. It makes me feel I'm unclean, and can never belong there, any more than I can
become a child again.

LADY: You feel all this already?

STRANGER: That's how far I have come; and it seems to
me as though I lay chopped to pieces in Medea's cauldron,
being slowly boiled; I shall either dissolve into nothing, or
arise renewed. It all depends on Medea's skill.

LADY: You talk like an oracle. Couldn't you become a
child again?

STRANGER: I'd have to start at the cradle. And I'd have
to be the right child this time.

LADY: Exactly. But wait while I go into St. Elizabeth's
chapel. If the café was open, I should beg you not to
drink. But luckily it's shut.

> The STRANGER *sits down again and draws in the
> sand. Six* MOURNERS *dressed in brown enter, with*
> FUNERAL GUESTS. *One carries a banner with the
> insignia of the Carpenters' Guild, and brown crêpe;
> another, a large axe decorated with spruce twigs; a
> third carries a cushion with a speaker's gavel on it.
> They stand outside the café and wait.*

STRANGER: Excuse me. Whose funeral was this?

FIRST GUEST: A carpenter. [*Makes a noise like a clock
ticking.*]

STRANGER: A real carpenter? Or the insect kind that
lives in walls and goes tick-tock?

SECOND GUEST: Both. But mostly the insect kind. What
did you say it was called?

STRANGER [*to himself*]: The rogue! He's trying to trick
me into saying death-watch beetle. But I'll say something
else to annoy him. [*Aloud.*] You mean a goldsmith?

SECOND GUEST: No, I didn't mean that. [*Makes the ticking sound again.*]

STRANGER: Are you trying to frighten me? Or is the dead man working miracles? I'm not afraid and I don't believe in miracles. Strange, though, that you mourners are wearing brown. Why not black? It's cheap, looks good and is practical.

THIRD GUEST: To our foolish eyes it is black, but if Your Honour so commands, it is brown.

STRANGER: You seem a strange company, and I feel an unease which I'd like to attribute to that wine I drank last night. But if I say those are spruce-twigs around that axe, I suppose you'll tell me they're — well, what are they?

FIRST GUEST: That's a grape-vine.

STRANGER: I guessed they wouldn't be spruce-twigs. Look, now the café's opening. At last.

> *The café is opened. The* STRANGER *sits down at a table and is served with wine. The* GUESTS *sit at the empty tables.*

STRANGER: You must have been glad to see the back of your late companion, since you make haste to wet your throats.

FIRST GUEST: Well, he was a good-for-nothing. Couldn't take life seriously.

STRANGER: And drank, no doubt?

SECOND GUEST: He did.

THIRD GUEST: And let others support his wife and children.

STRANGER: Ah, that was wicked of him. But no doubt that's why such fine words are being spoken over his coffin. Would you mind not pushing my table while I'm drinking?

FIRST GUEST: I've a right to when I'm drinking.

STRANGER: When you are, yes. There's a big difference between you and me.

The MOURNERS *murmur. The* BEGGAR *enters.*

STRANGER: Hullo, here's that beggar picking around again.

BEGGAR [*sits at a table*]: Landlord! A bottle of hock!

LANDLORD [*comes out with a document*]: Off! You'll get nothing here. You haven't paid your taxes. Here's the court finding, your name, your age and your character.

BEGGAR: *Omnia serviliter pro dominatione.* I'm a free man, with a University education and I have refused to pay taxes because I don't wish to be conscripted into society. A bottle of hock!

LANDLORD: If you don't clear off, you'll get a free trip to jail.

STRANGER: Can't you two settle this matter somewhere else? You're disturbing your customers.

LANDLORD: Well, I want you as a witness that I'm acting within the law —

STRANGER: I think the whole thing's idiotic. Can't a man enjoy the small pleasures of life simply because he hasn't paid his taxes?

LANDLORD: I see! You're one of those fellows who go round telling people to ignore their responsibilities.

STRANGER: No, this is going too far. Do you realize that I am a famous man?

The LANDLORD *and* MOURNERS *laugh.*

LANDLORD: Notorious, more like! Wait a moment. Let me see. This description could fit. [*Reads from the document.*] Thirty-eight years old, brown hair, blue eyes, no fixed occupation, abandoned his wife and children, holds subversive views on social questions, and gives the impression of not being in full command of his senses. Doesn't it fit?

STRANGER [*gets up, pale and crushed*]: What is this?

LANDLORD: Bless my soul, but it does fit!

BEGGAR: Perhaps it is him and not me.

LANDLORD: Looks like it. Now why don't you two trot along?

BEGGAR [*to* STRANGER]: We'd better go.

STRANGER: We? This is beginning to look like a plot.

> *The church bells ring. The sun breaks through and lights up the coloured rose window above the church door, which opens and reveals the interior of the church. Organ music: Ave Maris Stella is sung.*

LADY [*comes out of church*]: Where are you, what are you doing? Why did you call me again? Must you hang on to a woman's skirts like a child?

STRANGER: Yes, now I am afraid. Things are happening here which can't be explained naturally.

LADY: I thought you weren't afraid of anything, even death.

STRANGER: No, not of death. But of — the other thing. The unknown.

LADY: Listen, my friend. Give me your hand and I'll take you to a doctor. You're ill. Come.

STRANGER: Perhaps. But first tell me one thing. Is all this a carnival, or — are these people real?

LADY: They seem to be real —

STRANGER: But that beggar. He's a horrible creature. Does he really look like me?

LADY: If you go on drinking, you'll become like him. Go into the post-office now and collect your letter. Then come with me.

STRANGER: No, I won't go into the post-office. It's probably only a summons.

LADY: But suppose it isn't?

STRANGER: It'll be bad news of some kind.

LADY: Do as you please, but no one can escape his destiny. I feel as though higher powers had conferred about us, and decided our fate.

STRANGER: You too? Do you know, just now I heard the gavel fall, the chairs pushed back and the servants sent out. Oh, this torture! No, I won't go with you.

LADY: What have you done to me? When I went into that chapel, I couldn't pray. A candle went out on the altar and a cold wind blew on my face just as I heard you call me.

STRANGER: I didn't call. I just longed for you.

LADY: You're not the weak child you pretend to be. Your power is extraordinary. I'm frightened of you.

STRANGER: When I'm alone I'm as weak as a paralytic, but once I have hold of someone I become strong. Now I want to be strong, so I will go with you.

LADY: Perhaps you can free me from my ogre.

STRANGER: Are there such things?

LADY: I call him that.

STRANGER: Good. Then I will go with you; to fight with trolls, to liberate princesses, to kill ogres — that is to live!

LADY: Come, my liberator.

She draws the veil from her face, kisses him swiftly on the mouth and hastens out. The STRANGER *stands for a moment bewildered and dazed. A high-pitched chorus of women's voices approaching a shriek is heard from the church. The illuminated rose window suddenly becomes dark; the tree above the bench stirs; the* MOURNERS *rise from their places and look up at the sky, as though seeing something unusual and alarming. The* STRANGER *hurries out after the* LADY.

Scene 2. At the DOCTOR'S

A courtyard enclosed by three rows of houses — single-storeyed wooden buildings with tiled roofs and small windows. To the right, glass doors and a verandah. Left, outside the windows, a rose-hedge and beehives. In the centre of the yard is a heap of wood, shaped like an oriental cupola; beside it, a well. Over the centre of the middle wall rises the top of a tall walnut tree. In the right-hand corner is the gate to the garden. By the well is a large tortoise. Right, the entrance down to the cellar. An ice-chest and a rubbish-bin. Outside the verandah, tables and chairs.

SISTER [*enters from the verandah with a telegram*]: Here is bad news, brother.

DOCTOR: When wasn't there?

SISTER: But this time! Ingeborg is coming home, with — guess whom?

DOCTOR: Wait a moment. I know, because I have long sensed that this would happen, and longed for it. This writer — I have admired him, learned from him and wished to know him. Now he is coming, you say? Where did Ingeborg meet him?

SISTER: In town, it seems. Probably in that literary salon she frequents.

DOCTOR: I have often wondered if this man can be someone I was at school with. The name is the same. I hope so — that boy had something fateful about him, and now that he's a man, he should have fulfilled those tendencies.

SISTER: Don't let him enter your house. Go away, pretend you have to see someone.

DOCTOR: No. One cannot run away from one's fate —

SISTER: You never shrank from anything. Are you going to grovel before this imaginary monster that you call Fate?

DOCTOR: Life has taught me to. I have wasted much time and strength struggling against the inevitable.

SISTER: But why do you let your wife go round compromising herself, and you?

DOCTOR: You know why. Because, when I released her from her vows, I offered her a life of freedom, in contrast to what she regarded as a prison. Anyway, I couldn't love her if she obeyed me or if I was able to command her.

SISTER: So you make a friend of your enemy.

DOCTOR: Now, now.

SISTER: And you let her bring into your house the man who will destroy you. Oh, if you knew how boundlessly I hate that man!

DOCTOR: I know, I know. His latest book is loathsome. But it suggests that he suffers from some mental sickness.

SISTER: Then they should have put him away.

DOCTOR: Some people say that, but I do not feel he has gone that far —

SISTER: That's because you're so eccentric yourself, and have a wife who is raving mad.

DOCTOR: I can't deny that mad people have always exercised a strong attraction for me. At least eccentricity is never banal. [*A steamer's whistle is heard.*] What was that? Someone cried out!

SISTER: You're nervous. It was only the steamer. But I beg you — please go!

DOCTOR: I think I'd like to — but I can't. Do you know, when I stand here, I see his portrait there in my study. And the sunshine casts a shadow which makes him look like — it's horrible! Do you see who he looks like?

SISTER: He looks like the Evil One. Go!

DOCTOR: I can't.

SISTER: At least defend yourself —

DOCTOR: I usually do. But this time it's like an approaching storm. How many times have I not wished to run away but been unable to! It's as though the earth was of iron and I a magnet. If disaster strikes, it is not of my choice. They've just come in through the gate.

SISTER: I heard nothing.

DOCTOR: But I, I hear them. And now I see them too. It is he, my old schoolfriend. He did something once in school — I was blamed, and punished for it. But he acquired the nickname Caesar, I don't know why.

SISTER: And this man —

DOCTOR: Yes, such is life. Caesar!

LADY [enters]: Good afternoon, husband. I've a nice surprise for you.

DOCTOR: So I've heard. He is welcome.

LADY: He's in the guest room changing his collar.

DOCTOR: Are you happy with your capture?

LADY: He is certainly the unhappiest person I have ever met in my life.

DOCTOR: That's saying a lot.

LADY: Yes; he suffers for all mankind.

DOCTOR: I'm sure. Go to him, sister, and show him down to us.

SISTER goes.

DOCTOR: You've had an interesting journey?

LADY: Yes; I've met many strange people. Have you had any patients?

DOCTOR: No, the surgery's been empty all morning. My practice seems to be declining.

LADY [*sympathetically*]: I'm sorry. I say, aren't you going to bring the wood-pile in? It'll get damp out there.

DOCTOR [*without reproach*]: I know. And I should kill the bees and pick the fruit in the garden, but I can't seem to care about anything —

LADY: You're tired.

DOCTOR: Tired of everything.

LADY [*without bitterness*]: And you have a bad wife, who can't be of any help to you.

DOCTOR [*gently*]: You mustn't say such things, when I don't say them.

LADY [*turns to the verandah*]: Here he is.

The STRANGER *enters, dressed more youthfully than in the opening scene. He steps in from the verandah with a forced ease; seems to recognize the* DOCTOR, *cringes and stumbles forward, but recovers himself.*

DOCTOR: Welcome to my house.

STRANGER: Thank you.

DOCTOR: You bring good weather. We need it — it's been raining here for six weeks —

STRANGER: Not seven? It usually rains for seven weeks after St Swithin's Day. But I'd forgotten, that hasn't come yet. How stupid I am! Hm!

DOCTOR: I'm afraid our simple way of life in this small town will seem dull to you who are used to the pleasures of the capital.

STRANGER: Oh, no — I am as little at home there as here. Forgive my asking, but haven't we met before? When we were young?

DOCTOR: Never.

The LADY *has seated herself at the table, and is knitting.*

STRANGER: You're sure?

DOCTOR: Quite sure. I have followed your literary career from its beginning and, as I know my wife has told you, with the greatest interest, so that if we had met I should have remembered it, at any rate your name. However — here you see how a country doctor lives.

STRANGER: If you knew how a so-called liberator lives, you wouldn't envy him.

DOCTOR: I can imagine — I've seen how people love the chains that bind them. Perhaps it is ordained, since it is so.

STRANGER [*listens*]: That's strange. Who is playing the piano next door?

DOCTOR: I don't know who it can be. Do you know, Ingeborg?

LADY: No.

STRANGER: It's Mendelssohn's Funeral March. It follows me everywhere. I don't know if it's only in my head, or —

DOCTOR: Do you have auditory hallucinations?

STRANGER: Not hallucinations, but little things that have actually happened persecute me. Can't you hear music?

DOCTOR *and* LADY: Yes, of course.

LADY: And it is Mendelssohn.

DOCTOR: He's very fashionable now.

STRANGER: Yes, I know, but that someone should be playing it just now, here — [*Gets up.*]

DOCTOR: If it will reassure you, I'll go and enquire. [*Goes out on to the verandah.*]

STRANGER [*to* LADY]: I'm stifling here. I can't spend a night under this roof. Your husband looks like an ogre, and in his presence you turn into a pillar of salt. Murder has been committed in this house. There are ghosts here, and I shall leave as soon as I get the chance.

DOCTOR [*from outside*]: Yes, the postmistress is playing the piano.

STRANGER [*nervously*]: Oh. That's all right, then. This is a strange home you have here, Doctor. Everything is unusual. That wood-pile, for instance —

DOCTOR: Yes. It's been struck by lightning twice —

STRANGER: How horrible. But you still keep it there?

DOCTOR: Yes, just because of that. And this year I've raised it six feet. But also because it gives me shade in the summer. Like Jonah's gourd. But when autumn comes, he'll go into the woodshed —

STRANGER [*looks around*]: And you have Christmas roses — which flower in summer. Where did you get them? Everything here is as though time was going backwards —

DOCTOR: Oh, those. Well, I have a patient here who's a little mentally disturbed —

STRANGER: In this house?

DOCTOR: Yes, but he's a quiet fellow. He simply broods over the aimlessness of Nature, and thinks it stupid that Christmas roses should freeze in the snow, so he puts them in the cellar and plants them in the spring.

STRANGER: You have a madman in the house? That's disagreeable.

DOCTOR: He's very peaceable.

STRANGER: How did he become mad?

DOCTOR: Who can tell? Mental illness is not like bodily illness.

STRANGER: Is he — around?

DOCTOR: The madman? Yes, he's walking in the garden arranging the universe. But if he bothers you, we'll lock him in the cellar.

STRANGER: Why do they allow such wretches to live?

DOCTOR: One never knows if they're ready —

STRANGER: For what?

DOCTOR: For what follows.

STRANGER: Nothing follows life.

    Pause.

DOCTOR: Who knows?

STRANGER: It's horrible here. Do you have corpses too?

DOCTOR: Yes. In the ice-chest here. Some nice bits and pieces, which I must send along to the medical board. [*Takes out a leg and arm.*] Look.

STRANGER: It's like Bluebeard's castle.

DOCTOR [*sharply*]: What do you mean by that? [*Glances sharply at the* LADY.] You think I murder my wives? Eh?

STRANGER: Good heavens, no, I can see that you don't. But — you do have ghosts here, don't you?

DOCTOR: I should say we do! Ask my wife.

    He moves behind the wood-pile, so that he is invisible to the LADY *and the* STRANGER.

LADY [*to* STRANGER]: You can speak normally. My husband is a little deaf, though he can lip-read.

STRANGER: Then I'll take the opportunity to say that I've never had a more agonizing half-hour in my life. We stand here talking the most utter nonsense, simply because

no one has the courage to speak his thoughts. I was in
such a state just now that I was seriously think of taking out my knife and opening a vein to cool myself down,
but now I feel inclined to speak plainly and blow him to
blazes. Shall we tell him straight out that we intend to go
away together, and that you've had enough of his lunacy?

LADY: If you talk like that, I shall come to hate you. One
should always behave like a gentleman.

STRANGER: How nicely you've been brought up.

The DOCTOR *moves into their view. They continue.*

STRANGER: Will you run away with me, before the sun
goes down?

LADY: Sir —

STRANGER: Why did you kiss me yesterday?

LADY: Sir —

STRANGER: Imagine if he can hear us! He looks so sly —

DOCTOR: Well, Ingeborg, how shall we amuse our guest?

LADY: Our guest doesn't expect to be amused. He is not
accustomed to pleasure —

The DOCTOR *blows a whistle. The* MADMAN *comes
into sight in the garden. He wears a laurel wreath on
his head and is curiously dressed.*

DOCTOR: Caesar! Come here!

STRANGER [*disturbed*]: Is his name Caesar?

DOCTOR: No, that's a nickname I gave him after a boy
who was at school with me —

STRANGER [*uneasily*]: What is this?

DOCTOR: Well, it's a strange story. But I got the blame.

LADY [*to* STRANGER]: Who ever heard of a child being
destroyed by that?

The STRANGER *winces. The* MADMAN *enters.*

DOCTOR: Come in and bow to the great writer, Caesar.

MADMAN: Is that the great writer?

LADY [*to* DOCTOR]: Why must you bring the madman in, when it upsets our guest?

DOCTOR: Now, Caesar, don't be rude, or you'll be whipped.

MADMAN: He's Caesar, all right, but he isn't great. He doesn't know which came first, the chicken or the egg. But I know.

STRANGER [*to* LADY]: I'm going. Have you tempted me into an ambush, or what am I to believe? In a moment he'll probably let out the bees to amuse me.

LADY: You must trust me implicitly, however things may appear. And don't talk so loud.

STRANGER: But he'll never leave us, this frightful ogre. Never.

DOCTOR [*looks at his watch*]: Well, if you'll excuse me, I must go and visit a patient. I'll be back in an hour. I hope you won't get bored waiting.

STRANGER: I'm used to waiting for what never comes.

DOCTOR [*to* MADMAN]: Caesar, you scoundrel, come here. I'll shut you in the cellar. [*Goes out with the* MADMAN.]

STRANGER [*to* LADY]: What is this? Who is persecuting me? You assure me that your husband feels friendly towards me; I believe you, and yet he can't open his mouth without wounding me. Every word he spoke pierced me like a needle. And there's that funeral march again — it really is being played. And that Christmas rose again. Why does everything recur? Dead men and beggars and madmen and human destinies and childhood memories. Come away. Let me liberate you from this hell.

LADY: That was why I brought you here. And also so that no one would be able to say that you had stolen another man's wife. But I must ask you one thing. Can I trust you?

STRANGER: You mean my feelings?

LADY: We won't speak of them; we have excluded them. And they'll last as long as they will last.

STRANGER: You mean, for material support, then? Yes, I've a lot of money due to me. I need only write or send a telegram —

LADY: Then I trust you. Very well. [*Puts her knitting in her pocket.*] Go out through that gate. Follow the lilac hedge and you'll see a wooden door. Open it and you'll find yourself on the high road. Meet me in the next village.

STRANGER [*hesitates*]: I don't like back doors. I'd rather have fought him in the open —

LADY [*with a gesture*]: Hurry!

STRANGER: Come with me.

LADY: Very well. But then I'll go first. [*Turns and blows a kiss towards the verandah.*] My poor ogre!

ACT TWO

Scene 1. A hotel room

The STRANGER. *A* PORTER. *The* LADY.

STRANGER [*with a travelling bag in his hand*]: You have no other room?

PORTER: None at all.

STRANGER: But I don't want to sleep in this one.

LADY: They haven't another, dearest, and all the other hotels are full.

STRANGER [*to* PORTER]: Leave us.

> The LADY *falls into a chair without removing her overcoat or hat.*

STRANGER: Is there anything you'd like?

LADY: Yes. For you to kill me.

STRANGER: I can understand that. Refused everywhere because we're not married, the police after us, and now we find ourselves in this hotel, the last in the world I'd choose — and this room, number eight. There's someone fighting against me. There's someone.

LADY: Is this number eight?

STRANGER: You've been here before too?

LADY: And you?

STRANGER: Yes.

LADY: Let's get out of here — on to the street, into the forest, anywhere —

STRANGER: I'd like to. But I'm as tired as you are, after this dreadful chase. Do you know, I felt our journey would end here — I resisted, I tried to go somewhere else, but the trains were late, they didn't come, and we had to come here, to this room. It's the Devil's work; but we'll get to grips, he and I!

LADY: It seems we shall never find peace, on this earth.

STRANGER: It's amazing how nothing has changed here. That permanently withering Christmas rose — there it is again. And that picture, the Hotel Breuer in Montreux. I've stayed there too.

LADY: Did you go to the post-office?

STRANGER: I was waiting for you to ask that. Yes, I went. In reply to five letters and three telegrams I'd sent, there was just a telegram, saying my publisher had gone abroad for a fortnight.

LADY: Then we're finished.

STRANGER: Pretty well.

LADY: And in five minutes the porter will come to ask for our passports, and then the manager will ask us to leave.

STRANGER: Then there'll be only one thing left —

LADY: Two.

STRANGER: But the other's impossible.

LADY: What is the other?

STRANGER: To go to your parents, in the country.

LADY: You read my thoughts already.

STRANGER: We can no longer have any secrets from each other.

LADY: Then our dream is finished.

STRANGER: Perhaps.

LADY: Go and send one more telegram.

STRANGER: I should, but I can't do anything any more. I don't any longer believe in any future to my labours. Someone has paralysed me.

LADY: And me. We had decided never to talk about the past, but we drag it with us. Look at this wallpaper. Do you see the picture those flowers make?

STRANGER: Yes, it's him. Everywhere, everywhere! How many times — ! But I see someone else in the pattern of that tablecloth — ! Is this real? No, it must be a delusion. I'll be hearing that funeral march any moment, and then it'll be complete. [*Listens.*] There it is!

LADY: I hear nothing.

STRANGER: Then — I'm going —

LADY: Shall we go home?

STRANGER: The last and worst resort. To come as vagabonds, as beggars — no, that's impossible.

LADY: But it's — no, it's too much. To come in shame and dishonour, and bring grief to them — for me to see you humiliated, and you me. We could never respect each other again.

STRANGER: It's true, it would be worse than death. And yet — somehow I feel it's inevitable, and I begin to long for it, to get it over with, since it must be.

LADY [*takes out her knitting*]: But I have no wish to be insulted in your presence. There must be some other way. If we were married — we could do it quickly, my other marriage isn't strictly legal according to the laws of the country where it happened. We only need to go and get ourselves married by the same priest who — but this is humiliating for you —

STRANGER: It's like everything else. This honeymoon is beginning to be like a pilgrimage — or a gauntlet —

LADY: You're right. And in five minutes the manager will come and turn us out. The only way to end these humiliations is to swallow the final — hush! I hear footsteps.

STRANGER: I feel you're right. Well, I'm ready. I'm ready for everything now, and since I can't fight the invisible, I'll show how long I can endure it. Lend me your jewellery — I'll redeem them when my publisher gets back, if he hasn't got drowned bathing or been killed in a railway accident. When one's as ambitious for honour as I am, the first thing one must be ready to sacrifice is one's honour.

LADY: Since we're agreed, don't you think we'd better leave this room voluntarily? Oh, God! Here he comes. The manager.

STRANGER: Let us go. The gauntlet of the waiters, the chambermaids, the bootboys and the porter — the blush of shame and the pallor of anger. The beasts of the forest have their holes, but we must flaunt our shame. At least lower your veil.

LADY: This is freedom.

STRANGER: And I the liberator.

They go.

Scene 2. By the sea

A hut on a cliff by the sea. Outside, a table with chairs. The STRANGER *and the* LADY *are in light-coloured clothes and look younger than in the previous scene. The* LADY *is knitting.*

STRANGER: Three days of happiness and peace with my wife. Now the old unease returns.

LADY: What are you afraid of?

STRANGER: That this won't last.

LADY: Why do you think that?

STRANGER: I don't know. I feel it must end, suddenly, horribly. There's something false in this sunshine and calm. And I feel that happiness is not part of my destiny.

LADY: But everything's settled. My parents accept the situation, my husband has written to say he understands —

STRANGER: What's the use, what's the use? Fate spins her web, I hear again the gavel fall, the chairs pushed back from the table. The sentence is pronounced, but it must have been decided before I was born, because I began to serve my punishment even in childhood. There isn't a moment in my life on which I can look back with joy —

LADY: And you got everything you asked from life.

STRANGER: Everything. But I forgot to ask for gold.

LADY: Are you back there again?

STRANGER: Do you wonder?

LADY: Hush!

STRANGER: Why do you always knit? You look like one of the Fates, drawing that wool through your fingers. No, don't stop. The most beautiful sight I know is a woman bent over her work, or her child. What are you knitting?

LADY: Only a shawl.

STRANGER: It looks like a net of nerves and knots: your thoughts. I imagine the inside of your brain must look like that —

LADY: If I had half the thoughts you think I have. But I have none at all.

STRANGER: Perhaps that's why I find such contentment with you. I find you complete. I can't imagine life without you. The clouds have gone, the sky is blue, the breeze warm — feel how it strokes your face! This is life; yes, now I am alive, just now! I feel myself swell and stretch, rarefy, become boundless; I am everywhere, in the sea which is my blood, in the mountains which are my skeleton, in the trees, in the flowers. And my head reaches to heaven. I look out over the Universe which is I, I feel the strength of the Creator within me, for I am the Creator. I should like to take this globe into my hand and knead it into something completer, more lasting, more beautiful. I should like to see all creation happy — born without pain, living without grief, and dying calmly joyful. Eve, will you die with me, now, this moment, for in another moment the agony will return?

LADY: No, I'm not ready to die.

STRANGER: Why?

LADY: I think I still have something left undone. Perhaps I have not suffered enough —

STRANGER: You think that is the purpose of life?

LADY: It seems so. But please do one thing for me.

STRANGER: Well?

LADY: Don't blaspheme like you did just now, and don't liken yourself to God. When you do, you remind me of Caesar in his cellar at home —

STRANGER [*disturbed*]: Caesar? How can you know? Tell me!

LADY: If I hurt you, I didn't mean it. I was stupid to say "home". Forgive me.

STRANGER: Were you only thinking of blasphemy when you likened me to Caesar?

LADY: Yes.

STRANGER: It's strange, I believe you when you say you don't want to wound me. And yet you do, like everyone else I meet. Why?

LADY: Because you're hyper-sensitive.

STRANGER: There you are again. You mean I'm paranoiac?

LADY: I swear I didn't mean that. Now the demons of discord and suspicion have come between us. Drive them away while there's time!

STRANGER: You mustn't say I blaspheme when I say what so many have said: "Look, we are gods!"

LADY: Oh, if it's true, why can't you help yourself and us?

STRANGER: Can't I? Wait. We are only beginning.

LADY: If the end is like the beginning, Heaven help us!

STRANGER: I know what you are afraid of. I had a surprise I meant to keep for you, but I won't torment you any longer. [*Takes out a registered, unopened letter.*] Look.

LADY: The money has come!

STRANGER: This morning. Who can destroy me now?

LADY: Don't talk like that. You know who can destroy us.

STRANGER: Who?

LADY: He Who punishes human pride.

STRANGER: And courage. Especially courage. This was my Achilles' heel, and I have borne everything except this damned lack of money, which always trapped me.

LADY: Forgive my asking, but how much have you received.

STRANGER: I don't know, I haven't opened it yet. But I know roughly how much there should be. Let me see. [*Opens letter.*] What is this? No money, only a note from the bank to say I have nothing in my account. Can this be right?

LADY: I begin to believe what you said just now.

STRANGER: That I am damned? Yes. But I fling my damnation back where it came from. You up there! I curse You!

LADY: Don't! You frighten me.

STRANGER: Fear me if you like, but don't despise me. Now the gauntlet is down, and you'll see a bout between champions. [*Opens his coat and waistcoat and gazes threateningly upwards.*] Come on! Strike me with Your lightning, if You dare! Scare me with Your thunder, if You can!

LADY: Don't talk like that!

STRANGER: Yes! Just like that! Who dares to wake me from my dream of love? Who snatches the beaker from my mouth, and women from my arms? Jealous powers, be they gods or devils. Petty-bourgeois gods, who answer an honest challenge with pinpricks from the rear; who refuse to meet a man on his own ground, but taunt him with unpaid bills and sneak in through the back door to humiliate him before his servants; who won't fight with honest weapons, but must hoot and spit; I defy them! These mighty powers and masters, I defy them!

LADY: May Heaven forgive you!

STRANGER: The sky is still blue and silent, the sea still blue and foolish. Hush; I hear a poem coming. I call it that when a theme begins to stir in my head. First I hear the rhythm. This time it is like the tramping of hooves, the jingle of spurs; the clash of swords; but a fluttering too, as when a sail bellies. Banners!

LADY: No, it is only the wind in the trees —

STRANGER: Hush! Now they are riding over a bridge — a wooden bridge, and there is no water in the river, only stones. Wait! Now they are reading a prayer, men and women. A *Te Deum*. Now I see — do you know where? — in your shawl — a big kitchen, white, with lime-washed walls; three small windows, deep-set, with lattices and flowers. In the left-hand corner stands a stove, in the right a dining-table with pine benches; and over the table in the corner hangs a black crucifix. Beneath it burns a lamp. But the ceiling is of sooty brown beams — and on the walls hangs mistletoe, rather withered —

LADY [*frightened*]: Where do you see all this? Where?

STRANGER: In your shawl.

LADY: Do you see any people there?

STRANGER: I see an old, a very old man sitting at the kitchen table. With a hunting-bag. But his hands are clasped in prayer. And on the floor an old woman is kneeling. Now I hear the prayer again. It seems to come from outside, on the verandah. But the two in the kitchen look as though they were made of white wax or honey. And over it all lies a veil. No, this is no poem. [*Awakes.*] This is something else.

LADY: It is reality. It is the kitchen in my parents' home,

where you have never been. The old man was my grandfather, the forester; the woman, my mother. She was
praying — for us. It is six o'clock — when the servants read
prayers on the verandah —

STRANGER: It's horrible. Am I seeing into the future too?
Yet it was beautiful. The room, snow-white, with mistletoe and flowers. But why are they praying for us?

LADY: Yes, why? Have we done wrong?

STRANGER: What is wrong?

LADY: I have read that Wrong does not exist, and yet — !
I so long to see my mother again. Not my father, he disowned me, as he disowned my mother —

STRANGER: Why did he disown her?

LADY: Who knows such things? The children least of all.
Let us go home. I long to.

STRANGER: To the lion's den, the snake pit. One more or
less, why not? For your sake I will do it, but not as a
prodigal son. For your sake I will go through fire and
water —

LADY: You cannot know that.

STRANGER: But I can usually guess.

LADY: It is a hard journey. They live on a mountain. The
house can only be reached on foot.

STRANGER: It sounds like a fairy tale. But I seem to have
read or dreamed something like this.

LADY: Perhaps you have. But everything you will see is
real — a little strange, perhaps, but people are sometimes
strange. Are you ready?

STRANGER: Quite ready, for whatever may happen.

LADY [*kisses him on the forehead and makes the sign of
the cross, simply and shyly, without affectation*]: Come!

Scene 3. On the highway

A mountain landscape. Rear right, on a peak, stands a chapel. The highway, lined by fruit-trees, winds downstage. Between the trees can be seen Calvaries, small chapels of expiation, and crosses commemorating accidents. Downstage a signpost with a notice: "Begging is forbidden in this parish."

The STRANGER. *The* LADY.

LADY: You are tired.

STRANGER: I won't deny it. But what humiliates me is that I am hungry, because our money is finished. I never thought that would happen to me.

LADY: It seems we must be ready for everything, for I think we are fallen from grace. Look, my boot has split. We shall look like beggars.

STRANGER [*points at the signpost*]: And begging is forbidden in this parish. Why do they have to write it in such big letters?

LADY: It's been there for as long as I can remember. I haven't been here since I was a child. The road seemed quite short then, the mountains less high, the trees smaller. And I think we used to hear birds sing.

STRANGER: Birds sang for you all the year round, poor child. Now they sing only in the spring — and it is nearly autumn. But then you danced down this endless road of Calvaries, picking flowers at the foot of the crosses — [*A distant hunting-horn is heard.*] What's that?

LADY: It's Grandfather coming back from hunting. The good old man. Let's hurry and get there before dark.

STRANGER: Is it far?

LADY: Not very. We have only the mountain to cross, and then the river.

STRANGER: That's the river I hear, then?

LADY: Yes. That's where I was born and brought up. I was eighteen before I crossed to this shore, to see what made the distance so blue. Now I have seen it.

STRANGER: You're crying.

LADY: The good old man! When I stepped into the boat, he said: "There lies the world, child. When you have seen enough, come back to your mountain. The mountains hide." I have seen enough. Enough!

STRANGER: Let us go. The road is long, and it is beginning to grow dark.

They take up their things and go.

Scene 4. At the gorge

The narrow entry to a gorge. It is lined by steep mountains covered with pine forests. Downstage a hovel. Against its door stands a broom, on the shaft of which hangs a buck's horn. Left, a smithy, the open door of which emits a red glow. Right, a flour mill. In the background, the gorge, with a millstream and bridge. The mountains form gigantic human profiles.

As the curtain rises the SMITH *is standing in the door of the smithy and the* MILLER'S WIFE *in the door of the mill. As the* LADY *enters they make a gesture to each other and disappear through their doorways. The* LADY *and* STRANGER *have ragged clothes. The* LADY *goes towards the smithy.*

STRANGER [*enters*]: They hid. Because of us, I suppose.

LADY: I don't believe that.

STRANGER: What a strange landscape this is! And how disquieting! Why is that broom there, and that grease-horn? Probably because it's their normal place, but they make me think of witches. Why is the smithy black and the mill white? Because one is sooty and the other floury, but just now when I saw the blacksmith standing in the glow of his fire facing the white miller's wife, I thought of an old poem — ! But do you see those giants up there? No, it's intolerable. Can't you see your ogre, whom I saved you from? It's his profile. Look! There!

LADY: It's only the mountain —

STRANGER: It is the mountain, but it's still him.

LADY: Don't ask me why we see him.

STRANGER: Conscience pricks when one is hungry and tired, it sleeps when one is full and rested. Isn't it like a curse that we have to arrive like beggars? Do you see how ragged we are after climbing through these thorn bushes? I think someone is fighting me —

LADY: Why did you challenge God?

STRANGER: Because I want to fight openly, not with unpaid bills and empty purses. Even so; here is my last shilling. Let the god of the river take it, if he exists. [*Throws a coin into the stream.*]

LADY: We needed that for the ferryman. When we enter the house now we must first ask for money —

STRANGER: When did we talk about anything else?

LADY: You despise money —

STRANGER: Like everything else.

LADY: Everything is not contemptible. There are good things —

STRANGER: I haven't noticed them.

LADY: Come with me and you'll see.

STRANGER: Very well. I'll come.

He shrinks as he is about to pass the smithy.

LADY [*who has gone ahead*]: Are you afraid of the fire?

STRANGER: No. But —

> *The hunting-horn is heard distantly. He runs past the smithy after her.*

Scene 5. In the kitchen

A large kitchen with whitewashed walls. Three windows in the right-hand corner (two in the rear wall, one in the right wall). The windows are small and set in deep niches containing flower pots. The roof is sooty brown, with beams. In the left corner, a stove with pots, etc., of copper, iron, pewter and wood. In the right corner, a crucifix with a lamp. Beneath it a square table with benches against the wall. Sprigs of mistletoe hang here and there. A door upstage. Outside can be seen the workhouse; through the rear windows, the church. By the stove are baskets for the dogs, and the beggars' table.

The OLD MAN *is seated at the table under the crucifix with his hands clasped. His hunting-bag lies in front of him. He is in his eighties, strongly built with white hair and a full beard, and is dressed as a forester. The* MOTHER *is kneeling in the centre of the room. She is grey-haired, approaching fifty, dressed in black and white. From outside can be clearly heard the voices of men, women and children singing the final bars of the prayer: "Holy Mary, Mother of God, pray for us poor sinners, now and at the hour of our death. Amen."*

OLD MAN *and* MOTHER: Amen.

MOTHER: Father. Two tramps have been seen by the river. They were ragged and dirty and had been in the water. When the boatman asked for their fare they had nothing. Now they're sitting in the sheep-hut drying their clothes.

OLD MAN: Let them sit.

MOTHER: Never close your door to a beggar. It may be an angel.

OLD MAN: That is true. Let them come.

MOTHER: I'll put some food out here on the beggars' table, if it won't disturb you.

OLD MAN: By all means.

MOTHER: Shall I give them some of the cider?

OLD MAN: Yes. You can light a fire too. They'll be frozen.

MOTHER: It's a little late to make up a fire. But if you wish it, Father —

OLD MAN [*looks out through the window*]: Yes, do it.

MOTHER: What are you looking at, Father?

OLD MAN: The river has risen. I'm wondering what I've wondered for seventy-five years. When shall I reach the sea?

MOTHER: Are you sad this evening, Father?

OLD MAN: *Et introibo ad altarem Dei; ad Deum qui laetificat juventutem meam.* Yes, I am sad. *Deus, Deus meus; quare tristis est anima mea, et quare conturbas me?*

MOTHER: Put your trust in God.

The MAID *enters and makes a sign to the* MOTHER, *who goes over to her. They whisper. The* MAID *goes.*

OLD MAN: I heard you. My God! Must I endure this too!

MOTHER: You don't have to meet them. You can go up to your room.

OLD MAN: No, I shall accept them as a penitence. But why do they come like this, as tramps?

MOTHER: I expect they lost their way and had an accident. Do you think — ?

OLD MAN: But that she should bring her — her husband here, with her! It's shameless.

MOTHER: You know Ingeborg. She always thinks everything she does is right and proper. Have you ever known her be ashamed of anything she's done, or suffer correction? Yet she's not shameless, quite the reverse. And everything she does, however tasteless, somehow seems right for her.

OLD MAN: Yes. And somehow one can't be angry with her. She always feels she's not responsible, isn't even touched by insults; it's as though she denied her own existence, or was two women, one sinning, the other absolving. But this man! I've never hated anyone as much as I do him. He sees nothing but evil everywhere. And I've never heard as much evil of any man as I have of him.

MOTHER: I know, Father. But perhaps Ingeborg has some destiny to fulfil in this man's life, and he in hers. Perhaps they have to torment each other until they find peace —

OLD MAN: You may be right. But I don't want to have any share in something I find shameless. Must I have this man under my roof? But I must endure it, like everything else. I've deserved it.

MOTHER: In God's name, then.

The LADY *and the* STRANGER *enter.*

MOTHER: Welcome to you both.

LADY: Thank you, Mother.

The OLD MAN *rises and studies the* STRANGER.

LADY: God's peace be with you, Grandfather. This is my husband. Give him your hand.

OLD MAN: I want to look at him first. [*Approaches the* STRANGER, *places his hands on his shoulders and looks him in the eyes.*] Why have you come to my house?

STRANGER [*simply*]: Only to keep my wife company, at her request.

OLD MAN: If that is true, you are welcome. I have had a long and stormy life, and have at last found, in solitude, a certain peace. I beg you not to disturb it.

STRANGER: I do not come to beg for anything, and I shall take nothing with me when I go.

OLD MAN: That answer displeases me; we all need each other. I may even need you. One never knows, young man.

LADY: Grandfather!

OLD MAN: Yes, child. I do not wish you happiness, for there is no such thing, but I wish you strength to endure your fate. Now I shall leave you. Your mother will see to your needs. [Goes.]

LADY [to MOTHER]: Did you put that food out for us, Mother?

MOTHER: On the beggars' table? — No, no — I didn't realize —

LADY: Yes, we must look like beggars. We got lost on the mountain. If Grandfather hadn't sounded his horn —

MOTHER: Grandfather gave up hunting long ago.

LADY: Then it must have been someone else. Well, Mother, I'll go to the rose room and make it ready.

MOTHER: Go, child. I'll follow you.

The LADY *wants to say something, but cannot. She goes.*

STRANGER [to MOTHER]: I've seen this room before.

MOTHER: And I've seen you. I've been waiting for you.

STRANGER: As one awaits misfortune?

MOTHER: Why do you say that?

STRANGER: Because I usually bring misfortune with me.

But since I must be somewhere, and cannot change my fate, I have no scruples —

MOTHER: Then you're like my daughter. She has no scruples, and no conscience —

STRANGER: Oh?

MOTHER: You thought I meant ill; but I can't stand here and speak ill of my child. I only made the comparison because I assumed you knew her character as I do.

STRANGER: I haven't noticed those characteristics in Eve.

MOTHER: Why do you call Ingeborg Eve?

STRANGER: By inventing a name for her I made her mine. I shall recreate her as I wish her to be —

MOTHER: In your own image? [*Smiles.*] Country witches carve an image of the one they want to destroy and give it the name of their intended victim. So you calculate through this new Eve of yours to destroy her whole sex?

STRANGER [*looks at the* MOTHER *in amazement*]: Damn it — ! Forgive me, you are my wife's mother, but I know you to be religious. How can you have such thoughts?

MOTHER: They are yours.

STRANGER: This is beginning to be interesting. I came expecting a country idyll and find myself in a witch's kitchen.

MOTHER: Not quite. But you forgot, or didn't know, that I am a woman who was shamefully abandoned by a man, and that you are a man who shamefully abandoned a woman.

STRANGER: That's plain speaking. Well, now I know where I am.

MOTHER: And I'd like to know where I am. Can you support two families?

STRANGER: Yes, if all goes well.

MOTHER: All doesn't go well in this life. Money can vanish.

STRANGER: But my talent is a capital asset which will not vanish.

MOTHER: It's been known to happen.

STRANGER: I've never met anyone who so knew how to drain a man's courage —

MOTHER: Arrogance needs to be drained. Your last book wasn't so good.

STRANGER: You've read that too?

MOTHER: And know your secrets. So don't try to fool me. One small thing which bothers me. Why didn't you pay the boatman?

STRANGER: My Achilles' heel again! I threw away my last shilling. Can't you talk about anything but money here?

MOTHER: Oh, we can. But in this house we do our duties first and take our pleasures afterwards. So you came on foot because you hadn't any money?

STRANGER: Yes

MOTHER [*smiles*]: And perhaps you haven't eaten, either?

STRANGER: No.

MOTHER: You're a schoolboy, a lazy good-for-nothing —

STRANGER: I've been through a lot in my life, but I never found myself in a situation like this —

MOTHER: I almost pity you. I'd be inclined to laugh if you weren't so pathetic. You'll be the cause of many tears. Now you've got what you want, stick to the woman who loves you. If you throw her over you'll never smile again. You'll forget what happiness was.

STRANGER: Is that a threat?

MOTHER: No. A warning. Now go and eat your supper.

STRANGER [*indicates the beggars' table*]: At that table?

MOTHER: You mock poverty; you may not always do so. I've known it happen before.

STRANGER: I'll soon believe nothing is impossible. This is the worst I've ever known.

MOTHER: Oh, no. There's worse possible. Just you wait.

STRANGER [*miserably*]: Yes. I expect anything now.

> *He goes. The* MOTHER *is left alone. The* OLD MAN *enters.*

OLD MAN: Well. That was no angel.

MOTHER: Not a good one, anyway.

OLD MAN: Ssh! You know how superstitious the people are round here. Well, as I was going down to the river, I heard some of them talking. One said that his horse shied at "him"; another that his dogs flew at him, so that he had to tie them up; the ferryman swore that his boat rose in the water when "he" stepped into it. Of course it's just superstition, but —

MOTHER: But?

OLD MAN: Well, only that a magpie flew in through the window, and it was shut, through the glass, into their room. But perhaps I didn't see right.

MOTHER: I expect not. But why does one sometimes see wrong — and in the right place?

OLD MAN: That man's very presence makes me ill. I feel a tightness in my chest when he looks at me.

MOTHER: We must get rid of him. I don't think he'll be happy here.

OLD MAN: No, I don't see him growing old here. I got a letter last night warning me against him. For one thing, the police are after him —

MOTHER: The police? In your house!

OLD MAN: Yes, it's some question of money. But I beg you — the laws of hospitality, even towards beggars, even towards enemies, are sacred. Leave him in peace for a few days till he has recovered from this mad chase. You see how Providence has got her claws into him. His soul must be ground in the bruising-mill before he goes into the sieve!

MOTHER: I wouldn't mind being the instrument of Providence in this case.

OLD MAN: Don't confuse Providence with revenge.

MOTHER: I'll try not to. If it's possible.

OLD MAN: Good night.

MOTHER: Do you think Ingeborg has read his latest book?

OLD MAN: Hardly. How could she bind herself to a man with such views?

MOTHER: You're right. She can't have. Well. Now she shall.

ACT THREE

Scene 1. The rose room

A room in the forester's house, furnished in a simple but homely manner. The walls are washed in rose-pink; the curtains are of thin rose-red muslin. Flowers stand in the small latticed windows. Right, a desk and bookshelf. Left, an ottoman with a canopy of rose-red curtains above. Chairs and tables in old German style. Upstage, a door; outside, a landscape and the workhouse, a dark gloomy building with uncurtained windows. The sun is shining brightly.

The LADY *is seated on the ottoman, knitting. The* MOTHER *is standing with a red-bound book in her hand.*

MOTHER: You don't want to read your husband's book?

LADY: No, not that book. I promised him not to.

MOTHER: Don't you want to know the man to whom you've entrusted your destiny?

LADY: What purpose would it serve? We're happy as we are.

MOTHER: You don't make great demands of life.

LADY: Why should I? Demands never get satisfied.

MOTHER: I can never decide whether you're wiser than any of us, or just stupid.

LADY: I don't know anything about myself either.

MOTHER: As long as the sun shines and you've enough to eat, you're content.

LADY: Yes. And when the sun doesn't shine, I think: "It is ordained so."

MOTHER: To change the subject, do you know he's being sued for debt?

LADY: What poet isn't?

MOTHER: Which is he, a fool or a knave?

LADY: Mother, he's neither. He's — different. The only tiresome thing is, I can never say anything that he hasn't heard before. It means we don't talk much, but he's happy just to have me with him. And I'm happy to have him.

MOTHER: So? You've reached calm waters already. Then it won't be long before you hit the rapids. But don't you think if you read his new book it might give you something to talk about with him?

LADY: Perhaps. You can leave it there if you like.

MOTHER: Take it and hide it. It'll be a nice surprise for him when you quote something from his latest masterpiece.

LADY [*puts the book in her pocket*]: Here he comes. He seems to know when anyone's talking about him. Even at a distance.

MOTHER: If only he knew when others were suffering for him. Even at a distance.

> *She goes. The* LADY *is left alone for a few moments. She opens the book and glances at it; seems amazed; and puts it back in her pocket.*

STRANGER [*enters*]: Your mother's been here. And you were talking about me. I can almost hear the echo of her voice. I can feel her words poison the air and see them darken the sunlight. I think I can even see the impress of her body in the air — there! She leaves a smell after her like a dead snake.

LADY: How nervous you are today.

STRANGER: Terribly. Some bungler has overtuned my nerves, and now he's playing on them with a horsehair bow, so that they scream like a partridge — you don't know what it's like. There's someone here who is stronger than I. Someone who goes round with a lantern and searches me out wherever I am. Do you have witches in this part of the country?

LADY: Don't turn your back on the sunshine. Look at the beautiful landscape, and you'll feel calmer.

STRANGER: No. I can't look at that workhouse. I feel it was built there just for my sake. And there's always a mad-woman standing there, waving at me.

LADY: Do you think you've been badly treated here?

STRANGER: In a way. No — but they stuff me with delicacies, as though I was being fattened for slaughter, and yet everything rankles, because it isn't well wished. I feel their hatred like — like when you open an ice-chest. Can you imagine, I feel a cold wind everywhere, although the air's quite still and it's terribly hot! And I keep hearing that damned mill —

LADY: But it isn't grinding now.

STRANGER: Yes. It grinds, it grinds —

LADY: My dear, there is no hatred here. Only infinite
compassion —

STRANGER: And there's something else. Why do people
cross themselves when I walk on the road?

LADY: That's only because the people here pray silently
as they walk. It's their custom. What was in that letter you
got this morning?

STRANGER: Enough to make my hair stand on end, and
make me want to spit in the face of destiny. I'm being
sued for alimony by my children's guardians. Have you
ever seen anyone in such a humiliating situation? It's not
my fault; I've money due to me, but I can't get it. I can
do what's asked of me, I want to, but I'm not allowed to.
Is that my fault? No. But I get the shame. This is not the
work of nature, but of the devil.

LADY: But why?

STRANGER: Exactly! Why? Why is man born into this
world an ignorant being, ignorant of laws, customs and
conventions, which through his ignorance he breaks and is
therefore punished? Why does one enter manhood full of
noble intentions, only to be driven into every kind of contemptible action which one loathes? Why, why?

LADY [*who, unnoticed by him, has been reading the book
and not listening*]: It must have some purpose, though we
cannot fathom it.

STRANGER: If it is to make us humble, as some assert, it's
a bad way to do it, for it only makes me proud. Eve!

LADY: You mustn't call me that.

STRANGER [*starts*]: Why not?

LADY: I don't like it. It's as though I were to call you
Caesar —

STRANGER: Are we there now?

LADY: Where? What do you mean?

STRANGER: Did you mean something else by that name?

LADY: Caesar? No, I didn't. Now I'm beginning to understand.

STRANGER: Good. Then allow me to drive the knife home myself. I am Caesar, the schoolboy who did something for which another boy got the blame. That other boy was your husband — the ogre. Thus it amuses Fate to spin her web. A noble pleasure! [*The* LADY *hesitates and is silent.*] Say something!

LADY: I can't.

STRANGER: Say that he became an ogre because as a child he lost faith in the existence of divine justice, through being innocently punished for someone else's crime. Say it, and I shall say how I suffered twenty times over for that crime, and emerged from the religious crisis which it caused so chastened that I have never since committed a similar act.

LADY: It isn't that. It isn't that.

STRANGER: What, then? Is it that you can no longer respect me?

LADY: Not that either.

STRANGER: Then it is because I shall always feel ashamed in your presence, and then it will be finished between us.

LADY: No!

STRANGER: Eve!

LADY: Don't! You wake evil thoughts in me —

STRANGER: You have broken your promise. You have been reading my book.

LADY: Yes.

STRANGER: That was foolish. You should not have done that.

LADY: I meant well, only well.

STRANGER: Good intentions may have evil consequences. Now I am trapped, though I set the trap myself. Why must everything recur, everything? Childish follies and adult crimes. That one should reap evil where one has sown evil is fair enough; but when does a good act have its reward? What kind of a being is He Who writes down every misdeed, large or small? No human being does that. Men may forgive, but the gods, never.

LADY: Don't talk like that, please? Say that you can forgive.

STRANGER: I am not petty, I think you know that; but what have I to forgive you?

LADY: Oh — more than I can say —

STRANGER: Say, and then perhaps we shall be quits.

LADY: He and I used to read the curse of Deuteronomy over you — because you had destroyed his life.

STRANGER: What curse is that?

LADY: In the Bible, the one the priests read in chorus at the beginning of Lent.

STRANGER: I don't remember it. But what matter, one more or less?

LADY: In our family, it is a tradition that whoever we curse, the curse comes home.

STRANGER: I don't believe in that. Though I don't doubt that evil goes out from this house. But may it return on the heads of those who send it! That is my prayer. According to the laws of the land it should be my duty to put a bullet through my head. But I can't while I have not fulfilled my duties. Imagine — I can't even die! And my right to do that was the last religious belief I'd retained. The powers are cunning. I have heard that a man can wrestle with God and have some hope of success, but even Job

couldn't fight with Satan. Shall we have a little talk about
you now?

LADY: Not yet. Soon, perhaps. Reading your dreadful
book — I've only glanced at it, a few lines here and there —
has been like eating of the tree of knowledge. My eyes are
opened, and I know now what evil is and what good is. I
didn't before. And now I see how evil you are. Now I
know why you wanted to call me Eve. But if sin came
into the world through the first mother, forgiveness came
through another mother. We were cursed for the one,
redeemed for the other. You will not destroy my sex
through me, but I may have another purpose to serve in
your life. We shall see.

STRANGER: You *have* eaten of the tree of knowledge.
Goodbye.

LADY: Are you leaving?

STRANGER: What else can I do? I can't stay here.

LADY: Don't go.

STRANGER: I must. To clear up my affairs. I'll go and
say goodbye to the old people, then I'll come back to
you. I won't be a minute. [*Goes.*]

LADY [*stands for some seconds as though frozen; then
goes to the door and looks out*]: No. He's gone. Gone.

   She sinks brokenly to her knees.

Scene 2. The asylum

*The refectory of an old abbey. It resembles a simple,
whitewashed semi-circular church, but the walls show
stains of damp which resemble curious figures.
   Eating tables with food bowls. At the end of
each table, a lectern for the reader. Upstage, the door
to the chapel. Candles burn on the tables. On the left,
a painting of Michael slaying Satan.*

At a long eating-table on the left sits the STRAN-
GER *in a white invalid's dress, alone with his food
bowl. At a table to the right sit the* MOURNERS IN
BROWN *from Act One; the* BEGGAR; *a* WOMAN
IN MOURNING *with* TWO CHILDREN; *a* WOMAN
who resembles the LADY *but is not the* LADY, *and
who knits instead of eating; a man who resembles the*
DOCTOR *but is not he; others who resemble the*
MADMAN, *the* GRANDFATHER, *the* MOTHER *and
the* BROTHER; *the* PARENTS *of the "Prodigal", etc.
All are dressed in white, over which they wear gauze
habits of different colours. Their faces are waxen yellow and white like those of corpses, and they all look
and move like ghosts.*

As the curtain rises, all except the STRANGER
are concluding the Lord's Prayer.

STRANGER [*rises and goes to the* ABBESS, *who is standing at the serving table*]: Mother, let me speak to you for
a moment.

ABBESS [*in a black and white Augustine dress*]: Yes, my
son.

They come downstage.

STRANGER: First of all; where am I?

ABBESS: In the Abbey of Good Hope. We found you on
the mountain above the gorge, with a cross you had
broken from a wayside Calvary, with which you were
threatening someone in the clouds whom you imagined
you saw. You were in a fever and had fallen down a preci-
pice. We found you unhurt but in a delirium; we brought
you here to the hospital and put you to bed. You have
been in a delirium ever since, and though you complained
of a pain in one of your hips we could find no wound.

STRANGER: What did I say in my delirium?

ABBESS: The usual things men say in fevers. You reproached yourself with everything imaginable, and thought
you saw your victims, as you called them.

STRANGER: And then?

ABBESS: You talked mainly of money. You wanted to pay for your treatment. I tried to assure you that we take no payment here, but do all for charity —

STRANGER: I want no charity. I don't need that.

ABBESS: It is indeed more blessed to give than to receive. But it takes a noble spirit to receive and be grateful.

STRANGER: I don't need to receive anything and I don't ask anything. I will not be forced into gratitude.

ABBESS: Hm! Hm! Hm!

STRANGER: Tell me, why will none of these people sit at the same table with me? They get up and go away.

ABBESS: They are afraid of you.

STRANGER: Why?

ABBESS: The way you look.

STRANGER: The — way I look? But how do they look? Are they real?

ABBESS: If you mean, do they exist — yes, in that sense they are terrifyingly real. They may look strange to you because you still have a fever. Or there may be another reason.

STRANGER: But I seem to know them all. I see them as though in a mirror. And they're only pretending to eat. Those two over there are like my parents — at first sight, that is. I've never feared anything before, because life meant nothing to me, but now I begin to be frightened.

ABBESS: If you don't believe they are real, let us ask the Confessor to introduce them to you.

She makes a sign to the CONFESSOR, *who approaches.*

CONFESSOR [*in Dominican dress, black and white*]: Sister!

ABBESS: Tell our invalid who these people are.

CONFESSOR: That won't take long.

STRANGER: May I ask you something first? Haven't we met before?

CONFESSOR: Yes. I sat by your sick-bed while you were in a fever, and heard your confession —

STRANGER: My confession!

CONFESSOR: Yes. But I could not grant you absolution, for my impression was that what you were telling me were hallucinations.

STRANGER: How do you mean?

CONFESSOR: There was hardly a crime or a vice to which you did not plead guilty, including some so terrible that we require the strictest penitence before we can grant absolution. Now that you have regained consciousness, I must ask if there is any ground for these self-accusations.

The ABBESS *moves away.*

STRANGER: Have you any right to ask that?

CONFESSOR: No, I have not. You are right. But you wanted to know who these people are? Well, they are not the happiest of mankind. There, for example, we have a madman called Caesar, who lost his reason through reading the books of a certain author whose notoriety is greater than his fame. And there a Beggar, who won't admit that he is a Beggar because he can read Latin and claims that he has been liberated. And there a Doctor, also called an ogre; his story is well known. And a father and mother who grieved to death for a depraved son who raised his hand against them. He did not follow his father's bier to the churchyard and in a state of drunkenness profaned his mother's grave; for that he must answer himself. There sits his poor sister, whom he drove out into the winter snow, according to his own account. And there an abandoned wife with two neglected children. And there a woman who knits. You know them all. Go and greet them.

During this speech the STRANGER *has turned his back on the company. Now he goes and sits at the table left, still with his back towards them. When he raises his head he sees the picture of Michael and drops his eyes. The* CONFESSOR *goes over and stands behind the* STRANGER. *A Catholic requiem is heard from the chapel.*

CONFESSOR [*whispers to the* STRANGER *as the music is heard softly*]:

> *Quantus tremor est futurus*
> *Quando judex est venturus*
> *Cuncta stricte discussurus.*
> *Tuba mirum spargens sonum*
> *Per sepulchra regionum*
> *Coget omnes ante thronum.*
> *Mors stupebit et natura*
> *Cum resurget creatura*
> *Judicanti responsura*
> *Liber scriptus proferetur*
> *In quo totum continetur*
> *Unde mundus judicetur.*
> *Judex ergo cum sedebit*
> *Quidquid latet apparebit*
> *Nil inultum remanebit.*

He goes to the lectern by the table right. He opens the breviary. The music ceases.

CONFESSOR: Now let us continue with our reading. "But it shall come to pass, if thou wilt not hearken unto the voice of the Lord thy God, to observe to do all His commandments and His statutes which I command thee this day; that all these curses shall come upon thee and overtake thee. Cursed shalt thou be in the city and cursed shalt thou be in the field. Cursed shall be thy basket and thy store. Cursed shalt thou be when thou comest in and cursed shalt thou be when thou goest out."

OTHERS [*whisper*]: Cursed!

CONFESSOR: "The Lord shall send upon thee cursing, vexation and rebuke, in all that thou settest thine hand unto for to do, until thou be destroyed and until thou perish quickly; because of the wickedness of the doings, whereby thou has forsaken Me."

OTHERS [*aloud*]: Cursed!

CONFESSOR: "The Lord shall cause thee to be smitten before thine enemies; thou shalt go out one way against them, and flee seven ways before them; and shall be removed into all the kingdoms of the earth. And thy carcase shall be meat unto all fowls of the air, and unto the beasts of the earth, and no man shall fray them away. Thou shalt betroth a wife, and another man shall lie with her; thou shalt build an house, and thou shalt not dwell therein; thou shalt plant a vineyard and shalt not gather the grapes thereof. Thy sons and thy daughters shall be given to other people, and thine eyes shall look and fail with longing for them all the day long; and there shall be no might in thy hand. And among the nations shalt thou find no ease, neither shall the sole of thy foot have rest; but the Lord shall give thee a trembling heart, and failing of eyes and sorrow of mind. And thy life shall hang in doubt before thee; and thou shalt fear day and night, and shalt have none assurance of thy life. In the morning shalt thou say: 'Would God it were even!' And at even shalt thou say: 'Would God it were morning!' And because thou servest not the Lord thy God with joyfulness, and with gladness of heart, for the abundance of all things; therefore shalt thou serve Him in hunger and in thirst, and in nakedness and in want of all things; and He shall put a yoke of iron upon thy neck, until He have destroyed thee."

OTHERS: Amen!

The CONFESSOR *has been reading quickly and loudly, without addressing himself to the* STRANGER.

The OTHERS, *except the* LADY, *who is knitting, have listened and cursed, without seeming to notice the* STRANGER, *who has been sitting with his back to them, quiet and hunched. He rises to go. The* CONFESSOR *goes towards him.*

STRANGER: What was that?

CONFESSOR: The curse of Deuteronomy.

STRANGER: Oh — it was that! I seem to remember it contained a blessing too.

CONFESSOR: For those who keep His commandments.

STRANGER: I see. I can't deny it shook me a little, for a moment. I don't know whether this is a trial to test me, or a warning to heed. However, my fever still seems to be with me, so I'll go and find a real doctor.

CONFESSOR: As you please. But make sure it's the right one.

STRANGER: Of course, of course.

CONFESSOR: One who can cure these "beautiful pangs of conscience".

ABBESS: If you ever need charity, you know where it can be found.

STRANGER: No, I don't.

ABBESS [*softly*]: I will tell you. In a rose-red room, by a broad, flowing river.

STRANGER: Yes! In a rose-red room — ! Let me see. How long have I been lying here?

ABBESS: Three months.

STRANGER: Three months? Ah! Have I been sleeping, or where have I been? [*Looks out through the window.*] Yes, it's autumn. The trees are bare, the clouds wear their cold colour. Memories begin to awake. Do you hear a mill turning, a horn calling, a river rushing, a forest whispering, and — a woman crying? Yes, you are right. Only there is charity. Goodbye! [*Runs out.*]

CONFESSOR [*to* ABBESS]: The madman! The madman!

Scene 3. The rose room

The curtains have been removed and the windows gape like brown holes at the darkness outside. The furniture is covered with brown dustsheets and is pushed forward into the middle of the room. The flowers are gone and the big, black iron stove is lit.
The MOTHER *stands ironing white curtains by the light of a single candle. There is a knock on the door.*

MOTHER: Come in.

STRANGER [*enters*]: Good evening. Where is my wife?

MOTHER: Oh, it's you. Where have you come from?

STRANGER: I think from Hell. But where is my wife?

MOTHER: Which one?

STRANGER: That question is justified. Everything is justified, except me.

MOTHER: There's a reason; and it's good you've noticed it. But where have you been?

STRANGER: Whether it was a poorhouse, a madhouse or an ordinary hospital, I don't know. I like to think it was a hallucination. I've been ill and lost my memory. I can't believe three months have gone. But where is my wife?

MOTHER: I should ask you that. When you left her she went away. To look for you. Whether she's tired of looking, I don't know.

STRANGER: It looks terrible here. Where's the old man?

MOTHER: Where no griefs torment him.

STRANGER: Dead?

MOTHER: Yes. He is dead.

STRANGER: You speak as though I were to blame for that too.

MOTHER: Perhaps.

STRANGER: He didn't look that sensitive. And showed himself capable of strong hatred.

MOTHER: No. He could only hate evil, in himself and others.

STRANGER: Then I am blamed unjustly. For that too.

Pause.

MOTHER: What are you looking for here?

STRANGER: Charity.

MOTHER: At last. But tell me. What happened after you left here?

STRANGER: I fell on the mountain and hurt my hip. I lost consciousness. If you talk sensibly to me I'll tell you the rest.

MOTHER: I'll talk sensibly.

STRANGER: Well, then. I woke in a bed of red steel bars, and three men were pulling on a rope which ran between two blocks, and each time they pulled it felt as though I was being stretched a yard longer —

MOTHER: You'd dislocated your hip, and they were trying to re-set it.

STRANGER: You're right. I hadn't thought of that. But then — yes, then I lay there and saw my whole life unreel in a kind of panorama from my childhood, through my youth, right up to. . . . And when it was finished, it began to unreel again — and the whole time, I heard a mill turning — and I hear it still. Yes, now it's here too!

MOTHER: It can't have been a pretty spectacle.

STRANGER: No. And in the end I came to the conclusion that — I was a dreadful blackguard.

MOTHER: Why do you use that expression?

STRANGER: I know you'd rather I said "an evil person". But anyone who says that about himself seems to me to be bragging, and there's a kind of cocksureness about it that I haven't yet attained to.

MOTHER: You still have doubts?

STRANGER: Yes. About many things. But I begin to believe one thing —

MOTHER: Yes?

STRANGER: That there are things — and powers — that I didn't believe in before.

MOTHER: Have you also realized that neither you nor any other human being controls your curious destiny?

STRANGER: I — think I did realize that.

MOTHER: Then you've got somewhere.

STRANGER: But there's something else. I'm — bankrupt. I've lost the power to create. And I can't sleep at night —

MOTHER: Oh?

STRANGER: What people call — night mares. And the worst is, I no longer dare to die, because I'm no longer sure that death puts an end to misery.

MOTHER: I see.

STRANGER: But the worst thing of all is that I've developed such a loathing for myself that I'd gladly get rid of that self, but I can't see any possibility of doing so. If I were a Christian, I couldn't obey the commandment to love my neighbour as myself, because that would mean I would hate my neighbour, which I do. I know it's true that I am a great blackguard, and I've always suspected it, but because I didn't want to be life's fool I've always kept a wary eye on "the others" — and when I saw that they weren't any better than myself, I became angry when they tried to master me.

MOTHER: Yes, but you've got it wrong. You thought it was just a matter between yourself and the rest of mankind. It's between you and Him —

STRANGER: Who?

MOTHER: The Invisible One Who steers our destiny.

STRANGER: May I see Him?

MOTHER: You will be dying when you do.

STRANGER: No!

MOTHER: Where did you get this accursed spirit of rebelliousness? If you won't bend like the rest of us, you must be broken like a straw.

STRANGER: I don't know where I got this damned obstinacy. I tremble when I see an unpaid bill, but if I could climb Mount Sinai and confront the Almighty, I wouldn't cover my face.

MOTHER: Blessed Jesus! To talk like that! I think you are a child of the Evil One.

STRANGER: That seems to be the general opinion of me around here. But I've heard that those who are close to the Evil One are usually favoured with honour, possessions and gold, especially gold. Do you think I come into that category?

MOTHER: You will bring a curse on my house.

STRANGER: Then I will leave your house.

MOTHER: Tonight? No. Where will you go?

STRANGER: In search of the one person whom I do not hate.

MOTHER: Are you sure she will receive you?

STRANGER: Quite sure.

MOTHER: I'm not.

STRANGER: But I am.

MOTHER: Then I must make you unsure.

STRANGER: You can't do that.

MOTHER: I can.

STRANGER: You're lying.

MOTHER: Now we're not speaking sensibly any longer, so we'll stop. Can you sleep in the attic?

STRANGER: Anywhere. But I shan't sleep.

MOTHER: Then I'll wish you a good night; whether you think I mean it or not.

STRANGER: There aren't rats in the attic, are there? I'm not afraid of ghosts, but I don't like rats.

MOTHER: It's lucky you're not afraid of ghosts, because — no one's ever stayed a whole night up there. Whatever it is.

STRANGER [*hesitates a moment, then*]: You are the most malignant person I've ever met. But that's because you're religious.

MOTHER: Good night.

Scene 4. The kitchen

It is dark, but the moon outside casts restless shadows on the floor from the window lattices as the storm clouds run by.

In the corner, right, beneath the crucifix, where the OLD MAN *used to sit, his hunting-horn, gun and hunting-bag hang on the wall. A stuffed bird of prey stands on the table. The windows are open and the curtains flap; and dishcloths, aprons and hand-towels hanging on a line flutter in the wind, the soughing of which can be heard. In the distance a waterfall roars; now and then the wooden floor bangs.*

STRANGER [*enters, half-dressed, with a candle in his hand*]: Is there anyone there? No one. [*Comes in with the candle, which renders the shadow-play less distinct.*] What's that moving on the floor? Is there anyone here? [*Goes towards the table, but stops as though petrified when he sees the bird of prey.*] Jesus Christ!

MOTHER [*enters, dressed, with a candle*]: Are you still up?

STRANGER: Yes, I couldn't sleep.

MOTHER [*gently*]: Why, my son?

STRANGER: There was someone walking upstairs.

MOTHER: Impossible. There's no room above that one.

STRANGER: That's what disturbed me. But what's that moving on the floor like snakes?

MOTHER: The moonlight.

STRANGER: Yes, it's the moonlight. And there is a stuffed bird. And there are kitchen cloths. Everything's normal and natural — it's just that that disturbs me. Who's that knocking? Has someone been shut out?

MOTHER: No, it's a horse kicking in the stable.

STRANGER: Really?

MOTHER: Yes, there are horses that suffer from the night mare.

STRANGER: What is a night mare?

MOTHER: Who knows?

STRANGER: Let me sit down for a moment.

MOTHER: Sit down, and let me talk seriously to you. I

was cruel to you last night, and I ask you to forgive me. But because I am so cruel, I use religion as I use a hair shirt and a stone floor. If it will ease your mind, I will tell you what the night mare is; it is my evil conscience. Whether it is I or somebody else that punishes me, I don't know, and I don't think I have the right to ask. Now tell me what happened to you in that room.

STRANGER: I really don't know. I didn't see anything, but when I went in I felt someone was there. I looked with my candle, but found no one. Then I went to bed. And then someone began to walk with heavy steps above my head. Do you believe in ghosts and spirits?

MOTHER: No. My religion forbids that. But I believe in the power of conscience to create means of chastisement.

STRANGER: Well. . . . After a moment I felt an icy stream of air against my breast, groping until it found my heart. Then my heart went cold, and I had to get out of bed —

MOTHER: And then?

STRANGER: Then I found myself pinned to the floor, and I saw the whole panorama of my life unroll before me, everything, everything. And that was the worst.

MOTHER: Yes. I know all that. I have been through it. There's no name for that sickness, and only one cure —

STRANGER: What?

MOTHER: You know. You know what children have to do when they've done wrong.

STRANGER: What must they do?

MOTHER: First, ask for forgiveness.

STRANGER: And then?

MOTHER: Try to make things right.

STRANGER: Isn't it enough to suffer according to one's deserts?

MOTHER: No. That's just revenge.

STRANGER: Well, what else?

MOTHER: Can you make good a life you've destroyed? Can you undo a wicked deed?

STRANGER: No, that's true. But I was forced to do that deed. I was forced to take, because nobody gave me. But shame on Him Who forced me! Ah! [*Puts his hand to his breast.*] Ah! Now He's here, in this room! He's tearing the heart from my breast! Ah!

MOTHER: Humble yourself.

STRANGER: I can't!

MOTHER: On your knees!

STRANGER: I won't.

MOTHER: Christ have mercy upon you. Lord have mercy! [*To the* STRANGER.] On your knees to Him Who was crucified for us! Only He can undo what has been done.

STRANGER: No, not to Him! Not to Him! And if I'm forced to do it, I'll take it back — later.

MOTHER: On your knees! My son!

STRANGER: I can't kneel! I can't! Help me, Eternal God!

　　Pause.

MOTHER [*mutters a swift prayer, then*]: Well. Do you feel better?

STRANGER [*collects himself*]: Yes. But do you know what that was? It wasn't death. It was annihilation.

MOTHER: Annihilation of the godhead in you. We call that spiritual death.

STRANGER [*earnestly, without irony*]: I see. Now I begin to understand.

MOTHER: My son. You have left Jerusalem and are on the

road to Damascus. Go there; by the same road you came.
And plant a cross at every station, but stop at the seventh.
You don't have to suffer fourteen, like Him.

STRANGER: You speak in riddles.

MOTHER: Well. . . . Get up. Go and search out those to
whom you have something to say. First your wife.

STRANGER: Where?

MOTHER: Search. But don't forget the one you call the
ogre —

STRANGER: Never!

MOTHER: I hear you said that when it was suggested that
you should come here. But, as I told you, I was expecting
you.

STRANGER: Why?

MOTHER: For no reason that you would call rational —

STRANGER: Just as I saw this kitchen — in — an ecstasy,
if you like —

MOTHER: I regret now that I tried to part you from Ingeborg. You and she were meant to meet. Go now, and
search her out. If you find her, good. If not, perhaps it
was intended so. It is beginning to grow light. The dawn is
here. The night is over.

STRANGER: And what a night!

MOTHER: You will remember it.

STRANGER: Not all of it. But I shall remember some.

MOTHER [*looks out through window; as though to herself*]: O morning star, why hast thou fallen so far from
heaven?

   Pause.

STRANGER: Have you noticed that before the sun rises,
we mortals shiver? Are we children of darkness, that we
tremble before the coming of the light?

MOTHER: Do you never tire of asking questions?

STRANGER: Never. You see — I long for the light.

MOTHER: Go now. And peace be with you.

ACT FOUR

Scene 1. At the gorge

The landscape is as before, but it is autumn and the trees are bare. There is a noise of hammering from the smithy, and the mill is turning. The SMITH stands in his doorway, left; the MILLER'S WIFE right. The LADY is dressed in a jacket and a patent-leather hat, but is in mourning. The STRANGER wears Tyrolean Alpine dress — a woollen jacket, knee-breeches, mountain boots, a staff, and a green huntsman's hat with a blackcock's feather in it. Over his clothes he wears a brown "Kaiser's cloak", with a cape and hood.

LADY [*enters in travelling clothes, tired and distressed*]: Has a gentleman in travelling clothes passed this way?

The SMITH and MILLER'S WIFE shake their heads.

LADY: Can you give me shelter for the night?

They shake their heads again.

LADY [*to SMITH*]: May I stand in your doorway and warm myself for a moment?

The SMITH pushes her back.

LADY: May God reward you as you deserve!

She goes; is seen a moment later on the bridge; then disappears.

STRANGER [*enters in travelling clothes*]: Has a lady in

travelling dress gone across the river? [*They shake their heads. To the* MILLER'S WIFE]: Can you sell me a crust of bread? I have money. [*She rejects the money.*] Have you no charity?

An echo in the distance imitates his voice: "Charity!" The SMITH *and the* MILLER'S WIFE *utter a long and high-pitched laugh, which is answered by the echo.*

STRANGER: I like that. An eye for an eye, a tooth for a tooth. That always helped to ease my conscience.

He enters the gorge.

Scene 2. On the highway

Again, the landscape is as before, but it is autumn. The The BEGGAR *is sitting outside a chapel of expiation with a lime-twig and a starling in a cage.*

STRANGER [*enters dressed as in the preceding scene*]: Tell me, beggar. Have you seen a lady in travelling dress pass this way?

BEGGAR: I've seen five hundred. And I'd be obliged if you'd stop calling me beggar. I work now.

STRANGER: Oh, it's you.

BEGGAR: *Ille ego qui quondam* –

STRANGER: What work do you do?

BEGGAR: I keep a starling. He whistles and talks –

STRANGER: He's the one who works, then?

BEGGAR: Yes. I've become independent.

STRANGER: Do you catch birds, too?

BEGGAR: Oh, the lime-twig. No, that's just for appearances.

STRANGER: You care about appearances?

BEGGAR: What else matters? Who cares about what's inside?

STRANGER: Is that your philosophy?

BEGGAR: My whole metaphysical system. It may seem rather an outdated viewpoint, but —

STRANGER: Say something serious. Tell me your history.

BEGGAR: Oh, what's the use of rooting in dunghills? Forget the past, friend, forget it. Do you think I'm always as merry as this? No, it's only when I meet you. You're so bloody funny.

STRANGER: How can you laugh with a whole life wasted behind you?

BEGGAR: Now you're being personal. But if a man can't laugh at adversity, even other people's, how's he to go on living? Listen. If you follow these wheel-tracks in the mud, you'll come to the sea, and there the road ends. Sit down there and rest for a while, and you'll see things differently. You get so many accidents on this road — religious worries, painful memories — they keep your mind from the rose room. But just follow the tracks. If it gets a bit muddy now and then, just stretch your wings and try to fly. Talking of flying, I once heard a bird sing something about Polycrates' ring. How he'd got all the glory of the world but didn't know what to do with it. So he went round proclaiming the worthlessness of the life he'd managed to create out of the emptiness he'd found in riches. I wouldn't say it was you if I couldn't swear to it. And once when I asked you if you knew who I was, you replied that you weren't interested. I offered you my friendship, but you refused it and said: "Be off!" But I don't take offence or bear grudges, so I'll just give you this good advice. Follow the tracks.

STRANGER [shrinks aside]: No, you won't fool me again.

BEGGAR: Sir! You only think bad of people, so you only get bad in return. Try to think good for once. Try.

STRANGER: I'll try. But if people betray me, I have the right to —

BEGGAR: You never have that right.

STRANGER [*as though to himself*]: Who reads my secret thoughts, who turns my soul inside out, who persecutes me? Why do you persecute me?

BEGGAR: Saul, Saul, why persecutest thou me?

> The STRANGER, *with a gesture of horror, goes. The sound of the funeral march is heard, as before. The* LADY *enters.*

LADY: Have you seen a gentleman pass this way?

BEGGAR: Yes, there was a poor chap here just now, hobbling along.

LADY: The man I am looking for isn't lame.

BEGGAR: This one wasn't exactly that. But he seemed to have hurt his hip, so he couldn't walk properly. Well, I won't be hard. Look there in the mud.

LADY: Where?

BEGGAR [*points*]: There. See that wheeltrack? Beside it there's a heavy footprint —

LADY [*looks at it*]: It's him. Yes, they are heavy. Shall I be able to catch him up?

BEGGAR: Follow the tracks.

LADY [*takes his hand and kisses it*]: Thank you, my friend. [*Goes.*]

Scene 3. By the sea

> *The same landscape as before, but winter. The sea is blue-black; on the horizon clouds tower like giant heads. In the distance three white, dismantled masts*

of a wrecked ship, like three crosses, project from the water. The table and bench still stand under the tree, but the chairs are gone. There is snow on the ground. Now and then a bell-buoy sounds.

The STRANGER *enters left, stops for a moment and looks out to sea. Then he goes out right, behind the hut. The* LADY *enters left; seems to follow the* STRANGER'S *footprints in the snow and goes out right, in front of the hut. The* STRANGER *re-enters right, goes left, finds the* LADY's *footprints, stops and looks back right. The* LADY *enters, runs to embrace him, but staggers back.*

LADY: Are you pushing me away?

STRANGER: No. But someone seems to stand between us.

LADY: Someone does. So; I've found you. But —

STRANGER: Yes. It is winter now, as you see.

LADY: And I feel the cold stream out of you.

STRANGER: I got frozen there. In the mountains.

LADY: Will it never be spring again?

STRANGER: Not for us. We have been driven from Paradise and must wander among stones and thistles. And when our feet and hands are bleeding we must rub salt in one another's wounds. And that mill is turning; and it will never stop, for the stream will never run dry.

LADY: I suppose you are right.

STRANGER: But I don't want to yield to the inevitable. I don't want us to tear each other apart. I shall offer myself to the gods as a placatory sacrifice. I shall say: "I am the guilty one." It was I who taught you to loose your bonds, I who tempted you. You can blame me for everything. What we did, and the consequences —

LADY: You can't bear it alone.

STRANGER: There are moments when I feel I can bear all the world's sin and grief and dirt and shame. There are moments when I believe that my sins and crimes are themselves my ordained punishment. Do you know, a little while ago I lay in a fever and among other things — there were so many things — I dreamed that I saw a crucifix with Him on it. And when I asked the Dominican — there was a Dominican there, among many others — I asked him what this might mean, and he replied: "You will not let Him suffer for you, so suffer yourself." That is why mankind has grown so sensitive to its own agonies.

LADY: And why our consciences become so heavy, now that we must bear the burden alone.

STRANGER: Have you — reached that point too?

LADY: Not yet. But I am on the way.

STRANGER: Put your hand in mine and let us go together.

LADY: Where?

STRANGER: Back — the way we came. Are you tired?

LADY: Not any longer.

STRANGER: Several times I fell. But then I met a strange beggar — perhaps you remember him? — the one they said was like me. And he told me to try to think good of his intentions. I tried — just to see — and —

LADY: Yes?

STRANGER: Things got better. Since then I have found the strength to go on.

LADY: Let's go together.

STRANGER [*turns to the sea*]: It's growing dark, and the clouds are gathering.

LADY: Don't look at the clouds.

STRANGER: And down there. What's that?

LADY: Only a wrecked ship.

STRANGER [*whispers*]: Three crosses! What new Golgotha awaits us?

LADY: They are white. That means good.

STRANGER: Can any good ever happen to us again?

LADY: Yes. But not yet.

STRANGER: Let us go.

Scene 4. The hotel room

As before. The LADY *is seated knitting beside the* STRANGER.

LADY: Say something.

STRANGER: No. I've only had evil thoughts since we came back here.

LADY: Why did we have to come back to this dreadful room?

STRANGER: I don't know. It was the last thing I wanted to do. So I began to long to come here — to suffer.

LADY: And you have suffered.

STRANGER: Yes. I no longer hear any songs, or have good visions. Each day I hear the mill grind, and see that dreadful panorama, which grows and grows. And at night —

LADY: Why did you cry in your sleep?

STRANGER: I had a dream —

LADY: A real dream?

STRANGER: Terrifyingly real. Now you see my curse — I *must* talk about it, and whom can I tell but you? But I mustn't tell you, because then I shall touch the door to that closed room —

LADY: The past.

STRANGER: Yes.

LADY [*simply*]: There is always something trivial in those sealed rooms.

STRANGER: I suppose so.

Pause.

LADY: Tell me.

STRANGER: I fear I must. Well, I dreamed I saw — your former husband married to my former wife. So that my children had him for their father —

LADY: Only you could imagine that.

STRANGER: I hope you're right. [*Sighs.*] But I saw him maltreat them. [*Gets up.*] Then I strangled him, of course, and — no, I can't go on. But I shall have no peace until I know. And to do that I must go and see him, in his own home.

LADY: Has it come to that?

STRANGER: I've felt on the verge of it for a long time, and now there's no help for it. I must see him.

LADY: Suppose he won't see you?

STRANGER: I shall go as a patient, and tell him about my illness.

LADY [*frightened*]: You mustn't do that.

STRANGER: I understand. You mean he might have me put away? Well, I must risk that. I *need* to risk everything — my freedom, my life, my well-being. I must suffer enough to bring my soul up into the daylight; I long for a torture to restore my sense of feeling equal with society, so that I don't have to go on feeling in debt. So; down into the snake pit, and the sooner the better.

LADY: If I could go with you —

STRANGER: You don't need to. My sufferings will suffice for both of us.

LADY: Then I shall call you my liberator, and the curse I once invoked on you shall become a blessing. Do you see that it is spring again?

STRANGER: I noticed it in that Christmas rose. It's beginning to wither.

LADY: But don't you feel that there is spring in the air?

STRANGER: Yes. I think that chill is beginning to leave my heart.

LADY: Perhaps the ogre will be able to cure you completely.

STRANGER: We'll see. He may not be so dangerous after all.

LADY: He is certainly not so cruel as you.

STRANGER: But my dream! Imagine —

LADY: — If it was only a dream! My wool is finished now, and my useless task. It has got dirty —

STRANGER: But it can be washed.

LADY: Or dyed a new colour.

STRANGER: Rose-red.

LADY: Never!

STRANGER: It is like a scroll —

LADY: With our saga on it.

STRANGER: Written in mud, and tears, and blood.

LADY: Our saga will soon be done. Go and write the last chapter.

STRANGER: Then we shall meet at the seventh station. Where we started.

ACT FIVE

Scene 1. At the DOCTOR's

The scene is as before, except that the wood-pile is half its former size, and on the verandah stands a bench with surgical instruments — knives, saws, forceps, etc. The DOCTOR *is busy polishing his instruments.*

SISTER [*enters from the verandah*]: There's a patient asking for you.

DOCTOR: Do you know him?

SISTER: I haven't seen him, but here's his card.

DOCTOR [*reads it*]: Well! This goes beyond anything I've ever — !

SISTER: Is it him?

DOCTOR: Yes. I respect courage, but such brazenness as this I find cynical. It's almost like a challenge. However, show him in.

SISTER: Are you serious?

DOCTOR: Absolutely. But if you wish, you can talk to him a little. In your brazen way.

SISTER: I'd already decided to.

DOCTOR: Good. You do the ground work. I'll add the veneer.

SISTER: Never you fear! I'll tell him everything you're too kind to say.

DOCTOR: Never you mind my kindness. And hurry up, so I don't start feeling unkind. But shut the doors!

The SISTER *goes.*

DOCTOR: What are you doing by that rubbish bin again,

Caesar? [*The* MADMAN *enters.*] Tell me, Caesar. If your enemy comes and rests his head on your knees, what would you do?

MADMAN: Cut it off.

DOCTOR: That is not what I taught you.

MADMAN: No, you say I should heap coals of fire on it. But I think that's wicked.

DOCTOR: I think so too, really. It's crueller, and more cunning. Better to take some small revenge, then he feels he has made amends and his debt is settled.

MADMAN: If you understand these things better than I do, why ask me?

DOCTOR: Shut up, I'm not talking to you. Right; we'll take his head off. And then, we'll see.

MADMAN: It depends on how he behaves.

DOCTOR: Quite right. How he behaves! Hush! Be off, now.

STRANGER [*enters from verandah, disturbed but with a certain air of resignation*]: Doctor.

DOCTOR: Yes.

STRANGER: You are doubtless surprised to see me here —

DOCTOR [*earnestly*]: I gave up being surprised a long time ago. But I see I must start again.

STRANGER: Will you grant me a private conversation?

DOCTOR: On any subject regarded as proper among civilized people. Are you ill?

STRANGER [*hesitantly*]: Yes.

DOCTOR: Why do you come to me?

STRANGER: You should be able to guess.

DOCTOR: I do not wish to. What is wrong with you?

STRANGER [*hesitantly*]: I can't sleep.

DOCTOR: That's not an illness, it's a symptom. Have you been to a doctor about it before?

STRANGER: I was a patient in — an institution. I had a fever — but it was a very strange fever.

DOCTOR: What was strange about it?

STRANGER: May I ask you — can one walk in a delirium?

DOCTOR: Yes, if one is mad. But only then.

The STRANGER *gets up, but sits down again.*

DOCTOR: What was the name of the hospital?

STRANGER: The House of Good Hope.

DOCTOR: There is no hospital of that name.

STRANGER: Is it a monastery, then?

DOCTOR: No. A madhouse.

The STRANGER *gets up.*

DOCTOR [*gets up and calls*]: Sister! Shut the front door. And the little door to the main road. [*To the* STRANGER.] Please sit down. I have to shut these doors for fear of tramps. The district's full of them.

STRANGER [*calms himself*]: Doctor; a straight question. Do you think I am mad?

DOCTOR: One never gets an honest answer to that question, you know — or believes it, if the answer is yes. So it doesn't matter what I say. But if you think your soul is sick, go and find a priest.

STRANGER: Wouldn't you care to take on that job for a minute?

DOCTOR: No. I lack the calling.

STRANGER: If —

DOCTOR [*interrupts*]: Anyway, I haven't the time. I'm about to get married.

STRANGER: My dream.

DOCTOR: I thought it might help you to know that I've consoled myself, as the saying is — might even make you happy — it's the usual reaction — but I see it increases your sense of suffering. There must be some reason for that. I must investigate. How can it trouble you that I am marrying a widow?

STRANGER: With two children?

DOCTOR: One moment. One moment. Ah, I see! What a hellish notion, just like you. If there is a hell, you ought to be in charge of it. Your inventiveness in finding new methods of punishment exceeds my wildest imaginings — and people call me the ogre!

STRANGER: But it could happen.

DOCTOR [*interrupts*]: For a long time I hated you, as you perhaps know, because you did something unforgivable which destroyed my good name. But as I grew older and wiser, I realized that if my punishment was unjustified at the time, I had nevertheless deserved it for other things which had not been found out. And anyway you were a child and had enough of a conscience to punish yourself, so that needn't worry you either. Was that why you came?

STRANGER: Yes.

DOCTOR: Then will it content you if I say: "Go in peace"? [*The* STRANGER *looks at him questioningly.*] Or did you think I was going to have you put away, or saw you up with that instrument over there? Or kill you, perhaps? What was it you once said, "Why do they allow such wretches to live"? [*The* STRANGER *looks at his watch.*] You'll have time to catch the boat.

STRANGER: Will you give me your hand?

DOCTOR: No, I can't do that. I mustn't. Anyway, what help will it be if I forgive you, if you haven't the strength to forgive yourself? There are situations when the only help is to undo what has been done; and in this case there is no help, or hope.

STRANGER: "The Good Hope".

DOCTOR: Things haven't been that bad. You challenged Fate, and you were broken. There's no shame in a good fight. I did the same, but as you see I've cut down my wood-pile. I don't want to have lightning in my house. I don't play with that kind of thing any longer.

STRANGER: One more station, and my journey will be done.

DOCTOR: Never, sir. Goodbye.

STRANGER: Goodbye.

Scene 2. The street corner

As in Act One. The STRANGER *is seated on the bench under the tree, drawing in the sand.*

LADY [*enters*]: What are you doing?

STRANGER: I am drawing in the sand. Still.

LADY: Don't you hear any songs?

STRANGER [*points to the church*]: Yes, but from in there. There's someone I wronged without knowing it.

LADY: I thought our wandering was near our end, now that we are back here.

STRANGER: Where we started. In the street, between the café and the church. And the post-office. The post-office! P, o, s, t — I say, didn't I leave a registered letter here, uncollected?

LADY: Yes, because it contained something bad —

STRANGER: Or a writ. [*Strikes himself on the forehead.*] There it is again!

LADY: Go and fetch it. And believe it may contain something good.

STRANGER [*ironically*]: Good?

LADY: Believe it. Try to imagine it.

STRANGER [*goes into the post-office*]: I'll try.

> The LADY *walks up and down, waiting. The* STRANGER *comes out with a letter.*

LADY: Well?

STRANGER: I am ashamed. It was money.

LADY: You see. All this misery, all these tears — for nothing.

STRANGER: Not for nothing. It seems horrible, this game, but perhaps it's not. I wronged the Invisible One when I suspected Him of —

LADY: Hush! Don't try to shift the blame.

STRANGER: No. It was my own stupidity. Or wickedness. I didn't want to become life's fool, and so I became it. But the powers —

LADY: Have returned the changeling. Let us go.

STRANGER: Yes. Let us return to your mountains and hide ourselves with our griefs.

LADY: Yes. The mountains hide. But first I must light a candle to my blessed Saint Elizabeth. [*The* STRANGER *shakes his head, deprecatingly.*] Come.

STRANGER: Well. I can always go in with you. But I won't stay.

LADY: You don't know. Come. In there you will hear new songs.

STRANGER [*goes after her to the church door*]: Perhaps

LADY: Come.

Parts II and III of this translation of TO DAMASCUS were broadcast in a shortened form by the British Broadcasting Corporation on Radio 3 on 11 July 1971 (and repeated on 17 October 1971). The cast was:

NARRATOR	Martin Friend
THE CONFESSOR (who also appears in a different guise as THE BEGGAR)	Edward Kelsey
THE MOTHER	Eva Stuart
THE STRANGER	Stephen Murray
THE LADY (INGEBORG)	Zena Walker
CAESAR	Brian Hewlett
THE DOCTOR	John Rye
A NURSE	Katherine Parr
A PROFESSOR	John Ruddock
A VOICE	Martin Friend
A WHORE	Olwen Griffiths
A BARMAID	Katherine Parr
ANOTHER VOICE	Brian Hewlett
A POLICEMAN	Trevor Martin
SYLVIA	Elizabeth Proud
THE TEMPTER	John Gabriel
EVE	Elizabeth Proud
THE PRIOR	Trevor Martin
FATHER MELCHIOR	John Ruddock

Special sound and music by Malcolm Clarke of the B.B.C. Radiophonic Workshop.

Directed by Charles Lefeaux

PART II
(1898)

CHARACTERS*

THE STRANGER
THE LADY
THE LADY'S MOTHER
THE MADMAN (CAESAR)
A MIDWIFE
A NURSE
A MAID
THE DOCTOR
THE LADY'S FATHER
A PROFESSOR
FIRST WHORE
SECOND WHORE
A BARMAID
A POLICEMAN
THE CONFESSOR ⎫
THE BEGGAR   ⎬ (the same person)
THE DOMINICAN ⎭
THREE CHILDREN
A MAN
A WOMAN
SISTERS OF MERCY, BANQUET GUESTS, MUSICIANS,
WHORES, DOWN-AND-OUTS, etc.

* Strindberg's own "List of Characters" prefaced to the play
contains only the Stranger, the Lady, the Lady's Mother, the Lady's
Father, The Confessor-Beggar-Dominican, the Doctor and Caesar.
(Translator's note)

SCENES

Act 1. Outside the house

Act 2. The laboratory
The rose room

Act 3. The inn
The prison
The rose room

Act 4. The inn
The gorge
The rose room

ACT ONE

Outside the house

*Right, a terrace, on which the house stands. Below,
the highway runs upstage to a dense pine-forest and a
criss-crossing vista of mountains. Left, the river bank
is indicated, though the river itself is not visible.*

*The house is white, with small latticed windows
in sandstone frames. The walls are covered with vines
and rambler roses. Outside, up on the terrace, is a
fountain; along the edge of the terrace hang pumpkin-
plants, with big yellow flowers. Fruit trees line the
highway, and a memorial cross commemorates an
accident.*

*Through the terrace a staircase leads on to the
road with flower pots on the balustrade. At the foot
of the steps is a bench. The road runs in downstage
right, winds past the terrace, which juts out like a
headland, and continues upstage. From the left the
sun shines brightly.*

The MOTHER *is seated on the bench at the foot
of the steps. The* DOMINICAN *stands in front of her.*

DOMINICAN:* You sent for me on an important family
matter. Tell me about it.

MOTHER: Father; I am a woman who has been sorely tried
by life. I don't know how I have sinned that I should be so
out of grace with God.

DOMINICAN: It is a sign of grace to be tested by the
Almighty, and salvation awaits those who endure.

MOTHER: I have sometimes told myself so, but there are
limits to suffering —

* The same person as the CONFESSOR and the BEGGAR.
(Strindberg's footnote)

DOMINICAN: There are no limits. Suffering is boundless, like grace.

MOTHER: First, my husband left me, to go away with another woman.

DOMINICAN: Let him go. He will return, and on his knees.

MOTHER: Then my only daughter was married to a doctor. She left him and came here with a stranger, whom she introduced as her new husband.

DOMINICAN: That I do not understand. Divorce is not permitted in our church.

MOTHER: No. But they crossed the frontier, where other laws apply, and he being, an Old Catholic,* got a clergyman to marry them.

DOMINICAN: That is no true marriage, and it cannot be dissolved since it never existed. But it can be declared void. Who is this man?

MOTHER: To be honest, I wish I knew. I know one thing, which makes my cup overflow. He is divorced, with a wife and children living in poverty.

DOMINICAN: A difficult case, but we shall find an answer. What else?

MOTHER: He is a poet, said to be famous in his own country —

DOMINICAN: And godless, no doubt?

MOTHER: He was. But since he made this second marriage, he has not had a day's happiness. Fate, as he calls it, laid its hand on him, and the iron rod of chastisement drove him here as a destitute beggar. Misfortune after misfortune smote him, and I was beginning to pity him when he went away. He collapsed while wandering in the forest, and was

* The Old Catholics were a religious group who separated from the Roman Catholic community in Germany after the Vatican Council in 1870–71. (Translator's note)

taken by merciful souls who found him to an asylum, where he lay sick for three months without our knowing where he was.

DOMINICAN: Wait. Last year a man was brought in the way you describe to our Abbey of the Good Hope, where I am confessor. In his fever he opened his heart to me, and there was scarcely a crime he did not claim to have committed. When he came to his senses he said he remembered nothing. To test his heart and reins I employed the secret apostolic power which is granted to us and read what we call the small curse over him to see what effect that would have. When a secret crime has been committed, the curse of Deuteronomy is read over the suspect. If he is innocent, it will not harm him; but if he is guilty, it will be as the blessed Paul says: "He is delivered unto Satan for the destruction of his flesh, that his spirit may be saved."

MOTHER: Ah, God! It is he.

DOMINICAN: The same: your son-in-law. Strange are the ways of Providence. My words found their mark?

MOTHER: Yes, and then — When he slept here he was awoken by a mysterious force that he said froze his heart —

DOMINICAN: Did he have fearful visions?

MOTHER: Yes.

DOMINICAN: And was tormented by those pangs of which Job speaks? "When I say, my bed shall comfort me, then Thou scarest me with dreams and terrifiest me through visions, so that my soul chooseth strangling and death rather than life." That is as it should be. But were his eyes opened?

MOTHER: Yes; but only to find his sight transformed. As his misfortunes grew and he could no longer explain them by natural causes, and no doctor could cure him, he began to realize that he was wrestling with higher powers —

DOMINICAN: — that wished him evil, and so were evil. That is the usual way. And then?

MOTHER: He got hold of some evil books that taught him that such evil powers could be defied.

DOMINICAN: So; he is looking into the hidden that should remain hidden. Well; did he succeed in exorcizing these powers of chastisement?

MOTHER: He says so. And he seems to have found peace at night.

DOMINICAN: So he believes. But because he refused to love truth, God will trouble him so that he will believe what is false.

MOTHER: Then he must take his punishment. But he has changed my daughter too. She used to be neither hot nor cold. But now she's on the way to becoming evil.

DOMINICAN: How do they manage together, as husband and wife?

MOTHER: Half the day like angels. The other half they torment each other like devils.

DOMINICAN: That is the way. They will torment each other until they reach the Cross.

MOTHER: If they don't part.

DOMINICAN: Already!

MOTHER: They've left each other four times, but always come back. It's as though they were chained together. And a good thing, for there's a child on the way.

DOMINICAN: Let the child come. Children have a power that renews dying souls.

MOTHER: Please God. But it seems to be a new source of trouble between them. They're already quarrelling about the child's name. And she's jealous of his children by his former marriage because he can't swear he'll love the new child as much as he does them, and she demands that he shall promise this, unconditionally. There's no bottom to their hell.

DOMINICAN: Only be patient. He has challenged the powers, which has brought him to us, and our prayers are stronger than his resistance. They are as infinite as they are mysterious.

> The STRANGER *appears on the terrace. He wears a hunting-coat and a panama hat, and carries an alpine staff.*

DOMINICAN: Is that him up there?

MOTHER: Yes. That is my new son-in-law.

DOMINICAN: He is remarkably like your previous one. [*Makes the sign of the cross in the air.*] See how troubled he is. Now he'll stiffen like an icicle — look! In a moment he'll cry out.

STRANGER [*has stopped suddenly and stands quite still; clutches his heart and cries*]: Who is that down there?

MOTHER: I.

STRANGER: But you aren't alone.

MOTHER: No. I have company.

DOMINICAN [*makes the sign of the cross again*]: Now he will fall like a hewn tree.

> The STRANGER *crumples and falls to the ground.*

DOMINICAN: I will go now. If he saw me, he would break. But I will soon be back. You can see he is in good hands. Goodbye. Peace be with you. [*Goes.*]

STRANGER [*gets up and comes down the steps*]: Who was here?

MOTHER: A traveller. Sit down, you look so pale.

STRANGER: I felt dizzy for a moment —

MOTHER: You always find new words for things. But they don't help. Sit down on that bench.

STRANGER: No, I don't want to sit here. People are always passing.

MOTHER: I've sat here since I was a child, and watched life run by like the river down there. I've watched people on that road, playing, haggling, begging, cursing, dancing. I love this bench and I love the river down there, though every year it nibbles away our inheritance. Last spring it took all our pasture land, so that we had to sell our stock. These last years the property has lost half its value, and when they've finished draining the tarn and the marsh, the river will rise and engulf the house. We've fought it in the courts for ten years, but always lost. We shall go under. It's inevitable, like fate.

STRANGER: Fate is not inevitable.

MOTHER: If you think you can fight it, take care.

STRANGER: I already have.

MOTHER: Oh dear, are you back there again? You learn nothing from the chastisement of Providence.

STRANGER: Yes, to hate. Can one love what is evil, and does evil?

MOTHER: I'm not a scholar, but I read in a book yesterday that Eumenides means the Kindly Ones.

STRANGER: That's true. But it's a lie that they *are* kindly. I know only one good Fury. Mine.

MOTHER: You call Ingeborg a Fury?

STRANGER: She is; and a powerful one. Her inventiveness in tormenting me exceeds my own worst nightmares. If I get out of her hands alive I shall emerge as pure as gold from the furnace.

MOTHER: You've got what you deserve. You wanted to create her in your own image, and you've succeeded.

STRANGER: Completely. But where is my Fury?

MOTHER: She went out. Along the road.

STRANGER: Down there? Then I shall go to meet my destruction. [*Goes upstage.*]

MOTHER: You can still joke? You wait.

> The MOTHER *is alone for a few moments until the* STRANGER *has disappeared. Then the* LADY *enters right. She is in summer clothes and carries the post-bag, with opened letters in her hand.*

LADY: Are you alone, mother?

MOTHER: He's just gone.

LADY: Here is the post. It's all for Job.

MOTHER: Do you open his letters?

LADY: All of them. I want to know the man with whom I have joined my destiny. I suppress anything that might swell his pride. I isolate him so that he may keep his electricity and perhaps blow himself up.

MOTHER: How clever you've grown.

LADY: Yes. He's become so foolish now, that he tells me all his secrets, so that soon I'll hold his fate in my hand. Would you believe it, he's experimenting with electricity now! He says he's going to harness lightning, so that it'll give him light, heat and power. Well, let him. But I see from his letter that he's started corresponding with alchemists. About making gold.

MOTHER: Is he going to make gold now? Is he sane?

LADY: That's the big question. The lesser question is whether he's a charlatan.

MOTHER: Do you suspect him?

LADY: I believe all evil of him. And all good. Within the same day.

MOTHER: What other news?

LADY: The ogre's around. His marriage plans have broken down, and he's become a melancholic, has given up his practice and tramps the roads.

MOTHER: Poor man. He was my son-in-law, in spite of everything, and he had a good heart beneath that rough exterior.

LADY: I know. He was only an ogre so far as he was my husband. As long as I knew he was all right and on the way to finding peace, I was at peace. Now he'll haunt me like an evil conscience.

MOTHER: Have you a conscience?

LADY: I never used to have. But reading my husband's writings has opened my eyes. Now I can see the difference between good and evil.

MOTHER: He'd forbidden you to read his books and hadn't foreseen the consequences of your disobedience.

LADY: Who can anticipate all the consequences of one action?

MOTHER: What more evil have you in your bag, Pandora?

LADY: The worst. Ah! Can you imagine, mother — his first wife is planning to marry again!

MOTHER: That should make you both happy.

LADY: Don't you know that his worst nightmare is that his wife should marry again and his children have a step-father?

MOTHER: If he can bear that alone, he's not the man I thought.

LADY: Do you think he's that sensitive? Doesn't he say himself that in this era an educated gentleman should never be surprised at anything?

MOTHER: People say so many things. But when it comes to the point —

LADY: But in the bottom of Pandora's bag there's a present which isn't unlucky. Look. His little son's portrait.

MOTHER [*looks at it*]: He looks an angel.

LADY: Such a lovely face, so sweet an expression — one feels good simply by looking at it. Do you think my child will be as beautiful? Tell me, do you think so? Say yes, or I shall be miserable. I already love this little person, but I feel I could hate him if my child is not as beautiful. Yes — I'm already jealous.

MOTHER: When you came here after your honeymoon, I hoped your unhappiness might be over. But I see now, that was only the beginning.

LADY: I, too, am prepared for anything. And I don't think this skein can be untangled. It must be cut.

MOTHER: But you've made things more difficult for yourself by intercepting his letters.

LADY: Formerly, when I lived my life like a sleepwalker, I was able to take the pain from any hurt simply by kissing it. Now that he has made me think, I'm not so resilient. [*Puts the letters in her pocket.*] Here he comes. Hush, now.

MOTHER: One thing. Why do you let him walk about in your first husband's summer suit, like a ghost?

LADY: It amuses me to torment and humiliate him. I've got him to think it suits him, and that it used to belong to my father. When I see him in the ogre's clothes, I feel I've got both of them in my power.

MOTHER: God have mercy on us! How cruel you've become!

LADY: Perhaps that's my purpose. If I have one, in this man's life.

MOTHER: Sometimes I wish the river would rise and

drown us all as we slept. Then, if it washed the house for a thousand years, it might wash away the sin on which it was built.

LADY: Is it true, then, that my grandfather, the notary, dishonestly acquired other people's property? I have heard that this estate consists of what rightly belonged to widows and orphans, and was stolen from bankrupts and the land of the dead — and bribes —

MOTHER: Speak no more of that. The tears of the wronged have swollen to a lake, and people say it is that that is now being tapped, and will cause the river to wash us away.

LADY: Can't it be prevented, legally? Is there no justice on the earth any longer?

MOTHER: Not on the earth; but in heaven, and that's what will now drown us children of sinners. [*Goes up the steps.*]

LADY: It is not enough, then, that we have our own tears. We must inherit other men's too.

STRANGER [*enters*]: Did you call me?

LADY: No. I only drew you. I didn't want you.

STRANGER: I felt you were meddling with my fate in some bestial way. You didn't take long to learn my tricks.

LADY: And others, too.

STRANGER: I beg you; don't touch my destiny with your clumsy fingers. I am Cain, you see, and the powers have cursed me; but the powers allow no mortal to meddle in their vengeance. You see this scar on my forehead? [*Lifts his hat.*] It means: vengeance is mine, saith the Lord.

LADY: Is that hat too tight for you?

STRANGER: No. But it burns me. Like this coat! If I didn't know it would please you, I'd have thrown all this lot in the river. Do you know that when I go into the village, people call me doctor? They mean of course your husband, the ogre. And I always seem to be unlucky. If I

ask: "Who planted this tree?", people reply: "The
doctor." If I ask who owns the green chest, people say:
"It is the doctor's." And when it isn't the doctor's, it is
the doctor's wife's. That's you. This identification of me
with someone else makes my position here intolerable.
I'd like to go away —

LADY: You've tried six times, without success.

STRANGER: Yes. But the seventh time, I shall succeed.

LADY: Try.

STRANGER: You say that as though you were sure I
would fail.

LADY: I am sure.

STRANGER: Torment me in some other way, dear Fury.

LADY: I can, too.

STRANGER: In some new way. Try to say something
cruel that the other one didn't say.

LADY: The other one. You mean your wife. Charming of
you to remind me of her.

STRANGER: Everything that lives and moves, everything
that is dead and stiff, recalls the past.

LADY: Until that comes which shall wipe out the past, and
bring light.

STRANGER: You mean your child, which you are expecting.

LADY: *Our* child!

STRANGER: Do you love it?

LADY: From today I have begun to love it.

STRANGER: Today? What has happened, then? Five
months ago you wanted to go to a lawyer and get a
divorce because I wasn't prepared to take you to a quack
doctor and have it aborted.

LADY: That was then. Now I feel differently.

STRANGER: Now? [*Looks around, as though sniffing the air.*] Now? Has the post come?

LADY: You're still quicker than me. But soon the pupil will outdo the master.

STRANGER: Were there any letters for me?

LADY: No.

STRANGER: Give me the parcel, then.

LADY: How could you hear that?

STRANGER: Give me the parcel, since your conscience differentiates so sensitively between letters and parcels.

LADY [*holds out the post-bag, which she has been hiding behind her*]: Here.

> The STRANGER *takes out the photograph, studies it carefully and puts it in his pocket.*

LADY: What was it?

STRANGER: The past.

LADY: Was it beautiful?

STRANGER: Yes. As beautiful as the future can never be.

LADY [*sombrely*]: You shouldn't have said that.

STRANGER: I know. I'm sorry.

LADY: Can you suffer?

STRANGER: Twice as much now, for I suffer when you suffer. And when, in self-defence, I wound you, it is I who run the fever.

LADY: In other words, you are powerless against me.

STRANGER: Yes. Especially now, when you are protected by the innocent child you carry beneath your heart.

LADY: He will be my avenger.

STRANGER: Or mine.

LADY [*with tears in her voice*]: Poor creature. Born in sin and shame, born for hatred and revenge.

STRANGER: It's a long time since I heard that tenderness in your voice.

LADY: Yes.

STRANGER: It was that tone that first trapped me, because it was like a mother's when she talks to her child.

LADY: When you say that word "mother", I feel I could almost believe good of you. But the next moment, I think: it's only a new way to deceive me.

STRANGER: What harm have I really done you? [*She hesitates.*] Answer! What harm have I done you?

LADY: I don't know.

STRANGER: Think of something. Say this: "I hate you because I can't deceive you."

LADY: Can't I? Poor you.

STRANGER: Then you have some poison in the pocket of your dress.

LADY: Yes, I have.

STRANGER: What can it be? Who's that coming along the road?

LADY: The harbinger.

STRANGER: Is it a man or a ghost?

LADY: A ghost from the past.

STRANGER: He's wearing a frock coat and a laurel wreath. But he's barefoot.

LADY: It is Caesar.

STRANGER [*confused*]: Caesar? That was my nickname at school.

LADY: Yes. But it is also the nickname of the madman who lived with my — former husband, if you will excuse the expression.

STRANGER: Is the madman free, then?

LADY: So it seems.

CAESAR [*enters upstage, wearing a frock-coat but no shirt-collar, and a laurel wreath on his head. He is barefoot, and generally of bizarre appearance*]: Why don't you salute me? You should say: "Hail, Caesar!" For I am master now. The ogre has gone mad, since the Great One went off with his wife, whom he himself had stolen from her first lover, or fiancé or whatever they call it nowadays.

STRANGER [*to* LADY]: There's poison for us both. [*To* CAESAR]: Where is your servant, or slave, or doctor, or keeper, then?

CAESAR: He'll be here soon. But don't be frightened. He has no poison or dagger. He only has to show his face and all living things fly from him. The trees shed their leaves and the dust on the road runs before him in a whirl-wind, like the pillar of cloud before the children of Israel.

STRANGER: Now, listen —

CAESAR: Quiet while I speak! And sometimes he thinks he's an ogre, and says he wants to eat up a little child as yet unborn, which is really his by rights, as the first-comer. [*Goes.*]

LADY [*to* STRANGER]: Can you exorcize that demon?

STRANGER: I can't touch demons that live in sunlight.

LADY: You made a boast this morning which has now recoiled on you. You said: "Invisible things that creep in the night and fight in the dark, are cowards; but let them come in the daylight, when the sun is shining." Now they have come.

STRANGER: And that pleases you?

LADY: Yes. Almost.

STRANGER: What a pity I don't get pleasure when you suffer. Let us sit on the bench — the bench of the accused. I expect we'll have more visitors.

LADY: No, let us go.

STRANGER: No. I want to see how much I can bear. Besides, each turn of the rack is like a crime wiped off my punishment slate.

LADY: But I can't bear any more. Look, here he comes himself. Oh, God! This man whom I once thought I loved.

STRANGER: Thought? Yes; these are all illusions, and yet not just illusions. Go. I will face him alone.

> The LADY *starts to climb the steps, but has not reached the top when the* DOCTOR *enters upstage. He has long grey hair hanging down his neck, and is dressed in a panama hat and a hunting-coat exactly like the* STRANGER's. *He affects not to notice the* STRANGER *and sits down on a stone on the other side of the road opposite the* STRANGER *on his bench. He takes of his hat and mops his brow.*

STRANGER [*who has become impatient*]: What do you want?

DOCTOR: Only to see the house where I was once happy. Where *my* roses bloomed —

STRANGER: A gentleman would choose a time when the present owners were away. If only to save himself from appearing ridiculous.

DOCTOR: Ridiculous? I wonder which of us two is the more ridiculous?

STRANGER: For the moment, I suppose it is I.

DOCTOR: Yes. But I don't think you realize the full extent of your absurdity.

STRANGER: What do you mean?

DOCTOR: I mean, that you want to own what I have owned.

STRANGER: Go on.

DOCTOR: Have you noticed that we are identically dressed? Good. Do you know why that is? Because you are wearing the clothes which I forgot to take away. In this era an educated gentleman shouldn't expose himself to such ridicule.

STRANGER [*throws off his hat and coat*]: Damn that woman!

DOCTOR: Put up with it. Other men's clothes have been fatal ever since Nessus. Go inside and change, and I'll sit here and watch and listen as you settle your score in private with that "damned woman". Don't forget the stick.

> *The* LADY *has run up towards the house, but falls on the steps. The* STRANGER *stands confused.*

DOCTOR: The stick! The stick!

STRANGER: Not for the woman's sake, but for the child's, I beg you — be merciful.

DOCTOR [*wildly*]: I see, so there's a child too! *Our* house, *our* roses, *our* clothes, not forgetting the bedclothes, and *our* child! I am everywhere in your house, I sit at your table, lie in your bed; I am in your blood, in your lungs, in your brain; I am everywhere, and you cannot touch me. When midnight strikes I will breathe ice on your heart so that it will stop like a broken clock. When you sit at your desk I shall come with an invisible poppy to drug your mind and confuse your understanding, so that you'll see visions which you won't be able to distinguish from reality. I shall lie in your path like a stone to make you stumble. I shall become a thorn to prick your hand when you pluck the rose. My spirit will stretch over you like a spider's web and, through the woman you stole from me, I shall lead you like a ringed bull. Your child shall become

mine and I shall speak through its mouth. In its eyes you
will see mine, so that you will spurn it from you like an
enemy. Goodbye, house, goodbye, rose room. No happiness will flower there for me to envy.

He goes. The STRANGER *has all this time been sitting
on the bench listening speechlessly like an accused in
the dock.*

ACT TWO

Scene 1. The laboratory

*A garden pavilion in rococo style, with high windows.
In the middle stands a large desk with diverse chemistry
and physics apparatus. Two copper wires run down
from the ceiling to an electroscope on the middle of a
table, fitted with small bells to register the tension of
atmospheric electricity. On a table left stands a large
old-fashioned electricity machine with a glass disc,
brass conducting rods and a Leyden battery. The
stands are lacquered red and black. Right, a big old-
fashioned fireplace with tripods, crucibles, tongs,
bellows, etc. Upstage, a door leads out to a landscape.
It is cloudy and sombre weather, but now and then
red sunlight shines into the room. A brown cloak with
a cape and hood hangs by the fireplace. Beside it stand
a travelling bag and an alpenstock.*

The STRANGER. *The* MOTHER.

STRANGER: Where is . . . Ingeborg?

MOTHER: You know better than I do.

STRANGER: Well; she's at the lawyer's, to get a divorce —

MOTHER: Why?

STRANGER: Because — no, it's so absurd you wouldn't believe me.

MOTHER: Tell me.

STRANGER: Well, she wants a divorce because I didn't give that mad husband of hers a thrashing. She says I'm a coward.

MOTHER: I don't believe it.

STRANGER: No, there you are. You only believe what you want to believe. The rest is lies. Do you find it compatible with your interests to believe that she stole my letters?

MOTHER: I don't know.

STRANGER: I wasn't asking whether you knew, but whether you believed.

MOTHER [*changes the subject*]: What's this you're working on?

STRANGER: An experiment with atmospheric electricity.

MOTHER: Is that a lightning conductor you've led in on to your desk?

STRANGER: Yes. But there's no danger. As soon as any disturbance starts in the atmosphere, the bells ring.

MOTHER: It's blasphemy. Black magic. Take care. What are you doing in that fireplace?

STRANGER: Making gold.

MOTHER: You believe that?

STRANGER: You think I'm a charlatan? I can't blame you, but don't judge too quickly. I expect to be getting confirmation of my analysis any time now.

MOTHER: Well, that's as it may be. But what are you planning to do if Ingeborg doesn't come back?

STRANGER: She'll come. Though once the child is born, she may leave me.

MOTHER: You're so sure of things.

STRANGER: Yes, I'm still sure. One feels that as long as the bond holds. But once it's broken, one still feels it, horribly clearly.

MOTHER: But when you're freed from each other, you may still be bound together by the child. One can't tell.

STRANGER: I know. So I've fortified myself against that with an ambition which will fill the emptiness of my life.

MOTHER: Gold, and honour, you mean?

STRANGER: Precisely. The most indestructible of human illusions.

MOTHER: You still build on illusions?

STRANGER: What else should I build on, since everything is an illusion?

MOTHER: When you wake from that dream, you'll see a reality you never dreamed of.

STRANGER: When I wake.

MOTHER: You wait. Now I'll go and shut the windows, before the thunderstorm begins.

STRANGER [goes upstage]: That'll be interesting. [A hunting-horn is heard in the distance.] Who's that blowing again?

MOTHER: Nobody knows. And it bodes no good.

> She goes. The STRANGER fingers the electroscope, turning his back to the open window. Then he takes a book.

STRANGER [reads aloud]: "When Adam's race of giants had so increased that they felt strong enough to venture an assault on the gods, they began to build a tower that would reach to heaven. Then the gods were seized with fear, and to protect themselves they forestalled the con-

spiracy by confusing the giants' tongues and their understanding, so that when two of them met they could not
comprehend each other, even when they spoke the same
tongue. Since then the gods have ruled through discord:
divide, and rule. And discord is maintained through people
supposing that they have discovered the truth, but the
only prophets who are believed are false prophets. But
when any mortal finds out the secrets of the gods, nobody
believes him and he becomes insanely convinced that no
one *will* believe him. Since when all mortals have been
more or less mad, especially those who are supposed wise,
and the madmen are the only sane men; for they see, hear
and feel what is invisible, inaudible and intangible, but
can never convey their experience to others." Thus saith
Sohar, the wisest of all wise books, which therefore no
man believes. I shall build no Tower of Babel, but I shall
lure the gods into my rat-trap and then I shall send them
down to the nether powers beneath the earth to be neutra-
lized. The Schedim above have set themselves between
mortals and the Lord of Sabaoth, which is why joy, freedom and happiness have vanished from the earth.

> *The* LADY *enters. Distraught, she throws herself on
> the floor before the* STRANGER, *embraces his feet
> with her arms and bows her head to the floor.*

LADY: Help me! Help me! And forgive me!

STRANGER: Get up, for God's sake. Get up! Stop this.
What has happened?

LADY: Alas! In my anger I have acted like a lunatic, and
am caught in my own net.

STRANGER [*raises her up*] : Get up, uncomprehending
child, and tell me what this is.

LADY: I went to the public prosecutor, and —

STRANGER: Asked for a divorce.

LADY: That was my intention. But when I got there, I
accused the ogre of trespass and attempted murder —

STRANGER: But he has done neither.

LADY: No, but I accused him of them. And as I stood there he came himself and charged me with malicious prosecution. So then I went to my lawyer and he said I must expect at least a month in prison. Imagine — my child will be born in prison! How shall I escape this? Help me. You can help me. Tell me what to do.

STRANGER: I can help you. But don't take your revenge on me afterwards because I helped you.

LADY: How you distrust me! But hurry, and tell me.

STRANGER: Well, we can blame me. Say that I sent you.

LADY: How kind you are — after all! And now I shall be quite cleared of all this?

STRANGER: Dry your tears, child, and stop worrying. But tell me something else. Was it you who left this purse here? [*She looks embarrassed.*] Tell me.

LADY: Has that happened before too?

STRANGER: Yes. He — the other one — wanted to find out whether I was a thief. The other time it happened, I cried, because I was still a child.

LADY: Oh, no!

STRANGER: You really are the most wretched person I know.

LADY: And that is why you love me?

STRANGER: No, not because of that. Have you stolen my letters too? Answer: yes! So you want to make me out a thief too, with this purse.

LADY: What's that you have on the table there?

STRANGER: Lightning.

> *There is a flash of lightning, but no thunder.*

LADY: You're frightened!

STRANGER: Yes, sometimes. But not of what you are afraid of.

The DOCTOR's *face appears at the window, with distorted features.*

LADY: Is there a cat in the room? I feel so uneasy?

STRANGER: No, I don't think so. But I feel there is someone here.

LADY [*turns and sees the face, screams, and runs to the* STRANGER *for protection*]: Oh — it's he!

STRANGER: Where? Who?

The DOCTOR'S *face disappears.*

LADY: There, in the window! It's he!

STRANGER: I see no one. You must be mistaken.

LADY: I saw him. The ogre. Can't we kill him?

STRANGER: We could. But it wouldn't help. He has an immortal soul, and it is bound to yours.

LADY: If one had known before.

STRANGER: It's in the catechism.

LADY: Let us die, then.

STRANGER: That was once my religion. But now I no longer believe that death is the end of things, so all we can do is go on — fight, and suffer.

LADY: How long must we suffer?

STRANGER: As long as he suffers and our conscience flays us.

LADY: Let us try to defend ourselves against our consciences. Let us seek excuses for our wanton conduct; let us hunt out his faults —

STRANGER: Try.

LADY: You can say that. Since I know he is unhappy, I can see only his good qualities, and you suffer by the comparison.

STRANGER: You see how wisely things are arranged. His sufferings make him a saint, and make me hateful and ridiculous. This is hopeless. We have murdered a human soul. We are murderers.

LADY: Whose fault is that?

STRANGER: The fault of whoever rules human destinies so insanely.

There is a flash of lightning. The electric bells ring.

LADY: Blessed Jesus! What is that?

STRANGER: The powers answering us.

LADY: Have you a lightning conductor in this room?

STRANGER: The priest of Baal would bring down fire from heaven.

LADY: Now I am afraid — afraid of you. You are terrifying me!

STRANGER: There. You see.

LADY: Who are you, that you dare to defy heaven and play with human destinies?

STRANGER: Get up and calm yourself. Listen to me, believe in me, grant me the respect I deserve, and I will raise both of us high above this swamp into which we have descended. I will kiss your sick conscience so that it will be healed like a wound. Who am I? I am he who has done what no man has done before. I am he who shall overturn the golden calf and the tables of the money-lenders. I hold the fate of the world in my crucible, and within a week the richest of the rich shall be poor, the false god of gods, gold, will have ceased to rule, all will be equally poor, and the children of men will creep lost around the earth like ants whose hill has been kicked to pieces.

LADY: How will that help us?

STRANGER: Do you think I made gold to enrich myself? No, to destroy the order of the world. To destroy, do you hear? I am the destroyer, the annihilator, the world-burner, and when everything lies in ashes I shall wander starving among the ruins and rejoice at the thought: it is I who have done this, I who have written the last page of the world's history, which is now finished.

> The DOMINICAN's *face appears at the open window,* *unnoticed by them.*

LADY: So this was the hidden meaning of your last book. It was not fiction.

STRANGER: No. But to achieve this I had to find a duplicate self that could take into itself everything that binds my spirit. So that my soul might rediscover its pure fire, which would enable it to rise into the ether, pass beyond the powers, and arrive at the throne to lay the complaints of mankind at the feet of the Almighty —

> The DOMINICAN *makes the sign of the cross and* *vanishes.*

STRANGER: Who is here? Who is this terrible being who persecutes me and paralyses my spirit? Did you see anyone?

LADY: No, no one.

STRANGER: But I sense him. [*Clutches his heart.*] Do you hear, do you hear? Afar off, far, far away, a prayer is being read. Do you hear?

LADY: Yes, I hear. But it is not a prayer. It is the curse of Deuteronomy. [*Cries.*] Ah!

STRANGER: Then it must be the House of Good Hope —

LADY: Ah! Ah!

STRANGER: My dearest. What is it!

LADY: Say that word again. Dearest!

STRANGER: You are sick.

LADY: Not sick, but in pain. But — joyful pain. Go and
ask my mother to make my bed ready. But first, give me
your blessing.

STRANGER: You ask *me* to — ?

LADY: Say you forgive me. I may die if our baby takes my
life with him. Say you love me.

STRANGER: I can't say that word.

LADY: You don't love me?

STRANGER: When you ask that, I feel that I don't. It's
terrible, but I feel I hate you.

LADY: At least give me your hand. As you would to someone in need.

STRANGER: I want to, but I can't. There's someone in me
that rejoices in your suffering; but it isn't me. I'd like to
take you in my arms and suffer with you, but I may not.
I can't!

LADY: Hard as stone.

STRANGER [*with controlled emotion*]: Perhaps not. Perhaps not.

LADY: Come to me.

STRANGER: I can't move. It's as though someone had
taken possession of my soul, and I'd have to kill myself
to kill him.

LADY: Think of your child —

STRANGER: I can't do that either. He will bind me to the
earth.

LADY: If we have done wrong, we have been punished.
Dear God! Won't it soon be enough?

STRANGER: Not soon. But some day.

LADY [*falls to the floor*]: Oh — help me! Have mercy.
I'm dying.

> The STRANGER *stretches out his hand to her, as
> though released from a paralysis. She kisses his hand.
> He raises her and leads her towards the door.*

Scene 2. The rose room

> *A room with rose-coloured walls (as in Part I). Small
> windows with iron bars and pots of plants. Rose-
> coloured curtains; white and rose furniture. Upstage,
> a door leading to a white bedroom. When the door is
> opened, a big bed is visible, with a canopy and white
> hangings. Right, an exit door. Left, a stove with a
> coal fire. In front of the fire is a metal bath covered
> with a white cloth. A cradle in white, rose and light
> blue. Baby clothes are spread around. A green dress
> hangs on the wall, right.*
>
> Four SISTERS OF MERCY *are kneeling facing
> the upstage door, dressed in Augustine black and
> white. The* MIDWIFE, *in black, is by the fire. The*
> NURSE, *in black and white Breton folk costume. By
> the upstage door the* MOTHER *stands listening. The*
> STRANGER *is seated in a chair right, reading a book.
> Beside him hang a hat and a brown cloak with cape
> and hood. On the floor, a small suitcase.*

SISTERS OF MERCY [*sing a psalm. The others, except
the* STRANGER, *occasionally join in the words.*]:

*Salve, Regina, mater misericordiae;
Vita dulcedo, et spes nostra, salve.
Ad te clamamus, exules filii Evae;
Ad te suspiramus gementes et flentes
In hac lacrymarum valle.*

> The STRANGER *gets up and goes to the* MOTHER.

MOTHER: Stay where you are. A new creature is being
born, another is dying. You care about neither.

STRANGER: Who knows? When I want to come in, I mustn't, and when I don't want to, I must. Now I want to come in.

MOTHER: She doesn't want to see you. Anyway, your presence is superfluous. Only the child matters now.

STRANGER: To you. But to me, I still matter.

MOTHER: The doctor forbids anyone to come in. A life is in danger.

STRANGER: What doctor?

MOTHER: Are you back there again?

STRANGER: Yes, thanks to you. An hour ago you hinted that the child wasn't mine. You'd call your daughter a whore to hurt me. You're just about the most loathsome person I know.

MOTHER [*to the* SISTERS]: Sisters! Pray for this unhappy creature.

STRANGER: Stand aside and let me in — for the last time! Stand aside!

MOTHER: Leave this room, and this house.

STRANGER: If I did you'd send the police after me within ten minutes for having abandoned my wife and child.

MOTHER: If I did, it'd only be to have you sent to that hospital you know.

MAID [*enters upstage*]: Excuse me, sir. Madam asks if you'll do something for her.

STRANGER: What is it?

MAID: She wants a letter from her dress. It's hanging in here.

STRANGER [*looks around, sees the green dress, goes over and takes a letter from the pocket*]: This letter is addressed to me. It must have been opened two days ago. Stolen, in other words. Charming!

MOTHER: Forgive her. She's sick.

STRANGER: She wasn't sick two days ago.

MOTHER: But she is now.

STRANGER: But not two days ago. [*Reads the letter.*]
But I do forgive her. In the moment of victory.

MOTHER: Victory?

STRANGER: Yes. I've done what no man has done before.

MOTHER: Gold — ?

STRANGER: This letter is confirmation from the greatest
authority living. I must go now, to meet him.

MOTHER: Go — now?

STRANGER: You have just ordered me to.

MAID: Madam would like to see you, sir.

MOTHER: You hear!

STRANGER: No. Now I don't want to. You have called
my wife, your daughter, a whore, and my unborn child a
bastard. Keep them. You have murdered my honour.
There is nothing left for me but to seek it elsewhere.

MOTHER: Can't you forgive?

STRANGER: Yes. I forgive you — and go. [*Puts on the
brown cloak and hat, picks up the suitcase and stick.*]
Because if I stayed, I should soon become worse than I
am. That innocent creature who should have ennobled
our wretched existence, you have defiled in its mother's
womb. It will only be a seed of discord, a chastiser, an
avenger. Why should I stay here to let myself be torn to
pieces?

MOTHER: Have you no sense of duty?

STRANGER: Yes; the most important one. To save my
soul from total destruction. Goodbye!

ACT THREE

Scene 1. The banquet at the inn

*A banqueting hall. Long tables decked with flowers
and candelabra. Dishes of peacocks and pheasants in
full plumage, boars' heads, lobsters, oysters, salmon,
asparagus, melons, grapes. A music platform in the
right corner upstage with eight* MUSICIANS. *At the
table of honour sits the* STRANGER *in full evening
dress, with tails; beside him, a* GUEST *similarly
dressed, with decorations; a* PROFESSOR *in academic
tails with decorations; the others are in black tails with
order-ribbons of varying degrees of splendour. At the
second table a few wear tails, but the others are in
black morning coats. Those at the third table wear
smart ordinary suits. At the fourth table sit tattered
and dirty figures of bizarre appearance. The tables are
so arranged that the top table is farthest to the left
and the fourth on the extreme right, so that the figures
at this fourth table are invisible to the* STRANGER.
Among them, nearest to the audience, are the
DOCTOR *and* CAESAR, *shabbily dressed.*

The GUESTS *have reached the dessert, and gold
cups stand before them. The* MUSICIANS *are playing
Mendelssohn's Funeral March very softly. The* GUESTS
are chatting among themselves.

DOCTOR [*to* CAESAR]: The atmosphere's a bit forced,
don't you think, Caesar? And they've rushed us through
the meal.

CAESAR: It's all humbug, that's my opinion. He hasn't
made gold. It's all lies. Like everything else.

DOCTOR: So I've heard, though I wouldn't know. In these
enlightened times, anything goes.

CAESAR: That Professor in the chair is supposed to be an authority. But what's he a professor of?

DOCTOR: I don't know. Metallurgy, I suppose. Or applied chemistry.

CAESAR: Can you see what ribbon it is he's wearing?

DOCTOR: Nothing I know. Some foreign shit, I expect.

CAESAR: You get all sorts at these subscription banquets.

DOCTOR: Hm!

CAESAR: You mean we — ? Hm. Well, I admit we're not the best dressed here, but if it's a question of intelligence —

DOCTOR: Caesar, you're a certified lunatic in my charge. You should avoid the subject of intelligence.

CAESAR: I never heard such cheek. You idiot, don't you know I've been paid to keep an eye on you, since you went off your head —?

PROFESSOR [*raps on the table*]: Gentlemen!

CAESAR: Hear, hear!

PROFESSOR: Gentlemen! Our little society is today honoured by the presence of the great man whom we welcome as our guest of honour. When your committee —

CAESAR [*to* DOCTOR]: That's the government. Eh?

PROFESSOR: When your committee asked me to give expression to their admiration and gratitude, I at first hesitated to accept this flattering responsibility. But when I compared my own inadequacy with that of others, I felt that neither party could truthfully be said to lose by the comparison.

VOICES: Hear, hear!

PROFESSOR: Gentlemen! This century of great discoveries is now crowned by the most sensational of all discoveries — prophesied by Pythagoras, paved by Albertus and Paracelsus, and achieved at long last by our guest of honour.

Permit me to present a humble token of our admiration to the greatest man of this great century. From our society this laurel wreath. [*Places a laurel wreath on the* STRANGER's *head.*] And from your committee — this! [*Hangs a glittering decoration round the* STRANGER's *neck.*] Gentlemen! Three cheers for the great Maker of Gold!

ALL [*except the* STRANGER]: Hip-hip-hip-hurrah!

> *The* MUSICIANS *play chords from the Funeral March. During the latter half of the* PROFESSOR's *speech, servants have exchanged the gold cups for dull pewter ones and now begin to remove the peacocks and pheasants. The music continues slowly. The* GUESTS *chatter.*

CAESAR: Aren't we going to get a taste of that before they take it away?

DOCTOR: It's all humbug. Except about the gold-making —

STRANGER [*raps on the table*]: Gentlemen! I have already prided myself on being a man who is not easily fooled —

CAESAR: Hear, hear!

STRANGER: And not easily carried away. But the sincerity of your noble tribute has moved me, and when *I* say moved me, I mean it.

CAESAR: Bravo!

STRANGER: Of course, there are doubters, and there are moments in every man's life when even the strongest is assailed by doubt. I must confess that I too have sometimes doubted; but, after finding myself the subject of your sincere and heartfelt tribute, and attending this regal banquet — for it is regal — and learning that the government itself —

A VOICE: The committee. The committee.

STRANGER: The committee, if you prefer — has seen fit so flatteringly to reward my humble talent, of which posterity alone can be the true judge, I can no longer doubt — I *believe*! [*The* COMMITTEE MEMBER *on the* STRANGER's *left tiptoes out.*] Yes, gentlemen, this is the noblest, the most beautiful moment in my life, for it has enabled me to rediscover the most precious thing a man can have: belief in myself.

CAESAR: Magnificent! Bravo!

STRANGER: Thank you. Gentlemen! Your health!

> *The* PROFESSOR *rises. The* OTHER GUESTS *rise too, and mingle. The* MUSICIANS *withdraw, leaving only two of their number.*

A GUEST [*to* STRANGER]: Capital, my dear sir, capital.

STRANGER: Superbly organized.

> *All the* GUESTS *in full evening dress tiptoe out. The* LADY'S FATHER, *an old dandy of military mien with a monocle, walks over to the* DOCTOR.

LADY'S FATHER [*to* DOCTOR]: By Jove, are you here?

DOCTOR: Yes, Father-in-law. I am here, and everywhere where *he is*.

LADY'S FATHER: You mustn't call me father-in-law any longer. Anyway, I'm *his* father-in-law now.

DOCTOR: Does he know you?

LADY'S FATHER: No, he hasn't had that privilege, and I prefer to remain incognito to him. Is it true that he has made gold?

DOCTOR: They say so. But what's certain is that he left his wife while she was in labour.

LADY'S FATHER: You mean I may expect another son-in-law soon? Well, lads, I don't like this. All this chopping and changing rather sours the pleasure of being a father-in-law. Nobody ever asks my opinion. I suppose it's no wonder, considering. . . .

> *The tables have now been cleared; even the cloths and candelabra are gone, so that the wooden boards and trestles stand bare. A big stone pitcher is carried in, and stone mugs of the cheapest kind are set out on the top table.* CAESAR *raps for attention, and the poorest* GUESTS *seat themselves at the top table around the* STRANGER. *The* LADY'S FATHER *sits astride a chair and stares at the* STRANGER.

CAESAR: Gentlemen! This banquet has been described as regal, not that the service has been regal, quite the contrary, it's been deplorable, but the man we're here to honour is a king, a king in the world of intellect. That's something only I can appreciate — [A GUEST *titters.*] Shut up, you drunk! But he is more than a king, for he is a man of the people, the humble people, a friend of the oppressed, the protector of madmen, the comforter of fools. Whether he has made gold, well, that I don't know, I don't care, and personally I don't believe it. [*Murmurs. Two* POLICEMEN *enter and sit by the door. The* MUSICIANS *descend and sit at the table.*] But if he has, then he has solved all the problems the newspapers have been posing over the past fifty years. But this is only speculation —

STRANGER: Gentlemen!

A DRUNK: No, don't interrupt.

CAESAR: It's just loose speculation, without any real evidence. The analysis may be wrong.

ANOTHER DRUNK: Don't talk rubbish.

STRANGER: If it would interest you, gentlemen, to hear the grounds on which I made this claim —

CAESAR: No! We don't want to hear!

LADY'S FATHER: One moment! I think justice demands

that the accused should be allowed to explain himself. Let him briefly expound his secret.

STRANGER: I don't want to give away my secret, and there's no need. I have confided my findings to the appropriate authority.

CAESAR: I never heard such humbug. We don't believe authorities, we're free-thinkers. Who ever heard of such cheek? Are we expected to accept the word of a huckster, a charlatan, a quack?

LADY'S FATHER: One moment, my good people.

During the preceding dialogue, a prettily decorated screen with palms and birds of paradise has been removed, revealing a squalid taproom with a bar behind which a BARMAID *is dispensing drinks to down-and-outs and whores.*

STRANGER: Have I been invited here to be insulted?

LADY'S FATHER: Not at all. Our friend here is somewhat exuberant in his phraseology, but he has not as yet said anything insulting.

STRANGER: Do you not regard the word charlatan as insulting?

LADY'S FATHER: He did not intend that seriously.

STRANGER: Even in fun I regard the word quack as deeply offensive.

LADY'S FATHER: He did not use that word.

STRANGER: What? I appeal to you, gentlemen! Did he not say quack?

ALL: No! He never said it!

STRANGER: Where am I? What kind of company is this?

A DRUNK: Is there anything wrong with us? Eh?

Murmurs. The BEGGAR *comes forward on crutches and strikes the table with a crutch, smashing the mugs.*

BEGGAR: Mr Chairman! May I speak? [*He smashes more of the crockery.*] I have never been a man who has been easily fooled, gentlemen, but this time I have been. My friend there, in the seat of honour, has convinced me that I have been sadly deceived in my assessment of his intelligence and powers of judgement. There are limits to sympathy and there are limits to cruelty. It pains me to see true merit dragged in the mud and this man deserves a better fate than that into which his folly has led him.

STRANGER: What do you mean?

During the BEGGAR's *speech the* LADY'S FATHER *and* DOCTOR *have slipped out. The top table is now entirely occupied by* DRUNKS *and* BEGGARS. *The customers in the taproom are now standing in groups staring at the* STRANGER.

BEGGAR: This. You, who regard yourself as the Man of the Century, have accepted an invitation from a club of drunks to acclaim you as a man of science —

STRANGER [*rises*]: But the committee —

BEGGAR: Yes, the committee of this drinking club has given you its highest award in the shape of that medal, which you will have to pay for yourself.

STRANGER: And the Professor?

BEGGAR: He calls himself that, but he isn't one. He's just a teacher, and that uniform he was wearing, which no doubt deceived you, was that of a palace clerk.

STRANGER [*tears off his wreath and order-ribbon*]: Very well. But who was the old gentleman with the monocle?

BEGGAR: That was your father-in-law.

STRANGER: Who is responsible for this charade?

BEGGAR: It's no charade. It's perfectly serious. The Professor approached you on behalf of "Society", which is the name of this club, and asked if you would be their guest. You accepted; so it was quite serious.

Two WHORES *come forward with a dustbin suspended on a pole and put the dustbin on the top table.*

FIRST WHORE: If you're the one who makes gold, buy us a drink.

STRANGER: What does this mean?

BEGGAR: This is the last item on the agenda of the banquet, and it means: gold is only garbage.

STRANGER: If that were true, garbage could be exchanged for gold.

BEGGAR: Well, that is the philosophy of this drinking club, and you must accept the philosophy of your hosts.

SECOND WHORE [*sits down by the* STRANGER]: Do you recognize me?

STRANGER: No!

SECOND WHORE: Oh, come on. You don't need to be coy at this time of night.

STRANGER: I suppose you're meant to be one of my victims. And I one of your first hundred seducers.

SECOND WHORE: Not the way you mean. But just after I'd been confirmed, I'd read a book you'd written, and it said it was the duty of every man and woman to let their impulses bloom freely. Well, I let mine. And here's the result.

STRANGER [*gets up*]: Perhaps I may go now?

BARMAID [*comes forward with a bill*]: Not till you've paid this, you don't.

STRANGER: I? But I haven't ordered anything.

BARMAID: I wouldn't know about that. But you're the last member left.

STRANGER [*to* BEGGAR]: Is this part of the arrangements too?

BEGGAR: That's right. And as you know, everything has to be paid for. Even honour.

STRANGER [*takes out a visiting card and hands it over*]: Here is my card. You will be paid tomorrow.

BARMAID [*puts the card in the dustbin.*]: Hm! I don't know this name, and I've thrown lots of these into the dustbin before now. I want money.

BEGGAR: Look, madam, I guarantee that this gentleman will pay —

BARMAID: Oh, so you're going to cheek me too? Officer! Here a moment.

POLICEMAN: What's all this? Another unpaid bill, eh? You come with me to the station and we'll settle this little matter. [*Writes in his notebook.*]

STRANGER: I'd rather that than stand here and argue. [*To* BEGGAR.] I don't mind a joke, but I didn't expect such deadly earnest as this.

BEGGAR: One must be prepared for everything when one challenges such mighty powers as you have. And let me whisper this. Be prepared for worse. For the worst!

STRANGER: To think I could let myself be fooled so — so — !

BEGGAR: These Belshazzar's feasts always end with a hand coming out and writing — a bill. And another hand taking hold of your shoulder and leading you to the place of reckoning. Well, at least it's a royal reckoning.

POLICEMAN [*puts a hand on the* STRANGER]: You finished talking?

WHORES *and* BEGGARS: The gold-maker! The gold-maker can't pay! Hurrah! He's going to jail! He's going to jail!

SECOND WHORE: I feel sorry for him.

STRANGER: You pity me! Thank you for that, though I don't deserve it. *You* can feel pity!

SECOND WHORE: Yes. That's something I learned from you, too.

> *The scene grows dark. A medley of décors ensues — a landscape, a palace and a room descend and come forward, while the characters and the furniture disappear. At length the* STRANGER, *who has been standing as though paralysed and asleep, also vanishes and out of the confusion emerges a prison cell.*

Scene 2. The prison

> *Right, a door. Above the door, a grille, through which a ray of sunlight casts a patch of light on the left-hand wall, where a big crucifix hangs. The* STRANGER *is seated in his hat and brown cloak at a table, looking at the patch of light. The door is opened and the* BEGGAR *is let in.*

BEGGAR: What are you thinking about?

STRANGER: I'm sitting here wondering why I'm sitting here, and then I wonder where I was last night.

BEGGAR: Where do you think you were?

STRANGER: I think I was in hell. Or that I dreamed it all.

BEGGAR: Wake up, then. Now you must face reality.

STRANGER: Tell me. It's only ghosts I'm frightened of.

BEGGAR [*takes out a newspaper*]: First, it says here that the great scientist who declared that you had made gold has withdrawn his certificate. He says you deceived him, and the newspaper calls you a charlatan.

STRANGER: Damnation! Who am I fighting against?

BEGGAR: Adversity, like other men.

STRANGER: No, this is something else —

BEGGAR: Your own credulity, then?

STRANGER: No, I'm not credulous, and I know I'm right.

BEGGAR: What good is that if no one else knows it?

STRANGER: If only I can get out of here, I'll clear the whole matter up.

BEGGAR: The bill for the banquet has been paid, so that charge has been dropped —

STRANGER: Who paid it?

BEGGAR: Your "Society", I suppose. Or your government, or whatever those drunks were.

STRANGER: Then I can go?

BEGGAR: Yes. But there's something else —

STRANGER: Go on.

BEGGAR: But an educated gentleman like you mustn't take it amiss —

STRANGER: I think I know.

BEGGAR: The announcement's on the front page.

STRANGER: In other words, she has already re-married, and my children have a stepfather. Who is he?

BEGGAR: Whoever he is, don't kill him, for he is blameless. You left her.

STRANGER: My children. Oh, God! My children!

BEGGAR: I see you weren't expecting this. But why not look around? I mean, at your age — and with your education —

STRANGER [distraught]: Oh, God! My children!

BEGGAR: Educated gentlemen don't cry, you know. Now

listen, my lad. When disasters like this happen, a gentleman either — well, you tell me.

STRANGER: Shoots himself.

BEGGAR: Or?

STRANGER: No. Not that.

BEGGAR: Yes, my little lad. Precisely that. He throws out
a sheet-anchor. Just to see —

STRANGER: That's hopeless. Hopeless.

BEGGAR: Yes, it is. Absolutely hopeless. And you can live
another fifty years calmly contemplating the harm you've
done.

STRANGER: You ought to be ashamed.

BEGGAR: *I* ought?

STRANGER: Have you ever known anyone go through
what I've gone through?

BEGGAR: Look at me.

STRANGER: I don't know what your life has been.

BEGGAR: No. In all the time you've known each other, it
has never occurred to you to ask. Once when I offered
you friendship you turned up your nose, and fell splash
into the arms of our friends, "Society". Good luck with
them, and goodbye. For now.

STRANGER: Don't go.

BEGGAR: You want someone to keep you company when
you walk out of here?

STRANGER: Why not?

BEGGAR: It hasn't occurred to you that I might not want
to be seen with you?

STRANGER: No, it didn't really.

BEGGAR: Well, it's the truth. Do you think I want to be

suspected of being involved in all these scandals that are all over the papers?

STRANGER: *You* refuse to keep *me* company?

BEGGAR: Even a beggar has his pride, and doesn't like being mocked.

STRANGER: He won't go with me! Am I so poor?

A sad lullaby is heard as though at a distance.

STRANGER: What is that?

BEGGAR: A mother singing at her child's cradle.

STRANGER: Why do I have to be reminded of that just now?

BEGGAR: To realize what you lost for the sake of an illusion.

STRANGER: If I *was* mistaken, then it's the devil's work, and I lay down my arms.

BEGGAR: Please do it as quickly as possible, then.

STRANGER: Not yet! [*A prayer is heard being read afar off.*] What's that? [*A long call is heard on a hunting-horn.*] It is the unknown hunter! [*The funeral march is heard.*] Where am I? [*He stands still as though in a trance.*]

BEGGAR: Yield, or be broken.

STRANGER: I cannot yield.

BEGGAR: Break, then.

> The STRANGER *falls. We see the same confusion of scenes that we saw at the beginning of this scene.*

Scene 3. The rose room

The same as in Act Two, Scene 1. The SISTERS OF MERCY *are still on their knees, but are now reading from their prayer-books. The* MOTHER *is standing by the door upstage, the* LADY'S FATHER *by the door right.*

SISTERS: *Exules filii Evae, ad te suspiramus gementes et flentes in hac lacrymarum valle.*

MOTHER [*approaches the* FATHER]: Hullo, are you back?

FATHER [*humbly*]: Yes.

MOTHER: Your beauty's thrown you over, then?

FATHER: Don't be crueller than you need.

MOTHER: You say that! You, who gave my wedding presents to your mistress, who had so little honour that you asked me to choose your own presents to her, and wanted to pick my brains about colours and clothes — ! What do you want here?

FATHER: I heard that my daughter —

MOTHER: Your daughter is hovering between life and death, and you know she regards you as an enemy. So please go, before she knows you are here.

FATHER: You're right. I have no answer to that. But let me sit in the kitchen. I'm so tired, so tired.

MOTHER: Where were you last night?

FATHER: At the club. But tell me, isn't her husband here?

MOTHER: Must I spell out our misery to you? Don't you know what has happened to your daughter?

FATHER: Yes, yes — I know. What a husband, *what* a husband —

MOTHER: He's not the only one. Go downstairs now, and sleep yourself sober.

FATHER: The sins of the fathers —

MOTHER: Don't get maudlin.

FATHER: I don't mean my sins, of course. Our parents'. You know. And now they say they're going to drain the lake up there, so the river'll rise —

MOTHER [*pushes him out through the door*]: Ssh! Fate will lay her finger on us in her own time, without you tempting her.

MAID [*enters upstage*]: Madam says she wants to see the master.

MOTHER: Her husband, she means.

MAID: Yes, the master — madam's husband.

MOTHER: He left, just a minute ago.

STRANGER [*enters*]: Is the child born yet?

MOTHER: No, not yet.

STRANGER [*clutches his forehead*]: Why is that? Can it take so long?

MOTHER: Long? What do you mean?

STRANGER [*looks round*]: I don't know what I mean. But — how is the mother?

MOTHER: The same as she was a minute ago.

STRANGER: A minute ago?

MOTHER: I thought you were going back to your gold-making.

STRANGER: I don't understand. Perhaps there's some hope, then. . . . Was that nightmare just a nightmare?

MOTHER: You look as though you were sleepwalking.

STRANGER: Do I? I wish I was. The one thing I feared, I would fear no longer.

MOTHER: He Who rules your destiny seems to know your vulnerable points.

STRANGER: Even when I had only one left, He found

that out — luckily only in a dream. Blind powers! Evil powers!

MAID [*enters again*]: Excuse me, sir, madam asks if you will do her a favour.

STRANGER: She's like an electric eel — she delivers her blows from a distance. What friendly favour does she want now?

MAID: There's a letter in the pocket of her green coat.

STRANGER: Ugh! Nothing good'll come of that. [*Takes a letter from the green coat, which is hanging beside her dress by the stove.*] This is the end! I dreamed this, and now it is true. My children have a stepfather.

MOTHER: Whom are you going to blame for that?

STRANGER: Myself. No one. I have lost my children.

MOTHER: You will have a new one here.

STRANGER: Imagine if he should be cruel to them. Imagine!

MOTHER: Then you'll have their suffering on your conscience. If you have one.

STRANGER: Imagine if he should — strike them!

MOTHER: Do you know what I'd do in your place?

STRANGER: Yes. I know what you'd do. But I don't know what I shall do.

MOTHER [*to the* SISTERS]: Pray for this man.

STRANGER: No, not that. Not that. It won't help, and I don't believe in it.

MOTHER: But you believe in your gold?

STRANGER: Nor in that either. That's finished. Everything's finished.

MIDWIFE [*enters upstage*]: A child is born. Praised be the Lord!

MOTHER *and* SISTERS: The Lord be praised!

MIDWIFE [*to* STRANGER]: Your wife has given you a daughter.

MOTHER [*to* STRANGER]: Don't you want to see your child?

STRANGER: No. I will not bind myself again to anything on this earth. I fear lest I should come to love it, and then you would tear the heart out of my body. Let me go, out of this air, which is too clean for me. Don't let the innocent child come near me, for I am lost and damned, and for me there can be no joy, no peace, no grace.

MOTHER: My son, now you speak wisdom. Without malice, and without deceit. I applaud your decision. You are superfluous here, and would be plagued to death amongst women. Go in peace.

STRANGER: Not in peace. But I shall go. Goodbye.

MOTHER: Unhappy sons of Eve! A fugitive and a vagabond shalt thou be on the earth.

STRANGER: Because I murdered my brother.

ACT FOUR

Scene 1. The inn

The banqueting room of Act Three; but it is now drab, with unpainted wooden tables and benches. BEGGARS, DOWN-AND-OUTS *and* WHORES. *Here and there* CRIPPLES *sit drinking by the light of candles. The* STRANGER *and the* SECOND WHORE *are drinking aquavit, a bottle of which stands on the table. The* STRANGER *is drinking heavily.*

SECOND WHORE: Don't drink so much.

STRANGER: What? Are you a moralist too?

SECOND WHORE: No, But I don't like to see a man I respect degrade himself.

STRANGER: I came here to degrade myself. Dirt hardens the skin against the thorns of life. I came to find comfort in foul surroundings. And I chose your company because you were the person I most despised of everyone I knew, and yet had retained a spark of humanity. You took pity on me when no one else did — not even myself. Why?

SECOND WHORE: I don't know.

STRANGER: Do you know there are moments when you're almost beautiful?

SECOND WHORE: Listen to him!

STRANGER: Yes. And you're like someone I once loved.

SECOND WHORE: Thanks very much.

BARMAID: Don't talk so loud, there's a sick man in here.

STRANGER: Tell me, have you ever loved anyone?

SECOND WHORE: We don't use that word, but I know what you mean. Yes, I had a lover, and we had a child.

STRANGER: That was unwise.

SECOND WHORE: I thought so. But he said the time for emancipation had come, when all bonds would be broken, all barriers torn down, and —

STRANGER [*tortured*]: What happened then?

SECOND WHORE: Then he left me.

STRANGER: He was a swine. [*Drinks.*]

SECOND WHORE [*looks at him*]: Do you think so?

STRANGER: Of course.

SECOND WHORE: You're a hard man.

STRANGER [*drinks*]: Am I?

SECOND WHORE: Don't drink so much. I want to see you high up, high above me. So you can lift me to your level.

STRANGER: Child, what illusions you have. I, lift you? I, who am at the bottom of the pit? No, I'm not, it isn't I who am sitting here, for I am dead. I know my soul is somewhere else, far away, far, far away. . . . [*Stares vacantly.*] Where a great river runs like molten gold in the sunshine, and roses flower with vines upon a wall; and a white pram stands beneath an acacia tree. But the child sleeps, for its mother sits by it knitting, knitting a long, long strip which comes out of her mouth, on which is written: "Blessed are they that mourn, for they shall be comforted." But it isn't true. I never find it. Tell me, isn't there thunder in the air, it feels so close and oppressive — ?

SECOND WHORE [*looks out through window*]: No, I can't see any clouds outside —

STRANGER: That's strange. There's lightning.

SECOND WHORE: You're mistaken.

STRANGER: One, two, three, four, five — now there should be thunder. But there's none. I've never been afraid of thunder before today. Tonight, I mean. Is it day or night?

SECOND WHORE: Night, of course.

STRANGER: Yes, it's night. Night.

During this scene the DOCTOR *has come in and sat down behind the* STRANGER *without the latter seeing him.*

BARMAID: Don't talk so loud, there's a sick man in here.

STRANGER [*to* WHORE]: Give me your hand.

SECOND WHORE [*dries it on her apron*]: Why?

STRANGER: Your hand is white and beautiful. But look at mine. It's quite black. Don't you see that it is black?

SECOND WHORE: So it is.

STRANGER: Black already. Perhaps mouldering too? Has my heart stopped? [*Puts his hand on his heart.*] Yes, it has. I'm dead, then, and I know when it happened. To think that one can walk around and be dead. But where am I, then? Are all these people dead too? They look as though they'd risen out of the sewers, or as though the poorhouse, the hospital and the jail had spewed them out. Workers of the night, suffering, moaning, cursing, quarrelling, tormenting each other, defiling each other, envying each other, as though they possessed anything worthy of envy! The fire of sleep runs in their veins, their tongues cleave to their mouths, which are parched with cursing, and they quench the fire with water, fire-water which brings them a new thirst, fire-water which itself burns with a blue flame and burns out the spirit like a prairie fire which leaves nothing but red sand. [*Drinks.*] Burn! Quench! Burn! Quench! But what won't burn is memory — memory of the past. How can one burn memories?

BARMAID: Don't talk so loud, please, there's a sick man in here. He's already asked for the sacrament.

STRANGER: May he go to hell, and quickly!

The OTHERS *murmur in horror.*

BARMAID: Take care! Take care!

SECOND WHORE [*to* STRANGER]: Do you know that man who's sitting behind you, staring at you?

The STRANGER *turns round. He and the* DOCTOR *stare at each other for a moment without saying anything.*

STRANGER: Yes, I used to know him.

SECOND WHORE: He looks as though he'd like to eat the back off you.

The DOCTOR *seats himself opposite the* STRANGER *and stares at him.*

STRANGER: What are you looking at?

DOCTOR: At your grey hair.

STRANGER [*to* WHORE]: Am I grey-haired too?

SECOND WHORE: Why, of course.

DOCTOR: And at your pretty companion. You have good taste sometimes. Sometimes not.

STRANGER: And sometimes we share the same taste. Unluckily for you.

DOCTOR: That's not kind. But you've murdered me twice in your life, so murder on.

STRANGER [*to* WHORE]: Let's get out of here.

DOCTOR: You sense my presence! You feel me from afar off! But I reach you as the thunder reaches you, even were you to hide yourself in the earth or at the bottom of the sea! Try to feel me!

STRANGER [*to* WHORE]: Help me out of here. Lead me — I can't see —

SECOND WHORE: No, I don't want to go yet. And I don't want to be bored.

DOCTOR: Quite right, lady of pleasure! Life is grim enough without our having to bear other people's suffering, especially when it's of their own making. But that man doesn't bear his, he makes his wife bear it.

STRANGER: What was that? Wait. She accused me falsely of trespass and attempted murder.

DOCTOR: And now he's blaming her.

> The STRANGER *puts his head into his hands and lets it sink on to the table. A violin and a guitar play in the background.*

DOCTOR [*to* WHORE]: Is he ill?

SECOND WHORE: He must be out of his mind. He says he's dead.

In the distance the reveille is sounded — first the drums, then a bugle, but very faintly.

STRANGER: Is it morning? The night is over, the sun rises, and the ghosts go back to sleep in their graves. I will go too. Come.

SECOND WHORE [*moves towards the* DOCTOR]: No, I told you.

STRANGER: You too, my last friend? Am I so repulsive that even a whore won't keep me company?

DOCTOR: You must be.

STRANGER: I don't believe it, though everyone says so. I don't believe anything, because every time I've believed anything, I've been made a fool. But tell me one thing — hasn't the sun risen yet? A little while ago I heard a cock crow and a dog bark. And now they're ringing the Angelus. Have they put out the lights? It's so dark.

DOCTOR [*to* WHORE]: He's blind.

SECOND WHORE: My God, I believe you're right.

STRANGER: No, I can see you. But not the lights.

DOCTOR: The twilight is falling for you. You have played with the lightning and stared too deeply at the sun. That's forbidden.

STRANGER: We are born with a longing to stare at the sun, but may not. It's only envy.

DOCTOR: What have you that is worth envying?

STRANGER: Something that you will never understand, and that only I can appreciate.

DOCTOR: You mean the child?

STRANGER: You know I didn't mean that. If I had meant that, I'd have said: "Something you can never *have*."

DOCTOR: Are you back there again? Then I shall express myself equally plainly. You took what I had left.

SECOND WHORE: Ugh! No, I've had enough of this. You're a couple of pigs. [*Gets up and sits down elsewhere.*]

STRANGER: We've all sunk pretty low. But I believe that the lower I sink, the closer I come to a goal: the end.

BARMAID: Don't talk so loud, there's a man dying in here.

STRANGER: Yes, there's a smell of corpses about.

DOCTOR: Perhaps it's us.

STRANGER: Can one be dead without knowing?

DOCTOR: The dead say you can't feel the difference.

STRANGER: You frighten me. Is it possible? And all these shadows, whose faces I seem to recognize — memories of childhood, the school bench, the swimming-bath, the gymnasium — ! [*Clutches his heart.*] Ah! Ah! Now he approaches, the Terrible One, who sucks my heart from my breast — ! He comes, the Invisible One, who has persecuted me for so long! [*Distraught.*] He's here!

> *The doors are thrown open and a* CHOIRBOY *comes in, carrying a lantern of blue glass which throws a blue light on the* GUESTS. *He rings a silver bell, and they all howl like wild beasts. Then the* DOMINICAN *enters with the sacrament. The* BARMAID *and* WHORE *throw themselves on their knees, the* OTHERS *howl. The* DOMINICAN *raises the monstrance. All kneel. The* CHOIRBOY *and the* DOMINICAN *go into the room left. The* BEGGAR *enters and goes over to the* STRANGER.

BEGGAR: Come away from here. You're ill, and there's a summons out for you.

STRANGER: A summons? By whom?

BEGGAR: Your wife.

DOCTOR: The electric eel strikes from a distance. She sued me once for slander, because I refused to let her sleep out at nights.

STRANGER: Sleep out at nights?

DOCTOR: Yes. Don't you know the woman you've been married to?

STRANGER: I heard she was engaged before she married you.

DOCTOR: That was the term used. She was a married man's mistress. She talked her way into his studio and modelled naked for him, and then sued him for rape.

STRANGER: And you married this woman?

DOCTOR: She seduced me and then sued me for breach of promise. I had to marry her. She employed two detectives to see I didn't run away. And you married this woman!

STRANGER: I learned early in life that there is no point in discriminating when all are alike.

BEGGAR: Come away from here. You'll regret it if you don't.

STRANGER [to DOCTOR]: Was she always religious, this woman?

DOCTOR: Always.

STRANGER: And tender, kind-hearted, self-sacrificing?

DOCTOR: Utterly.

STRANGER: Can one make sense of this?

DOCTOR: No, but one can go mad thinking about her. So one accepted her as she was — bewitching, intoxicating.

STRANGER: Yes. But then one is defenceless against one's pity for her, and that's why I don't want these lawsuits, because I can't defend myself without accusing her, and I don't want that.

DOCTOR: You were married before. How was that?

STRANGER: Just the same.

DOCTOR: It's like chewing henbane, that kind of love. You see suns where no suns are, and stars where no stars are. But it's fun while it lasts.

STRANGER: But afterwards! Afterwards!

BEGGAR: Come away! He's sitting here poisoning you, and you won't see it. Come!

STRANGER [gets up]: Poisoning me? Do you think he's lying?

BEGGAR: Every word's a lie.

STRANGER: I don't believe you.

BEGGAR: No, you only believe lies. Well, it serves you right.

STRANGER: Has he been lying? Has he?

BEGGAR: How can you be such a fool as to believe your enemy?

STRANGER: He is my friend, for he has told me the bitter truth.

BEGGAR: Eternal powers! Save his reason. He thinks everything evil is true, and everything good a lie. Come away, or you're lost.

DOCTOR: He's lost already, like a broken egg. Now he'll be whipped into a froth, and atomized, and become part of the great pancake. All right, then. Go to hell. [To the OTHERS.] Howl, victims! Howl! [The GUESTS howl.] And no more womanly pity! Howl, woman!

The WHORE *makes a gesture of repulsion with her hand.*

STRANGER [to BEGGAR]: That man is not lying.

Scene 2. The gorge

A gorge with a stream, and a footbridge over it. In the foreground, the ruins of a smithy and a mill. Fallen trees lie across the stream. Above the pine-trees behind is a starry sky, with Orion clearly visible. The foreground is covered with snow, the background is in the full green of summer. The STRANGER *and the* BEGGAR *enter.*

STRANGER: I'm frightened. The stars hang so low tonight, as though they'll fall on me like drops of molten silver. Where are we?

BEGGAR: In the gorge by the stream. You should know the place.

STRANGER: Oh, I know it. I know it. I've not forgotten my honeymoon. But where is the smithy? And the mill?

BEGGAR: Destroyed. The lake was drained a week ago. The stream rose, the river rose, and everything was destroyed. The meadows, the ploughland, the orchards.

STRANGER: And that peaceful house?

BEGGAR: It was purged of its ancient sin. But the walls stand.

STRANGER: And the inhabitants?

BEGGAR: They have gone abroad. The saga is done.

STRANGER: Then my saga is also done. I have not a single comforting memory left. The last one was killed by that poisoner –

BEGGAR: For whom you prepared the poison. Give up the fight now.

STRANGER: Yes. Now I give up.

BEGGAR: Then the time for settlement is at hand.

STRANGER: I have settled my debts. If I have erred, surely I've been punished.

BEGGAR: The others don't think so.

STRANGER: I've stopped bothering about the others since
I saw that the powers that control the destinies of men
tolerate no helpers. My crime was that I wanted to liberate
mankind —

BEGGAR: Liberate them from their responsibilities, and
criminals from their sense of guilt, so that they lost all
conscience. You're not the first nor the last to dabble in
the Devil's work. *Lucifer a non lucendo!* But when a
sinner grows old he turns monk — thus wisely are things
ordained — and then he becomes divided against himself
and seeks to drive out Beelzebub with his own rod of fire.

STRANGER: That's what I shall be driven to.

BEGGAR: Yes. What you least wanted. You must preach
against yourself from the rooftops; you must rend your
web, thread by thread; you must flay yourself alive at
every street corner, and show your bleeding flesh. That
needs courage. But a man who has played with lightning
is no coward. Oh, sometimes, when night comes and the
invisible ones who can only be seen in the dark ride your
chest like a hobby-horse, then you will be afraid — even
of the stars, but mostly of the mill of sin, that grinds and
grinds the past, the past, the past. But one of the seven-
and-seventeen wise ones asserts that the greatest victory is
the victory over one's self; but the fools will not believe
that, so they too are deceived, for they only believe what
the nine-and-ninety unwise ones have said a thousand
times.

STRANGER: Enough! Tell me, isn't there snow on the
ground here?

BEGGAR: Yes. It's winter here.

STRANGER: And over there, it's green?

BEGGAR: There it is summer.

STRANGER: And growing light?

Bright sunlight is seen over the bridge.

BEGGAR: Yes, it's light there and dark here.

STRANGER: And who are these coming towards me?

> THREE CHILDREN *in summer clothes, two* GIRLS *and a fair-haired* BOY, *run on to the bridge from the right.*

STRANGER: My children! Hallo, there! [*They look at him unrecognizingly.*] Gerda! Erik! Thyra! It's me!

> *The* CHILDREN *seem to recognize him, and turn away, right.*

STRANGER: They don't know me any longer. They don't *want* to know me!

> A MAN *and a* WOMAN *enter right. The* CHILDREN *dance out left. The* STRANGER *falls on his face on the ground.*

BEGGAR: That's what you've got to expect. That's the way life goes. Get up, now.

STRANGER [*gets up*]: Where am I? Where have I been? Is it spring, winter or summer? What century am I in, what continent? Am I a child or an old man, a man or a woman, a god or a devil? Who are you? Are you *you* or are you me? Are these my entrails I see around me, are those stars or the nerves within my eyes, is that a river or my tears? Hush! Now I've leaped forwards a thousand years in time, and I'm beginning to shrink, to concentrate and crystallize. Wait a little. Soon I shall be re-created. Out of the dark pool of chaos the lotus will push its head into the sun and say: "It is I." I must have slept for a thousand years; and I dreamed that I exploded and became ether, felt no more, suffered no more, knew no joy, only peace and equilibrium. But now! Ah! Now I suffer as though I were the whole human race. I suffer, and have no right to complain —

BEGGAR: Suffer, my friend. The agony will pass the sooner.

STRANGER: No. This is the suffering of eternity.

BEGGAR: And only a minute has passed.

STRANGER: I can't bear it!

BEGGAR: Then you must seek help.

STRANGER: What's this? It isn't over yet!

> *It grows light over the bridge.* CAESAR *enters and runs down from the bridge. Then the* DOCTOR *enters right, bare-headed, with a crazed look. He makes a movement as though wishing to throw himself into the stream.*

STRANGER: He has been avenged so fully that he does not prick my conscience.

> *The* DOCTOR *goes out right. The* SISTER *enters right, looking for him.*

STRANGER: Who is this?

BEGGAR: His sister. She has no husband and no one to look after her, now that her brother has gone mad and been destroyed by grief.

STRANGER: That is harder. Unhappy creature, what can one do for you? If I share her suffering, does that help her?

BEGGAR: No.

STRANGER: Oh, pangs of conscience, why do you come afterwards and not before? Can you help me out of this, beggar?

BEGGAR: No. No human being can. Let us go on.

STRANGER: Where to?

BEGGAR: Just come.

Scene 3. The rose room

The LADY *is seated by the cradle, dressed in white*

and knitting. Her green dress hangs by the door, right.
The STRANGER *enters and looks round in amaze-*
ment.

LADY [*simply and gently, with no trace of reproach*]: Ssh!
Come here, and I'll show you something beautiful.

STRANGER: Where am I?

LADY: Ssh! Look at the little visitor who came while you
were away.

STRANGER: They said the river had destroyed everything.

LADY: Why do you believe everything people want you to
believe? The river has gone, but this little creature has
something that protects herself, and hers. Don't you want
to see your daughter? [*He approaches the cradle. She lifts*
the hood.] Do you see how beautiful she is? Isn't she?
[*He frowns.*] Look at her.

STRANGER: Everything is poisoned. Everything.

LADY: Yes, perhaps.

STRANGER: Don't you know that *he* has lost his reason
and is wandering the countryside followed by his sister
searching for him? And he's in rags, and drunk —

LADY: Oh, God, God!

STRANGER: Reproach me.

LADY: You reproach yourself. I would rather give you
advice. Go to the Abbey of Good Hope. There is someone
there who can free you from the evil you fear.

STRANGER: That place where they cursed and bound me?

LADY: They can free you too.

STRANGER: I think you're trying to cheat me. I don't
believe you any more.

LADY: Nor I you. So let this be our last meeting.

STRANGER: I suppose it was meant to be. I only wanted to make sure we felt the same.

LADY: Surely you see that we can never build any happiness on the suffering of others. So we must part. It's the only way to save him. I have my child to fill my life, and you your ambitions —

STRANGER: You still mock me?

LADY: No, why should I? You have solved the great riddle —

STRANGER: Hush! No more of *that*, even if you believe it.

LADY: But everyone believes it.

STRANGER: No one believes it any more.

LADY: It's in today's paper that someone in England has made gold, and that his analysis has been confirmed.

STRANGER: You've been fooled.

LADY: No! My God, he won't believe he's right.

STRANGER: I believe nothing any more.

LADY: Look at the paper. It's in the pocket of that dress.

STRANGER: That green witch's dress which once bewitched me between the café and the church one Sunday afternoon. That will bring me no good.

LADY [*goes over and takes out a newspaper and a big envelope.*]: Look for yourself.

STRANGER [*tears the paper in two*]: I don't need to look.

LADY: He won't believe. He won't believe. But the Academy is holding a banquet for you next Saturday.

STRANGER: Oh, is that there too? The banquet!

LADY [*hands him the envelope*]: And there is your diploma of honour. Read it, man!

STRANGER [*tears the envelope*]: Are they giving me a medal too?

LADY: Whom the gods wish to destroy they first strike blind. You intended no good with your discovery, and that's why you weren't permitted to make it alone.

STRANGER: Now I shall go — I don't want to stand here and flaunt my dishonour to the world. I've become a laughing-stock and all I want to do is hide, bury myself alive — I dare not die.

LADY: Go, my friend. We are leaving for abroad in a few days.

STRANGER: So that at least was true. Then the solution is at hand.

LADY: The solution to that riddle: why did we have to meet?

STRANGER: Why did we have to meet?

LADY: To torment each other.

STRANGER: Was that all?

LADY: You were to free me from an ogre who was no ogre, and so you became one. And I was to free you from evil by taking all your evil on my head. I did, but you only became more evil. My poor liberator, now you stand bound hand and foot, and no magician can free you.

STRANGER: Goodbye. And thank you. For everything.

LADY: Goodbye. And thank you. For this. [*Indicates the cradle.*]

STRANGER [*goes upstage*]: Perhaps I should say goodbye in there too?

LADY: Do that, my friend.

> The STRANGER *exits through the door upstage. The* LADY *goes to the door right and admits the* DOMINICAN (*the* BEGGAR).

THE CONFESSOR:* Is he ready?

LADY: All he wants is to leave the world and bury himself in a monastery, unhappy man.

CONFESSOR: Then he wouldn't believe that he is the great discoverer that he *is*?

LADY: No. He can believe good of no one, not even himself.

CONFESSOR: That is the divine punishment. That he should believe lies, because he will not believe the truth.

LADY: Ease his burden if you can.

CONFESSOR: No. That will make him arrogant, and he will accuse God of malice and injustice. And this man is a demon who must be kept chained. These revolutionaries misuse their gifts to do evil, and the human capacity for evil is boundless.

LADY: For the sake of the . . . affection you once felt for me, ease his burden just a little, where he suffers most and is least guilty.

CONFESSOR: I may not. But you can. Let him leave you in the belief that there is some good in you, and that you are not as your former husband painted you. If he believes you, I will later free him, as I once bound him when he bared his soul to me as he lay in fever at the Abbey of Good Hope.

LADY [*goes upstage and opens the door*]: Very well.

STRANGER [*enters*]: There he is, the Terrible One! How did he come here? But — it's the beggar!

CONFESSOR: Yes, it is your terrible friend, who has come to collect you.

STRANGER: Have I — ?

CONFESSOR: Yes. You forswore your soul to me once,

*Strindberg now calls him this. (Translator's note)

when you lay sick and felt that madness was approaching. Then you promised to serve the good powers, but when you recovered you broke your promise. That is why you were stricken with conscience, and wandered in torment, unable to find peace.

STRANGER: Who are you, who dare to meddle with my destiny?

CONFESSOR: Ask her.

LADY: He is the man to whom I was first engaged. When I left him, he dedicated his life to the service of God.

STRANGER: So?

LADY: So you need not feel so badly about what you did when you punished my infidelity and — the other one's lack of conscience.

STRANGER: His crime cannot excuse mine. Anyway, it's probably untrue like everything else, and you're only saying it to comfort me.

CONFESSOR: Unhappy spirit!

LADY: And a damned one.

CONFESSOR: No. [*To* LADY.] Say some good of him.

LADY: He wouldn't believe it. He only believes evil.

CONFESSOR: Then let me. A beggar came once and asked him for water; but he gave him wine and let him sit at his own table. You remember?

STRANGER: No. I don't bother with such trivialities.

CONFESSOR: Pride! Pride!

STRANGER: Why not pride? It's the last trace of our divine ancestry. Come now, before darkness falls.

CONFESSOR: "The whole world shined with a clear light, and none were hindered in their labour. Over these only was spread a heavy night, an image of the darkness which

would afterwards receive them. But yet were they unto
themselves more grievous than the darkness."

LADY: Do not hurt him.

STRANGER [*passionately*]: How sweetly she can speak,
yet is so evil. Look at those eyes! They can't weep, but
they can caress, sting, lie. And yet — "Don't hurt him."
Look — she's afraid I will wake her child, the little abomin-
ation that took her from me. Come, priest, before I change
my mind.

PART III
(1901)

CHARACTERS*

The Stranger
The Confessor
Sylvia
The Lady
Maja
A Woman
Thyra
Erik
The Tempter
Caesar
A Chief Magistrate
Florian, a Defendant
The Mayor
The Dead Woman's Father
A Seduced Woman
Eve
The Serpent
The Stranger's First Wife
The Prior
Father Uriel
Father Clemens
Father Melchior
Pilgrims, Venus Worshippers, Witnesses,
   Monks, etc.

*Strindberg's own list of characters as prefaced to the play names only the Stranger, the Lady, the Confessor, the Prior, the Tempter, the First Wife, Her Present Husband (who in fact never appears), Erik, Thyra, Gerda, and "Bipersoner" ("minor characters".) He also omitted to append a list of scenes. (Translator's note)

SCENES

1. A river bank

2. A crossroads

3. A terrace

4. Higher up the mountain

5. A dining-room

6. The same

7. A chapter hall

8. A picture gallery

9. The sanctuary

Scene 1

*The foreground comprises one bank of the great river.
Right, a tongue of land with old willow-trees. Centre
stage, the river flows stilly. The background is the
further bank, consisting of a high mountain covered
with forest. Above the treetops towers the monastery,
a huge square building, completely white, with two
rows of small windows. The facade is broken by the
chapel, with two towers in Jesuit style; the chapel
door is open, so that at a certain moment the monstrance on the altar is illuminated by the rays of the
sun.*
    *On the nearer shore, which is low and sandy,
grow purple and yellow loose-strife. A barge floats
there. Left is the ferryman's hut. It is an evening in
early summer, and the sun is low. The foreground,
the river and the further shore are all in shadow. The
leaves of the forest on the further shore sway in a
gentle breeze. Only the monastery is in sunlight.*
    The STRANGER *and the* CONFESSOR *enter
right. The* STRANGER *is in alpine dress, plus his
brown cloak with its hood and cape, a staff and a
night-bag. He limps somewhat. The* CONFESSOR *is
in black and white Dominican dress. They stop where
a willow hides the monastery from them.*

STRANGER: Why do you lead me by these steep and
crooked paths, which never end?

CONFESSOR: Such is the way, friend. But we are nearly
there.

    He leads the STRANGER *forward so that the latter
sees the monastery. Overcome by the sight, he takes
off his hat and puts down his night-bag and staff.*

CONFESSOR: Well?

STRANGER: I never saw anything so white on this dusty earth, except in dreams. When I was young I dreamed of such a house, where peace and purity dwelt. Hail, white house! Now I am home.

CONFESSOR: But first we must wait for the pilgrims. This river bank is called the shore of farewell. Here you say goodbye before the ferryman rows you over.

STRANGER: Haven't I said enough goodbyes? My whole life has been a thorn-path of goodbyes — hotel-lobbies, jetties, railway stations, the waving of tear-stained handkerchieves.

CONFESSOR: And yet your voice trembles with the pain of parting.

STRANGER: I miss nothing. I want nothing back.

CONFESSOR: Not even youth?

STRANGER: That least of all. What would I do with its capacity for suffering?

CONFESSOR: And for joy?

STRANGER: I have never known joy. I was born with a thorn in my flesh, and every time I groped for joy it pricked my finger and Satan brushed my cheek.

CONFESSOR: Sinful joys.

STRANGER: Not so sinful. My own home, a wife, children; duties, thoughts of others. No, I was born out of grace, life's unwanted child, hunted, harried — cursed.

CONFESSOR: Because you disobeyed God's commandments —

STRANGER: Which Paul says no man *can* obey. But *I* must. Why just me? Because I had to be the whipping-boy. Because more was demanded of me than of other men. [*Cries.*] Because I never received justice!

CONFESSOR: Are you back there, rebellious spirit?

STRANGER: Yes, *there*, always *there*! Shall we cross the river?

CONFESSOR: Do you think a man may enter the white house before he is ready?

STRANGER: I am ready. Try me.

CONFESSOR: Very well. The first monastic vow is: humility.

STRANGER: And the second, obedience. I was born with neither. That is why I want to face the trial.

CONFESSOR: And show your pride in humility.

STRANGER: Call it what you like. All things are meaningless to me now.

CONFESSOR: All? The world and its best gifts, the innocent joys of childhood, the happy warmth of home, the recognition of your fellow-mortals, the satisfaction of duties fulfilled — all meaningless?

STRANGER: To me. Because I was born with no sense of joy. There have been times when I have been envied, but I have not understood what people envied me for: my torment when I failed, my fear when I succeeded that my success would not last long.

CONFESSOR: That is true. Life gave you everything you wanted, even, at the end, a little gold. They even put up a statue to you, I seem to recall.

STRANGER: A statue? To me?

CONFESSOR: Do you believe in monuments? Mm?

STRANGER: Not at all. But a monument suggests a certain recognition which neither envy nor lack of understanding can nullify.

CONFESSOR: You think so? I have always thought that human greatness depends on other men's opinions, and that as opinions change greatness can swiftly shrink to nothing.

STRANGER: I've never bothered about other people's opinions. Only my own.

CONFESSOR: Indeed?

STRANGER: And no one has been as uncompromising towards himself as I. Or so humble! Everyone demanded that I should respect them while they were all trampling on me and spitting at me. When I finally discovered that I had duties to the immortal soul with which I had been temporarily endowed, I began to demand that people should respect this immortal soul, and was immediately condemned as the proudest of the proud — and by whom? By the proudest of those who were small and humble.

CONFESSOR: Now you're contradicting yourself —

STRANGER: I quite agree. But life consists of contradictions. The rich are spiritually poor. The little millions have power, and the great act as servants to the little millions. I've never met such pride as in humble people; I've never found an uneducated man who didn't regard himself as qualified to condemn education and turn his back on it. I've always found the worst of the deadly sins among religious people — I mean self-righteousness. I used to be religious when I was young, and I was never so wicked as I was then. The better I thought myself, the worse I became!

CONFESSOR: Then what do you seek here?

STRANGER: I told you before, but I'll repeat it. Death without dying.

CONFESSOR: To kill your flesh, to kill your old self? That is good. Hush, now. Here come the pilgrims on their wooden rafts to celebrate the feast of Corpus Christi.

STRANGER [looks towards the right and is amazed]: What is this?

CONFESSOR: It is people who believe in something.

STRANGER: Help my unbelief, then.

The sun falls on the monstrance in the church so that it shines like a window in the sunset.

STRANGER: Has the sun entered the church, or — ?

CONFESSOR: The sun has entered the church.

The first raft enters right. Children in white with garlands on their heads and lighted candles in their hands stand around an altar covered with flowers. On the altar is a white banner with a golden lily. As the raft glides slowly by, they sing.

PILGRIMS:
Beati omnes qui timent Dominum,
Qui ambulant in viis ejus.
Labores manuum tuarum quia manducabis;
Beatus es et bene tibi erit.

They glide out. A second raft enters with young boys on one side of it and young girls on the other. It carries a banner with a rose.

SECOND PILGRIMS:
Uxor tua sicut vitis abundans,
In lateribus domus tuae.

They go out. A third raft enters with husbands and wives. It has a banner with fruit — figs, grapes, pomegranates, melons, ears of corn, etc.

THIRD PILGRIMS:
Filii tui sicut novellae olivarum,
In circuitu mensae tuae.

They go out. A fourth barge, with older men and women, and a banner with a snow-covered pine-tree.

FOURTH PILGRIMS:
Ecce sic benedicetur homo
Qui timet Dominum.

They go out.

STRANGER: What was that they were singing?

CONFESSOR: A pilgrims' song.

STRANGER: Who wrote it?

CONFESSOR: A royal person.

STRANGER: Here? What's his name? Has he written anything else?

CONFESSOR: At least fifty songs; and his name is David,
the son of Jesse. But he didn't always write psalms. When
he was young, he had other interests, and — well, never
mind.

STRANGER: Can we go now?

CONFESSOR: In a moment. But I have one or two things
I must tell you first.

STRANGER: Yes?

CONFESSOR: But you mustn't get angry, or start having
regrets.

STRANGER: I won't.

CONFESSOR: Well. You see, on this bank you are a well-
known, one might say a famous man. But on that other
bank you will be quite unknown to the brothers — just an
ordinary, simple human being.

STRANGER: Oh? Don't they read in the monastery?

CONFESSOR: Yes. But nothing frivolous. Only serious
books.

STRANGER: But surely they read newspapers?

CONFESSOR: Not the kind that talk about you.

STRANGER: Then my life's work does not exist beyond
the river?

CONFESSOR: What work?

STRANGER: I see. Very well. Can we go now?

CONFESSOR: At once. Is there no one you wish to say
goodbye to?

STRANGER [*after a moment*]: Yes. But it isn't possible.

CONFESSOR: Have you seen *anything* impossible?

STRANGER: Not really. Not since I saw what happened to me.

CONFESSOR: Well, whom would you like to meet?

STRANGER: I once had a daughter. I called her Sylvia. She sang all day like a nightingale. It's some years since I saw her and she must be sixteen by now. But I'm agraid that if I did see her again, I might want to go on living.

CONFESSOR: You fear nothing else?

STRANGER: What else should I fear?

CONFESSOR: That she might have changed.

STRANGER: She could only have changed for the better.

CONFESSOR: Are you sure?

STRANGER: Yes.

CONFESSOR: She will come. [*He goes down to the bank and beckons right.*]

STRANGER: Wait. I wonder if this is wise.

CONFESSOR: It can do no harm.

> *He beckons again. A boat rowed by a young* GIRL *appears on the river. She is in summer clothes and bare-headed, with fair hair hanging loose. She steps out of the boat behind the willow. The* CONFESSOR *withdraws towards the ferryman's hut, though he remains visible to the audience. The* STRANGER *waves to the* GIRL, *who waves back. She runs up, throws herself into the* STRANGER's *arms and kisses him.*

GIRL: Father! Dear Father!

STRANGER: Sylvia, my beloved child!

SYLVIA: What on earth are you doing up here in the mountains?

STRANGER: And how did you get here? I thought I'd hidden myself well.

SYLVIA: Why should you hide?

STRANGER: You mustn't ask too many questions. What a big girl you've become! And I've grown grey.

SYLVIA: No, you're not grey. You're as young as when we last met.

STRANGER: When we last met?

SYLVIA: When you left us. [*He does not reply.*] Aren't you glad to see me again?

STRANGER [*dully*]: Yes.

SYLVIA: Well, show it, then.

STRANGER: How can I be happy when this is goodbye for ever?

SYLVIA: Where are you going?

STRANGER [*points to the monastery*]: Up there.

SYLVIA [*worldly-wise*]: To the monastery? Yes, now I think, perhaps that's best.

STRANGER: What do you mean?

SYLVIA [*pitying yet well-meaning*]: I mean, when one has a misspent life behind one — [*Soothingly.*] Oh, did that hurt you? Tell me one thing —

STRANGER: You tell me one thing, my beloved child, which worries me more than anything. You've got a step-father —

SYLVIA: Yes.

STRANGER: Well?

SYLVIA: He's a really nice person —

STRANGER: With all the virtues I lacked?

SYLVIA: Aren't you glad we're in better hands?

STRANGER: Good, better, best. Why aren't you wearing a hat?

SYLVIA: George is carrying it.

STRANGER: Who is George, and where is he?

SYLVIA: My friend. He's waiting down there on the bank.

STRANGER: Are you engaged?

SYLVIA: Good heavens, no.

STRANGER: Do you intend to marry?

SYLVIA: Never.

STRANGER: I see it in your marbled cheeks, like those of a child who has got up too early. I hear it in your voice, which no longer resembles the nightingale but the jay. I feel it in your kisses, which burn cold like the sun in May. Your cold eyes tell me that you have a secret of which you are ashamed but of which you would like to boast. How are your brother and sister?

SYLVIA: Thank you. They're well.

STRANGER: Have we anything more to say to each other?

SYLVIA [coldly]: Perhaps not.

STRANGER: You look so like your mother.

SYLVIA: How can you know? You were never able to see her as she was.

STRANGER: So knowing, and so young.

SYLVIA: I've learned from you. If you only knew yourself.

STRANGER: Have you more to teach me?

SYLVIA: Perhaps. But people didn't think it proper in your time.

STRANGER: My time; which was, and is no longer. Just as Sylvia is no longer, only a name, a memory. [*Takes a travel-book from his pocket.*] Do you see this travel-book? Do you see those little marks there, from little fingers, and those, from little wet lips? You made those when you were five and sat on my knees in the train, when we saw the Alps for the first time. You thought it was heaven, but when I told you it was Die Jungfrau you asked to be allowed to kiss the name there in the book.

SYLVIA: I don't remember.

STRANGER: Beautiful memories go; the ugly ones remain. Do you remember nothing of me?

SYLVIA: Yes.

STRANGER: Ssh! I know what you mean. One night — yes — oh, horrible — horrible! Sylvia, my child, when I close my eyes I see a pale little angel who used to sleep in my arms when she was ill, who thanked me when I gave her a present. Where is she, where is she, whom I long for and who no longer exists, although she is not dead? You who stand there are a stranger whom I never knew and certainly don't want to see again. If Sylvia were dead and in her grave, at least I would have had a churchyard to visit with my flowers. Strange — she doesn't exist in death's kingdom or in this world. Perhaps she never did exist, and was just a dream like everything else.

SYLVIA [*soothingly*]: Poor Daddy!

STRANGER: There she is! No, it was only her voice. You mean my life was a failure?

SYLVIA: Yes, but why talk about it now?

STRANGER: Because I remember now, I once saved *your* life. You were ill for a month with typhoid, in dreadful pain. Your mother, who looked at things objectively, asked the doctor to free you from your agony by poison. By preventing this, I saved you from death and your mother from prison.

SYLVIA: I don't believe you.

STRANGER: But a fact can be a fact, even if you don't believe it.

SYLVIA: You dreamed it.

STRANGER: Who knows if I haven't dreamed everything — if I'm not dreaming now? I wish to God it were so.

SYLVIA: I must go now, Daddy.

STRANGER: Say goodbye, then.

SYLVIA: May I never write to you?

STRANGER: A dead girl write to a dead man? I shall have no more letters; and no more visits. But I'm glad we met, because now there is nothing on this earth that binds me any longer. [*As he goes left.*] Goodbye, dear girl — or should I say dear lady? You don't need to cry.

SYLVIA: I wasn't going to. Though I suppose I ought to. Well, goodbye. [*Goes out, right.*]

STRANGER [*to* CONFESSOR]: I'm well out of that, Confessor. It's a rare blessing when two people can part with mutual relief. Humanity's making great strides — fewer tears, more self-control. I've seen so many tears in my time. I find this drought almost disappointing. She's a strong girl — the kind of strength I once longed to have. And this was the most beautiful thing life had to offer — the child, the angel in the white-veiled cradle — there was a blue canopy over it when she slept, blue and arched like heaven. That was the best. How will the worst look?

CONFESSOR: You should be happy, not sad. But throw away that stupid travel-book. This is your last journey.

STRANGER: You mean this? Very well. [*Opens the book, kisses it and throws it into the river.*] Is there anything else I must do?

CONFESSOR: Yes. If you have any gold or silver, you must give it to the poor.

STRANGER: I've a silver watch. I never managed gold.

CONFESSOR: Give it to the ferryman, and he will give you a glass of wine.

STRANGER: The last glass! This is like an execution. Will they shave my head too?

CONFESSOR: Yes, later.

> *He takes the watch and hands it in at the ferryman's hut, whispering a few words in the doorway. He receives in return a bottle of wine and a glass, which he places on the table.*

STRANGER [*fills the glass but leaves it on the table*]: Will I get no wine up there?

CONFESSOR: No wine, and no women. You will hear songs, but not the kind that go with wine and women.

STRANGER: I've had enough of women. They no longer tempt me.

CONFESSOR: Are you sure?

STRANGER: Quite sure. But tell me one thing. What do you monks think of women, since you never let them set foot within your consecrated walls?

CONFESSOR: Still inquisitive?

STRANGER: And why may an abbess not receive confession, conduct mass or preach?

CONFESSOR: I shall not answer that.

STRANGER: Because your answer would have to agree with my feelings on — the subject.

CONFESSOR: If we did really agree on one thing, it would be no disaster.

STRANGER: Very good!

CONFESSOR: Drink up your wine.

STRANGER: No, I only want to look at it for the last time. It's beautiful.

CONFESSOR: Don't think too deeply. There are memories at the bottom of the glass.

STRANGER: And forgetfulness, and songs, and power. Imaginary, but all the more intense for that.

CONFESSOR: Wait a little, and I will go to the ferryman and book our passage.

STRANGER: Hush. I hear a song, and I see. . . . I saw for a moment, as when a flag is puffed out by a breeze, and then falls by its staff like a rag, and one sees only a rag. I saw my whole life in a moment, with its joys and sorrows, its beauty and squalor. But now I see it no longer.

CONFESSOR [goes left]: Wait a moment, and I will book our passage.

> The STRANGER *walks downstage so that the dying sun streaming through the trees from the right throws his shadow over the ground and the river. The* LADY *enters right in deep mourning. Her shadow falls in front of the* STRANGER.

STRANGER [who has at first been gazing at his own shadow]: Ha! The sun. It makes me into a bloodless image, a giant walking on the water, climbing the mountain, scaling the chapel roof — and now he goes out into space — to the stars — ha, now I'm up among the stars. [Sees the LADY's shadow beside him.] But who is persecuting me, who disturbs my voyage to heaven and seeks to climb on my shoulders? [Turns.] You!

LADY: I.

STRANGER: So black! Black and evil.

LADY: No longer evil. I am in mourning —

STRANGER: Whom do you mourn?

LADY: Our Mitzi —

STRANGER: My daughter! [*She spreads her arms to throw herself into his arms, but he turns aside.*] I congratulate the dead child, I pity you. To me it is all one.

LADY: Comfort me.

STRANGER: Charming! I am to comfort my fury, weep with my executioner, play for my tormenting spirit!

LADY: Have you no feelings at all?

STRANGER: None at all. The feelings I had I wasted on you, and others.

LADY: You are right. Reproach me.

STRANGER: No. I have neither the time nor the inclination. tion. Where are you going?

LADY: With the ferry.

STRANGER: That's bad luck for me. I am going the same way. [*She weeps into her handkerchief. He takes his handkerchief and dries her tears.*] Dry your tears, child, and be yourself. Be hard, be unfeeling, as you are.

> *She tries to put her arms round his neck. He strikes her gently on the fingers.*

STRANGER: Don't touch me! When your words and your looks lost their power over me, you always tried to touch me. Forgive the banal question, but are you hungry?

LADY: No, thank you.

STRANGER: You are tired. Sit down. [*She sits at the table. He throws the bottle and glass into the river.*] Well. What will you live for now?

LADY [*sadly*]: I don't know.

STRANGER: Where do you plan to go?

LADY [*weeps*]: I don't know.

STRANGER: So you're really in despair? You see no purpose in existence and no end to your misery! Well, what a coincidence. It's a pity they don't have monasteries for both sexes, or you and I would make a pair. Is the ogre alive?

LADY: You mean — ?

STRANGER: Your first husband.

LADY: He will never die.

STRANGER: Like a certain worm. Well, since we're far from the world and its petty-mindedness, tell me one thing. Why did you leave him and go with me, that time?

LADY: Because I loved you.

STRANGER: How long did that last?

LADY: Until I read your book, and the child came.

STRANGER: And then?

LADY: I hated you. I wanted to free myself of all the evil you had infected me with, but I couldn't.

STRANGER: Yes, that's probably what happened. Though what really happens, one is never allowed to know.

LADY: Has it ever struck you that one is never really allowed to know about anything? That one can live for twenty years with someone, one's brothers and sisters, one's parents, without knowing anything about them?

STRANGER: You've noticed that too? Since you're so perceptive, tell me this. How did you come to love me?

LADY: I don't know. But I'll try to remember. [*Pause.*] Yes, you were man enough to be impolite to a woman! You looked in me for human companionship, not just female companionship. I felt that this did honour to you; and to me.

STRANGER: Then tell me this too. Did you find me a misogynist?

LADY: A woman-hater? Every normal man is that, in his heart of hearts. Woman-worshippers are all twisted men.

STRANGER: You're not trying to flatter me?

LADY: A woman who flatters a man is not a normal woman.

STRANGER: I see you've been doing a lot of thinking.

LADY: That's the least important. It's when I haven't been thinking that I've understood most. Anyway, what I've been saying now was probably just what came into my head. It may be quite untrue.

STRANGER: Yes. But when it agrees with my own observations, it becomes very true to me. [*She weeps into her handkerchief.*] Now you're crying again.

LADY: I'm thinking of Mitzi. The most beautiful treasure we had — gone.

STRANGER: No, you were the most beautiful, when you sat up all night watching your child, that you had placed in your bed because her cradle was too cold. [*There are three hard knocks on the ferryman's door.*] Ssh!

LADY: What is that?

STRANGER: My companion, who is waiting for me.

LADY [*composes herself*]: I never believed life could offer anything so wonderful as a child.

STRANGER: Or anything so bitter.

LADY: Why bitter?

STRANGER: You've been a child yourself. And have you forgotten how when we were newly married we went to your mother dirty, ragged and penniless? I seem to remember she didn't think us so wonderful.

LADY: That's true.

STRANGER: And I — ! Yes, just now I met my Sylvia. I thought I would see all that is good and beautiful in a child in full flower, now that she has become a young girl —

LADY: Yes?

STRANGER: I found a withered rose, which had bloomed too early. Her breasts had sunk, her hair was sparse like an underfed child's, and her teeth were worm-eaten —

LADY: Ugh!

STRANGER: So don't grieve. Don't grieve for our little daughter. You might have had to grieve for a grown-up daughter, as I do.

LADY: So that is life?

STRANGER: Yes. That is life. And that is why I am going to bury myself alive.

LADY: Where?

STRANGER [*points up towards the monastery*]: There.

LADY: In the monastery? No, don't leave me. Stay with me, I'm so lonely, and so poor, so poor. When our child died, my mother cast me off, and ever since I've been living in an attic, with a seamstress. At first she seemed decent and good-natured, but then the lonely evenings became too long for her, and she started going out to look for company. And so we parted. Now I walk the roads owning nothing but the clothes I stand up in, nothing but my grief; that is my food and drink, it nourishes me and lets me sleep — I wouldn't lose it for all the world. [*The* STRANGER *weeps.*] You're crying — you! Let me kiss your eyes.

STRANGER: And you have suffered this because of me.

LADY: No! You have never done me any harm; but I drove you from your home and from your child.

STRANGER: I don't remember it; but that you should say it — ! You still love me, then?

LADY: Probably. I don't know.

STRANGER: And you'd like to start again?

LADY: Start again? That war? We mustn't do that.

STRANGER: You're right. We should only go on fighting. And yet — it's so painful to be parted.

LADY: Parted? The very word is loathsome.

STRANGER: What shall we do, then?

LADY: I don't know.

STRANGER: No. One knows nothing. That's why henceforth I am going to *believe*.

LADY: How do you know you'll be able to believe? Faith is a gift.

STRANGER: One can get a gift, if one prays.

LADY: Oh, if only one could pray! I've never been able to beg.

STRANGER: I've managed to learn. Why can't you?

LADY: One has to humble oneself first.

STRANGER: Life does that for one.

LADY: Mitzi, Mitzi, Mitzi — ! [*She has rolled up a shawl which she has been carrying on her arm, rests it on her lap like a baby and hums a lullaby to it.*] Imagine — I see her — look, here! She's smiling at me, but she's dressed in black — she must be in mourning too. How stupid I am! Of course she is, if her mother is. She's got two teeth and they're white — milk-teeth, babies always have milk-teeth. Can't you see her? I see her — I'm not dreaming, it's her —

> The CONFESSOR *comes out through the door of the ferryman's hut.*

CONFESSOR [*sternly, to the* STRANGER]: Come. Everything is ready.

STRANGER: No, not yet. I must put my house in order first, and arrange things for this woman. She was once my wife.

CONFESSOR: I see. You want to stay.

STRANGER: No, I don't want that, but I don't want to leave duties unperformed when I go. This woman is home-less and penniless.

CONFESSOR: What is that to us? The dead must bury their dead.

STRANGER: Is that your teaching?

CONFESSOR: No, yours. Mine bids me send a sister of mercy to take care of this unhappy woman, who — who — ! The sister will be here soon.

STRANGER: I rely on you.

CONFESSOR [*takes the* STRANGER *by the hand and leads him*]: Come, then.

STRANGER [*desperately*]: Lord Jesus Christ, help us all!

CONFESSOR: Amen.

> The LADY *has not been looking at the* CONFESSOR *or the* STRANGER, *but now she looks up and after the* STRANGER *as though wishing to leap up and hold him back. But she is prevented from doing this by the imagined baby which she has laid to her breast.*

Scene 2

> *A crossroads up in the mountains. To the right lie huts, to the left a dyke, on which sit sick people in blue clothes with reddened hands. Out of the dyke rise now and then jets of blue steam and small blue flames. When this happens the sick people stretch out their hands and cough. The foreground consists of the mountain, with pine-trees the tops of which are obliter-ated by a still grey mist.*
> *The* STRANGER *is seated at a table outside a hut. The* CONFESSOR *enters downstage right.*

STRANGER: At last!

CONFESSOR: Why do you say that?

STRANGER: You left me here a week ago, and said: "Wait till I come back."

CONFESSOR: Well! Didn't I warn you that the road up here was long and hard?

STRANGER: I can't deny it. How far have we come?

CONFESSOR: Five hundred yards. We have fifteen hundred left.

STRANGER: But where's the sun?

CONFESSOR: Up there, above the clouds.

STRANGER: Then we have to go through the clouds?

CONFESSOR: Of course.

STRANGER: But these invalids? They're strange company. Why these red hands?

CONFESSOR: I do not wish to soil my lips or your ears with unclean words, so I will speak in pretty riddles, which you as a poet should be able to understand.

STRANGER: Yes, do say something pretty. There's so much that's ugly here.

CONFESSOR: No doubt you know the signs of the zodiac, and how they correspond to certain metals? Well; then you know that Venus is represented by a mirror. This mirror was in olden times of copper, and this metal was called Venus and bore her sign. But now the back of the Venus mirror is covered with quicksilver, or Mercury.

STRANGER: The back of Venus is Mercury! Hm!

CONFESSOR: In other words, Mercury is the reverse of Venus. Of itself quicksilver is shiny like a calm sea, or a lake in high summer, but when Mercury touches sulphur and gets burned he goes red, red like new-drawn blood, like the cloth of the scaffold, like the lips of whores, the painted lips of whores, the lips of whores painted with cinnabar — do you understand yet?

STRANGER: Wait a moment. Cinnabar is quicksilver and sulphur —

CONFESSOR: Exactly. Mercury has to go into the fire when he comes too close to Venus. Have we discussed this enough now?

STRANGER: Then these are sulphur springs?

CONFESSOR: Yes. And the flames of sulphur cleanse and scour all that is rotten. So when the spring of life goes rotten, men are sent to the sulphur springs —

STRANGER: How does the spring of life go rotten?

CONFESSOR: When Aphrodite, born of the pure womb of the sea, lies on the earth! When Aphrodite Urania the divine demeans herself to Pandemos, all-faring Venus.

STRANGER: Why was desire born?

CONFESSOR: Clean desire was born to be satisfied, unclean to be stifled.

STRANGER: What is clean and what is unclean?

CONFESSOR: Are you back there again?

STRANGER: Ask these people —

CONFESSOR: Take care! [*Stares at the* STRANGER, *who shrinks.*]

STRANGER: You're choking me — I can't breathe —

CONFESSOR: Yes, I shall deprive you of air, which you use for rebellious words and questions that stink. Sit there, now, and I shall return. When you have learned patience and stood the test. But don't forget that I hear you, see you, know your thoughts, wherever I may be.

STRANGER: So this is a trial? I'm glad I know.

CONFESSOR: But you must not talk to the Venus worshippers!

> OLD MAJA *appears upstage. The* STRANGER *rises, frightened.*

STRANGER: Whom must I meet here now, at last? Whom? .

CONFESSOR: Who are you talking about?

STRANGER: That woman there, that old woman.

CONFESSOR: Why, who is that?

STRANGER [*cries*]: Maja! Listen to me! [*She vanishes. He runs after her.*] Maja, my friend, listen to me! She's vanished!

CONFESSOR: Who was it?

STRANGER [*sits*]: Oh, God! When I finally found her, she went, or — ! For seven years I've been searching for her. I've written letters, advertised —

CONFESSOR: Why?

STRANGER: Her fate is bound to mine. Listen. Maja was the nurse of my first child. Those were hard years — I strove with the Invisible One, and He did not bless my work. I wrote so that my brain and nerves dissolved like fat in alcohol. But it didn't suffice; I am one of those for whom nothing suffices. Well, a day came when I couldn't pay the servants' wages — it was horrible — I became a servants' servant, and they became my masters! In the end, to save at any rate my soul, I fled from the Almighty, out into the desert, re-found my soul in solitude, and began to live again. My first thought was — my debts. For seven years I looked for Maja, but in vain. For seven years I saw her shadow, from railway compartments, from the decks of steamers, in foreign cities, in distant lands, but I never caught her. For seven years I dreamed of her, for seven years I was ashamed, and when I drank a glass of wine I blushed with shame at the thought of old Maja, who was probably drinking water in a workhouse. I have tried to give to the poor the sum I owed her, but it didn't help. And now — I've found her, and lost her in the same moment — ! [*Gets up and goes questingly upstage.*] Explain this to me! I want to pay my debt, at last I can pay it, but I may not.

CONFESSOR: Madman! Do not bow before what you do not comprehend, and you will see that the explanation will come. Goodbye.

He goes. The LADY *enters pensively, and sits at the table opposite the* STRANGER.

STRANGER: You again? The same, and yet — so different. How beautiful you are; as beautiful as when I first saw you, and asked to be allowed to be your friend, your dog —

LADY: That you see me as beautiful, which I am not, shows that you have re-found the mirror of beauty in your eye. The ogre never saw anything beautiful in me, because he had nothing beautiful to see with.

STRANGER: But why did you kiss me that time? Why should you do that?

LADY: You've often asked me that, but I've never been able to answer because I didn't know. Now that I've been parted from you — and come up here to the mountains, where the air is cleaner — and the sun nearer — ssh! Now I see that Sunday afternoon, when you sat like a helpless and abandoned child with hurt eyes staring at your fate. You awoke in me a feeling of motherhood which I had never known before — and pity, pity for a human soul, overcame me — and I forgot myself —

STRANGER: You make me ashamed. And, yes, I feel now that it was like that —

LADY: But you took it as — something else. As —

STRANGER: Don't say it. You make me ashamed.

LADY: You thought so ill of me? Didn't you notice how

I dropped my veil between us, like the crusader's sword in the bridal bed?

STRANGER: You make me ashamed. I infected you with my lust. Ingeborg, you were of better stuff than me. You make me ashamed.

LADY: Now you are beautiful! So beautiful —

STRANGER: Oh, no. Not I. You are.

LADY: Ah — now I see what lies behind your mask. Now I see it — now I see what you had hidden. What I *thought* I would find in you — what I was looking for, looking for — ! Sometimes I thought you were a hypocrite, but we are not hypocrites. No, no, we cannot dissimulate —

STRANGER: Ingeborg — now, beyond the river, with life below us, behind us — how different everything seems. Now I see your soul as God made it, the angel which, because of Adam's sin, was cast down into a mortal prison. There is a heaven after all. It wasn't the beginning when we began, and it will not be the end when we end. Life is a fragment, without beginning and without end. That's why it is so hard to understand.

LADY [*gently*]: So hard, so hard. Tell me — now that we stand beyond guilt and innocence — how did you come to hate women?

STRANGER: Let me think. Hate? Women? Hate? I've never done that. Unfortunately — ! Ever since I was eight years old, I have always been infatuated with one of them, usually innocently, and three times I have been volcanically in love. But — I have always felt that women hated me. And they have always tormented me.

LADY: How strange!

STRANGER: Let me think a moment more. Perhaps I have been jealous of my individuality — afraid of anyone having influence over me. My first love made herself into a governess and a nanny. Besides — there are men who can't stand children and men who can't stand women — over them.

LADY: But you have described women as the enemies of mankind. Do you mean that?

STRANGER: Of course I meant it, since I wrote it. And I've written from experience, not theorized. I sought in woman an angel who would lend me her wings, and I fell instead into the arms of an earthbound spirit who suffocated me under bolsters which she filled with her wing-feathers. I sought an Ariel and found a Caliban. When I wanted to rise she dragged me down. And she always made me feel sinful.

LADY [*gently*]: Do you know what the great understander of women, Solomon, said? "And I find more bitter than death the woman whose heart is snares and nets, and her hands as bands. Whoso pleaseth God shall escape from her; but the sinner shall be taken by her."

STRANGER: And I was never agreeable in God's sight! Was it a punishment, then? It is possible. But I was never agreeable in anyone's sight, and never had a good word said of me. Did I never do anything good? Is it possible that a human being can ever have done *no* good? It is horrible never to have a good word said of one.

LADY: You did. But when anyone said good of you, you rejected it as though it burned you.

STRANGER: That's true. I remember now. But can you explain it?

LADY: Explain? You always ask for explanations of the inexplicable. "When I applied my heart to know wisdom . . . then I beheld all the work of God, that a man cannot find out the work that is done under the sun; because although a man labour to seek it out, yet he shall not find it; yea, further; although a wise man think to know it, yet shall he not be able to find it."

STRANGER: Who says that?

LADY [*takes a doll from her pocket*]: Ecclesiastes. This is Mitzi's doll. Do you see how she longs for her little mistress? She's quite pale. And she seems to know where Mitzi is, for she always looks up to heaven however I hold her. Look — her eyes follow the stars like a compass needle — she is my compass, which always shows me where my heaven is. But she ought to be dressed in black, of course, since she's in mourning, but we were so poor. Do you know why we never had any money? Because God was angry with us for our sins. "The just suffer no want."

STRANGER: Where did you learn that?

LADY: In the book where everything is written. Everything. [*Wraps the doll in her cloak.*] Look, she's beginning to feel cold. It's the clouds up there —

STRANGER: How do you dare to walk alone in these mountains?

LADY: The Lord is with me. What can men do to me?

STRANGER: Don't these sick people worry you?

LADY [*turns towards the dyke*]: I do not see them. I no longer see anything ugly.

STRANGER: Ingeborg. I wronged you, and you are on the way towards bringing me salvation. Do you know that it was my dream to find reconciliation through a woman? You don't believe it. But it is true. In the old days nothing was of any value to me if I couldn't lay it at a woman's feet. But as a sacrifice to beauty and goodness, not as a tribute to an ambitious tyrant. I wanted to give; but she wanted to take, not to receive. So I hated her. When I was most helpless and thought the end was near, I longed to sleep at a mother's breast, where I could bury my tired head and drink in the tenderness I had never been given.

LADY: You had no mother?

STRANGER: Scarcely. And I never felt any sense of kinship towards my father or my brothers and sisters. Ingeborg, I was the son of that servant of whom it is written: "Cast out this bondwoman and her son, for the son of this bondwoman shall not be heir with the free man's son."

LADY: Do you know why Ishmael was driven out? It is written in the same book: because he was a mocker. It goes on: "He will be a wild man, his hand shall be against every man, and every man's hand against him."

STRANGER: Is that there too?

LADY: Yes, my child. Everything is there.

STRANGER: Everything?

LADY: Everything. You'll find answers to all your questions there. Even the most inquisitive.

STRANGER: Call me your child, and I shall love you. And when I love someone, I want to serve, obey, be ill-treated, suffer, endure —

LADY: You should not love me, but your Creator —

STRANGER: He is cruel, like my father.

LADY: He is love itself, and you are hatred.

STRANGER: You are His daughter, and I am His rejected son.

LADY [soothingly]: Hush! Hush! Please —

STRANGER: If you knew what I have suffered this past week! I don't know what I've landed in.

LADY: What do you mean?

STRANGER: There's a woman in that hut who looks at me as though I had come to steal her last crust of bread. She says nothing, and that's the worst thing of all. I think she prays when she sees me —

LADY: What kind of prayers?

STRANGER: The kind one reads backwards to ward off those who have the evil eye — and who bring bad luck —

LADY: Strange. Have you heard that it is possible to distort a person's vision?

STRANGER: I have. But who can do that?

THE WOMAN [*comes forward to the table*]: Hullo. I suppose you're the gentleman's sister.

STRANGER: I suppose you could say that now.

WOMAN [*to* LADY]: What a blessing I've met someone at last that I can tell this to. He's so silent, this gentleman, you feel shy of speaking to him, specially as he seems bereaved, poor man. But I can tell his sister, and I'd like him to hear it. From the moment he set foot in my house, it was like a blessing had come on it. I'd had nothing but troubles — no lodgers, my only cow had died, my husband in an alcoholics' home, no food for my children. I prayed to God to send me help from above — for I knew I'd get none from down here. Then this gentleman came. It's not only that he gave me twice what I asked — he brought luck with him, and my house has been blessed. God bless you, good gentleman.

STRANGER [*rises, disturbed*]: Hush, woman. You blaspheme.

LADY: He will not believe. Oh, God, he will not believe. Look at me!

STRANGER: Now when I look at you, I believe. She blesses me! And I, who am damned, have brought blessing with me. How can I believe this? With me — me! [*Falls at the table and weeps into his hands.*]

LADY: He weeps. Tears, rain from heaven that softens the solid rock, have fallen on his stone heart. He weeps.

WOMAN: Why, he's got a heart of gold. And he's generous. And so good to my little ones.

LADY: You hear? You hear?

WOMAN: There's only one thing I don't understand about the gentleman. Not that I want to speak ill of him for it.

LADY: What was that?

WOMAN: Well, it's only a tiny thing, but —

LADY: Tell me.

WOMAN: He couldn't stand my dogs.

LADY: I like that in him, that he can't stand unclean beasts. I hate everything animal, in myself and in other human beings. But I don't hate animals, because I hate nothing that is created —

STRANGER: Thank you, Ingeborg.

LADY: **You see. I see your merits, though you don't believe it.** Here is the Confessor.

   The CONFESSOR *enters.*

WOMAN: I'd better go. The Confessor doesn't like me.

LADY: The Confessor loves all mankind.

CONFESSOR [*comes forward and addresses the* LADY]: And you most of all, my child, for you are goodness itself. Whether you are beautiful to the human eye I cannot see, but I know that you are because you are good. You were the bride of my youth — and you will always be my spiritual bride, for you gave me what the others could never receive from you. Spiritually I have lived your life, I have endured your sufferings; I have not shared your pleasures, for you have had none except your child. Only I perceived the beauty of your soul. My friend here sensed it, and that drew him to you — but his evil was too strong, and you had to absorb it into yourself to free him. You had to suffer all the torments of hell by being evil for his sake, suffering for his sake, that he might find reconciliation. Your task is accomplished. Go in peace.

LADY: Where shall I go?

CONFESSOR: Up there. Where the sun always shines.

LADY [*rises*]: Is there a place for me there too?

CONFESSOR: There is a place for everyone. I will show you the way.

He leads her upstage. The STRANGER *makes a movement.*

CONFESSOR: Are you impatient? Do not be.

He goes. The STRANGER *sits alone. The* VENUS WORSHIPPERS *get up, approach him and form a circle round him.*

STRANGER: What do you want with me?

VENUS WORSHIPPERS: Hail! Father!

STRANGER [*in torment*]: Why do you say that?

FIRST VENUS WORSHIPPER [THYRA]: Because we are your children. Your little ones.

STRANGER [*tries to escape, but they surround him*]: Leave me!

SECOND VENUS WORSHIPPER [*a pale boy*]: Don't you recognize me, father?

The TEMPTER *appears upstage by the crossroads left, and laughs.*

STRANGER [*to* SECOND VENUS WORSHIPPER]: Who are you? I seem to know you?

SECOND VENUS WORSHIPPER: I am your son, Erik.

STRANGER: Erik! You here?

SECOND VENUS WORSHIPPER: I am here.

STRANGER: God have mercy on you. And — my child, forgive me.

SECOND VENUS WORSHIPPER: Never! You have shown us the way to the sulphur spring. Is it far to the lake?

The STRANGER *falls.*

TEMPTER [*laughs*]: Tempters, rejoice!

VENUS WORSHIPPERS: Sulphur! Sulphur! Sulphur! And Mercury!

TEMPTER [*comes over and touches the* STRANGER *with his foot*]: You worm! I can make you believe anything! Thanks to your unbounded pride. You think you're the mainspring of the universe, the prime cause of all evil. The fool thinks he's taught young people to worship Venus, as though they didn't know how to do that before he was born. His pride is insufferable, and he has had the presumption to trespass on my preserve. Give him another broadside, false Erik!

> *The* SECOND VENUS WORSHIPPER *bends down and whispers in the* STRANGER's *ear.*

TEMPTER: There used to be seven deadly sins. They have become eight. I discovered the eighth. It is called despair. For to doubt the existence of goodness and not to hope for forgiveness is to call — [*He hesitates before the word "God", then says it as though it burned his lips.*] — God evil. That is defamation, denial, blasphemy. See how he cringes!

STRANGER [*gets up hastily and looks the* TEMPTER *in the eyes*]: Who are you?

TEMPTER: Your brother. Aren't we alike? Some of your features remind me of my own portrait.

STRANGER: Where have I seen your portrait?

TEMPTER: Everywhere. I'm often found in churches, though not among the saints.

STRANGER: I don't recall --

TEMPTER: Is it so long since you went to church? I'm usually shown together with St. George.

> *The* STRANGER *trembles throughout his body, and tries to flee, but cannot.*

TEMPTER: And sometimes with Michael. I don't always

have the best position; but things may change. All things
can change; some time, the last may be first. It's the same
with you. You're a little down just now, but that can
change too. If only you had the sense to choose better
company! You've had too many skirts round you, my
boy. Skirts stir up dust, and dust settles on one's eyes and
in one's lungs. Sit down, young man, and let's have a chat.
[*He leads the* STRANGER *jovially by the ear to the table.*]
Sit and tremble, sit and tremble, my lad. [*They sit.*] Well!
What shall we have? A little wine — and a little woman?
No? Yes, that's too old a trick — as old as Dr Faustus.
Bravo! We moderns require intellectual debaucheries. So —
you're on your way up there, to the holy men, who believe
that he who sleeps sins not; to the brave, who gave up the
battle of life because they suffered a few defeats; to the
binders, who bind souls instead of freeing them. Talking of
freeing, has a holy man ever freed you from the burden of
sin? No! Do you know why you've been oppressed for so
long by a sense of sin? Because asceticism and abstinence
have so weakened you that anyone can take possession of
your soul and set up shop there. They can even do it from
a distance. You've so managed to annihilate your own self
that you see with the eyes of others, hear with the ears of
others, think the thoughts of others. In a word, you've
committed spiritual suicide. Weren't you praising the
enemy of mankind just now — woman, who turned Paradise into hell? You needn't answer — I read the reply in
your eyes and hear it on your lips. You talk of pure love
for a woman. It's lust, lad, just lust for every woman, and
that's what we have to pay so dearly for. You say you
don't desire her? Why do you want to have her near you,
then? You need a friend? Take a man friend, then — lots
of men! You tried to persuade yourself that you weren't
a woman-hater. The little lady found the right answer to
that. Every healthy man is a woman-hater, but he can't
live without uniting himself to the enemy and fighting her!
It's perverse, effeminate men who are the woman-
worshippers. Which are you, now? Well, then you saw
these sick souls, and thought you were the cause of their

misery. Believe me, they're healthy lads, and in a few days they'll get their discharge and be back at their jobs. Yes, yes, yes — that false Erik is a sly dog. But you've gone so far that you can't tell your own children from other people's. You'd do well to get away from that lot. Well? Do you see now that I can free you — yes, me, though I'm no holy man. Now. Let's get old Maja! [*He whistles with his fingers.* OLD MAJA *enters.*]

TEMPTER: Here we are! Well, what do you want? To lodge a complaint against this lad?

OLD MAJA: No. He's a nice gentleman. Always was. But he had a nasty wife.

TEMPTER [*to* STRANGER]: You see! Never heard that before, did you? Other way round, wasn't it, always? That good angel whose life you've ruined — yes, we've heard all that. Well, old Maja, what's all this he's been saying? He's been torturing himself for seven years thinking he owes you money.

OLD MAJA: He did once owe me a little, but I got it back and with good interest — much better than what they give at the savings bank. Real honest and good of him it was.

STRANGER [*starts*]: What are you saying? Is it possible — that I could have forgotten — ?

TEMPTER: If you've got the receipt on you, Maja, show it to us.

OLD MAJA: The gentleman'll have that. But I've got the savings book, where he put the money in in his name. [*Takes out a savings book and hands it to the* STRANGER, *who reads it.*]

STRANGER: Yes, she's right. And now, I remember. But why these seven years' torment, of shame and dishonour — these sleepless nights of unending reproach? Why, why, why?

TEMPTER: You can go now, Maja. But first, say something good about this self-torturer. Can you recall no human trait in this wild beast, whom humanity has baited for years?

STRANGER [*to* OLD MAJA]: Hush! Do not speak! [*Puts his hands to his ears.*]

TEMPTER: Well, Maja?

OLD MAJA: Well, I know what they say about him, but that's about what he writes — and I haven't read that, because I can't read. And no one don't have to read it if they don't want to. But he was a real kind gentleman. Look, he's stopping his ears. Well, I don't like flattery, neither. But I'll whisper it to you, sir. [*Whispers to the* TEMPTER.]

TEMPTER: Ye-es — everyone who's thin-skinned gets baited like a wild beast. True; that's the general rule. Goodbye, Maja.

OLD MAJA: Goodbye, kind gentlemen. [*Goes.*]

STRANGER: Why have I suffered innocently for seven years?

TEMPTER [*points upwards*]: Ask up there.

STRANGER: I never got any answer from Him.

TEMPTER: No? Well, that's sometimes the way. Do you think I look good?

STRANGER: I can't say that.

TEMPTER: You look revoltingly evil too. Do you know why we look like this?

STRANGER: No.

TEMPTER: Our fellow mortals' hatred and evil have wiped off on to us. Do you know that up there there are authentic saints who have never done any wrong themselves but just sit and suffer for others — relatives who have committed unredeemed crimes, etcetera. These angels who have taken on themselves the sins of others end up like us by looking like gangsters. What do you think of that?

STRANGER: I don't know who you are, but you're the first person who has ever given me answers that might possibly reconcile me to life. You are —

TEMPTER: Well! Say it!

STRANGER: You are the liberator.

TEMPTER: And therefore —

STRANGER: And therefore the vulture claws your liver eternally. But listen. Has it never occurred to you that there is a good reason for this, as for everything else? Suppose that the earth is a prison in which dangerous criminals are incarcerated? Would it be sensible to let them loose? Would it be right?

TEMPTER: What a question! I've never really thought about that. Hm! Hm!

STRANGER: And have you thought of this? That we may be born guilty — ?

TEMPTER: That doesn't concern me. I stick to the present.

STRANGER: Good! But don't you think we may sometimes be punished in the wrong — place, and that this is why we cannot see the logic of it, although it may exist?

TEMPTER: The logic's there all right. But life is such a web of errors, faults and misdemeanours, all relatively harmless when measured against human weakness, yet punished with the most remorseless vengeance. Everything is revenged, even the things we do in ignorance. Who forgives? Mortals sometimes; divine justice, never.

A PILGRIM *enters upstage.*

TEMPTER: Look at him. A penitent. I wonder what he's done? We'll ask him. Welcome to this land of peace, traveller! Sit at our simple and ascetic board, whence all temptations are banished.

PILGRIM: Thank you, fellow-wanderer in the vale of sorrow.

TEMPTER: What is your present cause for grief?

PILGRIM: Nothing special. Rather the reverse. The hour of liberation has struck, and I'm going up there to receive absolution.

STRANGER: Wait a minute. Haven't we met before?

PILGRIM: I think we have.

STRANGER: Caesar! It's Caesar!

PILGRIM: I was, but am no longer.

TEMPTER [*laughs*] : Imperial acquaintances! Splendid! But tell us, tell us.

PILGRIM: I will tell you, now I have the right to speak and my penitence is done. When we met at a certain doctor's, I was imprisoned there as a madman supposed to be suffering from the delusion that I was Caesar. I shall now reveal the truth. I never believed that, though scruples of conscience compelled me to put a good face on it. A friend, a bad friend, had written evidence in his possession that I was the victim of a misunderstanding, but he held his tongue when he should have spoken, and I took his silence as a challenge to me to hold my tongue — and suffer. Why did I hold my peace and suffer? Well, when I was young I was once in great need. I was received as a guest in a house on an island far out in the sea, by a man who, despite unusual gifts, had been passed over in his profession because of his unweaning pride. Solitude had caused this man to brood and to have strange conceits about who he was. I noticed this but said nothing. But one day his wife told me that her husband was sometimes not wholly sane, and believed himself to be Julius Caesar. For many years I kept this secret conscientiously, for I was not by nature ungrateful. But life is a fox, and some years later this Caesar brutally interfered in my private life. In my anger I revealed the secret of his obsession, and made my former benefactor a laughing-stock, so that his life became unbearable. Now hear how Nemesis strikes! A year later I wrote a book — I am a writer, though I publish anonymously. In this book I described certain features of my family life — how I played with my daughter Julia — she was called Julia, like Caesar's daughter — and with my wife, whom we called Caesar's wife, because none spoke ill of her. Well, this game, in which my mother-in-law also took part, cost me dear. When I read the proofs of my book, I saw the danger. I said to myself: this will ruin you. I intended to strike these passages out, but my pen refused, and an inner voice said to me: let it stand. It stood; and I fell.

STRANGER: Why didn't you let your friend publish that letter, which would have explained everything?

PILGRIM: No. When disaster struck, I thought: this is the hand of God, you must suffer this for your ingratitude.

STRANGER: And you did suffer?

PILGRIM: Not a bit! I laughed, and put a brave face on it. And because I took my punishment unresistingly and meekly, the Lord lightened my burden, and the mockery of the world did not touch me.

TEMPTER: That's a strange story. But such is life. Shall we push on now? Let's shack up together, we who've been through the mill. Pull yourselves up by the roots, and we shall scale the heights!

STRANGER: The Confessor told me to wait for him.

TEMPTER: He'll catch up with you. They're holding an assizes up here today, and there's one particularly interesting case in which I may have to testify. Come, come, come!

STRANGER: Well, I suppose it doesn't matter whether I sit down here or up there.

PILGRIM [to STRANGER]: Who is that?

STRANGER: I don't know. He looks like an anarchist.

PILGRIM: Interesting appearance he has.

STRANGER: A sceptical fellow, who has seen life.

TEMPTER: Come, now, my children. I'll tell you some stories as we go. Come, come, come! [*They go out up-stage.*]

Scene 3. A terrace on the mountain

Right and left are mountain ledges. In the distant back-ground, a bird's-eye view of a river landscape, with towns, villages, farmland, forest, and, in the extreme distance, a glimpse of the sea. Downstage stands an apple-tree in full fruit. Beneath it is a long table with a chair at one end and benches along its sides. Down-stage right, a corner of the village hall. The cloud now hangs directly above the village. At the head of the table sits the JUSTICE; *on the benches, his* FELLOW MAGISTRATES. *The* DEFENDANT *stands on the* JUSTICE's *right, the* WITNESSES, *including the* TEMPTER, *on the left. The* PUBLIC, *including* CAESAR *and the* STRANGER, *stand here and there around the table.*

JUSTICE: Is the defendant present?

DEFENDANT: Present.

JUSTICE: This is a deeply deplorable business, which has caused much shame and grief to our little community. Florian Reicher, aged twenty-three, stands accused of hav-ing shot dead the betrothed of Fritz Schlipitska, with full intent to kill her. We have here a case of premeditated murder, and the demands of the law in such a case are clear and specific. Has the accused anything to say in his defence, or any mitigating circumstances to plead?

DEFENDANT: No.

TEMPTER: Wait.

JUSTICE: Who is that?

TEMPTER: Counsel for the accused.

JUSTICE: It is true that the defendant has the right to employ counsel. But in case I think the judgement of the people is already determined by the facts, and the murderer can scarcely regain our sympathy. Am I right?

THE PEOPLE: He is already condemned.

TEMPTER: By whom?

THE PEOPLE: By the laws, and by his deed.

TEMPTER: Have a care. In my capacity as counsel for the accused, I stand here to defend him, and thereby take the charge upon myself. I demand the floor.

JUSTICE: We cannot refuse it to you.

THE PEOPLE: Florian is already condemned!

TEMPTER: You must hear me first! Well. I had attained my eighteenth year — this is Florian speaking, you understand. My mind, nurtured by the tender care of a pious mother, was pure, and my heart knew no guile, for I had seen no evil and knew of none. Then I met — I, Florian — a young girl, who in my eyes, stood for all that was most beautiful in this sinful world — for she was goodness itself. I offered her my hand, my heart and my future. She accepted, and vowed to be faithful to me. Five years I was to serve my Rachel — and I did serve her, gathered straw after straw towards the little home we were to build. My whole life was grounded on this woman's love; and, since I myself kept my promises and my faith in her, I never doubted her. In our fifth year — I had built our cottage, and gathered some sticks of furniture for it — I discovered that she was playing with me, and had taken at least three lovers —

JUSTICE: Are there witnesses to this?

THE MAYOR: Three suffice. I, the Mayor, am one.

JUSTICE: Your Worship's own word is sufficient.

TEMPTER: Then I shot her — not from revenge, but to free

myself of the impure thoughts with which her faithlessness filled me. For however I strove to root her image from my mind, images of her lovers always arose and stole their way into my blood so that in the end I felt as though I was living in an unnatural relationship with three men, through a woman who had been common to all of us.

JUSTICE: In other words, jealousy.

DEFENDANT: Yes, jealousy!

TEMPTER: Yes, jealousy — that sense of purity which will not permit the heart to countenance adultery. Had I accepted it, or not been jealous, I would have entered a house of vice which I did not wish to enter. So she had to go, and my thoughts had to be cleansed from that mortal sin which alone is worthy of condemnation. That is all.

THE PEOPLE: The dead woman is guilty! The dead woman is condemned!

JUSTICE: The dead woman is guilty as instigator of the crime.

THE DEAD WOMAN'S FATHER: My lord! Judge of my dead child, and you, my countrymen! May I speak?

JUSTICE: As father of the dead woman, you may speak.

DEAD WOMAN'S FATHER: To this charge against the dead, let me reply. Maria, my child, has without question sinned most gravely, and is certainly the cause of this dead man's crime. Of that there can be no doubt.

THE PEOPLE: No doubt! She is the guilty one!

DEAD WOMAN'S FATHER: But let a father speak a word in explanation, if not in defence. When my Maria was fifteen she met a man who seems to have made it his aim in life to draw young girls to him as a fowler tempts small birds into his snares. He was no seducer in the ordinary sense, for he contented himself with binding their minds, ensnaring their feelings, and then spurning them, to see how, with broken hearts and wings, they suffered — from the agony of the heart, which exceeds all other agony. For three years Maria was at a hospital for the mentally sick. When she came out she was broken, broken into several pieces — one might say into several *people*. She was a good angel, and one half of her feared God — but the other half was a demon who blasphemed against all things holy. I saw her leave her mad dance and run to meet her beloved Florian. I heard her, in his presence, change her tongue and take on a different visage, so that I could have sworn on the Bible that it was a different person who stood there. Yet she seemed to me equally honest — in either image. Is she guilty, or is her seducer guilty?

THE PEOPLE: She is innocent! Who is the seducer?

DEAD WOMAN'S FATHER: He stands here!

TEMPTER: Yes. It was I.

THE PEOPLE: Stone him!

JUSTICE: The formalities must be observed. He must be heard.

TEMPTER: Thank you. Hearken, ye Argives! Well — I, the undersigned, born of poor but fairly honourable parents, was by nature one of those rare birds who seek their Creator when they are young — and, naturally, I did not find Him. Most old cuckoos do not seek Him until they are old, and with good reason. But my youthful quest was attended by a purity of heart and a modesty which made me a laughing-stock even to my nannies — you too will laugh when I tell you that I would only undress in the darkness of a cupboard! Now, however corrupted we may be by the coarsenesses of life, surely we cannot fail to see something beautiful, even, now that we are older, something touching in this? Yet being the men we are, we mock such childish innocence. You mock him, ladies and gentlemen.

JUSTICE [*gravely*]: You misjudge us.

TEMPTER: If so, my apologies. Well, he grew to manhood –
that is, I did — and walked into an ambush of snares set to
trap his innocence. I am an old sinner but I blush now —
[*He takes off his hat.*] — yes, look at me! — when I think
of the vision that greeted him of a world of Potiphar's
wives. There was not a woman who — no, for the sake of
humanity and the female sex, I will spare you ... Forgive
me! There were moments when I did not believe my own
eyes but thought the Devil must have distorted my sight.
The most sacred bonds — ! [*He bites his tongue.*] No,
peace. Mankind will think itself slandered. Well, till I was
twenty-five I fought against it, and yielded neither to the
world's mockery nor to. . . . ! Yes, I was called a Joseph,
and I was a Joseph! I was jealous of my virtue, I felt
wounded if a woman gave me an unchaste look. But in the
end, I fell, insidiously seduced. Then I became the slave of
my own passions. I sat at Omphale's feet and span her
wool, I was degraded to the very depths of degradation,
and suffered, suffered, suffered! But it was my body that
was degraded — my soul retained its integrity, I may even
say its purity. And I cherished innocent infatuations for
young, pure girls who I have no doubt sensed the sympathy
which drew us to each other. For, without boasting — or
with boasting — they were drawn to me. But I did not
want to cross the barrier. But they did. And when I shrank
from the brink, it broke their hearts — so they assured me.
In a word, I have never seduced an innocent girl. I swear it!
Am I therefore guilty of this young girl's grief which turned
into madness? Can it not rather be said in my favour that
I refused to take the step which would have brought about
her fall? Who casts the first stone at me? None of you.
Then I have misjudged my audience! And I, who thought
myself an object of mockery, have pleaded the cause of
my masculine innocence. I feel young again, and would
offer my apologies to the human race — had I not happened to see a cynical smile on the lips of the woman who,
when I was young, was *my* seducer. Step forth, woman,
and see the result of your seduction. See what seed it has
brought forth.

A WOMAN [*steps forward gravely and modestly.*] It was I. May I be heard, and tell my simple story about the man who first seduced *me*? He happens to be **present** —

JUSTICE: Good friends! I must call a halt to these proceedings, or we shall find ourselves back with Eve in Paradise —

TEMPTER: — who seduced Adam! That's where we *must* go back to! Eve! Call forth Eve! Eve!

He swings his stick in the air. The trunk of the apple-tree becomes transparent, and EVE *is visible, swathed in her hair and with a girdle about her loins.*

TEMPTER: Well, mother Eve, you seduced our father. You stand accused. How do you plead?

EVE [*simply, gravely*]: The serpent deceived me.

TEMPTER: Well answered! Eve has acquitted herself. Call forth the serpent. Serpent! [EVE *disappears.*] Let the serpent come forth!

The SERPENT *appears in the tree.*

TEMPTER: Here you see the seducer of us all. Well, serpent, who seduced you?

ALL [*shuddering*]: Hush, blasphemer!

TEMPTER: Serpent! Answer!

A clap of thunder and a flash of lightning. Everyone runs away except the TEMPTER, *who falls to the ground, and* CAESAR, *the* STRANGER *and the* LADY. *The* TEMPTER *recovers and adopts the posture of the statue of the Whetter or the Slave, still prone.*

TEMPTER: The prime cause — or — well, we may not know. But since the serpent is guilty, we are relatively innocent — though one mustn't tell mankind that. Anyway, the defendant seems to have got out of his troubles — and the court vanished like smoke! The moral? Do not stand in judgement. Judge not, ye judges!

LADY [*to* STRANGER]: Come with me.

STRANGER: But I want to hear this man.

LADY: Why? He's like a small child, he asks all the questions that can't be answered. You know the kind of things children want to know. "Daddy, why does the sun rise in the east?" Can you answer that?

STRANGER: Hm!

LADY: Or: "Mummy, who created God?" And you think that's profound? Come with me.

STRANGER [*struggles with his admiration of the* TEMPTER]: Yes, but that about Eve — that was new —

LADY: Oh, nonsense. I read that in my Scripture lesson when I was eight. And that we inherit the debts of our parents is Common Law. Come, my child.

TEMPTER [*gets up, shakes himself and limps up the mountainside right*]: Come with me, and I will show you the world, which you think you know but do not know.

LADY [*goes up mountainside left*]: Come here, my child, and I will show you God's beautiful world as I have learned to see it since the tears of sorrow washed the dust from my eyes. Come to me.

The STRANGER *stands uncertainly between them.*

TEMPTER: How did you see the world through your tears? As the willows on the riverbank mirror themselves in running water. A chaos of crooked lines in which trees seem to stand on their heads. No, child, with my binoculars dried by the fire of hatred, with my telescope, I see everything truly, precise and sharp as it really is.

LADY: What do you know of reality, child? It is not reality which meets your eye but the image of reality. And the image is only the appearance, not the thing itself. You fight for images and illusions.

TEMPTER: Listen to her! A little philosopher in skirts! By — Zeus, a debate like this in a mountain-sized lecture theatre — it calls for an audience to match! Heigh-ho!

LADY: I have mine here — my friend, my husband, my child. If he will listen to me, good — then things will be well with me, and with him. Come here, my friend. This is the way. This is Mount Garizim, where people bless; and that is Ebal, where men curse.

TEMPTER: Yes, this is Ebal where men curse. "Cursed by the earth, woman, for thy sake. In sorrow thou shalt bring forth children, **and thy desire shall be** to thy husband, and he shall rule over thee." And: "Cursed is the ground for **thy sake, O man; in sorrow shalt thou eat of it all the days** of thy life; thorns also and thistles shall it bring forth to thee; in the **sweat of thy face shalt thou eat bread, till** thou return unto the ground." Those are the Lord's words, not mine.

LADY: And God blessed the first man and woman; and God blessed the seventh day. But you, we, **we made it evil, and that is why** . . . But he who follows the word of **the** Lord, he dwells on Garizim, where blessings are dispensed. Thus saith the Lord: "Blessed be thou in the city and on the land. Blessed be thy basket, thy tray, thy coming in and thy going out; and the rain of heaven shall bless thy seed, that thy children may flourish. To many shalt thou lend, but from no man shalt thou borrow; thou shalt be over all but under none. And the blessing of God shall follow thee in all things, if thou but follow the Lord's commands." So come, my friend, and put your hand in mine. [*Falls on her knees with clasped hands.*] I beg you, by the love that once bound us, by the memory of a child that joined us, by the power of a mother's love — a mother's, a mother's, for that is how I loved you, you strayed child, whom I have sought in the dark hiding-places of the forest, and whom I at last found hungry and destitute for lack of love. Come back, child of sorrow, and hide your tired head against my breast, where you used to rest before you looked at the light of the sun.

During this scene her dress falls and she stands clothed in white with her hair flowing, full-bosomed.

STRANGER: My mother!

LADY: Yes, child, your mother. In life I was never able to caress you — higher powers forbade it. Why? I did not dare to ask —

STRANGER: My mother? But she is dead.

LADY: She was, but the dead are not dead; and a mother's love can conquer death. Do you know that? Come, my child, and I will repay the debt I owe you. On my lap I shall rock you to peace; I will wash you clean from the remorse and sin of — [*She omits the word her lips will not utter.*] I will wash the sweat of agony from your brow, I will warm white linen by the hearth of our home, the home you never had, outlaw, wanderer, son of Hagar the bond-woman, born a slave with all men's hands raised against you. The ploughers ploughed on your back and drew their furrows deep. Come. I will heal your wounds and suffer your torments. Come.

STRANGER [*has been weeping so that his whole body has been shaking. Now he goes to the mountainside, left, where the* MOTHER *is standing with open arms*]: I am coming.

TEMPTER: I have no power here. But we shall meet again. [*Goes.*]

Scene 4

Higher up the mountain. A landscape of crags in cloud, with marshland around. The MOTHER *is climbing so that the cloud begins to envelop her. The* STRANGER *remains standing below her.*

STRANGER: Oh, Mother, Mother! Why are you leaving me like this? Just when my dearest dream was coming true.

TEMPTER [*appears*]: What were you dreaming? Tell me.

STRANGER: My bright hope, my dark longing, and my last prayer. To be reconciled with mankind through woman —

TEMPTER: Through woman, who taught you to hate — ?

STRANGER: Exactly — because she bound me to the earth, like the round stone that shackles the slave around his foot to stop him running away.

TEMPTER [*laughs*]: Woman — always woman!

STRANGER: Yes, woman! The beginning and the end — at any rate for us men. To each other they signify nothing.

TEMPTER: In other words, nothing in themselves, everything to us, through us! Our honour and our shame; our highest joy, our deepest pain; our redemption and our fall; our reward and our punishment; our strength and our weakness.

STRANGER: Our shame! You are right. Answer me this riddle, you who are so wise. Whenever I took a woman, my own, my beautiful adored one, on my arm, in front of other men, I felt ashamed, as though of a weakness. Solve me that riddle.

TEMPTER: You felt ashamed? [*Pause.*] I don't know.

STRANGER: *You* cannot answer?

TEMPTER: No. I always suffered when I was with my woman among other men; I felt that she was defiled by their glances, and I through her.

STRANGER: And when she committed the deed of shame, the shame became yours! Why?

TEMPTER: The Eve of the Greeks was called Pandora, maliciously created by Zeus to torment men and to rule them. As a wedding gift she received a box containing all the disasters that could strike mankind. Perhaps we should look to Olympus rather than Paradise to solve this Sphinx's riddle. It will never be completely solved. I'm no wiser than you. And while I ponder the problem, I still enjoy the most beautiful thing that creation has given us. Go thou and do likewise.

STRANGER: The most beautiful of Satan's illusions, you mean. For she who is most beautiful to me may be hideous to others. But even to me, when she is evil, she can be uglier than any other woman on earth. Then what is beauty?

TEMPTER: An illusion; a reflection of *your* goodness. [*Puts his hand to his mouth.*] Damn it! The word slipped out! And now — now the demon is loose.

STRANGER: The demon? Yes! But how, if she is a demon, how can a demon make me pine for virtue and goodness? For that was the first effect she had on me. I saw her beauty and was seized with a passion to become like her and thereby worthy of her. At first I took exercises and steam baths, bought good clothes, even used cosmetics, but only made myself ridiculous. Then I began from the inside: I accustomed myself to think beautifully, speak beautifully, and act nobly. And lo, one day, when this new veneer had formed about my soul, I found I was an exact replica of her — so she said — and *she* was the one who first uttered the blessed words: "I love you." How can a demon ennoble us? How can a spirit of evil fill us with goodness? How — ? No, she was an angel. A fallen one, of course; and her love was a twisted beam from the great original, the eternal light that warms and loves — loves — loves!

TEMPTER: Look, old chap. Are we going to stand here like schoolboys spelling out the ABC of love?

CONFESSOR: What's this chatterbox saying? His whole life has been expended in talk, so that he's never achieved anything.

TEMPTER: I ought to have been a priest. But I never got the call.

CONFESSOR: While you're waiting for it, come and help me to find a drunk who has gone and drowned himself in this bog. He must be here, I've followed his footprints.

TEMPTER: That's him, lying under those branches.

CONFESSOR [*lifts some branches, revealing a dead body, clothed, with a young, white face*]: Yes. It's him. [*Looks meditatively at the corpse.*]

TEMPTER: Who was he?

CONFESSOR: Wonderful! Wonderful!

TEMPTER: He was beautiful. Hardly more than a boy.

CONFESSOR: No, my friends. He was fifty-four years old. And when I saw him a week ago, he looked sixty-four. His eyes were a greyish-yellow like the slime a snail leaves in its track, and red-rimmed with drink — and because he wept blood over his vices and his misery. His face was brown and puffy like a piece of liver on a butcher's slab and he hid himself in shame from the eyes of men. Even in his last moments he seems to have blushed for the broken mirror of his soul, for he hid his face beneath these branches. I saw him fight against his vice; I saw him, after he had been dismissed from his post as teacher, kneel and pray to God to free him. But . . . . Well, now he is freed. And look, now that his evil has been taken from him, all that was good and beautiful in him has returned. This is how he must have looked when he was nineteen. Sin is forced on us as a punishment — why? We may not know. "He who hateth the righteous shall himself become a criminal," someone has written. Or. . . I knew him when he was young. And now I remember — he was always particularly cruel towards anyone who did not drink. He condemned people, and damned them, at the same time as he worshipped his cult of the grape on his altar of pleasure. Now he is free. Free from his sins, from his shame, from his ugliness. Yes, he is beautiful in death — death the liberator! Mark that, you liberator, who cannot even liberate a drunkard from his evil passion!

TEMPTER: Crime as punishment! Yes, that's not bad. That's quite deep.

CONFESSOR: Yes, I think so. Now you've a new theme for debate.

TEMPTER: I think I'll leave you two gentlemen for a while. We shall meet again soon. [*Goes.*]

CONFESSOR: Well! I saw you together with a lady just now. So there are still temptations.

STRANGER: Not the way you mean.

CONFESSOR: How, then?

STRANGER: I could still imagine myself reconciled to life and women — through a woman. And through the woman who was once my wife and who now, purified and ennobled by sorrow and privation, has become what I once believed her to be. But —

CONFESSOR: But?

STRANGER: Experience has taught me that the nearer we are to each other, the farther we are, and the farther, the nearer.

CONFESSOR: I knew that from the beginning. Even Dante knew it, who all his life possessed Beatrice's soul, and Beethoven knew it, who was wedded in her absence to Theresa von Brunswick, another man's wife.

STRANGER: And yet . . . I can find salvation only through her.

CONFESSOR: Stay near her, then.

STRANGER: You forget one thing. We are divorced.

CONFESSOR: Good. Then a new marriage can begin, and a more promising one, since you are both new people.

STRANGER: Do you think — anyone would marry us?

CONFESSOR: I? That's asking too much.

STRANGER: I'd forgotten. But I suppose we shall find someone. But it won't be so easy to find a home.

CONFESSOR: You are sometimes lucky, though you don't want to know it. Down there by the river stands a little house,

quite new — the owner has never seen it. He was an English-
man who was going to get married, but at the last moment
she broke it off. His lawyer built it, and neither of the betrothed couple ever set eyes on it. So it's quite virgin.

STRANGER: Is it for rent?

CONFESSOR: Yes.

STRANGER: Right; then I'll take the plunge. And try to
start life afresh!

CONFESSOR: And go down?

STRANGER: Out of the clouds. Down there the sun still
shines. I find the air up here somewhat thin.

CONFESSOR: Right. Then we part again. For a while.

STRANGER: Where will you go?

CONFESSOR: Upwards.

STRANGER: And I downwards. To the earth, to the
mother with the soft breasts and the warm lap —

CONFESSOR: Until you long again for what is hard, and
cold and white. Farewell. Greet them down there from me.

They go their separate ways.

Scene 5

*A beautiful panelled dining-room, with a majolica-
tiled stove. In the centre of the room is a table covered
to profusion with flowers in vases. Two candelabra,
with many lighted candles. A large carved sideboard,
left. Right, two windows. Upstage, two doors. The left
one is open and reveals the* LADY's *salon, decorated
in light green and mahogany brown. A standard-lamp
of brass with a big lemon-yellow shade is lit. The right-
hand door is shut. Left, behind the sideboard, is the
entrance from the hall.*

Enter left the STRANGER *dressed as a bride-groom and the* LADY *dressed as a bride, radiant with youth and beauty.*

STRANGER: Welcome to my house, my beloved. To your home and my home, my bride. *Your* home, my wife.

LADY: Thank you, dearest. It is like a fairy tale!

STRANGER: Yes; a fairy tale. Which I have written for you.

They sit on either side of the table.

LADY: Is this real? It seems to me too beautiful.

STRANGER: I never saw you so young, so beautiful.

LADY: It is your eyes —

STRANGER: Which have learned to see. It was your goodness that taught them.

LADY: I learned through grief.

STRANGER: Ingeborg!

LADY: That is the first time you have called me by my name.

STRANGER: The first? I've never met Ingeborg before. I've never known you before, you who sit here in our home. Home! Blessed word — blessed possession, that I have never had before. Home and wife! You are my first, my only wife, for what *was, is* no longer, any more than the hour which has just passed.

LADY: Orpheus! You have sung life and beauty into these dead stones. Sing life into me too —

STRANGER: Eurydice, whom I brought back from the underworld! I will love life into you, I shall make a poem out of you. Now we shall find happiness, for we know the perils that we must avoid.

LADY: The perils, yes. . . It's so wonderful in here. It's as though the rooms were filled with invisible guests, welcoming us. Good spirits, blessing us and our home.

STRANGER: The candle-flames stand still in prayer; the flowers are thinking — and yet —

LADY: Hush! Out there sleeps the summer night, warm and dark. The stars hang huge and full of tears in the pines like Christmas candles. This is salvation. Hold it fast!

STRANGER [*to himself*]: And yet —

LADY: Hush!

STRANGER [*gets up*]: I hear a poem coming. It is yours.

LADY: You mustn't tell it to me. I can read it in your eyes.

STRANGER: I read it in yours. Anyway, I can't speak it, for it has no words. It has smell, it has colour — and if I spoke it, it would die. What is unborn is most beautiful. What is unachieved is dearest.

LADY: Hush! Our guests will go.

Silence.

STRANGER: This is happiness. But I cannot grasp it.

LADY: See it, breathe it. It is not there to be grasped.

Silence.

STRANGER: You are looking at your little room.

LADY: As green and light as a midsummer meadow. And someone is there. People!

STRANGER: My thoughts.

LADY: Your good and beautiful thoughts.

STRANGER: Which you have given me.

LADY: Had I something to give you, then?

STRANGER: You? Everything! But my hands were not free to receive them before. Not pure enough to touch your heart —

LADY: My dearest. At last we are finding reconciliation.

STRANGER: With mankind, and woman — through a woman! Yes, it has happened. Blessed be thou amongst women.

> *The lamp and the candles go out. The room becomes dark, though a faint light is visible from the yellow-shaded brass lamp in the* LADY's *room.*

LADY: Why has it grown dark? Ah!

STRANGER: Where are you, my dearest? Give me your hand. I'm afraid.

LADY: Here, my love.

STRANGER: That little hand, that was offered me in the darkness, that led me over stones and thorns. That soft, dear hand. Lead me to the light, to your warm, bright room, green like hope.

LADY [*leads him to the green room*]: Are you afraid?

STRANGER: White dove, with you the fearful eagle seeks shelter, while the thunder threatens; for the dove is at peace; she has not angered the powers of heaven —

> *They have reached the doorway. The curtain falls.*

Scene 6

> *The same. The table has been cleared, and the* LADY *is seated at it, doing nothing. She seems bored. Downstage right a window is open. Silence.*

STRANGER [*enters, with a sheet of paper in his hand*]: Listen to this.

LADY [*abstracted, submissive*]: Finished already?

STRANGER: Already? Are you serious? It took me seven days to write this one poem. [*Silence.*] Perhaps it will bore you?

LADY [*drily*]: No, not at all. [*The* STRANGER *sits at the table and looks at the* LADY.] Why are you looking at me?

STRANGER: I wanted to see your thoughts.

LADY: You've heard them.

STRANGER: That's nothing. I want to see them. [*Pause.*] What one says is the least important. [*Pause.*] May I read it? No, I mustn't. You're tired of me. [*She seems to want to speak.*] Your face says to me: enough! Now you have sucked me dry, eaten me hollow, killed me, my self, my personality. Now I reply: how, my beloved? I killed you, I who wanted to give you all of me, who let you take the best of me, that I had acquired through long experience and wanderings through the deserts and oases of art and poetry —

LADY: I don't deny it. But it wasn't mine.

STRANGER: Yours? What is yours? Other people's!

LADY: And yours? Other people's!

STRANGER: No! What I have lived is mine, and no one else's. What I have read has become mine, because I broke it to pieces like glass, re-smelted it and, from the shapeless mass, blew new glass, in new forms.

LADY: Fine. But I cannot become yours —

STRANGER: I have become yours.

LADY: What did you get from me?

STRANGER: You ask that?

LADY: And yet — I can't see that you think it. But I feel that you feel it is so. You wish I was far away.

STRANGER: I must be a distance from you to be able to see you. Now you are too close for me to focus on you, and your picture is indistinct.

LADY: The nearer, the farther!

STRANGER: Exactly. But when we part, we long for each other. And when we meet again, we long to part.

LADY: Do you think we love each other, then?

STRANGER: Yes. But not like ordinary people. Like extraordinary people. We are two water-drops that fear to come too close lest they should cease to be two and become one.

LADY: This time we knew the perils and wanted to avoid them. It looks as though they weren't to be avoided.

STRANGER: Perhaps they weren't perils, but hard necessities written into the immortal design like laws. [*Silence.*] Your love always felt like hatred. And when you made me happy, you envied me the happiness you had given me. And when you saw me unhappy, then you loved me.

LADY: Shall I leave you?

STRANGER: Then I shall die.

LADY: And if I stay, I shall die.

STRANGER: Let us die together, and live our love in a higher life — *our* love, which seems not to be of this world — in another room, where distance and closeness do not exist, where two are one, where speech and time and space are otherwise than here.

LADY: I wanted to die. But I don't want to . . . I think I am already dead.

STRANGER: The air is too strong up here.

LADY: You don't love me, if you can talk like that.

STRANGER: To be honest, there are moments when you don't exist for me. But there are moments when I feel your hatred like a suffocating smoke. Literally.

LADY: And when you are angry with me, I feel as though my heart was creeping out of my breast.

STRANGER: Then we hate each other —

LADY: And love each other —

STRANGER: And hate each other because we love each other. We hate each other because we are bound to each other; we hate the bond, we hate love; we hate the most beautiful thing, which is the bitterest thing, the best life has to offer. We are finished.

LADY: Yes.

STRANGER: What a farce life is if one takes it seriously! And what a tragedy if one plays the clown! You were to lead me towards the light. Your gentler destiny was to make mine gentler; I was to lift you over the marsh and the quicksands. But you longed to be back down there, and you wanted to convince me that down there was up here. Is it possible, I ask myself, that you took over the evil that was in me when I was freed from it, and that your goodness entered into me? If I have done you evil, I ask your pardon, and kiss the little hand that caressed and tore me — the little hand that led me into the darkness — led me on the long road to Damascus.

LADY: Is this goodbye? [*Silence.*] Goodbye, then?

> *Silence. She goes. The* STRANGER *collapses on a chair by the table. The* TEMPTER *pokes his head in through the window and rests there on his elbows, smoking a cigarette.*

TEMPTER: Ah, well. *C'est l'amour.* The mystery of mysteries, the riddle of riddles, the unpredictable of unpredictables.

STRANGER: Are you here?

TEMPTER: Always present when there's a row. And where love is, there are always rows.

STRANGER: Always?

TEMPTER: Always. I was at a silver wedding yesterday. Twenty-five years — that's not to be sniffed at — and they'd quarrelled for twenty-five years. Their whole love-relationship had been one long row, with a lot of small ones thrown in. And yet, they loved each other, they thanked each other for all the good times they'd had; the bad ones were forgotten, rubbed out. For a moment's happiness makes up for ten days' hell of kicking and biting. Yes; anyone who isn't prepared to take the bad won't get the good. The outer layers are bitter, bitter, but the little fruit inside is sweet.

STRANGER: It's horribly little.

TEMPTER: My dear friend, it is little, but good. But, tell me, why did your Madonna run away? No answer, because he doesn't know. Well, now we'll have to sub-let that villa. Here's the board. I'll hang it out. "For hire." One leaves, another comes. *C'est la vie, quoi?* Rooms for travellers.

STRANGER: Have you been married?

TEMPTER: Why, yes.

STRANGER: Why did that break up?

TEMPTER: Mainly — I don't know, perhaps it's a peculiarity of mine — mainly because — well, you know how a man marries to have a home to come home to, and a woman so as to get out. She wanted to get out, and I wanted to get in. I was so constituted that I couldn't go out with her because I felt she was soiled by other men's glances. In company, my wonderful wife became a grimacing little marmoset whom I couldn't bear to look at. So, I had to stay at home. And then, she stayed away. And when I saw her next, she was another person. She, my white virgin parchment, was scrawled with crows'-feet; her lovely clear features were distorted into reflections of the satyr-masks of other men; in her eyes I saw miniature photographs of bull-fighters and hussars. In her voice I heard the strange tones of strangers' voices; on our piano, which hitherto had known only classical harmonies, she now strummed strangers' jangling trivia; our table was littered with the literary choices of strangers. To sum up, my whole existence was perverted into a spiritual concubinage with men I had never met — which was against my nature, which has always craved women. And — need I say it? — the taste of these strange gentlemen was always diametrically opposed to my own. She developed a positive genius for sniffing out what I detested. She called it "protecting her personality". Can you understand that?

STRANGER: I understand it, but I wouldn't try to explain.

TEMPTER: And yet this woman swore that she loved me; and that I didn't love her. But I loved her so much that I didn't want to talk to anyone else — I felt I was being unfaithful to her if I found pleasure in anyone else's company, even a man's. I'd married to find female companionship, and to get this I gave up my friends; I'd married to find companionship, and instead found utter loneliness. So I kept house and home to provide a female companion for men I'd never met. *C'est l'amour, mon ami.*

STRANGER: One should never talk about one's wife.

TEMPTER: No. For if one praises her, people laugh, and if one speaks ill of her, everyone feels sorry for her. And if in the former instance one asks why they are laughing, one gets no answer.

STRANGER: Yes! One never really knows the woman one is married to. One never really gets hold of her — it's as though she didn't exist. What is woman?

TEMPTER: I don't know. Perhaps a grub or a chrysalis, from whose dozing life a man will some day be born. She is like a child, but is not one; is a kind of child, but not like one. She strains down when man pulls up, and pulls up when man strains down.

STRANGER: She always wants to hold an opinion opposite to her husband's; always expresses sympathy for what he hates; is the coarsest thing in existence beneath the most delicate surface; the most evil, beneath the tenderest. And yet! Every time I have been in love, the experience has always ennobled me —

TEMPTER: You, yes. But what about her?

STRANGER: Her? She has always developed backwards

during the period of our love. And has become coarser, and more malignant.

TEMPTER: Can you explain that?

STRANGER: No. But once, when I tried to solve these riddles by assuming that I was in the wrong, I decided that she was absorbing all that was evil in me and I all that was good in her.

TEMPTER: Do you think woman especially false?

STRANGER: Yes and no. That she tries to hide her weaknesses only means that she is ambitious and has a sense of shame. Only whores are honest, and that's why they're cynical.

TEMPTER: Say something a little kinder about women.

STRANGER: Once I had a girl. She soon noticed that when I drank I became uglier than usual; so she begged me to give it up. I remember one evening, we'd been talking for hours in a café. When it got towards ten o'clock she told me to go home and not drink any more. We said goodnight and parted. A few days later I learned that she had left me that evening to go on to a big party where she had drunk till morning. "Well," I said — and at that time I looked only for good in women — "she wished me well, but had to befoul herself this once to advance her career."

TEMPTER: That's a noble thought, and a defensible one. She wanted you to be better than she was, higher and purer, so that she could look up to you. Can you argue that away equally nobly? Woman is always malignant towards her husband, and discontented with him, and he is always good and grateful to her. He does everything to meet her wishes, and she does everything to torment him.

STRANGER: That isn't true. It can look like that sometimes, of course. Yes, I once had a girl who attributed to me all the faults she had herself. For example, she was deeply in love with herself, and so called me egotistical. She drank, and called me a boozer. She seldom changed her linen, and called me dirty. She was jealous, even of my men friends, and called me Othello. She was domineering, and called me Nero. She was mean, and called me Harpagon.

TEMPTER: Why didn't you answer her?

STRANGER: You know why. If I'd ever told her what she was like, I'd have lost her. And it was her I wanted.

TEMPTER: At any price! Yes, that's the fountain-spring of humiliation. You got used to holding your tongue, and found yourself caught in a web of falsehoods.

STRANGER: Wait a moment. Don't you think married people mix their personalities, so that they can't distinguish between Mine and Yours, can't differentiate their personalities or tell one's faults from the other's? My jealous mistress who called me Othello confused me with herself — identified me with herself —

TEMPTER: It sounds a plausible theory.

STRANGER: Yes — you see, one can get much deeper into the root of things if one stops asking: "Whose fault is it?" When husbands and wives fall out, it's a kingdom divided against itself, which is the greatest of all disharmonies.

TEMPTER: There are moments when I believe that a woman cannot love a man.

STRANGER: Perhaps. For to love is an active verb, and woman is a passive noun. He loves, she is loved; he asks, she only answers.

TEMPTER: Then what is woman's love?

STRANGER: Her man's.

TEMPTER: Good! And that's why, when her husband ceases to love her, she is free of him.

STRANGER: Then, yes; but also —

TEMPTER: Hush! Someone's coming. A visitor!

STRANGER: A lady or gentleman?

TEMPTER: A lady. . . and a gentleman. But. . . the gentleman is staying outside. He's turning and going towards the forest. That's interesting!

STRANGER: Who is it!

TEMPTER: Well; look for yourself.

STRANGER [*looks out through the window*] : It is she! My first love —

TEMPTER: Who seems now to have left her second husband. . . and is coming here with number three, who, to judge from certain movements of his back and calves, seems to be slinking off after a somewhat stormy scene. Well, well! But she has not perceived his sly purpose. Very interesting! I'll hide and listen.

   He disappears. The FIRST WIFE *knocks.*

STRANGER: Come in.

   She enters. Silence.

FIRST WIFE [*confused*]: I came to lease a flat —

STRANGER: By all means.

FIRST WIFE [*hesitates*]: If I had known, I would not have come.

STRANGER: What difference does it make?

FIRST WIFE: May I sit down for a moment? I am tired.

STRANGER: Please.

   They sit on opposite sides of the table, as the STRANGER *and the* LADY *had done in the preceding scene.*

STRANGER: It's a long time since we sat like this.

FIRST WIFE: With flowers and candles on the table. One evening —

STRANGER: When I was dressed as a bridegroom and you as a bride —

FIRST WIFE: And the candle-flames stood still in prayer, and the flowers mused —

STRANGER: Is your husband outside?

FIRST WIFE: No.

STRANGER: You are still looking for — what does not exist?

FIRST WIFE: Doesn't it?

STRANGER: No. And I always told you so. But you didn't believe me, but had to find out for yourself. Have you found out now?

FIRST WIFE: Not yet.

STRANGER: Why did you leave your husband? [*Silence.*] Did he hit you?

FIRST WIFE: Yes.

STRANGER: How could he so forget himself?

FIRST WIFE: He was angry.

STRANGER: Why was he angry?

FIRST WIFE: For nothing.

STRANGER: Why was he angry for nothing?

FIRST WIFE [*rises*] : No, thank you. I'm not going to sit here and take insults. Where is your wife?

STRANGER: She has just left me.

FIRST WIFE: Why?

STRANGER: Why did you leave me?

FIRST WIFE: Because I felt how you wanted to leave me. In order not to be left alone, I went.

STRANGER: I suppose you're right. But how did you read my thoughts?

FIRST WIFE [*sits again*]: How? We didn't need to talk to reveal our thoughts.

STRANGER: But we did one thing wrong when we lived together. We accused each other of evil thoughts before they had become actions. Instead of living in reality, we lived in what was implied. For example, I once saw you accept with pleasure the unclean glances of a stranger, and accused you of infidelity.

FIRST WIFE: You were wrong — but you were right. My thoughts sinned.

STRANGER: Don't you think my habit of accusing you in advance stopped you doing wrong?

FIRST WIFE: Let me think. Yes, you're right. But in my anger at your incessant spying on my private thoughts, which belonged to me —

STRANGER: No, they belonged to both of us —

FIRST WIFE: If you like. But I regarded them as mine, and felt you had no right to intrude there. And when you did, I hated you, and in self-defence I accused you of being suspicious to the point of insanity. Now I can say it — your suspiciousness was never unjustified. It was really clairvoyance.

STRANGER: Ah! . . . Do you know, in the night-time, after we had said goodnight and gone to sleep as friends, I could still wake and feel your hatred spraying poison over me so that I had to leave our bed to avoid being suffocated. One night I woke and felt a pressure on my brain. I saw you were lying awake holding your hand near my mouth. I thought you were getting me to inhale poison from a bottle, and to make sure, I seized your hand.

FIRST WIFE: I remember.

STRANGER: What did you do then?

FIRST WIFE: Nothing. I just hated you.

STRANGER: Why did you hate me?

FIRST WIFE: Because you were my husband. Because I ate your bread.

STRANGER: Do you think it is always like this?

FIRST WIFE: I don't know. I expect so.

STRANGER: But you despised me sometimes, too.

FIRST WIFE: Yes, when you were ridiculous. A man in love is always ridiculous. Do you know the definition of absurdity? It's a man in love. Like a cock!

STRANGER: If every man who loves you women is ridiculous, how can you love them back?

FIRST WIFE: We don't. We put up with them. And look for someone else, who does not love us.

STRANGER: But when he begins to love you too, do you then look for a third?

FIRST WIFE: Perhaps.

STRANGER: Strange! [*Silence.*] I remember you always used to have an obsession for a type you called the Toreador, which I translated as knacker! In the end you got your Toreador. He gave you no children and didn't even keep you; he just beat you. The Toreador is always a brawler. [*Silence.*] One day I decided to try to compete with the Toreador. I began to cycle, take exercise, fence, etcetera. But then you began to loathe me. In other words: the husband must not be like that, but the lover may. Then you started getting obsessed with page-boys. That one who sat on the Brussels carpet and read bad poetry — my good poetry wasn't good enough for you. Is that a page-boy you've got now?

FIRST WIFE: Yes. But his poetry isn't bad.

STRANGER: Oh yes it is, my dear. I know him! He has borrowed my rhythms and turned them into organ-grinders' jingles.

FIRST WIFE [*gets up and goes towards the door*]: You're foul!

TEMPTER [*enters the door with a letter in his hand*]: A letter for you, madam.

> *He hands it to her. She reads it and collapses on to a chair.*

TEMPTER: A little farewell note. Ah, well. Everything's difficult at first — especially in love — and he who hasn't the patience to survive the early difficulties doesn't win the golden apples. Page-boys are always impatient! Unknown youth, have you had enough now?

STRANGER [*rises and takes his hat*]: Poor Anna.

FIRST WIFE: Don't leave me.

STRANGER: Yes, my friend. I must.

FIRST WIFE: Don't go. You were the best I had, in spite of everything —

TEMPTER: Are you two going to start again too? Well, it'd be a sure way to end this; for as sure as they get each other, they lose each other. What is love? Say something witty, each of you, before we part.

FIRST WIFE: I don't know what it is. All that is noblest and and most beautiful, and it has to decline into all that is foulest and most ugly.

STRANGER: A caricature of divine love.

TEMPTER: A plant that lives one year. It blooms during the engagement, goes to seed during marriage, and then droops towards the earth to wither and die.

FIRST WIFE: The most beautiful flowers do not seed. The rose is the flower of love.

STRANGER: And the lily that of innocence. It can seed, but will not open its white cup to anything but kisses.

TEMPTER: But reproduces itself by means of buds, from which new lilies spring as chaste Athene sprang fully grown from Zeus' head, not from his royal loins. Yes, my children,

I have come to understand many things, but not this: what my soul's beloved has to do with — [*Hesitates.*]

STRANGER: Say it.

TEMPTER: What true love, which is the marriage of souls, has to do with reproduction.

STRANGER *and* FIRST WIFE: Exactly!

TEMPTER: I have never understood how a kiss, which is an unborn word, a silent speech, a dumb language of two souls, can, by a sacred act, be transformed into — a surgical operation, which always ends in weeping and gnashing of teeth. I have never understood why that sacred first night, which should be the marriage of two souls in love, must end in bloodshed, strife, hatred, mutual contempt and — the mincing machine. [*Puts his hand over his mouth.*]

STRANGER: Perhaps that theory about the Fall is true. "In sorrow shalt thou bring forth children. . . "

TEMPTER: Yes. That one could understand —

FIRST WIFE: Who is this man?

STRANGER: Only a wanderer on life's quicksands.

The FIRST WIFE *rises.*

TEMPTER: Ready to go? Who goes first?

STRANGER: I.

TEMPTER: Where?

STRANGER: Upwards.

TEMPTER: I'll stay down here, halfway between —

Scene 7

The Gothic chapter hall. Upstage, open arcades lead out to the cloister and the monastery garden, in the centre of which can be seen a fountain with a portrait of Our Lady surrounded by tall white roses. Along the walls of the chapter hall, and fastened to them, are oaken choir-stalls. The PRIOR's *is in the centre of the wall on the right, somewhat raised. In the centre of the hall is a huge crucifix. The sun is shining on the portrait of Our Lady in the garden.*

The STRANGER *enters upstage. He is dressed in a coarse black monk's cloak, with a rope round his waist and sandals on his feet. He stops in the doorway and surveys the hall; then he walks to the crucifix and halts in front of it. The last verse of a hymn is heard from beyond the garden. The* CONFESSOR *enters upstage, dressed in black and white, with long hair, a long beard, and a very small tonsure which is barely noticeable.*

CONFESSOR: Peace be with you.

STRANGER: And with you.

CONFESSOR: What do you think of the white house?

STRANGER: I can only see black as yet —

CONFESSOR: You *are* still black; but you shall become so white, so white! Have you slept well this night?

STRANGER: Like a tired child. But tell me: why do I find so many closed doors?

CONFESSOR: You will gradually learn to open them.

STRANGER: It seems a large building.

CONFESSOR: It is boundless. It was started in the reign of Charlemagne, and has grown unchecked, thanks to the generosity of pious foundations. Undisturbed by the spiritual tempests and changes of the centuries, it stands upon its mountain as a monument to Western civilization: Christian faith buttressed by the wisdom of Greece and Rome.

STRANGER: It's not just a place of religion, then?

CONFESSOR: No. It embraces all the arts and sciences too. Libraries and museums, an observatory, laboratories — you will see them. We have farms and orchards too, and a hospital for laymen, with our own sulphur springs —

STRANGER: One question before the Chapter comes. Who is the Prior?

CONFESSOR [smiles]: He is — the Prior. Alone, incomparable, dwelling on the summits of human knowledge, and — well, you will soon see him.

STRANGER: Is it true that he is so old?

CONFESSOR: He has attained to an unusual age. He was born at the beginning of this century, which is now nearing its end.

STRANGER: And he has not always been a religious?

CONFESSOR: Not always a monk, but always a man of God. He was a minister once, seventy years ago; was twice University Chancellor; and an Archbishop — hush! The mass is ended.

STRANGER: He isn't one of those "advanced" priests, who pretends to vices he doesn't possess?

CONFESSOR: By no means. But he has seen life, and knows human nature, and is more human than priestly.

STRANGER: What about the other monks?

CONFESSOR: Wise men of strange and varied destinies —

STRANGER: Who have never really lived?

CONFESSOR: They have all lived, and many times. They have suffered shipwreck, started life afresh, gone to the bottom, risen again. You will meet them.

STRANGER: But it is the Prior who will question me. Don't think I intend to say yes to everything —

CONFESSOR: On the contrary. You must be yourself, and defend your views to the last ditch.

STRANGER: Do they allow one to say No here?

CONFESSOR: Here? You are a child, who have been living
in a child's world, where you played with thoughts and
words. And you lived under the illusion that something so
material as language could clothe something as subtle as
thoughts and feelings. We, who have discovered this to be
an illusion, we speak as little as possible, for we see and
sense what lies in each of our hearts. Through spiritual
exercises we have trained our senses so that we form a
single chain, and when complete agreement reigns among
us we experience a feeling of passion and harmony. The
Prior, who has the longest experience of such training,
feels when anyone's thoughts stray; he is like, in certain
respects, an engineer's galvanometer which registers when
and where there occurs a break in the line. So we can have
no secrets from each other, and therefore do not need
confession. Remember this well, when you stand before
the Prior's all-searching eye.

STRANGER: Is he going to cross-examine me?

CONFESSOR: Oh, no. Just a few customary questions,
with no hidden significance, before you face the practical
trials. Hush, here they are.

> He moves aside. The PRIOR enters upstage. He is
> dressed completely in white, with a raised white hood.
> He is a big man with long white hair, and a long white
> beard — the head of a Zeus. His face is pale but plump
> and unwrinkled. His eyes are big and surrounded by
> shadows, with powerful eyebrows. He radiates a still,
> majestic calm. He is followed by TWELVE FATHERS
> in black and white, with black cloaks and raised hoods.
> They all walk past the crucifix, bow, and proceed to
> their places.

PRIOR [after studying the STRANGER for some time]:
What do you seek here?

> The STRANGER is confused, searches for an answer,
> but finds none.

PRIOR [*gently, patriarchally, indulgently*]: Peace? Do you not?

The STRANGER *nods and silently mouths assent.*

PRIOR: But since life is an unending battle, how will you find peace among the living?

The STRANGER *cannot answer.*

PRIOR: You want to turn your back on life, because you felt that life had betrayed you — perhaps been unjust to you?

STRANGER [*whispers*]: Yes.

PRIOR: So you were the victim of injustice. And these injustices began so early in your childhood that you, an innocent child, could not imagine that you had committed any crime worthy of punishment. Well, once you were unjustly accused of stealing fruit; you were tormented into admitting the offence, tortured into telling lies and begging forgiveness for a fault you had not committed. Was it not so?

STRANGER [*in a firm voice*]: It was so.

PRIOR: Good. It was so. And you have never been able to forget it. Never! Now listen. You have a good memory. Do you remember *The Swiss Family Robinson*?

STRANGER [*starts*]: The Swiss Family Robinson?

PRIOR: Yes. Your history of torture dates from 1857, but around Christmas 1856, the previous year, you tore up a copy of *The Swiss Family Robinson* and, for fear of punishment, hid it under a cupboard in the pantry — [*The* STRANGER *stands amazed and crushed.*] The cupboard was oak-veneered, and there were clothes hanging in the upper part, and shoes in the lower. It seemed to you an enormous cupboard, for you were a little child, and it never occurred to you that it could be moved. But it could, and during a spring-cleaning that Easter the hidden evidence came to light. Fear drove you to blame it on a friend, and now it was he who had to undergo the torture, because appearances were against him and you had the reputation of honesty. Your history of torment dates from this event, and is its logical conclusion. You admit the logic?

STRANGER: Yes. Punish me.

CONFESSOR: No. I am no punisher, and I did similar things myself when I was a child. But will you now promise, for the rest of your life, to forget this private Calvary of yours and never to speak of it again?

STRANGER: I promise. If only the person I wronged could forgive me!

PRIOR: He has already done so. Am I not right, Father Isidor?

FATHER ISIDOR (*the* DOCTOR) [*rises*] : With all my heart.

STRANGER: Is it you?

FATHER ISIDOR: It is I.

PRIOR [*to* FATHER ISIDOR]: Father Isidor, say a word more. Just a word.

FATHER ISIDOR: Very well. It was in the year 1856 that I underwent this torture. But two years earlier I had already made one of my brothers undergo the same suffering by reason of a false accusation I had made against him. [*To* STRANGER.] So we are all guilty, and none of us is pure; and I don't suppose my victim had a clean conscience either. [*Sits.*]

PRIOR: Imagine if we all had to settle our accounts with each other, and with Eternal Justice! We are born with Adam's inheritance of sin. However — [*To* STRANGER.] You wanted to know something? Didn't you?

STRANGER: I wanted to know the innermost meaning of life.

PRIOR: The innermost? Then you wanted to know what no man may know. Father Uriel!

FATHER URIEL, *who is blind, rises.*

PRIOR [*to* STRANGER]: Look at this blind father. We call him Uriel, in memory of Uriel Acosta, of whom you perhaps know? [*The* STRANGER *shakes his head.*] Well; every young person ought to know about him. Uriel Acosta was a Portuguese of Jewish origin, but was brought up in the Christian faith. When he was still quite young he began to doubt — you understand — to doubt whether Christ really was God, and as a result he became converted to the Jewish faith. Then he began to doubt the teaching of Moses and the immortality of the soul, and as a result was handed over by the Rabbis to the Christian church to be punished. After a while he returned to the synagogue and the Jewish faith again. But his lust for knowledge knew no bounds and he continued his investigations until he found himself faced by a blank wall; and in despair at his failure to penetrate the ultimate mystery he took his life with a pistol. Look now at our good Father Uriel. He was once very young, and wanted to know; he always wanted to be in the forefront of every movement, and was a great discoverer of new philosophies. Incidentally, we were friends as boys; he is almost as old as I am. Well, around 1820 he began to discover the so-called philosophy of enlightenment, which had already been dead and buried for twenty years. Through this philosophy, which was a kind of panacea, a man could unlock every door, solve every riddle and vanquish every adversary. Everything became clear and simple. He was by now a confirmed opponent of all religions, and especially persecuted the mesmerists, as hypnotists were then called. In 1830, our friend became a Hegelian, a little late of course. Then he discovered God again, but in Nature and in Man himself, so that he found himself to be a little God. But unfortunately there were two Hegels, just as there were two Voltaires, and one of them, the later or right-wing Hegel, had evolved his Pantheism into a compromise with Christianity; so Father Uriel, anxious not to be behind the times, became a rationalist Christian, with the unfortunate consequence that he now had to challenge both rationalism and himself. For Father Uriel's sake, I shall cut this long, sad story short. In 1850, he became a materialist and, once again, an opponent of Christianity. In 1870 he became a hypnotist, in 1880 a theosophist, and in 1890 he decided to shoot himself. That was when I met him again. He was sitting on a bench in the Unter den Linden, and was blind. Uriel blind! And Uriel means: "God my light", and this was he who had spent a century brandishing the torch of knowledge at the head of every modern movement! [*To* STRANGER.] He wanted to know the meaning of life, you see; but it was not granted to him. So, now he *believes*. Is there anything else you wish to know?

STRANGER: I should like to ask one question.

PRIOR: Yes?

STRANGER: If Father Uriel had stayed with his first belief since 1810, people would have called him conservative or old-fashioned, but since he followed the natural development of the times and gave up his early faith, people say he abandoned the cause. In other words, whatever he had done, they would have abused him.

PRIOR: Do you mind what people say? Father Clemens, may I tell your story, how you minded what people said?

FATHER CLEMENS *rises and nods.*

PRIOR: Father Clemens is our greatest portrait-painter. In the world outside he is known by another name, and is widely famed. Well; Father Clemens was young in 1830. He felt a vocation for painting, and devoted himself to it with all his soul. The public, the critics, his teachers, his parents, all were agreed that he had mistaken his vocation, and the young Clemens minded what people said. He gave it up and turned to industry. He became a printer. When he was fifty, with his life behind him, his early paintings were discovered by a stranger, and were now acclaimed as masterpieces by the public, the critics, the teachers and his family. But now it was too late. And when Father Clemens complained of the world's cruelty, the world replied with a heartless grin: "Why did you let yourself

be fooled?" This so grieved Father Clemens that he came
here to us. And now he grieves no longer. Is it not so,
Father Clemens?

FATHER CLEMENS: That is correct. But that is not the
end of the story. My paintings of 1830 hung in a museum,
and were admired, until 1880. Then taste suddenly changed.
and one day it stood written in a respected newspaper that
my paintings were a disgrace to the museum. So they were
removed to the attic.

PRIOR [to STRANGER]: It's a good story, don't you
think?

FATHER CLEMENS: That isn't all. For by 1890 taste had
changed again, and a Professor in the Academy of Arts
wrote that it was a disgrace to the nation that my masterpieces should be hanging in an attic. So they were brought
down again and are now regarded as classics. But for how
long? There you see, young man, the worth of mortal fame!
Vanitas vanitatum vanitas!

STRANGER: Then is life worth living?

PRIOR: Ask Father Melchior, who has been tried, not
merely in the world of illusions, but also in that of errors,
untruths and contradictions. Go with him, and he will show
you our picture gallery, and tell you stories.

STRANGER: I will gladly go with anyone who can teach me
anything.

FATHER MELCHIOR *leads the* STRANGER *by the
hand out of the hall.*

Scene 8

*A picture gallery in the monastery. Most of the pictures
are portraits, and all of them have two heads.*

FATHER MELCHIOR: Well; first, a little landscape by an

unknown master. It is called *The Two Towers*. Perhaps you have been to Switzerland and seen the originals?

STRANGER: I have been to Switzerland.

FATHER MELCHIOR: Well. At the station of Amsteg on the Gotthard railway, you have seen a tower called Zwing-Uri; Schiller mentions it in *William Tell*. It stands there as a memorial to the horrible sufferings endured by the natives of Uri under the German emperors. Beautiful! And on the other, the Italian side of the Gotthard Pass, stands, as you know, the station of Bellinzona. There are many towers there, but the most remarkable is Castel d'Uri — a memorial to the horrible sufferings endured by the Italian cantons at the hands of the natives of Uri. You get the point?

STRANGER: You mean, freedom means the freedom to oppress others. That's my latest discovery!

FATHER MELCHIOR: Then we will proceed immediately to the portraits. Number One in the catalogue: Boccaccio. With two heads — all our portraits have two heads, at least. His story is well known. This great man started by writing licentious and godless romances dedicated to Queen Johanna of Naples, who seduced the son of St Birgitta. Boccaccio ended as a holy man in a monastery and had to lecture on Dante's Hell and the devils, which in his youth he had believed himself able to exorcise in a most extraordinary way. You see how the two faces regard each other, in confrontation?

STRANGER: Yes. But they lack the humour one would have expected in a man with such self-knowledge as friend Boccaccio.

FATHER MELCHIOR: Number Two. Yes — the two-headed Doctor Luther. The youthful champion of tolerance and the old defender of intolerance. Enough?

STRANGER: Quite enough.

FATHER MELCHIOR: Number Three, the great Gustav

Adolf, from your own country, receiving Catholic gold
from Cardinal Richelieu in order to fight for Protestantism
with an assurance of neutrality from the Catholic League.

STRANGER: How do the Catholics explain this triple
contradiction?

FATHER MELCHIOR: They say it's a lie. Number Four.
Schiller, author of *The Robbers,* elected an Honorary
Citizen of Paris by the French revolutionaries in 1792,
although he had been Chamberlain at the Court of Mein-
ingen since 1790 and the recipient of a pension from the
King of Denmark since 1791. The portrait shows the
Court Chamberlain (and friend of His Excellency Johann
Wolfgang von Goethe) in 1798, the year he actually
received the diploma of honour from the revolutionaries.
Think of it — the diploma of the Revolution of Terror in
1798, when the Directory had taken over and the Revolution was finished. I should have liked to have seen the
Chamberlain then, and his friend the Excellency! But it's
all one, for two years later, in 1800, he repays his diploma
with *The Bell*, in which he thanks them for their kindness
and tells the revolutionaries to keep calm. Well, that's life.
But what of it? We are enlightened people, and love both
The Robbers and *The Bell*, Schiller and Goethe.

STRANGER: The work survives, the author perishes.

FATHER MELCHIOR: Goethe — yes, he's Number Five.
Began with *The Cathedral of Strasbourg* and *Götz von
Berlichingen,* two battle-hymns for Gothic German art
versus Greece and Rome. Spent the second half of his life
fighting for classicism against Germanicism. Goethe versus
Goethe. Behold the famous godlike calm, harmony,
etcetera, all warring against itself in maximum discord. But
deflation becomes depression when the young romantic
school emerges and uses Goethe's *Götz* theories to de-
nounce Goethe's *Iphigenia*. His admirers usually pass over
in silence the fact that the "Great Heathen" ended by
converting Faust, in Part Two, and letting him be saved by
the Virgin Mary and her angels. Likewise the fact that the

"Mirror of Clarity" ended by finding everything "marvellous" and "rare", even the simplest things that had previously presented him with no problems. And his final longing was for more light. Ah, well. But what of it? We are enlightened and cherish our Goethe still.

STRANGER: And rightly.

FATHER MELCHIOR: Number Six — Voltaire. He has more than two heads. The atheist who spent his whole life defending God! The mocker who was mocked because he "believed in God like a child". Creator of the cynic Candide, who sings: "O lust, in the fire of my youth, I sought thy pleasures. Soon, amazed by the emptiness, my sweetness turned to bitterness. Now in the winter of my life, I find thee vanity." And Dr Pangloss, who thought he could fathom everything between heaven and earth by science and commonsense, ends by singing thus: "The pride of genius boasted it could embrace the sphere of knowledge. O mole, didst hope to embrace the boundless heavens? My knowledge is my sorrow: that all knowledge is vanity." But what of it? Voltaire is always good for a quote. The Jews quote him against the Christians, the Christians quote him against the Jews, for he was an anti-Semite — like Luther! Chateaubriand quoted him in the name of Catholicism; today the Protestants quote him against Catholicism. A lively fellow.

STRANGER: What's your opinion of him?

FATHER MELCHIOR: We don't have opinions here. We just have faith, as I told you before. Which is why we have only one head — placed directly above the heart. However — Number Seven. Napoleon — the child of the Revolution, the People's Emperor, the Nero of Liberty, the Oppressor of Equality and the Big Brother* of Fraternity. He is the cunningest of all the two-headed monsters, for he could laugh at himself, rise above his contradictions, change skins, change souls, and, after every transformation,

* This translation is not an anachronism, but literal. Strindberg's wording is *Broderskapets "stora bror"* (Brotherhood's "big brother").

emerge pure and radiant as a new-born child, free from
doubt, convinced of his own infallibility. There's only one
man comparable to him in that respect: Kierkegaard the
Dane. He was conscious from the first of the parthogenesis
of the soul — of its ability to give birth without copulation,
to plant shoots. Accordingly, and so as not to become life's
clown, he wrote under a series of pseudonyms, each of
them representing a "Stage on the Road of Life". But do
you know what happened? The Lord of life turned him
into a clown, despite all his precautions. Kierkegaard, who
spent his whole life fighting state religion and hack preaching, was forced by sheer necessity to end up as a hack
preacher himself. Ah, well. That's the way things can be!

STRANGER: The powers mock us —

FATHER MELCHIOR: They mock mockers, they humble
the proud, especially those who think that they alone
possess truth and knowledge. Well — Number Eight. Victor
Hugo. He multiplied himself unendingly. Peer of France,
Grandee of Spain, friend of kings, socialist author of *Les
Misérables*. The aristocrats of course call him a renegade
and the socialists a reformer. Number Nine. Count Fried-
rich Leopold von Stolberg. Wrote a fanatical defence of
Protestantism, and immediately became a Catholic.
Inexplicable behaviour for a sane man. A miracle, perhaps —
a miniature trip to Damascus? Number Ten, Lafayette.
The pioneer of liberty, the revolutionary; was forced to
leave France as a supposed reactionary because he wanted
to help Louis XVI, and was seized by the Austrians and
imprisoned in Olmütz as a revolutionary. Which was he?

STRANGER: Both.

FATHER MELCHIOR: Yes. Two opposites, making a
whole, a whole man. Number Eleven, Bismarck. The great
paradox, the honest diplomat who claimed to have discovered that the telling of the truth was the most cunning
of stratagems. He was forced — by the powers, eh? — to
spend the last six years of his life revealing himself as a
deliberate liar. You're tired? Let's stop.

STRANGER: Yes, my friend. If one clings to the same ideas all one's life, and sticks to one's opinions, one becomes outdated — it's the natural course of events — and one gets called conservative, old-fashioned, stationary. And if one goes on developing, moves with the times, renews oneself with the ever-youthful spirit of the age, they call you a turncoat and a renegade.

FATHER MELCHIOR: It's as old as the world. But does a wise man care what people call him? What one is when one is born, one is!

STRANGER: Then who dictates these incessant changes in the spirit of the age?

FATHER MELCHIOR: You ought to be able to answer that yourself. The spirit of the age is promulgated by forces which are self-developing — *apparently* in circles. Hegel, the philosopher of the New Age — who was dimorphic, since people swear both by a left-wing Hegel and a right-wing Hegel — best solved the contradictions of life, history and the spirit with his magic formula: thesis, assent; antithesis, dissent; synthesis, marry the two. Young man — relatively young man! You began life by saying Yes to everything; then as a principle you said No to everything. End by marrying these two principles. Stop being exclusive. Don't say: Either — Or. Say: Both — And. In a word, or rather two words: Humanity and Resignation!

Scene 9

The sanctuary of the chapel. A coffin lies open with a pall and two lighted candles. The CONFESSOR *enters, leading by the hand the* STRANGER, *who is dressed as a novice in white linen.*

CONFESSOR: Have you carefully considered the step you are about to take?

STRANGER: Carefully.

CONFESSOR: Have you any more questions to ask?

STRANGER: More questions? No!

CONFESSOR: Then wait here while I fetch the Chapter and the Brothers, that the ceremony may begin.

STRANGER: Yes! Let it happen!

The CONFESSOR *goes. The* STRANGER *ponders alone. The* TEMPTER *enters.*

TEMPTER: Ready?

STRANGER: So ready that I have no more answers left, even for you.

TEMPTER: At the edge of the grave. I understand. You will lie in a coffin and pretend to die. The old Adam will be exorcized with three shovelfuls of earth, and they will sing a *De Profundis*. Then you will rise from the dead, having renounced your old name, and you will be rebaptized with a new name like a little new-born child. What will you be called? [*The* STRANGER *does not reply.*] It stands written there. John: Brother John, because he preached in the wilderness, and —

STRANGER: Do not trouble me.

TEMPTER: Talk to me a little before you enter the long silence. They won't let you speak for a whole year.

STRANGER: All the better! In the end, words become a vice, like drink. And why speak when the words won't hide one's thoughts?

TEMPTER: Now that you stand on the edge of the grave, was life so bitter?

STRANGER: My life was.

TEMPTER: Did you ever know joy?

STRANGER: Yes, much joy. But it was always short, and seemed designed only to make worse the pain of losing it.

TEMPTER: Couldn't one put it the other way round, that the pain was given to enhance the joy?

STRANGER: One can *say* anything —

A WOMAN *with a baby for baptism crosses the stage.*

TEMPTER: Look. Another little mortal to be consecrated to suffering.

STRANGER: Poor child.

TEMPTER: A human saga beginning.

A BRIDAL COUPLE *cross the stage.*

TEMPTER: And there! The best of life — and the bitterest. Adam and Eve in Paradise, which in a week will be a Hell and in another fortnight a Paradise again —

STRANGER: The greatest joy! The greatest! The first, the last, the only thing that made life worth living. I, too, once sat in the sunlight — on a spring day, on a verandah — under the first green leaves of spring, and a small bridal crown crowned a head, and a white veil lay like a morning mist over a face that was not mortal — ! Then came the darkness.

TEMPTER: Whence?

STRANGER: From the light itself. That's all I know.

TEMPTER: Then it was only a shadow, for a shadow needs light, but darkness needs no light.

STRANGER: Enough! Or we shall never end.

The CONFESSOR *and the* CHAPTER *enter in procession.*

TEMPTER: Goodbye. [*Vanishes.*]

CONFESSOR [*with a big, black pall*]: O Lord, grant him eternal rest.

CHOIR: And let perpetual light shine on him.

CONFESSOR [*swathes the* STRANGER *in the pall*]: May he rest in peace!

CHOIR: Amen!

Introduction to
EASTER

STRINDBERG followed the first two parts of TO DAMASCUS with another symbolic play, ADVENT. But, though a powerful and interesting work, it was rejected by the theatres and was not performed during his lifetime. Since Strindberg had no source of income apart from his pen, he returned to writing realistic plays, of which in 1899 he completed no less than four: the acid tragi-comedy THERE ARE CRIMES AND CRIMES (about the adventures of a dramatist in Paris), and three historical dramas, THE SAGA OF THE FOLKUNGS, GUSTAV VASA and ERIK THE FOURTEENTH. He had calculated correctly; by the spring of 1900 THERE ARE CRIMES AND CRIMES, GUSTAV VASA and ERIK THE FOURTEENTH had all been staged in Stockholm and, more importantly, had all been successful, and THE SAGA OF THE FOLKUNGS was to be successfully staged the following year. The tide had turned for him at last. Twenty years before, in the early 1880s, he had — thanks not to his plays, but to his non-dramatic writings such as his novel THE RED ROOM, his satire THE NEW STATE and his short stories GETTING MARRIED — been the most discussed author in Sweden; but in the intervening years his fame had sadly declined. THE FATHER (1887) had been staged only once in Sweden, and had been a disaster; MISS JULIE (1888) had not been performed in Sweden at all, and CREDITORS, written the same year, had received only a single matinée. Who can wonder that he had, for six years from 1892 to 1898, turned his back on the theatre? His only real success on the Swedish stage had been with the slight fantasy LUCKY PETER'S JOURNEY in 1883; the acclaim that had been accorded to THE FATHER and CREDITORS in Paris in 1894 had not impressed his compatriots. But now, in 1900, he found himself accepted for the first time in his own country as a dramatist who mattered.

He followed ERIC THE FOURTEENTH, one of his
very finest plays, with two of his worst, GUSTAV ADOLF
and MIDSUMMER. It was forgivable, and hardly surprising; he had written seven plays in a little over eighteen
months. What is more surprising is how quickly he returned
to his best form. Some time in the summer of 1900, after
finishing MIDSUMMER, he produced a delightful short
play about marionettes, CASPER'S SHROVE TUESDAY,
and followed that with, even for him, an exceptional burst
of creative activity. Between 9 October 1900 and 5 January
1901, a period of eighty-seven days, he started and completed four of his most famous full-length plays, EASTER,
the two parts of THE DANCE OF DEATH and THE
VIRGIN BRIDE. Most amazingly, in the three weeks
between 9 and 31 October he somehow managed to write
both EASTER and Part I of THE DANCE OF DEATH,
neither of which shows any sign of hurried composition.

EASTER is a forerunner of the "chamber plays" (such
as STORM, THE BURNT HOUSE and THE GHOST
SONATA) which he was to write for his Intimate
Theatre seven years later. Like STORM and THE BURNT
HOUSE, and unlike TO DAMASCUS and the plays that he
wrote later, EASTER is a very still play. It takes place on
Good Friday in a small provincial town, when nothing
happens. Even from the street outside, nothing is heard
save the scraping of the creditor's stick and the squeaking
of his galoshes. The family background of the Heysts is
that of Strindberg's own childhood; his memories of his
father's bankruptcy, the visits of the police and the mocking glances and whispers of the neighbours, strongly colour
the play, as does the depression he had felt during the three
summers of 1897—9, which he had spent in the then empty
university town of Lund, a place where small collegiate
matters assumed monstrous proportions like the creditor
Lime's shadow on the blind (an idea which Strindberg got
from a shadow play called THE OGRE OF SKINFLINT
MOUNTAIN, Lime's jovial nickname for himself).

The character of Elis is very much a self-portrait, of the
arrogant, self-centred and intolerant husband that

Strindberg knew himself to be (he had portrayed himself
equally mercilessly as the dramatist Maurice in THERE
ARE CRIMES AND CRIMES). Eleonora was based on his
sister Elisabeth, who two years earlier had been taken into
a mental home. He felt closer to her than to any other
member of his family. "She was like a twin to me," he
wrote to Harriet Bosse after Elisabeth's death in 1904,
enclosing her photograph, and he felt that by her sufferings she had perhaps acted as a scapegoat for the sins
and shortcomings of the whole family, just as (he believed)
he himself might have done during his INFERNO period.
Eleonora was, by Strindberg's own admission, also partly
based on the title-character in Balzac's novel SÉRAPHITA,
which Strindberg greatly admired. Séraphita, like Eleonora
(and, he might have added, Prince Myshkin in Dostoyevsky's
THE IDIOT), was regarded as insane but was really a
superior being, a visitor from another world. In INFERNO,
Strindberg had written: "Swedenborg . . . had shown me
the only way to salvation: to seek out the demons in their
lair, within myself, and to destroy them — by repentance.
Balzac, as the prophet's adjutant, had taught me in his
SÉRAPHITA that 'remorse is the impotent emotion felt
by the man who will sin again; repentance alone is effective,
and brings everything to an end.'" That is one of the main
themes of EASTER; Elis, at the beginning of the play, feels
only egocentric remorse, and slowly comes to realize that
this is not enough.

In a letter which Strindberg wrote to Harriet Bosse but
never sent, he expatiated further on the character of
Eleonora. "Because of a family tragedy, Eleonora has
entered into a state of mind which some would call sick,
whereby she enters into a rapport (telepathic), now with
her relatives, now with all mankind and finally with the
Supreme Being, so that she suffers with all living things and
becomes Christ in man." He was to create a similar character in Agnes in A DREAM PLAY, though Agnes is not
mentally unbalanced as Eleonora is. As Martin Lamm has
observed, her mental state resembles Strindberg's own
during his stay in Lund after his INFERNO crisis, when

his persecutions had ceased but his hypersensitivity and religious brooding remained, and he only half-believed that he belonged to the living. Remembering his own state of mind at that time, he insisted to the various actresses who played the part that they should "not give the traditional representation of a mad person".

The creditor Lime was probably based on a police superintendent named Lindberg whom Strindberg had known in Lund, a ferocious-looking man who turned out upon closer acquaintance to be wise and gentle. In the play Strindberg calls him Lindkvist, which means lime-twig, a deliberate reference to the lime-trees of Elis' childhood which signified the peace to which he longed to return and to which Lime finally helps him to return. ("The lime-trees stand there still, the punt lies under the willows by the shore.") Thus the word Lindkvist symbolizes both chastisement and peace; at first Elis can think of it only as signifying the former, and it is with the greatest reluctance that he at length accepts that there can be a more benevolent association. "Lime" in English has, like Lindkvist, a secondary, harsh meaning, of the lime that burns; so, it seems a better name for the creditor than a Swedish word which would be meaningless to English and American audiences.

The episode of the daffodil stemmed from a story that an astronomer named Elis Strömgren has told Strindberg. As a student, Strömgren had gone into a flower-shop one afternoon and taken a daffodil. The next day he went back and paid for it, but he and Strindberg often discussed the matter, and how narrow the gap was between a thoughtless act and a criminal one. The dove that dropped a twig at Elis' feet was an incident that had happened to Strindberg the previous Easter. "A dove, on Riddargatan," he told a friend, Nils Andersson, on 10 April 1900, "flew down before my feet, carefully deposited a twig and flew off. I tride to make myself believe it was an olive branch; but it was birch! and has been birch all the way!" The same thing happened to him more than once that spring, according to his OCCULT DIARY. The family name of Heyst, which is very un-Swedish, Strindberg took from the little Belgian resort of Heyst-sur-mer,

which he had visited in 1898.* Ironically, when Joseph
Conrad wrote his novel VICTORY in 1914, he called his
Swedish hero Heyst; one can only suppose that he had read
EASTER and assumed Heyst to be a typically Swedish name.

EASTER had its first performance at Frankfurt-am-
Main in March 1901, but it proved a fiasco. Three weeks
later, on 4 April (Maundy Thursday), came the Swedish
première, at the Royal Theatre in Stockholm, with
Harriet Bosse, who had become engaged to Strindberg the
previous month, as Eleonora; but here, too, it was tepidly
received, and managed only eight performances. It was not
until Strindberg's own Intimate Theatre revived it in 1908
that its qualities were recognized, but since then it has been
one of his most frequently performed plays in Sweden, and
indeed abroad. England first saw it, in a humble way, on 19
March 1922, when Pax Robertson staged it with a semi-
professional company for her Chelsea Art Theatre at the
Bedford Hall; she revived it several times at later Easters,
with herself as Eleonora. In 1927 Claud Gurney produced
it at the Oxford Playhouse, and the following year it was
performed at the Arts Theatre Club in London with Gwen
Ffrangcon-Davies as Eleonora and Peggy Ashcroft (then
aged twenty) as Christina. For details of subsequent London
productions, see pp. 637—9.

Despite being one of Strindberg's more popular plays
among theatre managers, EASTER is one of the most difficult to make work. More even than THE FATHER or MISS
JULIE, it depends on precise casting; if Eleonora is wrong,
however good an actress she may be, the play not only fails
but is liable to be an embarrassment. She must be innocent
without being mawkish, a most elusive combination to
attain; and she must be positive, not passive. She must have,
as Charles Morgan wrote in his *Times* review of the 1928

*It is interesting that he should have named the family after this
resort, for he had particularly disliked it. On 29 August 1898 he wrote
to his daughter Kerstin: "After five days of torture at Heyst, where
I was obliged to live with 200 people, have six dishes of various sorts
for dinner, and sit at table for over an hour, I was ripe for life in a
monastery." (Mary Sandbach's translation)

London production, "the fire that gives light to the symbol".
Elis, like all of Strindberg's self-portraits, is another problem,
largely because Strindberg has invested him with several
of his own more tiresome characteristics, especially his self-
pity. He, too, must be positive and rebellious, like the
Stranger in TO DAMASCUS; one has seen productions of
EASTER in which everyone behaved as though they were
drugged.

Charles Morgan, a perceptive admirer of Strindberg whose
admiration is the more surprising when one thinks how far
removed his own plays were from Strindberg's, thought
that the play contained a central flaw. In the same review,
he wrote: "We die continually that we may have continual
resurrection. This is Strindberg's answer. He states it with
extraordinary emphasis, with the passion of conviction. But
is it the passion of a conviction that he has forced upon
himself? Is his answer made thus, not because a truth within him would not allow it to be made otherwise, but
because he could no longer bear to stay answerless? Is this
the reason that the play, for all its high theme, its nobility
of approach, its courage in inquiry, is never moving? There
is a flaw in it somewhere. By the standard of THE FATHER
it is cold . . . The truth seems to be that Strindberg's
desperate swerving towards orthodoxy yielded him an
answer that was still no answer for him."

One can only reply that with the right delicate casting,
and the required sense of stillness, of people imprisoned in
a house waiting for release, EASTER can work magically in
a theatre. It is a play about prisoners; and, like (in their
very different ways) THE LADY FROM THE SEA and
ANTONY AND CLEOPATRA and MARY ROSE, a play
for a very special kind of actress. If such an actress is not
to hand, it is, like those plays, better left undone.

EASTER

(1900)

This translation of EASTER was commissioned by the Pitlochry Festival Theatre, and was first performed there on 26 April 1973. The cast was:

MRS HEYST	Madeleine Newbury
ELIS	Roger Forbes
ELEONORA	Deborah Benzimra
CHRISTINA	Norma Streader
BENJAMIN	Lionel Guyett
LIME	Brendan Barry

Directed and designed by Donald MacKechnie

CHARACTERS

MRS HEYST
ELIS, her son, a schoolmaster
ELEONORA, her daughter
CHRISTINA, ELIS' fiancée
BENJAMIN, a schoolboy
LIME (LINDKVIST)

ACT ONE

MAUNDY THURSDAY

*The whole forestage is occupied by a glass verandah
on the ground floor of a house, furnished as a living-
room. Centre, a large door leads to the garden, which
has a fence and a gate to the street. On the other side
of the street (which, like the house, stands on a rise),
can be seen the low fence of a garden sloping down
towards the town. Behind can be seen the treetops of
this garden, green with spring foliage. Above them is a
church spire and the gable of a large house.*

*The windows of the verandah, which occupy the
whole breadth of the stage, have curtains of light-
yellow flowered cretonne which can be drawn. A wall
mirror hangs on a window-post on the left of the door,
with a calendar beneath it.*

*Right of the upstage door is a big desk with books,
writing materials and a telephone. Left of this door
stand a dining-table, a stove with transparent panes and
a sideboard. Downstage right, a sewing-table with a
lamp. By it, two armchairs. Another lamp hangs from
the ceiling. Outside in the street is a gas-lamp. On the
left of the verandah, a door to the rest of the apartment; on the right, a door to the kitchen.*

The time is the present. *

Before the curtain rises, Haydn's Seven Words
on the Cross *is heard:* Introduction, Maestoso Adagio.

*A shaft of sunlight slants into the room from the
left on to one of the chairs by the sewing-table. On the
other chair, in the shadow,* CHRISTINA *sits threading
ribbons into a set of freshly ironed white curtains.*

ELIS *enters in an unbuttoned winter overcoat*

*I.e. 1900. (Translator's note)

carrying a large bundle of newspapers, which he puts on the desk. Then he takes off his overcoat and hangs it up, left.

ELIS: Good morning, Christina.

CHRISTINA: Good morning, Elis.

ELIS [*looks around*]: The double windows out; the floor scrubbed; clean curtains — yes, it's spring again! And they've hacked up the ice from the street, and the willow is flowering down by the river. Yes, it's spring. And I can hang up my winter coat. Oh, Christina, it's so heavy. [*Weighs the coat in his hand.*] As though it had drunk up all the sorrows of winter, the sweat of anguish and the dust of school.

CHRISTINA: And now you have your holiday.

ELIS: Yes! Easter! Five glorious days to relax, to breathe, to forget! [*Stretches out his hand to* CHRISTINA, *then sits in the armchair.*] Why look, the sun's come back. He went away in November, I remember the day he disappeared behind the brewery across the street. Oh, this winter! This long winter!

CHRISTINA [*gestures towards the kitchen door*]: Hush! Quiet!

ELIS: Yes, I shall be quiet; and I shall be happy that it's over. Ah, the blessed sun! [*Rubs his hands and pretends to be taking a shower.*] I want to bathe myself in sunshine, wash myself in light after all this darkness and dirt —

CHRISTINA: Hush! Hush!

ELIS: Do you know, I believe that peace is returning to us, and that adversity has grown weary —

CHRISTINA: Why do you think that?

ELIS: Well, for one thing, as I passed the cathedral just now, a white dove came flying towards me. She alighted on the pavement and let fall a twig she was carrying, right at my feet.

CHRISTINA: What kind of a twig?

ELIS: I suppose it couldn't have been an olive! But I believe it was a sign of peace. Just now I feel a blessed sense of calm and sunshine. Where's Mother?

CHRISTINA [*indicates*]: In the kitchen.

ELIS [*closes his eyes and is silent for a moment*]: I can *hear* it's spring! I hear the double windows are out. Do you know how I hear that? From the wheels of the carriages, mostly — but what's that? The chaffinch is singing! And they're hammering at the wharf, and there's a smell of oil-paint from the steamers, from the red lead.

CHRISTINA: Can you smell that from here?

ELIS: Here? Yes, it's true, we're here, but I was there, up there in the north, where our home is. How did we come to this dreadful town, where everyone hates each other and where one is always alone? Yes, it was poverty that brought us here, but with poverty came tragedy — Father's crime, and our little sister's illness. Christina, do you know if Mother has visited Father in prison?

CHRISTINA: I believe she's been there today.

ELIS: What did she say?

CHRISTINA: Nothing. She talked about other things.

ELIS: There's one blessing anyway. With the verdict came certainty and a kind of calm, once the newspapers had stopped their prying. A year has gone. In another year he'll be out, and then we can begin again.

CHRISTINA: How patiently you suffer.

ELIS: Don't say that. Admire nothing in me — I have only faults. Now you know. I'm sorry you wanted to believe otherwise.

CHRISTINA: If they were your own faults. But you're suffering for someone else's.

ELIS: What's that you're sewing?

CHRISTINA: The kitchen curtains, Elis dear.

ELIS: It looks like a bridal veil. When autumn comes, Christina, you'll be my bride, won't you?

CHRISTINA: Yes. But let's think of the summer first.

ELIS: Yes, the summer! [*Takes out a cheque-book.*] Look how much money I've saved already! And when school ends, we'll go north, to Lake Mälaren. Our cottage stands there waiting for us, as it stood in our childhood. The lime-trees stand there still, the punt lies under the willows by the shore. Oh, if only it were summer, so that I could bathe in the lake! This family dishonour has soiled my body and soul. I long for a lake to cleanse myself in.

CHRISTINA: Have you heard anything from your sister Eleonora?

ELIS: Yes, poor creature. She's unhappy, and she writes letters which break my heart. She wants to leave and come home, of course, but the head of the place won't let her, because she does things which would send her to prison. Do you know, sometimes I feel guilty, terribly guilty, because I said she ought to be put there?

CHRISTINA: My dear, you reproach yourself for everything. It was a kindness to send her where she can be taken care of, poor girl.

ELIS: That's true, and I suppose it's better the way it is. She's as well off there as she can be. And when I think how she ruined every chance we had of happiness, what a nightmare her sickness was to us, how it drove us to despair, I'm selfish enough to feel relieved — almost glad. The worst thing I could imagine now would be to see her enter that door. I am a swine, aren't I?

CHRISTINA: It's human to think so.

ELIS: And yet I suffer. Suffer, at the thought of her misery, and Father's.

CHRISTINA: Some people seem born to suffering —

ELIS: Poor Christina. You are entering a family that has been doomed since birth. If not earlier.

CHRISTINA: Elis! You don't know if these are trials or punishments.

ELIS: I don't know what it is for you — you are blameless.

CHRISTINA: A morning of tears may lead to an evening of joy. Elis, perhaps I can help you through this —

ELIS: Do you think Mother has a white evening tie?

CHRISTINA [*uneasily*]: Are you going out?

ELIS: I'm going to a dinner. Peter held his doctoral disputation yesterday — well, you know — and he's giving a dinner to celebrate it.

CHRISTINA: Do you want to go to that?

ELIS: You mean I should stay away, because he proved such a damned ungrateful pupil?

CHRISTINA: Well, he was rather disloyal. He promised he'd pay tribute to your thesis, and then stole from it without acknowledgement.

ELIS: Oh, that's always happening. I'm content to know that I've done what I've done.

CHRISTINA: Has he invited you?

ELIS: You're right, he hasn't! That's strange — he's been talking about this dinner for years, as though I was an automatic guest, and I've told everyone about it. If I don't get invited now, it'll be a public insult. Never mind, it won't be the first time. Nor the last.

[*Pause.*]

CHRISTINA: Benjamin's late. Do you think he'll get through his exam?

ELIS: He certainly should. With a credit in Latin.

CHRISTINA: He's a nice boy, Benjamin.

ELIS: Yes, very. But he's a bit of a brooder. You know why he lives with us?

CHRISTINA: Is it because — ?

ELIS: Because my father embezzled his trust fees — like so many others'. That's the terrible thing, Christina, that I have to see these orphans whom he robbed having to suffer the humiliation of being educated on charity. You can imagine what they must think of me. I have to keep on reminding myself of this so as to be able to forgive their cruelty.

CHRISTINA: I really think your father is better off than you are.

ELIS: So do I.

CHRISTINA: Elis, we should think of the summer. Not the past.

ELIS: Yes, the summer! Do you know, last night I was woken by students singing. They sang: "Yes, I am coming! O happy winds, tell the fields, tell the birds, I love them. Tell birch and lime-tree, lake and mountain, I long to see them again. See them as in the happy days of childhood." [*Rises, disturbed.*] Shall I see them again, shall I ever leave this dreadful town, this Ebal, the accursed mountain, and see Garizim once again? [*Sits down by the door.*]

CHRISTINA: Yes, yes! You will!

ELIS: But do you think I shall see *my* birches and lime-trees as I saw them before? Don't you think the same black cloud will hang over them as has hung over the landscape and our whole life down here ever since that day when — ? [*Points at the armchair, which is now in shadow.*] Look, now the sun has gone.

CHRISTINA: It will come back. And then it will stay longer.

ELIS: That's true. The days will grow longer and the shadows shorten.

CHRISTINA: We are moving towards the light, Elis. Believe me.

ELIS: Sometimes I do believe that, and when I think of the past and compare it with now, I am happy. Last year you were not sitting there, you had left me and broken our engagement. Do you know, that was the darkest hour of all. I literally died, bit by bit. But when you came back — I lived again. Do you remember why you left me?

CHRISTINA: No, I don't remember. I feel now there was no reason. I just felt I had to go — so I went. It was like sleepwalking. When I saw you again, I awoke and was happy.

ELIS: And now we shall never leave each other again. If you went now, I would really die. Here's Mother. Say nothing, let her live in her world of dreams, where Father is a martyr and all his victims rogues.

MRS HEYST *enters from the kitchen, wearing an apron and peeling an apple. She speaks amiably, somewhat naïvely.*

MRS HEYST: Good morning, children. Would you like your apple soup cold or hot?

ELIS: Cold, please, Mother dear.

MRS HEYST: That's a good boy. You always know what you want, and say what you don't. Not like you, Christina. Elis learned that from his father. He always knew what he wanted and what he was doing, and people can't stand that. That's why things went wrong for him.

But his day will come, and then he'll have justice and the others will get their deserts. Wait now, what was I going to say? Ah, yes. Do you know that Lime has come to live here? Lime, the worst scoundrel of them all?

ELIS [*rises, disturbed*] : Lime? He's come here?

MRS HEYST: Yes, he's living just across the street.

ELIS: Then we'll have to see him walk past every day. That too!

MRS HEYST: Let me talk to him just once, and he'll never show his face here again. I know his little secrets. Well, Elis, how did Peter manage?

ELIS: Oh, he did fine.

MRS HEYST: I'm sure he did. When are you going to do your doctorate?

ELIS: When I can afford it, Mother.

MRS HEYST: When I can afford it! That's no answer. And Benjamin? Has he passed his exam?

ELIS: We don't know yet. He'll be here any minute.

MRS HEYST: Mm. I don't altogether like Benjamin. He's so self-righteous. But we'll cure him of that. He's a good boy really. Oh, yes, and there's a parcel for you, Elis. [*Goes into kitchen.*]

ELIS: Strange how Mother knows everything. And understands. I sometimes think she isn't as stupid as she pretends.

MRS HEYST [*returns with parcel*] : Look, here it is, Lina had it from the postman.

ELIS: A present? I'm frightened of presents, ever since I once got sent a case of cobblestones. [*Puts the parcel on the table.*]

MRS HEYST: Well, I'll go back to the kitchen. Won't it be too cold for you with this door open?

ELIS: Not at all, Mother.

MRS HEYST: Don't hang your overcoat there, Elis. It looks so untidy. Well, Christina, will you have my curtains ready soon?

CHRISTINA: In a few minutes, Mother.

MRS HEYST: I like that Peter. He's my favourite. Aren't you going to his dinner, Elis?

ELIS: Yes, yes, of course I am.

MRS HEYST: Well, then, why say you want your apple soup cold if you're going out? You're such a muddlehead, Elis. Not like Peter. Now shut the doors when it gets chilly so you don't catch cold. [*Exits right.*]

ELIS: Dear old Mother. Always Peter. Is she trying to make you fond of him?

CHRISTINA: Me?

ELIS: Well, you know these fancies old women get.

CHRISTINA: What's in that parcel?

ELIS [*opens it and takes out a decorated bough of birch-twigs*]: A Lenten birch.

CHRISTINA: Who's it from?

ELIS: It doesn't say. Well, that's harmless enough. I'll put it in water, and it'll sprout like Aaron's rod. "Oh, birch-tree of my youth! . . . " And Lime is here.

CHRISTINA: Who is Lime?

ELIS: Our chief creditor.

CHRISTINA: *You* don't owe him anything, do you?

ELIS: Oh yes, we all do, all of us. Our family name is dishonoured, as long as any debt remains.

CHRISTINA: Change your name.

ELIS: Christina!

CHRISTINA [*puts aside her work, which is now finished*]: Thank you, Elis. I only wanted to test you.

ELIS: But you mustn't tempt me. Lime is a poor man, and needs his money. Everywhere that Father trod is like a battlefield strewn with dead and wounded. And Mother thinks he is the victim! Would you like to come for a walk?

CHRISTINA: And look for the sun? I'd love to.

ELIS: Do you understand this, that the Redeemer suffered for our sins and yet we have to go on paying for them? No one pays for me.

CHRISTINA: But if anyone did pay for you? Would you then understand — ?

ELIS: Yes, then I'd understand. Ssh! Here's Benjamin. Can you see if he looks happy?

CHRISTINA [*looks out through upstage door*]: He's walking so slowly. And now he's stopping by the fountain. And bathing his eyes.

ELIS: That too!

CHRISTINA: Wait till you know —

ELIS: Tears, tears!

CHRISTINA: Be patient.

> BENJAMIN *enters, friendly and respectful, but dejected. He carries some books and a portfolio.*

ELIS: Well, how did it go?

BENJAMIN: Badly.

ELIS: May I have a look? What went wrong?

BENJAMIN: I wrote "*ut*" with the indicative, although I knew it should take the subjunctive.

ELIS: Then you've failed. But how could you?

BENJAMIN [*helplessly*] : I just can't explain. I knew it
ought to be, I wanted to do it right, and I did it wrong.
[*Sits miserably at the dining-table.*]

ELIS [*sits at the desk and reads from* BENJAMIN's
portfolio] : Yes, here it is. The indicative. Oh, my God!

CHRISTINA [*with an effort*] : Well, better luck next time.
Life is long — so terribly long.

BENJAMIN: Yes.

ELIS [*sadly but without bitterness*] : Why must everything
happen at once? And you were my best pupil. What can I
expect from the others? My reputation as a teacher will be
destroyed, I shall get no more pupils, and then — everything's finished. [*To* BENJAMIN.] Don't take it so hard.
It's not your fault.

CHRISTINA [*urgently*] : Elis! Courage, for God's sake.
Courage.

ELIS: Where shall I find it?

CHRISTINA: Where you found it before.

ELIS: Things are different now. I seem to be out of grace.

CHRISTINA: It is a sign of grace to suffer innocently.
Don't let yourself be tempted to impatience. Stand the
trial, for it is only a trial, I know it —

ELIS: Can this next year for Benjamin be shorter than
three hundred and sixty-five days?

CHRISTINA: Yes. A calm spirit makes time seem shorter.

ELIS [*smiles*] : Kiss the wound, it'll feel better, like you
tell children.

CHRISTINA: Be a child, then and I will say it to you. Think
of Mother. She bears everything.

ELIS: Give me your hand. [*She does so.*] Your hand is
trembling.

CHRISTINA: No. I can't feel it.

ELIS: You are not as strong as you pretend.

CHRISTINA: I don't feel weak.

ELIS: Why don't you give me strength, then?

CHRISTINA: I have none to spare.

ELIS [*looks out through window*]: Do you know who's coming now?

CHRISTINA [*looks through window and drops to her knees, crushed*]: This is too much.

ELIS: The creditor. Who can take our furniture when he pleases. Lime, who has come to this town to sit in his web like a spider and watch the flies —

CHRISTINA: Turn your back on him.

ELIS [*gets up*]: No. I shall not turn my back. When you weakened just now, I grew strong. Now he's coming down the street. He has already spotted his prey —

CHRISTINA: At least go away from the window.

ELIS: No. Now he amuses me. His eyes seem to glint, as though he sees his prey struggling in his trap. Come on, then! He counts the steps to our gate — he sees from the open door that we are at home. But — now he's met someone and stopped to talk. He's talking about us, he's looking this way —

CHRISTINA: Pray God he doesn't meet Mother. She might abuse him and make him implacable. Don't let that happen, Elis.

ELIS: Now he's shaking his stick, as though vowing that mercy shall not preclude justice. He's unbuttoning his overcoat, to show that we haven't taken the clothes from his body. I can see from his lips what he's saying. How shall I answer him? "Good sir, you are right. Take everything, it belongs to you!"

CHRISTINA: That is all you can say.

ELIS: Now he's laughing. But — kindly, not cruelly. Perhaps he isn't so cruel, though he wants his money. If only he'd come now, and stop this blessed chatter. Now he's waving his stick again — creditors always have sticks. And leather galoshes that say "Swish, swish!" — like a birch. [*Puts* CHRISTINA's *hand on his left breast.*] Feel, Christina, how my heart thuds. I can hear it myself, like a piston in my right ear. Oh, God — now he's saying goodbye —and those galoshes! Swish, swish, like a Lenten birch — but he's got charms on his watch-chain. So he can't be penniless. Creditors always have charms of cornelian, like raw flesh which they've cut from their neighbours' backs. Listen to his galoshes — mrr, mrr, grr, grr, like wolves! Swish, swish! Look out! He sees me! He sees me! [*Bows towards the street.*] He bowed to me first! He's smiling! He's waving his hand! And — [*Falls weeping by the desk.*] He's walked past!

CHRISTINA: Thank God!

ELIS: He's gone. But he will come back. Let us go out into the sun.

CHRISTINA: And the dinner with Peter?

ELIS: As I haven't been invited, I shall stay away. Anyway, what should I do amid all that junketing? To meet a friend who has betrayed me? I should simply be suffering to please him.

CHRISTINA: Thank you for staying with us.

ELIS: You know it's what I want to do. Shall we go?

CHRISTINA: Yes, This way. [*Exits left.*]

ELIS [*as he walks past* BENJAMIN, *pats his head*]: Try to be brave.

    BENJAMIN *hides his face in his hands.*

ELIS [*takes the birch-bough from the dining-table and puts it behind the mirror*] : This was no olive branch the dove brought. It was a birch!

> *He goes out.* ELEONORA *enters upstage, a girl of sixteen with a pigtail down her back. She carries a yellow daffodil in a pot. Without seeing, or seeming to see,* BENJAMIN, *she takes the water carafe from the sideboard, waters the flower, puts it on the dining-table opposite* BENJAMIN, *looks at him and imitates his movements.* BENJAMIN *looks at her, amazed.*

ELEONORA [*with a gesture towards the daffodil*] : Do you know what that is?

BENJAMIN [*simply, naïvely*] : A daffodil, of course. But who are you?

ELEONORA [*friendly, yet sad*] : Well, who are you?

BENJAMIN [*as before*] : My name's Benjamin. I lodge here with Mrs Heyst.

ELEONORA: I see! My name's Eleonora and I am her daughter.

BENJAMIN: How strange that they've never talked about you.

ELEONORA: People don't talk about the dead.

BENJAMIN: The dead!

ELEONORA: I'm regarded as dead, because I've done something very wicked.

BENJAMIN: You!

ELEONORA: Yes. I've embezzled trust fees. That didn't matter so much, because stolen goods bring no joy. But my old father got the blame and was sent to prison, and that, you see, can never be forgiven.

BENJAMIN: How strangely and beautifully you talk. I'd never thought of that, that my inheritance could have been stolen.

ELEONORA: People should not be bound, they should be
set free.

BENJAMIN: Well, you have freed me, from the misery of
feeling cheated.

ELEONORA: So you are a ward?

BENJAMIN: Yes. And I must live with these unfortunate
people to help them repay their debt.

ELEONORA: You mustn't use hard words, or I shall go.
I'm so soft, I can't bear anything hard. But — you are
suffering all this because of me?

BENJAMIN: Because of your father.

ELEONORA: That's the same, for he and I are the same
person. [*Pause.*] I have been very ill . . . Why are you so
sad?

BENJAMIN: I've just failed in something.

ELEONORA: Why should that make you sad? "The rod
and reproof give wisdom, and he who hateth punishment
must die." What have you failed in?

BENJAMIN: I failed my Latin exam — though I was quite
sure I would pass.

ELEONORA: I see. You were quite sure, so sure you'd
have betted money on it?

BENJAMIN: I did.

ELEONORA: I can believe that. Well, you see, it happened
because you were so sure.

BENJAMIN: You think that was the reason?

ELEONORA: Of course it was. Pride goes before a fall.

BENJAMIN: I'll remember that next time.

ELEONORA: Yes, you must. And the sacrifice that pleases
God is a contrite spirit.

BENJAMIN: Are you a believer?

ELEONORA: Yes, I believe things.

BENJAMIN: I mean, are you religious?

ELEONORA: Yes, that's what I mean too. So if you say nasty things about God, who is my friend, I won't sit at the same table with you.

BENJAMIN: How old are you?

ELEONORA: For me there is no time and no place. I am everywhere and always. I am in my father's prison and in my brother's classroom, I am in my mother's kitchen and in my sister's shop far away in America. When things go well for my sister and she sells goods, I feel her happiness, and when things go badly for her I suffer, but I suffer most when she does something wrong. Benjamin, you are called Benjamin because you are the youngest of my friends. Yes, everyone is my friend. If you let me take care of you, I'll suffer for you too.

BENJAMIN: I don't understand your words but I think I understand your meaning. And now I want whatever you want.

ELEONORA: Then will you begin by stopping judging people, even those who are condemned as criminals?

BENJAMIN: Yes, but I must have a reason for it. I've read philosophy, you see.

ELEONORA: Oh, have you? Then you must help me to understand something a great philosopher said: "Those who hate the righteous shall themselves become criminals."

BENJAMIN: According to all logic, that means that one can be foredoomed to commit a crime —

ELEONORA: And that crime itself is a punishment.

BENJAMIN: That's really deep! It might have been said by Kant or Schopenhauer.

ELEONORA: I don't know them.

BENJAMIN: Where did you read it?

ELEONORA: In the Holy Book.

BENJAMIN: Really? Are there things like that there?

ELEONORA: What an ignorant, neglected child you are!
  If only I could bring you up!

BENJAMIN: You, Eleonora!

ELEONORA: But I'm sure you're not really evil. You look
  a good person. What is the name of your Latin teacher?

BENJAMIN: Lektor Ahlgren.

ELEONORA: I'll remember that. Oh, now they're hurting
  my father! They're being cruel to him. [*Stands still as
  though listening.*] Do you hear that groaning in the
  telephone-wires? That's the hard words that the beautiful
  soft red copper can't bear. When people talk badly about
  each other on the telephone, the copper complains, and
  accuses — [*In a hard voice.*] And every word is written in
  the book. And at the end of time comes the reckoning.

BENJAMIN: How stern you are!

ELEONORA: Not I, not I! How should I dare be that?
  I? I?

> She goes to the stove and opens the shutter, and
> takes out some torn pieces of white notepaper.
> BENJAMIN *gets up and looks at these, as* ELEONORA
> *arranges them on the dining-table.*

ELEONORA [*to herself*]: How can people be so thoughtless as to put their secrets in stoves? Wherever I go, I look
  at once in the stove. But I never misuse what I find, I
  wouldn't dare, or I'd get hurt. What's this? [*Reads.*]

BENJAMIN: It's a letter from Peter, arranging a meeting
  with Christina. I've been expecting this for a long time.

ELEONORA [*puts her hand over the paper*]: Oh, Benjamin,
  what have you been expecting? Tell me, you wicked
  creature, who believe only evil. This letter will only bring
  good. I know Christina — she is to be my sister-in-law.

And this meeting will save my brother Elis from an unhappiness. Will you promise me to **keep quiet about** this, Benjamin?

BENJAMIN: I don't think I should dare to talk about it.

ELEONORA: People who have secrets do such wicked things. They think they're wise, and are mad. But what's it to do with me?

BENJAMIN: Yes, why are you so curious?

ELEONORA: You see, it's my illness that I have to know everything, otherwise I get restless.

BENJAMIN: Know everything?

ELEONORA: It's a fault I can't overcome. But I know what the starlings say.

BENJAMIN: They can't talk, surely?

ELEONORA: Haven't you heard starlings that have been taught to talk?

BENJAMIN: Oh, been taught, yes.

ELEONORA: Then starlings can learn to talk. Now there are some that teach themselves — that's called auto-didactic — they sit and listen, of course, without our knowing, and then imitate us. Just now as I was coming here, I heard two talking in a walnut-tree.

BENJAMIN: What fun you are! But what did they say?

ELEONORA: "Peter," said one. "Judas!" said the other. "Same to you," said the first. "Fie, fie, fie!" said the other. But have you noticed that the nightingales only sing in the deaf and dumb folks' garden next door?

BENJAMIN: Yes, that's well known. Why do they do that?

ELEONORA: Because people with ears can't hear what the nightingales say. But the deaf and dumb hear it!

BENJAMIN: Tell me more stories.

ELEONORA: Yes, if you're nice.

BENJAMIN: How do you mean, nice?

ELEONORA: Well, you must never pick up what I've said.
You must never say: "First you said that, now you say
this." Shall I tell you more about birds? There's a wicked
bird called the rat-buzzard. As you can tell from his name,
he lives on rats. But because he's a wicked bird, it's got to
be made hard for him to catch the rats. So he can only
say one word, which sounds like when a cat says Miaouw!
Well, when the buzzard says Miaouw the rats run and hide
— but the buzzard doesn't know what he's saying, so he
often has to go without food, because he's so horrid.
Would you like to hear more? Or shall I tell you about
flowers? Do you know that when I was ill, I had to take
henbane, which makes your eyes like magnifying glasses.
Belladonna does the opposite, it makes everything smaller.
But now I can see further than other people, and I can
see the stars in broad daylight.

BENJAMIN: But the stars aren't up then, surely?

ELEONORA: How silly you are! The stars are always up.
Now I'm facing north and I can see Cassiopeia sitting
like a "w" in the middle of the Milky Way. Can you see
her?

BENJAMIN: No, I can't.

ELEONORA: Well, remember this, that one person *can*
see what another can't. So don't be too sure of your
eyes. Well, I was going to tell you about this flower that's
on the table. He's a daffodil that lives in Switzerland —
he has a cup that drinks sunshine, that's why he's yellow
and soothes pain. Just now I passed a flower-shop and
saw him and wanted to give him to my brother Elis. When
I tried to go in I found the door was shut, because today
is Confirmation day. Well, as I had to have the flower, I
took out my keys and tried them — would you believe,
my door-key fitted! I went in. Do you understand the
silent language of flowers? Every smell expresses a whole

lot of thoughts, and these thoughts swarmed all over me; and with my magnifying eye I looked into their minds, which no one has ever seen. And they talked to me of their sorrows, which the stupid gardener caused them — I don't call him cruel, because he's just thoughtless. Then I put down a crown on the counter with my card, and took the flower and went.

BENJAMIN: But how thoughtless of you! Suppose they miss the flower and don't find the money!

ELEONORA: That's true. You're right.

BENJAMIN: A coin can get lost, and if they only find your card, you're done.

ELEONORA: But surely no one can believe that I meant to steal it?

BENJAMIN [*looks at her*]: No?

ELEONORA [*looks at him and gets up*]: Oh! I know what you mean. Like father, like child! Oh, how stupid I've been! Haven't I? Well, what must be must. [*Sits.*] Let it happen.

BENJAMIN: Couldn't it be put right — ?

ELEONORA: Hush! Talk about something else. Lektor Ahlgren! Poor Elis! Poor all of us. But it's Easter, and we must suffer. There's a concert tomorrow, isn't there? And they're playing Haydn's *Seven Words on the Cross*. "Mother, behold thy son!" [*Weeps in her hands.*]

BENJAMIN: What was this illness you had?

ELEONORA: Not a sickness unto death, but to the glory of God. "I awaited good, and evil came. I awaited the light, and darkness came." How was your childhood, Benjamin?

BENJAMIN: I don't know. Boring! And yours?

ELEONORA: I've never had any. I was born old. I knew everything when I was born, and when I learned anything it was only like remembering. I knew that people were thoughtless and stupid when I was four, and so they were cruel to me.

BENJAMIN: Everything that you say, I feel I've thought, too.

ELEONORA: I expect you have. Why did you think my coin should get lost in the flower-shop?

BENJAMIN: Because what hurts us must always happen.

ELEONORA: You've noticed that too? Hush, someone's coming. [*Looks out upstage.*] I can hear — it's Elis! Oh, what fun! My only friend in the world. [*Sadly.*] But he isn't expecting me. And he won't be glad to see me. No, he won't. Certainly not. Benjamin, Benjamin, try to look kind and happy when my poor brother comes. I'll go inside, so you can warn him I'm here. But no hard words, that hurts me so — do you hear? Give me your hand. [BENJAMIN *holds out his hand. She kisses the top of his head.*] There! Now you are my little brother! God bless and protect you. [*Goes left and, as she passes* ELIS' *overcoat, strokes it affectionately on the sleeve.*] Poor Elis!

> *She goes out.* ELIS *enters upstage, troubled.*
> MRS HEYST *enters from the kitchen.*

ELIS: Hullo, Mother.

MRS HEYST: Is it you? I thought I heard a strange voice.

ELIS: I have news. I met the lawyer on the street.

MRS HEYST: Yes?

ELIS: The case is to go to appeal. And to save time, I have to read through the whole transcript of the trial.

MRS HEYST: ˙Well, that won't take you long.

ELIS [*indicates the papers on the desk*]: Oh, I thought it was all over and done with. And now I must go through it all again — all the accusations, the affidavits, the evidence. All again.

MRS HEYST: Yes, but then the Court of Appeal will free him.

ELIS: No, Mother. He has confessed.

MRS HEYST: Yes, but there may have been some technical error, the lawyer told me when I last spoke with him.

ELIS: He said that to comfort you.

MRS HEYST: Aren't you going out to dinner?

ELIS: No.

MRS HEYST: Now you've changed your mind again.

ELIS: Yes.

MRS HEYST: It's bad, doing that.

ELIS: I know, but I can't help it.

MRS HEYST: I thought I heard a strange voice that I recognized. I must have been mistaken. [*Points to over-coat.*] You shouldn't hang that coat there. I told you before. [*Exits right.*]

ELIS [*wanders left; sees the daffodil on the dining-table. To* BENJAMIN]: How did that flower get here?

BENJAMIN: A young lady brought it.

ELIS: A lady? What's this, now? Who was it?

BENJAMIN: It was —

ELIS: Was it — my sister?

BENJAMIN: Yes.

ELIS *sinks into a chair by the dining-table. Pause.*

ELIS: Did you talk to her?

BENJAMIN: Why, yes.

ELIS: Oh, God! Won't it soon be enough? Was she unpleasant to you?

BENJAMIN: She? No, she was so kind, so kind.

ELIS: Strange. Did she speak about me? Was she very angry with me?

BENJAMIN: No! On the contrary. She said you were the best friend she had in the world —

ELIS: How extraordinary!

BENJAMIN: And as she left, she stroked your coat, there on the sleeve —

ELIS: Left? Where did she go?

BENJAMIN [*points to door, left*]: In there.

ELIS: She's there now, then?

BENJAMIN: Yes.

ELIS: You look so happy and peaceful, Benjamin.

BENJAMIN: She spoke so beautifully to me —

ELIS: What did she talk about?

BENJAMIN: She told stories, and said a lot about religion —

ELIS [*gets up*]: And that made you happy?

BENJAMIN: Yes.

ELIS: Poor Eleonora! So unhappy herself, and she can bring such joy to others. [*Goes left, unwillingly.*] God help me!

ACT TWO

GOOD FRIDAY

Music before the curtain: Haydn, Seven Words on the Cross; *Largo No. 1:* "Pater dimitte illis".

*The scene is as before, except that the curtains
are drawn and illuminated by the gaslight from the
street. The ceiling lamp is lit, as is a small paraffin-
lamp on the dining-table. There is a fire in the stove.*

At the sewing-table ELIS *and* CHRISTINA *sit,
doing nothing.* ELEONORA *and* BENJAMIN *are
seated at the dining-table facing each other, reading,
the lamp between them.* ELEONORA *has a shawl
over her shoulders.*

Everyone is dressed in black. ELIS *and*
BENJAMIN *wear white bow ties.*

*On the desk the papers of the trial are spread.
The daffodil stands on the sewing-table. On the dining-
table is an old pendulum clock.*

*Now and then the shadow of a passer-by can be
seen on the curtains.*

ELIS [*softly, to* CHRISTINA] : Good Friday! God, how
long it is! And the snow has heaped itself on the pavements
like straw outside the house of a dying man. Every sound
has ceased — except the organ music. I can hear that even
from here.

CHRISTINA: I suppose Mother went to Evensong?

ELIS: Yes. She didn't dare to show herself at Mattins. She
can't bear the way people look at her.

CHRISTINA: They're strange, these people. They expect
us to keep out of sight. They don't think it's decent —

ELIS: Well, perhaps they are right.

CHRISTINA: For one man's error, a whole family excommunicated?

ELIS: Well, that's the way it is.

ELEONORA *moves the lamp towards* BENJAMIN,
so that he can see better.

ELIS [*indicating* ELEONORA *and* BENJAMIN]: Look at them!

CHRISTINA: Isn't it beautiful! How well they get on.

ELIS: What luck that Eleonora is so calm. Please God that it continues.

CHRISTINA: Why shouldn't it?

ELIS: Because — luck doesn't usually last so long. I'm scared of everything today.

BENJAMIN *moves the lamp over towards* ELEONORA, *so that she may see better.*

CHRISTINA: Look at them.

ELIS: Have you noticed how changed Benjamin is? He used to be so sullen and obstinate. Now he's become calm and gentle.

CHRISTINA: How radiant she is. Not just beautiful.

ELIS: She has brought with her an angel of peace, which walks invisible and breathes a silent calm. Even Mother seemed to find peace when she saw her — a peace I hadn't expected.

CHRISTINA: Do you think she's recovered now?

ELIS: Yes. If it weren't for this exaggerated sensitivity of hers. She's sitting there now reading the story of Christ's agony, and sometimes she cries.

CHRISTINA: Well, I remember we used to do that in school on Wednesdays during Lent —

ELIS: Don't talk so loud, she'll hear you.

CHRISTINA: Not now. She's so far away.

ELIS: Have you noticed how Benjamin has acquired a kind of dignity? Almost nobility.

CHRISTINA: That is suffering. Joy makes everything banal.

ELIS: I wonder — could it be love? Do you think they —?

CHRISTINA: Ssh! Don't touch the butterfly's wings, or it will fly away.

ELIS: They're looking at each other and only pretending to read. I don't hear them turning any pages.

CHRISTINA: Hush!

ELIS: Look, now she can't control herself —

> ELEONORA *rises, tiptoes towards* BENJAMIN *and puts her shawl around his shoulders.* BENJAMIN *makes a gently deprecating gesture, but submits.*
> ELEONORA *returns to her chair and pushes the lamp over to* BENJAMIN's *side of the table.*

CHRISTINA: Poor Eleonora. She doesn't know what a good creature she is.

ELIS [*gets up*]: Well, I'll get back to that transcript of the trial.

CHRISTINA: Can you see any purpose in all this reading?

ELIS: Only one. To keep Mother's hopes alive. But although I only pretend to read, like them, the words stick in my eyes like thorns. The affidavits, the arithmetic, Father's admissions — listen. "The defendant confessed amid tears . . . " So many tears, so many tears. And these papers — with all their stamps, like forged banknotes, or prison locks. And the ribbons and the red seals — they're like the five wounds of Christ — and the sentences that never end, the eternal agonies. Good Friday. Yesterday the sun shone, yesterday we went out to the country, at least in our dreams. Christina — imagine if we have to stay here this summer!

CHRISTINA: It would save us a lot of money. But it would be horrible.

ELIS: I don't think I'd survive it. Three summers I've spent here — and it's like a tomb. Midday, and one sees the long grey street wind like a soldiers' trench — not a soul, not a horse, not a dog. But out of the sewers the rats creep, because the cats are on summer holiday. And the few people left behind sit at their windows, spying on their neighbours' clothes — "Look, she's wearing her winter dress!" — and their neighbours' downtrodden heels, and their neighbours' faults. And out of the slums the cripples creep, noseless and earless, malignant and unhappy. During the winter they hide themselves, but now they sit on the main boulevard and sun themselves, as though they'd taken over the town. And where a few days earlier pretty children in pretty clothes played under the proud and gentle eyes of their pretty mothers, groups of tatter-demalions wander, cursing and tormenting each other. I remember a midsummer day two years ago —

CHRISTINA: Elis, Elis! Think of the future!

ELIS: Is it brighter there?

CHRISTINA: Let us believe so.

ELIS [*sits at the desk*]: If only it would stop snowing out there. So that one could go out, and walk.

CHRISTINA: My dear, yesterday afternoon you longed for the darkness to return so that we should be hidden from people's eyes. "The darkness is so beautiful, so merciful," you said. "It's like drawing the sheets over one's head."

ELIS: There you are. It's equally miserable, either way. [*Reads the documents.*] The worst thing in this trial is those impudent questions about Father's way of life. It says here that we held extravagant parties. One witness says he drank. No, it's too much! I can't go on. But I must. To the end. Aren't you cold?

CHRISTINA: No, but it isn't warm. Isn't Lina home?

ELIS: She's gone to Communion. You know that.

CHRISTINA: I suppose Mother'll be back soon?

ELIS: I'm always worried when she goes out. She bears so much and sees so much — and it's all painful.

CHRISTINA: There's a curious melancholy strain in your family.

ELIS: That's why only melancholy people have ever wanted to associate with us. Happy people avoided us.

CHRISTINA: Mother's just come in through the back door.

ELIS: Don't be impatient with her, Christina.

CHRISTINA: Of course not. She has the hardest task of us all. But I don't understand her.

ELIS: She hides her shame as best she can, and that makes her difficult. Poor Mother!

> MRS HEYST *enters in black, carrying a psalm book and a handkerchief.*

MRS HEYST: Good evening, children.

EVERYONE [*except* BENJAMIN, *who greets her silently*]: Good evening, Mother. dear.

MRS HEYST: You're all wearing black as though you were in mourning.

> *Silence.*

ELIS: Is it still snowing?

MRS HEYST: Yes, sleeting. It's cold in here. [*Goes over to* ELEONORA *and pats her.*] Well, little one, I see you're reading and studying. [*To* BENJAMIN.] You're not doing more than you need to.

> ELEONORA *takes her mother's hand and presses it to her lips.*

MRS HEYST [*restrains her emotion*]: There my child. There, there.

ELIS: You went to Evensong, Mother.

MRS HEYST: Yes. It was the rural dean preaching. I don't like him.

ELIS: Did you meet anyone you know?

MRS HEYST [*sits at the sewing-table*]: I wish I hadn't.

ELIS: I know whom you —

MRS HEYST: Lime! And he came up to me —

ELIS: How monstrous!

MRS HEYST: Asked how we were, and — imagine my horror, he asked if he might visit us this evening.

ELIS: On this day!

MRS HEYST: I was speechless. And he took my silence to mean yes. [*Pause.*] He may be here any moment.

ELIS [*rises*]: Here? Now?

MRS HEYST: He said he wanted to leave some paper which was urgent.

ELIS: He wants to take the furniture.

MRS HEYST: But he looked so strange. I didn't understand him.

ELIS: Well, let him come. He has the law on his side, and we must yield. We must receive him in a proper manner when he comes.

MRS HEYST: As long as I don't have to see him.

ELIS: Yes, you can stay in your room.

MRS HEYST: But he mustn't have the furniture. How should we live if he took all our things away? We can't live in empty rooms. Can we?

ELIS: The foxes have holes and the birds of the air nests. There are homeless people who live in the forest.

MRS HEYST: Scoundrels may live there, but not honest people.

ELIS [*at the desk*] : I must do some reading now, Mother.

MRS HEYST: Have you found any mistakes?

ELIS: No. I don't think there are any.

MRS HEYST: But I met the town clerk just now, and he said there might be some legal flaw, a doubtful witness or an unattested statement or an inconsistency. You can't be reading carefully.

ELIS: I am Mother, but it's all so painful —

MRS HEYST: By the way, I met the town clerk just now — oh, yes, I told you — and he said a burglary was committed in the town yesterday, in broad daylight.

> ELEONORA *and* BENJAMIN *prick up their ears.*

ELIS: Burglary? In this town? Where?

MRS HEYST: It seems it was in a flower-shop in Church Street. But the whole thing was very strange. It seems what happened was that the owner shut his shop to go to church, because his son, or it may have been his daughter, was going to be confirmed. When he came back around three o'clock, or perhaps it was four, it doesn't matter, well, the shop door was open and there were some flowers missing, a whole lot, one yellow tulip in particular, which was the first thing he noticed.

ELIS: A tulip! You'd have frightened me if you'd said a daffodil.

MRS HEYST: No, it was a tulip. I'm quite sure of that. Well, now the police are looking into it.

> ELEONORA *has risen, as though wishing to speak, but* BENJAMIN *goes to her and whispers something.*

MRS HEYST: Fancy committing a burglary on Maundy Thursday, when the boys and girls are being confirmed. They're just scoundrels, the whole town. That's why they put innocent people in prison.

ELIS: They don't suspect anyone, then?

MRS HEYST: No. But it was a strange thief. He took nothing from the till.

CHRISTINA: Oh, if only this day were over!

MRS HEYST: And if only Lina would come home. Oh, they were talking about Peter's dinner last night. The Governor himself attended.

ELIS: That surprises me. Peter was always meant to be so opposed to his politics.

MRS HEYST: Well, he must have changed his mind.

ELIS: He's not called Peter for nothing, it seems.

MRS HEYST: What have you got against the Governor?

ELIS: He's a blocker. He blocks everything. He blocked the new school, he blocked the rifle club, he tried to block school camps and people riding bicycles — and he blocked me!

MRS HEYST: I don't understand that. Well, no matter. Anyway, the Governor made a speech, and Peter thanked him —

ELIS: Moved, no doubt. And denied his teacher, saying: "I know not the man." And the cock crowed again! Wasn't there once a Governor called Pontius, surnamed Pilate?

> ELEONORA *makes a movement as though wishing to speak, but calms herself.*

MRS HEYST: You mustn't be so bitter, Elis. People are people, and one must put up with them.

ELIS: Hush! I hear Lime coming!

MRS HEYST: Can you hear in this snow?

ELIS: I hear his stick strike the stones and his leather galoshes! Go inside, Mother.

MRS HEYST: No, now I want to stay. I'll give him a piece of my mind.

ELIS: Please, Mother, do go. It'll be too painful.

MRS HEYST [*rises, upset*]: Perish the day I was born!

CHRISTINA: Mother, you mustn't blaspheme!

MRS HEYST [*with an exalted expression*]: "Wherefore do the wicked live, become old, yea, are mighty in power? Their houses are safe from fear, neither is the rod of God upon them. What is the Almighty, that we should serve Him? And what profit should we have, if we pray unto Him?"

ELIS [*cries*]: Mother!

MRS HEYST: My God, why hast Thou forsaken me? And my children? [*Exits left.*]

ELIS [*listening outside*]: He's stopped! Perhaps he thinks it's indecent. Or too cruel. But he can't think that, if he can write such dreadful letters. They were always on blue paper, and now I can never see a blue envelope without trembling.

CHRISTINA: What are you going to say to him? What will you suggest?

ELIS: I don't know. I can't think any longer, I can't reason. Shall I fall on my knees before him, beg him for mercy? Can you hear him? I can hear nothing but the blood thudding in my ears.

CHRISTINA: Let us be ready for the worst. He will take everything —

ELIS: And the landlord will come and demand security, which I can't provide. He'll need that because our furniture will no longer be here —

CHRISTINA [*looks into the street from behind the curtain*]: He isn't there any longer. He's gone.

ELIS: Ah! Do you know, Mother's apathy and submissiveness trouble me more than her anger!

CHRISTINA: She only pretends to be apathetic. She was

like a lioness the way she spoke those last words. Did you see how she grew?

ELIS: Do you know, when I think of Lime now, I see him as a jovial ogre who only wants to scare children. How have I come to feel that?

CHRISTINA: Thoughts come and go —

ELIS: What luck I wasn't at that dinner last night. I'd made up my mind to make a speech attacking the Governor. And that would have ruined everything for me, and for us all. It was very lucky.

CHRISTINA: You see!

ELIS: Thank you for your advice. You knew your Peter, Christina.

CHRISTINA: My Peter!

ELIS: I meant — mine. Look, here he is again! Oh, God!

On the curtain can be seen the shadow of a man hesitantly approaching. The shadow gradually grows until it is gigantic. Everyone in the room is terrified.

ELIS: The ogre! Look at the ogre that wants to devour us!

CHRISTINA: You should smile at him now, like the ogres in fairy tales.

ELIS: I can't smile any more.

The shadow grows small and disappears.

CHRISTINA: Look at his stick, then, and you must laugh.

ELIS: He's gone. Yes, now I can breathe, because he won't be back before tomorrow. Oh!

CHRISTINA: And tomorrow the sun will shine. It will be the eve of resurrection, the snow will be gone and the birds will sing.

ELIS: Go on talking like that. I can *see* everything you say.

CHRISTINA: If only you could see into my heart, if you could see my thoughts, my hopes, my innermost prayers, Elis, Elis, now when — [*Stops.*]

ELIS: What? Tell me.

CHRISTINA: Now when I — ask you something.

ELIS: Tell me.

CHRISTINA: It is a trial. Remember, it is a trial, Elis.

ELIS: A trial? An ordeal? Well?

CHRISTINA: Let me — No, I daren't. It could fail.

ELEONORA *pricks up her ears.*

ELIS: Why do you torment me?

CHRISTINA: I may regret it. I know I shall. Well. Elis, let me go to the concert this evening.

ELIS: Which concert?

CHRISTINA: Haydn's *Seven Words on the Cross*, in the Cathedral.

ELIS: With whom?

CHRISTINA: With Alice —

ELIS: And?

CHRISTINA: Peter.

ELIS: Peter?

CHRISTINA: There — you're angry. I'm sorry. But it's too late.

ELIS: Yes, it is rather late. But explain yourself.

CHRISTINA: I prepared you to accept that I couldn't explain myself. That was why I asked you to trust me implicitly.

ELIS [*gently*]: Go. I trust you. But it hurts me that you seek the company of this traitor.

CHRISTINA: I know. But this is to be a test.

ELIS: Which I shall not be able to pass.

CHRISTINA: You will!

ELIS: I want to, but I can't. You will go, in any case.

CHRISTINA: Give me your hand.

ELIS [holds it out] : Here.

> The telephone rings.

ELIS [answers it] : Hullo. There's no answer. Hullo. It answers with my own voice. Who is there? How strange. I hear my own words like an echo.

CHRISTINA: That happens sometimes.

ELIS: Hullo. This is horrible. [Rings off.] Go now, Christina. I don't want any explanations or excuses. I shall stand the test.

CHRISTINA: If you do, all will be well for us.

ELIS: I shall. [CHRISTINA moves towards the exit, right.] Why are you going that way?

CHRISTINA: My clothes are out there. Well. Goodbye for now. [Goes.]

ELIS: Goodbye, my friend. [Pause.] For ever! [Runs out left.]

ELEONORA: God help us, what have I done? The police are looking for the criminal, and if I am discovered — poor Mother, and poor Elis!

BENJAMIN [naïvely] : Eleonora, you must say that I did it.

ELEONORA: You? Dear child, can you bear another's guilt?

BENJAMIN: That is easy to do when one knows one is innocent.

ELEONORA: One must never deceive people.

BENJAMIN: Well, let me telephone to the flower-shop and tell them what happened.

ELEONORA: No. I have done something wrong, and I must be punished by being made restless. I have woken their fear of crime, and so I must be frightened.

BENJAMIN: But if the police come —

ELEONORA: That will be hard — but it must happen. Oh, if only this day were over! [*Takes the clock from the dining-table and moves the hands.*] Please, clock, go a little faster. Tick, tack, ping, ping, ping. Now it's eight. Ping, ping, ping. Now it's nine. Ten! Eleven! Twelve! Now it's Easter Eve. Now the sun will soon be up, and then we'll write on the Easter eggs. I shall write this: "Thine adversary hath desired thee, that he may sift thee as wheat; but I have prayed for thee."

BENJAMIN: Why do you torment yourself so, Eleonora?

ELEONORA: I? Torment myself? Think, Benjamin, of all the blossoming flowers, the bluebells, the snowdrops, which have to stay out in the snow all day and night, freezing in the darkness! Think how they must suffer. I suppose the night must be hardest, then it's so dark, and they're frightened of the dark and can't run away — so they stand there waiting for the day to come. Everything suffers, everything, but the flowers most of all. And the birds that fly from the south! Where shall they sleep tonight?

BENJAMIN [*naïvely*]: They sit in hollow trees, surely you know that.

ELEONORA: There aren't enough hollow trees for them all. I've only seen two hollow trees in the parks here, and owls live in them, and they kill little birds. Poor Elis, he thinks Christina has left him. But I know she will come back.

BENJAMIN: If you know that, why didn't you tell him?

ELEONORA: Because Elis must suffer. Everyone must

suffer today, on Good Friday, because they must remember Christ suffering on the Cross.

The sound of a police whistle is heard from the street.

ELEONORA [*jumps up*]: What was that?

BENJAMIN [*rises*]: Don't you know?

ELEONORA: No.

BENJAMIN: It was the police.

ELEONORA: Ah! Yes, it sounded like that when they came to take father. It was then that I became ill. And now they are coming and will take me.

BENJAMIN [*stands facing the upstage door in front of* ELEONORA]: No, they shan't take you. I shall protect you, Eleonora.

ELEONORA: That is good of you, Benjamin, but you mustn't —

BENJAMIN [*looks out through the curtains*]: There are two of them. [ELEONORA *tries to push* BENJAMIN *aside but he resists her gently.*] Not you, Eleonora. If that happened, I — wouldn't want to live any more.

ELEONORA: Go and sit on that chair, child. Go and sit down. [BENJAMIN *obeys unwillingly. She looks out through the curtains without concealing herself.*] It was only two boys. Oh, we of little faith! Do you think God is so cruel, when I have done nothing wrong, only acted thoughtlessly? It served me right. Why did I doubt?

BENJAMIN: But tomorrow the man will come to take the furniture.

ELEONORA: Let him come! And we must go! Leave everything — all the old furniture that Father gathered for us, and which I have seen since I was a little child. Yes — one must not own anything which binds one to the earth. Out on to the stony roads, and walk them with bleeding feet, for that road leads upwards, and that is why it's hard —

BENJAMIN: Now you are torturing yourself again, Eleonora.

ELEONORA: Let me! But do you know what I most dread being parted from? That clock there! He was there when I was born, and he has measured out my hours and my days — [*Lifts the clock from the table.*] Do you hear how he beats like a heart — just like a heart — and he stopped the hour Grandfather died, for he was here even then. Goodbye, little clock, may you soon stop again! Do you know, he used to go faster when we had bad luck in the house, just as though he wanted to get past the bad times, for our sake, of course! But when times were good, then he went slower so that we could be happy for longer. Nice clock! But then we had a nasty clock too — she has to hang in the kitchen still! She couldn't stand music, and as soon as Elis started playing the piano she began to strike, we all noticed it, not just me. And that's why she has to sit in the kitchen, because she was horrid. Lina doesn't like her either, because she won't stay quiet at night, and you can't boil eggs by her, they all get hard boiled, Lina says. Now you're laughing.

BENJAMIN: What else can I do?

ELEONORA: You're a nice boy, Benjamin, but you must be serious. Think of the birch there, behind the looking-glass.

BENJAMIN: But you talk so strangely, I have to laugh. And why should one always weep?

ELEONORA: If one doesn't weep in the vale of tears, where shall one weep?

BENJAMIN: Hm!

ELEONORA: You'd like to laugh the whole day, and that's why you've been made to suffer too. And I only like you when you're serious. Remember that!

BENJAMIN: Do you think we shall come through all this, Eleonora?

ELEONORA: Yes, most things will be all right once Good
   Friday is over, but not everything. Today the birch,
   tomorrow the Easter eggs. Today snow, tomorrow thaw.
   Today death, tomorrow resurrection.

BENJAMIN: How wise you are.

ELEONORA: Yes — I can feel already that the skies are
   clearing, that the snow is melting. It smells of melted
   snow already in here. And tomorrow the violets will
   flower on the south wall. The clouds have lifted, I can
   feel that when I breathe — oh, I know so well when the way
   is clear up to heaven. Go and draw the curtains, Benjamin.
   I want God to see us.

   BENJAMIN *gets up and obeys her. The moonlight
   falls into the room.*

ELEONORA: Do you see the full moon! It is the Easter
   moon. And now you know that the sun is still there,
   though it is the moon that gives us light!

ACT THREE

EASTER EVE

Music before the curtain: Haydn, Seven Words on the
Cross, No. 5; Adagio.
   *The scene is as before, but the curtains are open.
   The landscape outside is also unchanged, though the
   sky is overcast. The stove is lit; the upstage doors are
   closed.* ELEONORA *is seated in front of the stove
   holding a bunch of anemones.* BENJAMIN *enters
   right.*

ELEONORA: Where have you been for so long, Benjamin?

BENJAMIN: I wasn't long.

ELEONORA: I've missed you.

BENJAMIN: Where have you been, then, Eleonora?

ELEONORA: I've been to the market and bought anemones. Now I shall warm them. They'd frozen, the poor things.

BENJAMIN: Where is the sun?

ELEONORA: Behind the mists. There are no clouds today, only sea mists — you can smell the salt —

BENJAMIN: Did you see that the birds are still alive out there?

ELEONORA: Yes, and none falls to the ground without God willing it. But in the market there were dead birds —

ELIS [*enters right*] : Has the newspaper come?

ELEONORA: No, Elis.

> ELIS *walks across the room. When he is halfway,* CHRISTINA *enters left.*

CHRISTINA [*not looking at* ELIS] : Has the paper come?

ELEONORA: No, it hasn't come.

> CHRISTINA *goes across the room to the right, past* ELIS, *who exits left; neither looks at the other.*

ELEONORA: Ugh, how cold it's grown! There's hatred come into this house. As long as there was love here one could stand everything, but now, ugh, it's so cold!

BENJAMIN: Why do they ask about the newspaper?

ELEONORA: Don't you **understand? That's where it'll be** —

BENJAMIN: What?

ELEONORA: Everything. The burglary, the police — other things too —

MRS HEYST [*enters right*] : Has the paper come?

ELEONORA: No, Mother dear.

MRS HEYST [*exits right again*] : Tell me as soon as it arrives.

ELEONORA: The paper, the paper! Oh, if only the printing press had broken, if the editor had been taken ill — no, one mustn't say that. Do you know, I was with Father last night —

BENJAMIN: Last night?

ELEONORA: Yes, in my sleep. And then I was in America with my sister — the day before, she'd sold thirty dollars' worth of goods, and made five dollars' profit.

BENJAMIN: Is that a lot or a little?

ELEONORA: It's quite a lot!

BENJAMIN [*thoughtfully*] : Did you meet anyone you knew in the market?

ELEONORA: Why do you ask that? You mustn't be clever with me, Benjamin. You want to know my secrets, but you mayn't.

BENJAMIN: But you think you may know mine?

ELEONORA: Listen — the telephone-wires are humming. That means the newspaper has come out; and now people are telephoning. "Have you read —?" "Yes, I've read —" "Isn't it dreadful?"

BENJAMIN: What is dreadful?

ELEONORA: Everything! All life is dreadful. But we have to accept it. Think of Elis and Christina. They like each other, and they hate each other too, so that the thermometer drops when they walk through the room. She went to the concert last night and today they won't talk to each other. Why, why?

BENJAMIN: Because your brother is jealous.

ELEONORA: Don't use that word! Anyway, what do you know about it, except that it's an illness and therefore a

punishment? You mustn't meddle with what's evil, or
it'll touch you too. Just look at Elis. Haven't you noticed
how changed he is, since he began to read those papers —?

BENJAMIN: About the trial?

ELEONORA: Yes. Isn't it just as though all the wickedness
in them had entered his soul and was staring out through
his face and eyes? Christina feels this and so that she won't
be touched by his malice she makes herself an armour of
ice. Oh, those papers! If only I could burn them up! They
radiate malice and falsehood and revenge. So, my child,
you must keep yourself from what is evil and unclean,
keep it from your lips and from your heart.

BENJAMIN: You see everything.

ELEONORA: Do you know what will happen to me if
Elis and the others learn that it was I who bought the
daffodil in that unusual way?

BENJAMIN: What will they do to you?

ELEONORA: I shall be sent back — to where I came from,
where the sun never shines, where the walls are naked and
white as in a bathroom, where only weeping and wailing
is heard, where I have sat away a year of my life.

BENJAMIN: Where do you mean?

ELEONORA: Where people are tortured worse than in
prison, where the damned live, where unrest reigns and
despair keeps watch by night and day and whence no
one returns.

BENJAMIN: Worse than prison? Where do you mean?

ELEONORA: In prison people are condemned, but *there*
they are damned. In prison they question you and listen
to you, but there no one listens. Poor daffodil, it's your
fault. I meant so well and did such wrong.

BENJAMIN: But why don't you go to the flower-shop and
say: "This is what happened"? You're just like a lamb
waiting for the slaughter.

ELEONORA: When it knows that it must be slaughtered, it doesn't complain or try to escape. What else can it do?

ELIS [*enters left with a letter in his hand*]: Hasn't the newspaper come yet?

ELEONORA: No, brother.

ELIS [*turns and speaks into the kitchen*]: Lina, go out and buy a paper —

>   MRS HEYST *enters right.* ELEONORA *and*
>   BENJAMIN *are terrified.*

ELIS [*to* ELEONORA *and* BENJAMIN]: Go outside, children, for a moment, please.

>   *They go out left.*

MRS HEYST: You've got a letter?

ELIS: Yes.

MRS HEYST: From the asylum?

ELIS: Yes.

MRS HEYST: What do they want?

ELIS: They want Eleonora back.

MRS HEYST: They mustn't! She's my child!

ELIS: My sister.

MRS HEYST: What do you mean?

ELIS: I don't know. I can't think any longer.

MRS HEYST: But I can. Eleonora, the child of sorrow, has become the bringer of joy, though not of this world. Her restlessness has been transformed into peace, which she shares with others. Sane or not. To me she is wise, for she understands how to bear life's burdens better than me, better than any of us. Elis, am I sane, was I sane when I believed my husband innocent? I knew the evidence against him was tangible and overwhelming, and that he had himself confessed his guilt. And you, Elis, are you sane, if you can't see that Christina loves you? And you believe she hates you?

ELIS: It's a strange way to love.

MRS HEYST: No. Your coldness freezes her. It's you who hate. But you are unjust, and so you must suffer.

ELIS: How am I unjust? Didn't she go out last night with the friend who has betrayed me?

MRS HEYST: Yes, she did, and with your knowledge. But why did she go? You ought to be able to guess.

ELIS: No, I can't.

MRS HEYST: Very well. Then you must suffer as you do.

The kitchen door opens and a hand appears with a newspaper, which MRS HEYST *takes and passes to* ELIS.

ELIS: That was the worst blow. With her I could have borne the rest. But now my last ally is taken from me, and now I must fall.

MRS HEYST: Fall, but fall so that you can rise again. What's in the paper?

ELIS: I don't know. I'm afraid of the paper today.

MRS HEYST: Give it to me, I'll read it.

ELIS: No. Wait a moment —

MRS HEYST: What are you afraid of, what do you think's there?

ELIS: The worst that one could imagine.

MRS HEYST: That's happened to us already, so many times. Oh, Elis, if you knew my life — if you had been with me as I watched your father go step by step to his ruin, without my being able to warn all those he was taking with him. When he fell, I felt guilty too, for I

had known of his crime, and if the judge had not been a
wise man who realized my position as a wife, I would
have been punished too.

ELIS: What was it that destroyed him? I've never
understood.

MRS HEYST: Pride. Like all of us.

ELIS: Why should we who are innocent suffer for his sake?

MRS HEYST: Hush!

> Pause. She takes the newspaper and reads. ELIS
> stands uneasily at first, then begins to walk to and
> fro.

MRS HEYST: What's this! Didn't I say it was a yellow
tulip that had been stolen from the flower-shop?

ELIS: Yes, I remember clearly.

MRS HEYST: But here it says — a daffodil.

ELIS [fearfully]: Does it say that?

MRS HEYST [sinks into a chair]: It's Eleonora! Oh, my
God, my God!

ELIS: Then it isn't over.

MRS HEYST: Prison, or the asylum.

ELIS: She can't have done it, it's impossible! Impossible!

MRS HEYST: Now our family name will become public
and dishonoured once again —

ELIS: Do they suspect her?

MRS HEYST: It says that suspicions point in a certain
direction — it's clear enough what they mean.

ELIS: I'll speak to her.

MRS HEYST [rises]: Speak kindly! I can't any longer. She
is lost — found again, and lost. Speak to her. [Exits right.]

ELIS: Oh! [*Goes to the door, left.*] Eleonora, my child. Come here, I want to talk to you.

ELEONORA [*enters, her hair loose*]: I was putting up my hair.

ELIS: Never mind that. Tell me, my little sister, where did you get that flower?

ELEONORA: I took it.

ELIS: Oh, God!

ELEONORA [*hangs her head, crushed, her arms crossed over her breast*]: But I left the money there —

ELIS: Then you paid?

ELEONORA: Yes and no. It's always so difficult — but I didn't do anything wrong. I only meant well. Do you believe me?

ELIS: I believe you, sister. But the newspaper does not know that you are innocent.

ELEONORA: Dear Elis, then I must suffer too. [*Bows her head so that her hair hangs down over her face.*] What will they do to me now? Well, let them.

BENJAMIN [*enters left, distraught*]: No, you mustn't touch her. She's done nothing wrong. I know! It was me, me, me! [*Weeps.*] I did it.

ELEONORA: Don't believe him. It was me.

ELIS: Whom am I to believe? Whom am I to believe?

BENJAMIN: Me! Me!

ELEONORA: Me! Me!

BENJAMIN: Let me go to the police —

ELIS: Quiet, quiet!

BENJAMIN: No, I want to go, I want to go!

ELIS: Hush, children. Mother's coming.

MRS HEYST [*enters, deeply emotional, takes* ELEONORA *in her arms and kisses her*] : My child, my child, my beloved child! This is your home, and here you shall stay.

ELEONORA: Mother, you kissed me! You haven't done that for years. Why now, at last?

MRS HEYST: Because now — because the owner of the flower-shop is outside and begs us to forgive him for having caused so much trouble. The lost money has been found, and your name —

ELEONORA [*runs to* ELIS *and kisses him, then throws her arms around* BENJAMIN's *neck and kisses the top of his head*] : You dear child, you wanted to suffer for me. How could you want that?

BENJAMIN [*shyly, childishly*] : Because I like you so much, Eleonora.

MRS HEYST: Get dressed now, children, and go out into the garden. The sun's coming out.

ELEONORA: Yes — the sun's coming out. Come, Benjamin.

She takes his hand. They go out hand in hand.

ELIS: Can we throw the birch on the fire soon?

MRS HEYST: Not yet. There is one thing left.

ELIS: Lime?

MRS HEYST: He's standing outside. But he's acting very oddly. He's so friendly, I can't think why. But he won't stop talking, and keeps chattering about himself.

ELIS: Well, now that I've caught a glimpse of the sun I shan't be afraid to face the ogre. Let him come in!

MRS HEYST: But, Elis, don't provoke him. Providence has placed our fate in his hands, and the meek of heart — well, you know what happens to the proud.

ELIS: I know. Listen! Those galoshes — grr, grr, grr, swish, swish! Is he going to come in with them on? Why not? They're his carpets and furniture —

MRS HEYST: Elis, think of us all. [*Exits right.*]

ELIS: I do, Mother.

> LIME *enters right. He is an earnest oldish man of grim appearance. He has* grey *hair, with a wig and military sideboards. Big, bushy* black *eyebrows. Small clipped* black *mutton-chop whiskers. Round black horn-rimmed spectacles. Large cornelian charms on his watchchain; a Spanish cane in his hand. He is dressed in black with a fur coat; a top-hat in his hand; top-boots with leather galoshes, which squeak. As he enters he stares probingly at* ELIS, *and remains standing.*

LIME: My name is Lime.

ELIS [*defensively*] : Mine is Heyst. Please sit down.

> LIME *sits on the chair to the right of the sewing-table and stares fixedly at* ELIS. *Pause.*

ELIS: What can I do for you?

LIME [*formally*] : Hm. Yesterday evening I had the honour to notify you that I intended to pay you a visit. However, on reflection I felt it would be unseemly to discuss business on a sacred day.

ELIS: We are very grateful —

LIME [*sharply*] : We are *not* grateful. No! [*Pause.*] However, Yesterday I happened to visit the Governor — [*Pauses, and looks to see what impression his words make on* ELIS.] Do you know the Governor?

ELIS [*carelessly*] : I have not the honour.

LIME: Then you shall have the honour. He and I spoke of your father.

ELIS: I can well believe it.

LIME [*takes out a paper and puts it on the table*] : And he gave me this paper.

ELIS: I have been waiting a long time for this. But
before we proceed, I should like to ask you a question.

LIME [*curtly*] : Please do.

ELIS: Why do you not hand this paper to the legal authorities, so that we may at least be spared this painful and
drawn-out torture?

LIME: I see, young man.

ELIS: Young or not, I ask for no mercy, only justice.

LIME: I see. No mercy, no mercy! Look at this paper,
which I have put on the edge of the table here. Now I
put it back in my pocket. Justice, then; just justice. Now
listen, my friend. It happened once that I was robbed,
robbed of my money in a not very pleasant way. When I
then politely wrote to you and asked how much time you
needed to repay me, you replied discourteously. And
treated me as though I were a usurer intent on plundering
widows and orphans, although I was the one who had
been plundered and you were of the robber's party. But,
as I had more sense than you, I answered your discourteous
communication with one that was courteous, though brief.
You know my blue notepaper, don't you? I can have
lawyers' seals on it when I wish, but I don't always wish.
[*Looks round the room.*]

ELIS: Go ahead. The furniture is yours.

LIME: I wasn't looking at the furniture. I was looking to
see if your mother was here. No doubt she loves justice
as fondly as you do.

ELIS: I hope so.

LIME: Good. Do you know that if this justice that you
prize so highly had had its way, your mother, as accessory
before the fact, would have been punished as a common
criminal?

ELIS: Oh, no!

LIME: Yes. And it could still happen.

ELIS [*rises*] : My mother!

LIME [*takes out another paper, this time a blue one, and puts it on the table*] : Look! Now I put this paper on the edge of the table, and this one *is* blue — though it still bears no seal.

ELIS: Ah, God! My mother! Life is a circle.

LIME: Yes, my young lover of justice. Life is a circle. That's how it is. Suppose, now, I asked myself this question. You, Anders Johan Lime, born in poverty and brought up in privation and want, have you the right in your old age to deprive yourself and your children, yes, *your children*, of the support which you by your industry, forethought and self-denial, yes, *self-denial*, have scraped together penny by penny? Anders Johan Lime, where lies justice? You robbed no one, but if you advertise that you were robbed, you cannot live in this town any longer, for all men will shun the merciless ogre who demanded his own. Do you see, then, that there is a charity which shakes its fist at justice and transcends it? That is mercy.

ELIS: You are in the right. Take everything. It belongs to you.

LIME: I am in the right, but I dare not use that right.

ELIS: I will remember your children, and make no complaint.

LIME [*puts the paper back in his pocket*] : Good. Then we'll put the blue paper away again. Now let us go a step further.

ELIS: Excuse me. Do they really intend to prosecute my mother?

LIME: First let us go a step further. So you do not know the Governor personally?

ELIS: No, and I do not wish to know him.

LIME [*takes out the blue paper again and waves it*] : Not so fast, not so fast. The Governor, you see, was a childhood

friend of your father's, and he wishes to know you. Every
thought and action has its echo; every one. Don't you
want to visit him?

ELIS: No.

LIME: The Governor —

ELIS: Can we talk about something else?

LIME: You should be polite to me, you know. I am
defenceless — you have public opinion on your side, and
I have only justice. What have you against the Governor?
He doesn't like bicycles and free schools. Such are his
foibles. We need not exactly respect people's foibles, but
we can accept them, accept them and concentrate on
more important matters. In the major crises of life we
must take each other as we find us, with all our faults and
weaknesses, swallow each other, bones and all. Go to the
Governor!

ELIS: Never.

LIME: Is that the kind of man you are?

ELIS [bluntly]: Yes, that kind.

LIME [gets up and begins to walk in his creaking boots,
waving the blue paper]: That's not so good. Not so good.
Well, let's start again, from another angle. A vindictive
person intends to start an action against your mother.
That you can prevent.

ELIS: How?

LIME: Go to the Governor.

ELIS: No.

LIME [walks across and takes ELIS by the shoulders]: Then
you are the most contemptible wretch I have ever met in
my life. Well, then, I shall go to your mother myself.

ELIS: No. Please.

LIME: Will you go to the Governor, then?

ELIS: Yes.

LIME: Say that once more, and louder.

ELIS: Yes!

LIME: Than *that* matter's settled. [*Hands him the blue paper.*] There's *that* paper. [ELIS *takes it without reading it.*] Then we come to number two; which *was* number one. Shall we sit? [*They sit as before.*] You see, once we try to meet each other halfway, the road becomes half as long. Number two. My claim upon this house. Have no illusions; I neither can nor will give up what belongs to my family. I shall exact my claim to the last penny.

ELIS: I appreciate that.

LIME [*sharply*]: Oh, so you appreciate that, do you?

ELIS: I did not mean to be offensive —

LIME: No, I appreciate that. [*Raises his spectacles and stares at* ELIS.] Grr, grr! Swish, swish! The meat-red cornelians. The Ogre from Skinflint Mountain who doesn't eat children, only scares them. Yes, I'll scare you, I will, I'll scare you out of your senses. I'll have every stick of furniture out of here — I've got the inventory in my pocket, and if a single stick is missing, you'll go to the dungeon, where no sun nor star ever shines! Yes, I can eat widows and children when I'm provoked! Public opinion? Bah — I only need to move to another town. [ELIS *is speechless.*] You had a friend called Peter, Peter Holmblad. A linguist, and your pupil. But you wanted to exalt him into a kind of prophet. Well, he betrayed you; the cock crowed twice, eh? [ELIS *is silent.*] Human nature is unreliable, like matter and thought; Peter *did* betray you, I don't deny it, and I don't defend him. On that point! But the human heart is bottomless. Gold and dross lie mingled there. Peter was a false friend, but he was a friend, none the less.

ELIS: A false one —

LIME: A false one, yes, but a friend, none the less. And

this false friend has, unbeknown to you, done you a great service.

ELIS: That too!

LIME [*moves closer to* ELIS]: Life is a circle. Every action has its ghost which walks. Every one.

ELIS: Every bad action, yes. But good is only rewarded with evil.

LIME: Not always. Good actions have their echoes too. Believe me.

ELIS: I suppose I must, otherwise you'll plague the life out of me.

LIME: Not your life, but your pride and malice. Those I shall squeeze out of you.

ELIS: Go on.

LIME: Peter has done you a service, as I told you.

ELIS: I want no services from that man.

LIME: Are we back there? Now you listen to me. Thanks to your friend Peter, the Governor was induced to put in a word for your mother. So you are going to write a letter to Peter and thank him. Promise that.

ELIS: No. Anyone else in the world, but not him.

LIME [*moves closer*]: Then I must squeeze you again. Listen. You have money at the bank.

ELIS: Well, what's that to do with you? I am not responsible for my father's debts, am I?

LIME: Aren't you? Aren't you? Didn't you share in the eating and drinking which my children's money paid for in this house? Answer!

ELIS: I cannot deny that.

LIME: And since the furniture will not meet the sum of the debt, you will forthwith write out a cheque for the balance. You know the amount.

ELIS [*annihilated*] : That too?

LIME: That too. Come, write!

> ELIS *gets up, takes out his cheque-book and writes at the desk.*

LIME: Make it out to yourself or order.

ELIS: It won't be enough.

LIME: Then you must go out and borrow the rest. Every penny must be paid.

ELIS [*hands the cheque to* LIME] : Look, this is all I have. It is my summer and my bride. I have no more to give.

LIME: Then you must go out and borrow, as I said.

ELIS: That I cannot do.

LIME: Then you must find security.

ELIS: No one will stand security for a Heyst.

LIME: Now, I give you an ultimatum. Two alternatives: thank Peter, or pay me the full amount.

ELIS: I do not want to have anything to do with Peter.

LIME: Then you are the most contemptible of mortals! By a simple act of courtesy you can save your mother's home and the happiness of the girl you love, and you refuse! There must be some motive that you won't reveal. Why do you hate Peter?

ELIS: Kill me, but stop torturing me.

LIME: You are jealous of him! [ELIS *shrugs his shoulders.*] That's the truth. [*Gets up and walks up and down. Pause.*] Have you read the morning paper?

ELIS: Yes, unfortunately.

LIME: All of it?

ELIS: No, not all of it.

LIME: I see. So! Then you do not know that Peter is engaged?

ELIS: I didn't know that.

LIME: Nor to whom? Guess!

ELIS: How — ?

LIME: To a young lady named Alice, and it was decided yesterday at a certain concert at which your own betrothed acted as intermediary.

ELIS: Why did they have to keep it so secret?

LIME: Haven't two young people the right to have secrets of the heart from you?

ELIS: And for their happiness I must suffer these agonies?

LIME: Yes! Others have suffered to give you happiness. Your mother, your father, your sweetheart, your sister. Sit down, and I will tell you a story, a very short one.

> ELIS *sits unwillingly. During the scene which has passed, and that which follows, it grows lighter outside.*

LIME: It was about forty years ago. I came to the capital as a young man, alone, unknown and friendless, to look for work. I had only a few shillings, and it was a dark night. As I knew of no cheap hotel, I asked passers-by, but no one answered. I was in the depths of despair. Then a man came and asked why I was crying — I *was* crying. I told him of my predicament. He turned, took me to a hotel and comforted me with kind words. As I entered the lobby, the glass door of a shop was flung open and hit my elbow so that the glass smashed. The furious shopkeeper seized hold of me and demanded payment, otherwise he would call the police. Imagine my despair, with the prospect of a night on the street! The kind stranger, who had seen all this, intervened, took it on himself to call the police, and saved me. This man — was your father. So every action does have its echo, good ones too. For your father's sake, I cancel this claim. Take this paper and keep the cheque. [*Rises.*] Since you have difficulty is saying thank you, I shall leave at once, especially as I find it painful to be thanked. [*Goes towards the upstage door.*] Go instead at once to your mother and set her mind at peace. [*With a warding-off gesture to* ELIS *as the latter makes to approach him.*] Go!

> ELIS *runs out right. The upstage doors open, and* ELEONORA *and* BENJAMIN *enter, calm yet grave. They stop in terror as they see* LIME.

LIME: Well, children, come in. Don't be frightened! Do you know who I am? [*Puts on a voice.*] I am the Ogre from Skinflint Mountain, who scares little children. Grr! Grr! But I'm not so dangerous. Come here, Eleonora. [*Takes her head between his hands and looks her in the eyes.*] You have your father's good eyes, and he was a good man — but weak! [*Kisses her forehead.*] There, now!

ELEONORA: Oh, he is speaking kindly of Father! Can anyone think kindly of him?

LIME: I can. Ask your brother Elis.

ELEONORA: Then you can't want to hurt us!

LIME: No, my beloved child.

ELEONORA: Well, help us, then.

LIME: Child, I cannot save your father from his punishment, nor get Benjamin through his Latin — but the rest is already settled. Life does not give everything, and it gives nothing free. So you must help me. Will you?

ELEONORA: What can *I* do?

LIME: What day is it today? Look.

ELEONORA [*takes down the calendar from the wall*]: It is the 16th.

LIME: Good! Before the 20th you must get your brother Elis to pay a visit to the Governor and write a letter to Peter.

ELEONORA: Is that all?

LIME: Oh, my child! But if he fails to do this, then the ogre will come and gobble you up!

ELEONORA: Why must the ogre come and frighten children?

LIME: So that the children shall be good!

ELEONORA: That's right. The ogre is right! [*Kisses* LIME *on the sleeve of his fur coat.*] Thank you, kind ogre.

BENJAMIN: You must say Mr Lime.

ELEONORA: No, that's such a dull name.

LIME: Goodbye, children. Now you can throw the birch on to the fire.

ELEONORA: No, let it stay there. Children are so forgetful.

LIME: How well you know children, little girl. [*Goes.*]

ELEONORA: We can go to the country, Benjamin! In two months! Oh, if only they'll go quickly! [*Tears pages from the calendar and scatters them in the sunshine which is flooding into the room.*] Look how the days pass! April! May! June! And the sun is shining on them all! Look! Now you must thank God for helping us to get out to the country!

BENJAMIN [*shyly*]: Can't I say it silently?

ELEONORA: Yes, you can say it silently. For now the clouds have lifted, and we can be heard up there.

> CHRISTINA *has entered left and is standing motionless there.* ELIS *and* MRS HEYST *enter right.* CHRISTINA *and* ELIS *walk tenderly towards each other, but the curtain falls before they meet.*

Introduction to

THE DANCE OF DEATH

STRINDBERG wrote Part I of THE DANCE OF DEATH in October 1900, the same month in which he wrote EASTER. The contrast between the two plays is remarkable: EASTER is a play of reconciliation and hope, THE DANCE OF DEATH an expression of the blackest pessimism and hatred. But that he should have written the two plays practically simultaneously is not as incongruous as some critics have supposed. It was a part of Strindberg's paranoid-schizophrenic character that he alternated with bewildering rapidity between opposing moods. Taken together, the two plays portray him more accurately and fully than either work considered by itself.

After his return to Stockholm from Lund in the summer of 1899, he had spent much time with his sister Anna and her husband, Hugo Philp, a schoolmaster who had been a fellow-student of Strindberg's at Uppsala thirty years before. Philp had taken Strindberg's side in the family row of 1876 about the question of inheritance, as a result of which Strindberg's father had excommunicated both Strindberg and Anna; and he had also supported him in the controversy surrounding the publication of Strindberg's short stories, GETTING MARRIED, in 1884. Ten years later Strindberg, turning suddenly against his old friend as schizophrenics do, had written a spiteful character sketch of Philp in a volume of scientific stories-cum-essays, VIVISECTIONS; but the long-suffering Philps had visited and consoled Strindberg during his INFERNO crisis in Paris in 1896, and during this summer of 1899 they had him to stay at their house at Furusund, in the Stockholm archipelago. Their daughter Märta, as an old lady of over ninety, told me her memories of this summer; how Strindberg loved to sit in the evening sunlight with a glass of wine and listen to her playing classical music on the piano, "though he himself could only pick out a tune with

one finger". "He must have been a very difficult guest," I
suggested, but she said: "No. He was charming, and so
gentle." Then she was silent for a moment, and added: "Of
course, when the black mood was on him, then he was
terrible." Then another pause, and: "My mother was the
same." She rebuked me for pronouncing his Christian name,
August, in the French manner; she said it was always
pronounced exactly like the month in English.

Anna had been trained as a violinist and had won a
scholarship to Paris, but had declined it in order to marry
Philp. Gunnar Ollén — whose admirable book, STRIND-
BERGS DRAMATIK (Stockholm, 1961), so comprehensively
details the factual background of the plays — describes her as
having "a pronounced artistic temperament, like her brother",
thus confirming her daughter's account of her, and as
being "temperamental, restless and suspicious". Even when
she was eighty, her motto was: "Peace and calm are the
worst things I know." Märta tells that her mother was
always moving, always travelling, loved parties, was impossible with servants and extravagant with money. Hugo Philp
was a linguist and a wit, liked by his pupils. He adored his
wife, though he was unfortunately totally unmusical.
Intellectually and politically he was a radical, and remained
sceptical about Strindberg's recent conversion to religion.

For about a year, things went well between Strindberg
and the Philps. Anna, like Märta, would entertain him on
the piano, and also the violin, and the family would play
cards with him, which he enjoyed. In January 1900, Hugo
became seriously ill with diabetes; Strindberg would sit
with him, and they would talk about death. In May of that
year Hugo had an attack of dizziness. At the beginning of
June, Strindberg accompanied them, as in the previous
year, to Furusund; but later that month he quarrelled with
them, partly because Hugo defended some writers whom
Strindberg loathed, partly because Hugo rebuked him for
the way he had treated his first wife, Siri. Another reason
seems to have been that Strindberg felt a strong physical
attraction towards his sister, and was consequently jealous
of Hugo. He was, moreover, suffering from a throat infec-

tion which increased his ill-humour, and before the end of June he returned angrily to Stockholm.

As was his custom when friends suddenly, in his eyes, became enemies, he conceived a violent hatred for Hugo, and his diary for that summer contains many references to Hugo and Anna. On 10 August, he noted: "Walked past the Philps' house [in Stockholm]. The blinds were down; on them were visible two hens tied by the necks, tugging at the cord, one on either side of an urn." When they celebrated their silver wedding on 5 October, Strindberg did not attend. Dr Ollén rightly remarks that anger tended to bring out the best in Strindberg as a writer, and that, recognizing this, he welcomed it and rejected attempts at reconciliation, at least until he had transmuted his anger into creative activity.

Four days later, on 9 October according to his OCCULT DIARY, he began THE DANCE OF DEATH, and by 31 October he had finished Part I — which, like Part I of TO DAMASCUS, he at first conceived as a complete play in itself, with no thought of a sequel. He took the title from Saint-Saëns' *Danse Macabre*, which he originally intended to include as the music to which the Captain dances; but, since Ibsen had used that in JOHN GABRIEL BORKMAN four years previously, Strindberg switched to *The Entry of the Boyars*. He told his German translator, Emil Schering, that he had considered entitling the play THE VAMPIRE. Although he wrote the play very rapidly, he had made several notes and sketches for it earlier; at various stages of its development, he planned to make the chief character a ship's pilot, a sacked professor and a hospital doctor. The play was probably influenced by Swedenborg's DE COELO ET INFERNO, a work which Strindberg knew well. In this, Swedenborg tells how happy a marriage can be when it "stands under the influence of religion"; but some marriages he states, "stand under the influence of evil"; and these are called "marriages of Hell". Partners in such a marriage can talk to each other, and may even be drawn to each other through lust; "but inwardly, they burn with a murderous mutual hatred which is so great that it cannot be described".

THE DANCE OF DEATH would seem to have been clearly based on the Philps. Alice is an actress who has given up her theatre career for marriage, just as Anna had sacrificed her musical career; Edgar, like Hugo, is suddenly taken seriously ill; and Kurt, who covets Edgar's wife, just as Strindberg seems secretly to have coveted Anna, sits by the bedside of the husband he would like to replace, and comforts him. Like the Philps, Edgar and Alice have a silver wedding coming up; they even share the Philps' liking for a game of cards. Hugo Philp certainly supposed Edgar to be based on himself, for on reading the play he threw it into the fire. But Edgar was also (and there may have been other models) at least partly based on a customs officer named Ossian Ekbohrn whom Strindberg had known earlier and who lived just outside Stockholm at Sandhamn. In an essay written in 1894 entitled *Nemesis Divina*, Strindberg described Ekbohrn as "a junior officer, brutal, uneducated, his wounded vanity thirsting for revenge on a superior". He lives with his wife, having no contact with her, isolated by "his despotism and his bullying of the islanders who hate him . . . I play the humble sympathizer who admires his broad vision of life and the universe . . . I have won his wife's heart by becoming a lightning-conductor to divert her husband's violence . . . 'For God's sake, take care!' she says to me. 'You don't realize that my husband is half-mad.' " That is precisely the situation of Alice, Edgar and Kurt in THE DANCE OF DEATH. What is curious is that Kurt, a character with whom Strindberg clearly identified himself (in an earlier draft of the play, Strindberg calls him The Stranger, *Den Okände*, the name he had given to the main and patently autobiographical character in TO DAMASCUS), should be so passive; but if Strindberg was in fact physically attracted by his sister, he may have been unwilling to portray himself as the active partner in the near-affair.

Part II he wrote some time at the end of 1900, probably in December. Emil Schering, preparing his translation of Part I for the German public, had hinted to Strindberg that he thought it too blackly pessimistic for the German

theatres to stage, and Strindberg may have written the
sequel, with its more hopeful ending (at least as regards the
younger generation) to counter this. But his notes for Part I
show that he had in mind, even at that stage, to suggest that
feuding families can be united by their children — as was to
happen with him and the Philps, for in 1907 their son
Henry married Strindberg's daughter Greta.

Despite the (one would have thought) obvious dramatic power of the two plays, especially Part I, nearly five
years elapsed before either was staged. At length, in September 1905, Part I received its première, not in Sweden
but in Cologne, and the two parts were staged together
that autumn in Berlin. During the next few years, they
were enthusiastically acclaimed; but neither play was
seen in Sweden until 1909, when Strindberg's own Intimate
Theatre presented Part I. "First and last, the Captain must
look old!" Strindberg commanded August Falck, who was
rehearsing the part. "His ugliness, age and whisky must be
visible." In his reminiscences, FEM ÅR MED STRIND-
BERG (FIVE YEARS WITH STRINDBERG) (Stockholm,
1935), Falck paints a vivid picture of the dramatist advising
his actor-director:

" 'THE DANCE OF DEATH, my boy! That's my best
play!' Strindberg often repeated . . . 'The Captain! What a
part!' And he jumped up and acted it for me. 'A refined
demon! Evil shines out of his eyes, which sometimes flash
with a glint of satanic humour. His face is bloated with
liquor and corruption, and he so relishes saying evil things
that he almost sucks them, tastes them, rolls them round
his tongue before spitting them out. He thinks of course
that he is cunning and superior, but like all stupid people
he becomes at such moments a pitiful and petulant wretch.'

"And with sweet-sour, fawning expressions, with
gestures both jaunty and pitiful, he walked around or threw
himself down into a chair. What he particularly often liked
to act was the powerful scene when Alice, with a bored
expression, plays the march *The Dance of the Boyars*,
which incites and hypnotizes the Captain to dance — wildly
and clumsily, terrifyingly. At such moments he was an

excellent actor — a great dramatic talent. His vivid impersonation remains for ever in my mind's eye and echoes in my ear."

Part I received a mixed reception from the Swedish press when performed (as it had had when published in 1901). August Brunius mocked it as "a pathological study of various physical and spiritual illnesses: erotic hysteria and sclerosis of the heart and the like. A hospital theatre would be the most appropriate locale for THE DANCE OF DEATH." But other critics were more perceptive, and the play proved one of the Intimate Theatre's biggest successes, achieving eighty-five performances. Part II, which was presented two months later, was even more favourably received, and reached the respectable total of sixty-five performances. The role of Judith, the Captain's daughter, was played by a young actress named Fanny Falkner, who, though more than forty years Strindberg's junior, twice became briefly engaged to him — for five days in 1909 and for a single day in 1910.

Max Reinhardt, a great Strindberg pioneer, staged a famous production of both parts at the Deutsches Theater in Berlin in 1912, with Paul Wegener and Gertrud Eysoldt, and in November 1915 he brought his production to Stockholm, where it created a sensation. He began and ended Part I with Edgar and Alice seated on opposite sides of the stage with their backs to the audience, staring into space. Since then, THE DANCE OF DEATH, or at any rate Part I, has been one of Strindberg's most frequently performed plays, both in Sweden and abroad. London first saw it, briefly, in 1924, when George Merritt and Sybil Arundale acted the two parts, on separate evenings each for a single performance at the St George's Hall under the auspices of the Sunday Players. Part I was directed by Peter Godfrey in 1925 at his little Gate Theatre in Covent Garden, with Merritt again as the Captain, Molly Veness as Alice and Godfrey himself as Kurt, a production which was successful enough to be revived the following year. In 1928 Robert Loraine gave a famous performance in the play at the Apollo Theatre (the first Strindberg production seen in the West End), following his success with THE FATHER the previous year. Loraine took a somewhat free hand with the text, which resulted in a public row between him and the then Swedish Minister in London, Baron Erik Palmstierna.

In 1965, Paul Scofield and Mai Zetterling acted Part I with distinction on television, but it was not until 1966, thirty-eight years after Loraine's triumph, that the play was revived on the London stage. That year, Glen Byam Shaw directed both parts, in a single bill, at the Old Vic for the National Theatre, with Laurence Olivier as Edgar and Geraldine McEwan as Alice. Olivier, though his appearance hardly answered Strindberg's demand for "ugliness, age and whisky", gave a splendidly dynamic and scarifying performance. Another memorable interpretation of the role was that by Erich von Stroheim, in a film which he directed (in French, in Italy), in 1947; unfortunately, he had a very weak Alice.

On the occasion of the 1928 production, Charles Morgan, an outspoken champion of Strindberg in an age when most London critics regarded him as an impossible foreign crank, wrote an anonymous review in the *Times* which remains, fifty years later, a wonderfully valid assessment. "Loose, tangled and contradictory though this play often is, it leaves an astonishing, an almost unaccountable, impression of genius. To the coldly regarding eye it exhibits a crowd of faults — now of over-emphasis, now of forced movements towards a climax, now of rash inconsistency of structure; yet, as a beggar's cloak full of holes may have a kind of majestic beauty when the wind fills it, so this broken drama, having unmistakably the winds of vision in it, has beauty and dignity and power." One would add that nowadays we do not expect or particularly like a play to be what the 1920s regarded as "well-made", and that it is partly the jagged, uneven shape of Strindberg's dramas, with the characters veering sharply from mood to mood as people under the stress of violent emotion do, that makes him, more than Ibsen, the model for so many of our younger playwrights, both in England and in America.

THE DANCE OF DEATH

(1900)

PART I

CHARACTERS

EDGAR, Captain at the Artillery Fortress
ALICE, his wife, an ex-actress
KURT, Quarantine Master
JENNY
THE OLD WOMAN
THE SENTRY

SCENE

The interior of a circular fortress tower, of grey stone. Upstage, two large doors with glass panes, through which can be seen the seashore, with batteries. On either side of the gateway, a window with flowers and birds. Right of the doorway, an upright piano. Downstage of this, a sewing-table with two easy chairs. Left centre, a writing-table with a telegraph apparatus; downstage, a whatnot with photographic portraits. Beside this, a chaise-longue. Against the wall, a sideboard. A ceiling lamp. On the wall by the piano hang two big laurel wreaths with ribbons, flanking a portrait of a woman in theatrical costume. By the doorway a wardrobe with uniform paraphernalia, sabres, etc. Near it, a secretaire. Left of the doorway hangs a mercury barometer.

ACT ONE

Scene 1

It is a mild autumn evening. The doors of the fortress stand open, and an artilleryman can be seen at his post at the battery on the shore. He wears a helmet with bands. Now and then his sabre glitters in the red light of the setting sun. The sea is dark and still.

The CAPTAIN *is seated in the armchair on the left of the sewing-table, fingering a spent cigar. He is in a worn undress uniform with riding-boots and spurs. He looks tired and bored.* ALICE *is seated in the armchair on the right and is doing nothing. She looks tired and expectant.*

CAPTAIN: Won't you play something for me?

ALICE [*indifferent, but not snappish*]: What shall I play?

CAPTAIN: What *you* wish.

ALICE: You don't like my repertoire.

CAPTAIN: Nor you mine.

ALICE [*changing the subject*]: Do you want those doors open?

CAPTAIN: If you do.

ALICE: Let them be, then. [*Pause.*] Why aren't you smoking?

CAPTAIN: I can't stand strong tobacco nowadays.

ALICE [*almost amiably*]: Smoke something milder, then. It's your only pleasure, you say.

CAPTAIN: Pleasure? What's that?

ALICE: Don't ask me. I'm as ignorant on the subject as you. Don't you want your whisky yet?

CAPTAIN: I'll wait a little. What have you got for dinner?

ALICE: How should I know? Ask Christine.

CAPTAIN: Shouldn't we be getting some mackerel soon? It's autumn.

ALICE: Yes, it's autumn.

CAPTAIN: Outside and in! But, notwithstanding the chill that comes with autumn, outside and in, a grilled mackerel with a slice of lemon and a glass of white Mâcon is a thought not wholly to be despised.

ALICE: Quite the orator, aren't you?

CAPTAIN: Have we any Mâcon left in the cellar?

ALICE: I wasn't aware we'd had any cellar for the past five years.

CAPTAIN: You are always ill informed. Well, we'll have to lay some in for our silver wedding —

ALICE: You really intend to celebrate that?

CAPTAIN: Naturally.

ALICE: It would be more natural if we kept our misery private. Our twenty-five years of misery —

CAPTAIN: My dear Alice. Miserable it has been, but we have had our fun now and then. And one must enjoy the brief time one has, for after that, there is nothing.

ALICE: Is there nothing? If only we could be sure.

CAPTAIN: Nothing at all. Just a barrowload of muck to fertilize the garden.

ALICE: All this for a garden.

CAPTAIN: That's what life is. Don't blame me.

ALICE: All this. [*Pause.*] Has the post come?

CAPTAIN: Yes.

ALICE: Is the butcher's bill there?

CAPTAIN: Yes.

ALICE: How much?

CAPTAIN [*takes a piece of paper from his pocket and puts his glasses on his nose, but at once removes them*]: You read it. I can't see any more —

ALICE: What's wrong with your eyes?

CAPTAIN: Don't know.

ALICE: Age.

CAPTAIN: Oh, rubbish. Me!

ALICE: Well, not me.

CAPTAIN: Hm!

ALICE [*looks at the bill*]: Can you pay this?

CAPTAIN: Yes. But not now.

ALICE: Later. In a year, when you're retired on a small pension. And that'll be too late. And you'll be ill again —

CAPTAIN: Ill? I've never been ill. Just out of sorts, once. I'll live for twenty years.

ALICE: The Doctor thought otherwise.

CAPTAIN: The Doctor!

ALICE: Well, who else should know?

CAPTAIN: There's nothing wrong with me and there never has been. And never will be. I'll die with my boots on, as an old soldier should.

ALICE: Talking of the Doctor, you know he's giving a party this evening.

CAPTAIN [*disturbed*]: Well, so what? We aren't invited because we don't mix with them, and we don't mix with them because I despise them both. They're trash.

ALICE: You say that of everyone.

CAPTAIN: Because everyone is trash.

ALICE: Except you.

CAPTAIN: Yes, because I have behaved like a gentleman whatever life has thrown at me. That is why I am not trash.

   Pause.

ALICE: Do you want to play cards?

CAPTAIN: Why not?

ALICE [*takes out a pack of cards from the drawer of the sewing-table and begins to shuffle it*]: You know he's got the regimental band. For a private party!

CAPTAIN [*angry*]: That's because he sneaks off to town with the Colonel! Dirty little creeper. If I'd chosen to do that —

ALICE [*deals*]: I used to be friends with Gerda. But she cheated me —

CAPTAIN: They're all cheats. [*Peers at the trump marker.*] What are trumps?

ALICE: Put your glasses on.

CAPTAIN: They won't help. Come on.

ALICE: Spades are trumps.

CAPTAIN [*displeased*]: Spades?

ALICE [*plays a card*]: Anyway, it's not just them. The new officers' wives don't want anything to do with us either.

CAPTAIN [*plays and takes the trick*]: What does that matter? We never give parties, so we won't notice. I can manage alone. I always have.

ALICE: So have I. But the children. The children grow up without knowing anyone.

CAPTAIN: They'll have to find their own friends, in town. My trick! Have you any trumps left?

ALICE: I've got one. That's mine!

CAPTAIN: Six and eight make fifteen —

ALICE: Fourteen, fourteen.

CAPTAIN: Six and eight makes fourteen points to me. I think I've forgotten how to count. And two makes sixteen. [*Yawns.*] Your deal.

ALICE: You're tired.

CAPTAIN [*deals*]: Not at all.

ALICE [*listens*]: You can hear the music from here. [*Pause*] Do you think Kurt's been invited?

CAPTAIN: He came this morning, so he's had time to get his tails out, though not to visit us.

ALICE: Quarantine Master? Is there to be a quarantine here?

CAPTAIN: Yes.

ALICE: I mean he is my cousin, and we once shared the same name —

CAPTAIN: That was no honour.

ALICE: Look — ! [*Sharply.*] You forget about my family and I'll forget about yours.

CAPTAIN: Now, now! Are we going to start again?

ALICE: Does the Quarantine Master have to be a doctor?

CAPTAIN: No. He's just a kind of administrator and book-keeper. And Kurt's never been either.

ALICE: He's had a hard life —

CAPTAIN: He cost me money. And when he left his wife and children, he lost what honour he had.

ALICE: There's no need to be so harsh, Edgar.

CAPTAIN: Well, it's true. Remember what happened later in America? Well! I can't say I miss him. But he was a nice lad and I liked arguing with him.

ALICE: Because he always gave in.

CAPTAIN [*haughtily*]: Gave in, gave in, at least he was a man one could talk to. On this island there isn't anyone who understands what I say. It's a community of imbeciles —

ALICE: It's strange that Kurt should come just at the time of our silver wedding — whether we celebrate it or not —

CAPTAIN: Why is it strange? Oh, I see — yes, it was he who brought us together. Married you off, was the phrase they used.

ALICE: Well, he did, didn't he?

CAPTAIN: Oh, yes! He got some idea into his head — well, you should know best.

ALICE: It was just a whim —

CAPTAIN: Which we have had to suffer for. Not he.

ALICE: Yes. Think if I'd stayed in the theatre. All my friends are stars now.

CAPTAIN [*gets up*]: Oh, we're back there, are we? I'll have a whisky. [*Goes to the sideboard and pours a whisky and soda, which he drinks standing.*] We ought to have a rail to rest our feet on. Then we could dream we were in Copenhagen, at the American Bar.

ALICE: We must have one made, if it'll remind us of Copenhagen. Those were our happiest days, in spite of everything.

CAPTAIN [*drinks greedily*]: Yes! Do you remember Nimb's charlotte russe? [*Smacks his lips.*]

ALICE: No. But I remember the concerts at Tivoli.

CAPTAIN: You have such refined taste, my dear.

ALICE: You should be proud, at having a wife with taste —

CAPTAIN: I am.

ALICE: When you need to boast about her —

CAPTAIN [*drinks*]: They must be dancing at the Doctor's now. I can hear the trombones — [*hums in waltz rhythm*] — oompapa, oompapa —

ALICE: I can hear the Alcazar waltz. Yes — it's a long time since I danced a waltz —

CAPTAIN: Could you still manage it?

ALICE: Still?

CAPTAIN: We-ell? You're done with dancing, aren't you, like me?

ALICE: I'm ten years younger than you.

CAPTAIN: Then we are the same age, since the lady is always ten years younger.

ALICE: Stuff! You're an old man. I'm in my prime.

CAPTAIN: But of course! You can be delightful — to other men, when you try.

ALICE: Can we light the lamp now?

CAPTAIN: Why not?

ALICE: Ring, then.

> The CAPTAIN *walks heavily to the desk and rings the bell.* JENNY *enters right.*

CAPTAIN: Jenny, would you mind lighting the lamp, please?

ALICE [*sharply*]: Light the lamp!

JENNY: Very good, madam.

> *She lights the ceiling lamp. The* CAPTAIN *watches her.*

ALICE [*curtly*] : Have you dried the glass properly?

JENNY: Yes, all it needs.

ALICE: How dare you answer like that?

CAPTAIN: Alice — please —

ALICE [*to* JENNY] : Get out! I'd better light the lamp myself.

JENNY: Yes, I think you had. [*Walks towards door.*]

ALICE [*gets up*] : Go!

JENNY [*pauses*] : I wonder what you'd say if I did?
    ALICE *is silent.* JENNY *goes. The* CAPTAIN *walks over and lights the lamp.*

ALICE [*uneasily*] : Do you think she will go?

CAPTAIN: Wouldn't surprise me. We'll be in a hole if she does.

ALICE: It's your fault. You spoil them.

CAPTAIN: Nonsense. They're always polite to me.

ALICE: Because you cringe to them. You cringe to all servants, because you're a bully with a slave's mentality.

CAPTAIN: Now, now —

ALICE: Yes, you cringe to your men and your junior officers, but you behave like an equal with your equals and your superiors.

CAPTAIN: Pah!

ALICE: You're like all bullies. Do you think she'll leave?

CAPTAIN: Yes, if you don't go and talk nicely to her.

ALICE: I?

CAPTAIN: If I did, you'd say I was flirting with the servants.

ALICE: Think if she does go! Then I'll have to do all the work again, and ruin my hands.

CAPTAIN: I can imagine worse things. But if Jenny goes, Christine will go, and then we shan't get another servant to come to this island. The ferry pilot frightens off every girl who comes to apply, and if he forgets to, my sentries will.

ALICE: Yes, your sentries. Whom I have to feed in my kitchen, and whom you haven't the courage to order out —

CAPTAIN: If I did, they'd go too, and we'd be left without a garrison.

ALICE: But it's ruining us.

CAPTAIN: Which is why the mess committee intend to apply to His Majesty for a subsistence allowance —

ALICE: For us?

CAPTAIN: No, for the sentries.

ALICE [*laughs*]: You're crazy.

CAPTAIN: Yes, laugh a little for me. We need some mirth.

ALICE: I'll soon have forgotten how to laugh.

CAPTAIN [*lights his cigar*]: One must never forget that. It's a bit of a bore, though.

ALICE: It certainly isn't funny. Do you want to go on playing?

CAPTAIN: No, it tires me.

Pause.

ALICE: You know, it does annoy me that my cousin, our new Quarantine Master, should pay his respects to our enemies before he comes and sees us.

CAPTAIN: Oh, why bother about that?

ALICE: Well, did you see in the paper that the list of arrivals described him as "of independent means"? That means he must have come into money.

CAPTAIN: Independent means? Indeed! A rich relation! First we've ever had in this family.

ALICE: In your family. We've had plenty of rich ones in mine.

CAPTAIN: He's got hold of some money, so he's giving himself airs. But I know how to play him. He won't get a look at my cards.

The telegraph apparatus begins to click.

ALICE: Who's that?

CAPTAIN [*stands still*]: Quiet a moment, please!

ALICE: Well, go and see what it says.

CAPTAIN: I can hear. I hear what they're saying. It's the children! [*Goes to the apparatus and taps out a reply. The apparatus taps back. The* CAPTAIN *answers.*]

ALICE: Well?

CAPTAIN: Wait a moment. [*Taps the "stop" signal.*] It's the children. Judith is ill again. She's staying away from school.

ALICE: Again! What else did they say?

CAPTAIN: Money, of course.

ALICE: Why does Judith have to be in such a hurry? If she took her exams next year it'd be soon enough.

CAPTAIN: You tell her that and see what good it does.

ALICE: You should tell her.

CAPTAIN: How many times haven't I? You should know that children do as they please.

ALICE: In this house, anyway. [*The* CAPTAIN *yawns.*] Must you yawn in your wife's presence?

CAPTAIN: What else is there to do? Haven't you noticed

that every day we say the same things? When just now
you said your inevitable "In this house, anyway", I should
have replied as usual "It's not just *my* house". But since
I've given that answer five hundred times already, I merely
yawned. My yawn could mean "I can't be bothered to
reply", or "You are right, my angel", or "For God's sake
let's stop".

ALICE: You're being really charming tonight.

CAPTAIN: Won't it be time for dinner soon?

ALICE: Do you know the doctor has ordered supper from
the Grand Hotel? On the mainland.

CAPTAIN: No? Then they'll be having grouse. There's no
finer bird than grouse. But one mustn't roast it in lard.

ALICE: Ugh! Must you talk about food?

CAPTAIN: You prefer wine? I wonder what those
Philistines will drink with grouse.

ALICE: Shall I play for you?

CAPTAIN [*sits at his desk*]: The last resort! Yes, as long as
we don't have any of your funeral marches and jeremiads.
There's no need to underline the obvious. I can always fill
in the words. "Hear how miserable I am! Miaow, miaow!
Hear what a frightful husband I have! Brum, brum, brum!
Oh, if only he would die!" Kettledrums, fanfares! And we
end with the Alcazar waltz and a champagne gallop! Talking of champagne, we have two bottles left. Shall we open
them and pretend we've guests?

ALICE: No, we won't. They're mine. I bought them myself.

CAPTAIN: Always careful with the purse-strings, aren't
you?

ALICE: And you're always mean, to your wife at any rate.

CAPTAIN: Then I've no further ideas. Shall I dance for
you?

ALICE: No, thank you. You're too old to dance.

CAPTAIN: You should have a female companion to live with you.

ALICE: Thank you. You should have a male.

CAPTAIN: Thank you. That was tried, and the result was mutual dissatisfaction. But interesting, as an experiment — I mean, that as soon as a stranger entered the house, you and I became so happy — to begin with —

ALICE: But afterwards!

CAPTAIN: Yes, let's not talk of that.

There is a knock on the door, left.

ALICE: Who can that be at this hour?

CAPTAIN: Jenny doesn't usually knock.

ALICE: Go and open it, and don't shout "Come in!" as though you were in an office.

CAPTAIN [*goes towards the door*]: You don't like anything associated with work, do you?

Another knock.

ALICE: Well, open it!

CAPTAIN [*opens it and is handed a visiting card*]: It's Christine. Has Jenny left? [*Inaudible reply.*] [*To* ALICE]: Jenny's left.

ALICE: I'll have to be a housemaid again, then.

CAPTAIN: And I a valet.

ALICE: Can't we use one of the men from the kitchen?

CAPTAIN: One can't do that nowadays.

ALICE: That card can't have been Jenny's, surely?

CAPTAIN [*looks at the card through his glasses, then hands it to* ALICE]: You read it. I can't.

ALICE [*reads*]: Kurt! It's Kurt! Go out and greet him!

CAPTAIN [*exits left*]: Kurt! Well, how nice!

> ALICE *arranges her hair and seems to become alive.*
> *The* CAPTAIN *enters left with* KURT.

CAPTAIN: Well here he is, the renegade! Welcome, my dear chap. Good to see you.

ALICE [*to* KURT]: Welcome to my house, Kurt.

KURT: Thank you. It's been a long time.

CAPTAIN: What is it, fifteen years? And we've grown old —

ALICE: Oh, Kurt hasn't changed, I don't think.

CAPTAIN: Sit down, sit down! Now, first of all, what's your programme? Are you booked for dinner tonight?

KURT: I've been invited to the Doctor's, but I haven't promised to come.

ALICE: Then you'll stay with us?

KURT: That would seem the most natural thing, since you are my relatives. But the Doctor is my boss, and it might be awkward later —

CAPTAIN: What nonsense! I've never been scared of my bosses —

KURT: I didn't say I was scared. It just might be awkward.

CAPTAIN: On this island, I'm the master. You get behind me and no one will dare to harm you.

ALICE: Be quiet now, Edgar. [*Takes* KURT's *hand.*] Never mind about bosses and masters — you stay here with us. People will think that natural and correct.

KURT: Very well, then. You certainly make me feel welcome here.

CAPTAIN: Why shouldn't you be welcome? We've no quarrel, have we? [KURT *cannot conceal a certain embarrassment.*] What could there be? You were a bit thoughtless once, but you were young and I've forgotten it. I don't bear grudges.

ALICE *is embarrassed. They all sit at the sewing-table.*

ALICE: Well, you've been out in the wide world.

KURT: Yes. And now I'm back here with both of you —

CAPTAIN: Whom you married off twenty-five years ago.

KURT: I didn't quite do that, but never mind. It's good to see you're still together after twenty-five years —

CAPTAIN: Yes, we've managed. We've had our ups and downs, but as you say, we're still together. And Alice has no cause to complain; everything's gone fine, money has been pouring in. Perhaps you don't know that I am a famous author — in the educational field —

KURT: Oh, yes, I remember when we last saw each other, you'd published a rifle instruction handbook that had gone well. Do they still use it in the army schools —?

CAPTAIN: It's still in print, and it's still the best, though they've tried to replace it with an inferior one — which gets read, but is quite worthless.

Painful silence.

KURT: You've been abroad, I hear?

ALICE: Yes, we've been to Copenhagen. Five times, imagine!

CAPTAIN: Yes! You see, when I took Alice out of the theatre —

ALICE: Took? You?

CAPTAIN: Yes, I took you as a wife should be taken —

ALICE: How dashing of you.

CAPTAIN: But since it was subsequently shoved down my throat that I had cut short her brilliant career — hm! — I had to make up for this by promising to take my wife to Copenhagen — and that promise I have kept — like a gentleman! Five times we have been there! Five. [*Counts the fingers on his left hand.*] Have you been in Copenhagen?

KURT [*smiles*]: No. I've mostly been in America.

CAPTAIN: America? That must be a frightful country, nothing but gangsters.

KURT [*embarrassed*]: Well, it isn't Copenhagen.

ALICE: Have you — heard anything — from your children?

KURT: No.

ALICE: Forgive me, Kurt dear, but it was rather thoughtless of you to leave them like you did —

KURT: I didn't leave them. The court awarded custody to their mother —

CAPTAIN: Let's not discuss that now. I think you were well out of that mess.

KURT [*to* ALICE]: How are your children?

ALICE: Oh, fine, thank you. They're at school in town. They're almost grown up.

CAPTAIN: Yes, they're clever kids. The boy's got a brilliant brain. Brilliant. He's going onto the General Staff —

ALICE: If they take him.

CAPTAIN: If? He'll be Minister of Defence.

KURT: Changing the subject — there's going to be a quarantine here — bubonic plague, cholera and all that. As you know, I'll be working under the Doctor. What kind of a chap is he?

CAPTAIN: Chap? He isn't a chap. He's an ignorant rogue.

KURT [*to* ALICE]: How very unpleasant for me!

ALICE: He's not as bad as Edgar makes out, but I can't say I like him —

CAPTAIN: He's a rogue! And so are the others, the excise officer, the postmaster, the telephone woman, the chemist, the pilot, the — what does he call himself? — alderman — they're all a pack of rogues, which is why I have nothing to do with them.

KURT: Are you at loggerheads with all of them?

CAPTAIN: All!

ALICE: Yes, it's true. One really can't associate with such people.

CAPTAIN: Every bullying little bureaucrat in the country seems to have been sent here.

ALICE [*sarcastically*]: Every one!

CAPTAIN [*genially*]: Hm! Is that a reference to me? I am no bully, at any rate in my own house.

ALICE: I'd like to see you try.

CAPTAIN [*to* KURT]: You mustn't listen to what she says. I'm a very good husband, and my old lady's the best wife in the world.

ALICE: Kurt, would you like a drink?

KURT: Thank you, not now.

CAPTAIN: Have you become a — ?

KURT: I just don't drink much.

CAPTAIN: America?

KURT: Yes.

CAPTAIN: I don't go with moderation. A man ought to be able to hold his drink.

KURT: These neighbours of yours. In my job I shall have to meet them all — and it'll be tricky, because even if one doesn't want to get involved, one gets involved in other people's intrigues.

ALICE: You go and meet them. You'll always come back to us. We're your true friends.

KURT: Isn't it horrible to sit alone surrounded by enemies, like you do?

ALICE: It isn't nice.

CAPTAIN: It isn't at all horrible! I've had nothing but enemies all my life, and they've helped me on my way, not harmed me. And when I have to die, I shall be able to say that I owe nobody anything and have never received anything gratis. Every stick I own I've had to fight for.

ALICE: Yes, Edgar's path has not been paved with roses —

CAPTAIN: With thorns, stones, flints — I've had to trust in my own strength. Same with you?

KURT [*simply*]: Yes, I learned the inadequacy of that ten years ago.

CAPTAIN: Then you're pathetic.

ALICE: Edgar!

CAPTAIN: Yes, he's pathetic if he doesn't trust in his own strength. It's true that when the mechanism runs down you're a barrowload of shit to scatter over the garden, but as long as the cogs go round you must kick and fight, with your fists and your feet. As long as the threads hold together. That's my philosophy.

KURT [*smiles*]: You're fun to listen to.

CAPTAIN: But don't you think I'm right?

KURT: No, I don't.

CAPTAIN: Well, it's the truth, anyway.

> *During the preceding dialogue the wind has risen, and now one of the doors upstage bangs to.*

CAPTAIN [*rises*]: The wind's getting up. I felt it would. [*Goes over, shuts the door and taps the barometer.*]

ALICE [*to* KURT]: You'll stay with us for supper?

KURT: Thank you, if I may.

ALICE: But it'll be very simple. Our maid has left.

KURT: That'll suit me.

ALICE: Dear Kurt, you're so unpretentious.

CAPTAIN [*by the barometer*] : Extraordinary how the barometer's fallen. I felt it!

ALICE [*whispers to* KURT] : He's so nervous.

CAPTAIN: We ought to eat soon.

ALICE [*gets up*] : I'll go and see to it. You two sit down and philosophize. [*Whispers to* KURT.] Don't contradict him or he'll lose his temper. And don't ask why he never became a major.

> KURT *nods.* ALICE *goes right.*

CAPTAIN [*sits at sewing-table with* KURT] : Cook us something worth eating, now, old lady.

ALICE: Give me some money, and I will.

CAPTAIN: Always money!

> ALICE *exits.*

CAPTAIN [*to* KURT] : Money, money, money! I spend the whole day opening my purse, so that I've finally come to believe I *am* a purse! Do you know that feeling?

KURT: Oh, yes. The only difference was, I used to think I was a wallet.

CAPTAIN [*laughs*] : You've sucked that lemon too? These women! [*Laughs again.*] And you caught a real tartar.

KURT [*patiently*] : Let's forget that, now.

CAPTAIN: She was a proper pearl. Whereas mine's a good woman, for all her faults. She's all right. For all her faults.

KURT [*smiles good-humouredly*] : For all her faults!

CAPTAIN: Don't laugh, damn you.

KURT [*as before*] : For all her faults.

CAPTAIN: Yes, she's been a faithful wife, and an excellent mother — first-rate — it's just that — [*Glances at door*] — She's got a devilish temper. Do you know, there have been moments when I've cursed you for saddling me with her?

KURT [*amiably*] : But I didn't. Look here, old chap —

CAPTAIN: Oh, come on. You're talking rubbish, you forget things you don't want to remember. Oh, don't take it amiss, I'm used to ordering people about and swearing at them. You know me, I know you won't take offence.

KURT: Of course not. But I didn't get you your wife. Quite the opposite.

CAPTAIN [*in full spate, regardless*] : Life's odd though, don't you think?

KURT: I suppose it is.

CAPTAIN: And getting old. It isn't nice, but it's interesting. Oh, I'm no age, but I'm beginning to feel it. All one's acquaintances die off, and one feels so alone.

KURT: Lucky the man who has a wife to grow old with.

CAPTAIN: Lucky? Yes, I suppose you're right — one's children leave one too. You shouldn't have left yours.

KURT: But I didn't. They were taken from me —

CAPTAIN: Now you mustn't get angry when I mention it.

KURT: But it didn't happen —

CAPTAIN: Well, whether it did or not, it's forgotten now. But you're on your own!

KURT: One can get used to anything, my dear fellow.

CAPTAIN: Can one? Can one get used to — to being quite alone?

KURT: Well, look at me.

CAPTAIN: What have you been doing these fifteen years?

KURT: What a question! I mean, fifteen years —

CAPTAIN: They say you've come into money, and are rich.

KURT: I wouldn't say rich —

CAPTAIN: I'm not trying to touch you —

KURT: If you were, I'd gladly —

CAPTAIN: Thank you very much, but I have money. You see — [*looks at the door*] — there must be no want in this house. The day I had no money — she would leave me.

KURT: Oh, no —

CAPTAIN: No? I know it! Would you believe it, she always remarks on it when I'm out of money, just for the pleasure of impressing it on me that I don't look after my family.

KURT: But you have a big income, I remember your saying.

CAPTAIN: Certainly I have a big income. But it isn't big enough.

KURT: Then it can't be big, in the usual sense —

CAPTAIN: Life is strange and so are we.

The telegraph starts tapping.

KURT: What is that?

CAPTAIN: Only a time-signal.

KURT: Haven't you a telephone?

CAPTAIN: Yes, in the kitchen. But we use the telegraph because the telephone-operators repeat everything we say.

KURT: It must be dreadful for you all, living out here.

CAPTAIN: It's perfectly gruesome. All life is gruesome. Kurt, you believe in an after-life. Do you suppose we shall find peace — afterwards?

KURT: I suppose there'll be storms and strife there too.

CAPTAIN: There too. If there is any "there". Better if there is nothing.

KURT: Can you be sure that annihilation would happen without pain?

CAPTAIN: I shall die snap! without pain.

KURT: You're sure of that?

CAPTAIN: Yes. I know it.

KURT: You don't seem content with your existence?

CAPTAIN [*sighs*]: Content? The day I'm allowed to die, I shall be content.

KURT: You can't be sure of that. But tell me, what do you do in this house? What happens here? The walls smell of poison — one feels ill the moment one enters. I'd like to leave, if I hadn't promised Alice to stay. There are corpses under the floorboards; there's such hatred here, it's difficult to breathe.

> The CAPTAIN *slumps in his chair and stares vacantly ahead of him.*

KURT: What's the matter? Edgar! [*The* CAPTAIN *remains motionless.* KURT *slaps him on the shoulder.*] Edgar!

CAPTAIN [*comes to himself*]: Did you say something? [*Looks around.*] I thought it was Alice. Oh, it's you? Look, I — [*Becomes torpid again.*]

KURT: This is horrible! [*Goes to the door right, and opens it.*] Alice!

ALICE [*enters, wearing a kitchen apron*]: What is it?

KURT: I don't know. Look at him!

ALICE [*calmly*]: He goes off like that sometimes. I'll play some music, then he'll wake up.

KURT: No, don't do that. Let me look at him. Can he hear? Can he see?

ALICE: Now he can neither hear nor see.

KURT: And you can say that so calmly! Alice, what is going on in this house?

ALICE: Ask that thing.

KURT: That thing? He is your husband!

ALICE: To me he is a stranger, as much a stranger as he was twenty-five years ago. I know nothing about that man — except that —

KURT: Hush! He can hear you.

ALICE: He can hear nothing.

A bugle sounds outside.

CAPTAIN [*jumps up, takes his sabre and military cap*]: Excuse me! I must just inspect the sentries. [*Goes out through rear doors.*]

KURT: Is he ill?

ALICE: I don't know.

KURT: Is he out of his mind?

ALICE: I don't know.

KURT: Does he drink?

ALICE: Not as much as he boasts he does.

KURT: Sit down and tell me. But calmly, and the truth.

ALICE [*sits*]: What shall I say? That I have sat in this tower for a lifetime, a prisoner, kept from life by a man I have always hated, and whom I now hate so boundlessly that the day he died I would laugh for joy!

KURT: Why haven't you parted?

ALICE: You may well ask. We parted twice when we were engaged, we've tried to part ever since, every day — but we are welded together, and can't prise ourselves loose. Once we did part — in here, without leaving the house.

Once in five years! Now only death can part us. We know that, and so we await him as a liberator.

KURT: Why are you so alone, the two of you?

ALICE: Because he isolates me. First he rooted out all my brothers and sisters from the house — that's the phrase he used, rooted out. Then my woman friends, and others —

KURT: But *his* relatives? Did you root them out?

ALICE: Yes. They would have robbed me of my life, once they had robbed me of my honour. In the end I had to maintain contact with the outside world through that telegraph, because the telephone-operators eavesdropped on our conversations. I taught myself to use the telegraph, though he doesn't know that. You mustn't tell him, or he'll kill me.

KURT: Horrible! Horrible! But why does he blame me for your marriage? You remember how it was. Edgar and I were friends. He fell in love with you as soon as he saw you, came to me and begged me to act as intermediary. I refused, and — my dear Alice, I knew how cruel and tyrannical you could be — so I warned him, and when he persisted, I told him to get your brother to plead his cause to you.

ALICE: I believe you. But he's been lying to himself about it all these years, and you'll never be able to persuade him otherwise.

KURT: Well, let him blame me, if it'll make him feel easier.

ALICE: That's too much to ask —

KURT: Oh, I'm used to it. But what does hurt me is his saying that I abandoned my children. That's quite untrue —

ALICE: Oh, that's his way. He says what he thinks, and then believes it. But he seems fond of you, mostly because you don't contradict him. Do try to go along with us. I think you came here at a lucky moment for us. Really, it's an act of providence. Kurt, you must help us. We're the most miserable couple on earth. [*Weeps.*]

KURT: I've seen one marriage at close quarters — and that was frightening. But this is almost worse.

ALICE: You think so?

KURT: Yes.

ALICE: Whose fault is it?

KURT: Alice! The moment you stop asking whose fault it is, things will be easier. Try to accept it as a fact, as a trial, which must be endured —

ALICE: I can't! It's too much. [*Gets up.*] It's so hopeless.

KURT: Unhappy people! Do you know why you hate each other?

ALICE: No. It's got no logic — no grounds, no purpose — but no end. Can you imagine what he most fears from death? He fears that I shall re-marry!

KURT: Then he does love you.

ALICE: So it seems. But that doesn't prevent him hating me.

KURT [*as though to himself*]: It is what men call the hatred of love, and is born in hell. Does he like you to play for him?

ALICE: Yes, but only ugly tunes. This frightful *March of the Boyars*. When he hears that he becomes possessed and wants to dance.

KURT: Does *he* dance?

ALICE: Yes. He has these whims.

KURT: One thing — forgive my asking. Where are the children?

ALICE: Two of them died, did you know?

KURT: You've been through that too?

ALICE: What haven't I been through?

KURT: But the other two?

ALICE: They're in town. They couldn't live at home. He turned them against me —

KURT: And you turned them against him.

ALICE: Of course. And then we had political intrigues, canvassing, bribes — in the end we sent the children away so as not to destroy them. What should have been our bond divided us; what should have been a blessing became a curse. Sometimes I think we belong to a race that is cursed.

KURT: Well, yes, we are, Since we first sinned —

ALICE [*with a spiteful glance, sharply*]: What do you mean?

KURT: Adam and Eve.

ALICE: Oh. I thought you meant something else.

Embarrassed silence.

ALICE [*clasps her hands*]: Kurt! We're cousins, you've been my friend since childhood. I haven't always treated you as I should. But now I am punished, and you have your revenge on me.

KURT: Revenge! I have taken no revenge. Alice!

ALICE: Do you remember one Sunday, when you were engaged? I'd invited you to dinner.

KURT: Alice!

ALICE: I must talk — please. When you arrived we were out and you had to go away —

KURT: You'd been invited out yourselves. What does that matter now?

ALICE: Kurt! When, just now, I invited you to dine with

us, I thought there was something in the larder. [*Hides her face in her hands.*] And there's nothing, not even a piece of bread — [*Weeps.*]

KURT: Poor, poor Alice.

ALICE: But when *he* comes back and wants something to eat and there isn't anything, he'll get angry. You've never seen him angry. Oh, God, this humiliation!

KURT: Why not let me go out and get something?

ALICE: There *is* nothing to get on this island.

KURT: Look — I couldn't care less, but for his sake and yours — let me think up something, something . . . We must laugh it off as a joke. When he comes back, I'll suggest we have a drink, then I'll think up something — get him in a good humour, play some game with him, it doesn't matter what — You sit down at the piano and be ready.

ALICE: Look at my hands. What are they to play with? I have to scour the pots and dry the glasses, lay the fires, clean the house —

KURT: But you have two servants.

ALICE: We have to say we have, because he's an officer — but they're always leaving, so that sometimes we have none at all — most of the time. How shall I get out of this business about supper? Oh, if only the house would burn down — !

KURT: Alice! Don't say such things.

ALICE: Or the sea would rise and swallow us up!

KURT: No, no, no! I can't listen to you!

ALICE: What will he say, what will he say? Don't go, Kurt, don't leave me.

KURT: No, Alice. I won't go.

ALICE: Yes, but when you have gone —

KURT: Has he struck you?

ALICE: Me? Oh, no — then he knows I would go. One must cling to a little pride.

> *Offstage shouts of : "Halt! Who goes there?" "Friend."*

KURT [*gets up*] : Is that him?

ALICE [*frightened*] : Yes.

> *Pause.*

KURT: What on earth shall we do?

ALICE: I don't know, I don't know.

CAPTAIN [*enters upstage, in a good humour*] : There! Now I'm free. Well, Kurt, now she's had the chance to beat her breast. Makes your heart bleed, doesn't it?

KURT: What's the weather like out there?

CAPTAIN: There's a storm blowing up. [*Jovially, opening one of the doors slightly.*] Baron Bluebeard with the maiden in his tower! And outside stalks the sentry with drawn sabre, to guard the fair virgin. Along come her brothers, but there goes the sentry, see! Left, right! He's a good watchdog. Look at him! Tum-titti, tum-tum, tum-titti-tum! Shall we dance the sword dance? Kurt should see that.

KURT: No, let's have the *March of the Boyars* instead.

CAPTAIN: You know that? Alice, sit down in your apron and play. Play, I say!

> *She goes unwillingly to the piano. The* CAPTAIN *pinches her arm.*

CAPTAIN [*to* ALICE] : You've been telling lies about me.

ALICE: I?

> *The* CAPTAIN *turns away.* ALICE *plays the* March of the Boyars. *The* CAPTAIN *performs a Hungarian dance behind the desk, clashing his spurs. Suddenly*

he slumps to the floor, unnoticed by KURT *and*
ALICE. *She plays the piece to its conclusion.*

ALICE [*without turning her head*]: Shall we give an encore?

Silence. She turns and sees the CAPTAIN *lying
senseless, hidden from the audience by the desk.*

ALICE: Blessed Jesus!

*She stands with her arms crossed over her breasts, and
gives a sigh as of thankfulness and relief.*

KURT [*turns and runs over to the* CAPTAIN]: What's
happened? What is it?

ALICE [*tensely*]: Is he dead?

KURT: I don't know. Help me.

ALICE [*stays motionless*]: I can't touch him. Is he dead?

KURT: No. He is alive.

ALICE *sighs. The* CAPTAIN *gets up.* KURT *helps
him to a chair.*

CAPTAIN: What has happened? [*Silence.*] What has
happened?

KURT: You fell.

CAPTAIN: Did something happen?

KURT: You fell on the floor. Is something the matter?

CAPTAIN: With me? Nothing at all. Not that I'm aware of.
What are you staring at?

KURT: You're ill.

CAPTAIN: Rubbish. Go on playing, Alice. Ah! There it is
again! [*Clutches his head.*]

ALICE: There, you see. You are ill.

CAPTAIN: Don't shout. I'm just a bit dizzy.

KURT: We must get the Doctor. I'll go and telephone.

CAPTAIN: I don't want any doctor.

KURT: You must. We must get him, for our sake. Otherwise it'll be our responsibility.

CAPTAIN: If he comes, I'll kick him out. I'll put a bullet in him. Ah! There it is again! [*Clutches his head.*]

KURT [*goes to door, right*]: I'll go and telephone.

   He goes. ALICE *takes off her apron.*

CAPTAIN: Will you give me a glass of water?

ALICE: I suppose I must. [*Gives it to him.*]

CAPTAIN: Charming!

ALICE: Are you ill?

CAPTAIN: Forgive me for not being well.

ALICE: Do you want to nurse yourself, then?

CAPTAIN: You don't want to nurse me, do you?

ALICE: What do you think?

CAPTAIN: The moment is come for which you have waited so long.

ALICE: Yes. And which you thought would never come.

CAPTAIN: Don't be angry with me.

KURT [*enters right*]: It's monstrous — !

ALICE: What did he say?

KURT: He rang off, just like that.

ALICE [*to* CAPTAIN]: Well. Now you see the result of your arrogance.

CAPTAIN: I think I'm — feeling worse. Try to get a doctor from town.

ALICE [*goes to the telegraph*]: I'll have to telegraph, then.

CAPTAIN [*half-rises, amazed*] : Can — you — telegraph?

ALICE [*starts to work the machine*] : Yes. I can.

CAPTAIN: I see. Well, do it then. Damned liar she is. [*To* KURT.] Come and sit beside me. [KURT *does so.*] Hold my hand. I'm sitting and falling. Can you imagine that? Down — down — strange!

KURT: Have you had these attacks before?

CAPTAIN: Never!

KURT: While you're waiting for a reply from town, I'll go to the Doctor and talk to him. He's attended you before?

CAPTAIN: He has.

KURT: Then he knows your background. [*Goes towards exit, left.*]

ALICE: I'll get a reply soon. Thank you, Kurt. But come back quickly.

KURT: As quickly as I can. [*Exit.*]

CAPTAIN: He's a good fellow, Kurt. How he's changed!

ALICE: Yes, and for the better. I pity him, though, getting mixed up with us just now.

CAPTAIN: On our silver jubilee! I wonder how things are with him really? Did you notice, he didn't want to talk about that?

ALICE: Yes, I noticed. Though I don't think anyone asked him.

CAPTAIN: What a life he's had. And us! I wonder if everyone's life is like this?

ALICE: Perhaps. Though they don't talk about it, like we do.

CAPTAIN: Sometimes I have thought that misery attracts misery, and that happy people somehow avoid disaster. Which is why we shall never know anything but misery.

ALICE: Have you known any happy people?

CAPTAIN: Let me think. No. Yes. The Ekmarks.

ALICE: How can you say that? She had that operation
last year —

CAPTAIN: That's true. Well, I don't know. Yes, the Kraffts.

ALICE: Oh, yes! They all lived an idyllic existence — rich,
respected, nice children, good marriages — till the parents
were fifty. Then their cousin comes along, turns out to be
a criminal, gets sent to prison, and that was the end of
their happiness. Their name was plastered across every
newspaper, and they didn't dare show their face in the
street. The children had to be taken away from school . . .
Dear God!

CAPTAIN: I wonder what I've got.

ALICE: What do you think it is?

CAPTAIN: My heart, or my head. It's as though my soul
wanted to fly out of my body and disappear in a cloud
of smoke.

ALICE: Do you feel like some food?

CAPTAIN: Yes. What have we got for supper?

ALICE [walks uneasily across the room]: I'll ask Jenny.

CAPTAIN: She's left.

ALICE: Oh, yes, of course.

CAPTAIN: Ring for Christine to bring me some fresh
water.

ALICE [rings the bell]: Imagine — ! [Rings again.] She
doesn't hear.

CAPTAIN: Go outside and see if — imagine if she's left
too!

ALICE [goes over to door left and opens it]: What's this?
Her trunk's standing packed in the corridor.

CAPTAIN: Then she has left.

ALICE: This is hell! [*Begins to weep, falls to her knees and lays her head against a chair, sobbing.*]

CAPTAIN: And all at once! And of course Kurt has to come and see the mess we're in. Just to add an extra humiliation. He has to come, just now.

ALICE: Do you know what I think? I think he's gone too. And won't come back.

CAPTAIN: I can believe that of him.

ALICE: Yes. We are cursed —

CAPTAIN: What's that?

ALICE: Don't you see how everyone shuns us?

CAPTAIN: Let them! [*The telegraph starts tapping.*] There's your answer. Quiet, I'm listening . . . "No one has time." They're avoiding us. The scum!

ALICE: That's the result of abusing your doctors. And neglecting to pay them.

CAPTAIN: That's not true —

ALICE: Even when you could, you wouldn't pay them, because you despised their work, just as you have despised my work and everyone else's. Now they won't come. And the telephone's cut off, because you didn't think that worth having either. Nothing's worth anything to you except your rifles and cannons.

CAPTAIN: Don't stand there talking rubbish.

ALICE: Everything comes back. Life is a circle.

CAPTAIN: Superstitious nonsense! An old wives' tale.

ALICE: You'll see. Do you know we owe Christine six months' salary?

CAPTAIN: Well, she's stolen that much.

ALICE: But I've had to borrow money from her.

CAPTAIN: I can believe that of you.

ALICE: How ungrateful you are! You know I only did it so that the children could visit us.

CAPTAIN: Kurt chose a good time. He's a rogue, like the rest of them. And a coward. Didn't dare say he'd had enough of us and that it'd be more fun at the Doctor's ball. Probably knew we'd give him a rotten supper. That bastard hasn't changed.

KURT [*hastens in, right*] : My dear Edgar! Look, it's like this. The Doctor knows all about your heart —

CAPTAIN: Heart?

KURT: Yes. You've had a bad heart for some time. A hardening —

CAPTAIN: An ossifying of the heart?

KURT: And —

CAPTAIN: Is it dangerous?

KURT: Well —

CAPTAIN: It is dangerous!

KURT: Yes.

CAPTAIN: Death?

KURT: You must be very careful. First — no more cigars.

The CAPTAIN *throws away his cigar.*

KURT: And no more whisky. Then, you must go to bed.

CAPTAIN [*frightened*] : No, not that. Not bed. Then it's the end. Then one never gets up again. I'll sleep on the sofa tonight. What else did he say?

KURT: He was very friendly, and says he'll come at once if you ask him.

CAPTAIN: Friendly, was he, the hypocrite? I don't want to see him. Can I eat?

KURT: Not tonight. And for the next few days, only milk.

CAPTAIN: Milk? I can't stand the stuff.

KURT: You'll have to learn.

CAPTAIN: No, I'm too old to learn. [*Clutches his head.*] Ah! There it is again! [*Remains seated, staring.*]

ALICE [*to* KURT]: What did the Doctor say?

KURT: That he *may* die.

ALICE: Thank God!

KURT: Take care, Alice! Take care. And now, go and get a pillow and a blanket, and I'll lay him on the sofa. Then I'll sit in this chair, all night.

ALICE: And I?

KURT: You go to bed. Your presence seems to worsen his condition.

ALICE: Order, and I'll obey. I know you want to help us both. [*Goes towards exit, left.*]

KURT: Both, Alice. I'm taking no sides in this.

> *He picks up the water carafe and goes out right. The wind rises outside. Then the door upstage blows open and an* OLD WOMAN *of poor and disagreeable appearance peers in.*

CAPTAIN [*wakes, gets up and looks around*]: So! They've left me, the rogues. [*Sees the* OLD WOMAN *and is frightened.*] Who's that? What do you want?

OLD WOMAN: I only wanted to shut the door, kind sir.

CAPTAIN: Why? Why?

OLD WOMAN: Because it blew open just as I was going past.

CAPTAIN: You were going to steal, you old devil!

OLD WOMAN: There's not much to take here. Christine told me.

CAPTAIN: Christine!

OLD WOMAN: Good night, sir. Sleep well.

> *She shuts the door and goes.* ALICE *enters left with pillows and a blanket.*

CAPTAIN: Who was that at the door? Was there someone?

ALICE: Yes, old Maia from the workhouse. She was just walking past.

CAPTAIN: Are you sure?

ALICE: Are you frightened?

CAPTAIN: I, frightened? Of course not.

ALICE: If you won't go to bed, you'd better lie here.

CAPTAIN [*goes and lies on the chaise-longue*]: I *want* to lie here. [*Tries to take* ALICE's *hand but she draws it away.*]

> KURT *enters with the water carafe.*

CAPTAIN: Kurt, don't leave me.

KURT: I'll stay with you all night. Alice is going to bed.

CAPTAIN: Good night, then, Alice.

ALICE [*to* KURT]: Good night, Kurt.

KURT: Good night.

> ALICE *goes.* KURT *takes a chair and sits by the* CAPTAIN.

KURT: Won't you take off your boots?

CAPTAIN: No! A warrior must always be ready for action.

KURT: Are you expecting a battle?

CAPTAIN: Perhaps. [*Sits up in his bed.*] Kurt! You are the only person I have opened my heart to. Listen. If I die tonight — remember my children.

KURT: I will.

CAPTAIN: Thank you. I trust you.

KURT: Can you explain why you trust me?

CAPTAIN: We haven't been friends, I don't believe in friendship, and our two families were born enemies and have always fought each other —

KURT: And yet you trust me!

CAPTAIN: Yes! And I don't know why. [*Silence.*] Do you think I am going to die?

KURT: Like everyone else. There'll be no exception made for you.

CAPTAIN: Are you bitter?

KURT: Yes. Are you afraid of death? The wheelbarrow and the garden?

CAPTAIN: Suppose it isn't the end!

KURT: Many think it's not.

CAPTAIN: What then?

KURT: Just surprises, I suppose.

CAPTAIN: But one knows nothing for sure.

KURT: No, that's just it. So one must be prepared for everything.

CAPTAIN: You aren't so stupid as to believe in hell?

KURT: Don't you, who are in the midst of it?

CAPTAIN: I was only speaking metaphorically.

KURT: The way you described yours wasn't metaphorical. Poetic or otherwise.

　　Silence.

CAPTAIN: If you only knew the agonies I suffer.

KURT: Bodily?

CAPTAIN: No, they aren't bodily.

KURT: Then they must be spiritual. There's no third kind.

Pause.

CAPTAIN [*raises himself in his bed.*] : I don't want to die!

KURT: Just now you were longing for annihilation.

CAPTAIN: Yes, if it's painless.

KURT: But it isn't.

CAPTAIN: Is this annihilation, then?

KURT: The beginning of it.

CAPTAIN: Good night.

KURT: Good night.

Scene 2

The same. The lamp is beginning to gutter. Through the windows and the glass panes of the upstage doors can be seen an overcast morning. The sea is rolling. A sentry stands at the battery as before. The CAPTAIN *is lying on the chaise-longue, asleep.* KURT *sits on a chair beside him, pale and spent with lack of sleep.*

ALICE : [*enters left*] : Is he asleep?

KURT: Yes, since sunrise.

ALICE: What sort of a night?

KURT: He's slept in snatches. But he's been talking so much.

ALICE: What about?

KURT: He's been going on about religion like a schoolboy. Seems to think he's solved the problems of existence. Finally, towards dawn, he discovered the immortality of the soul.

ALICE: *His* soul, of course.

KURT: Absolutely! He really is the most arrogant creature I've ever met. "*I* am, therefore God exists."

ALICE: So you've realized that. Look at those boots. With them he'd have trampled the earth flat, if he'd had the chance. With them he has trampled on other men's fields and flowers, other men's hearts and my brain. Now the wild boar feels the hunter's knife.

KURT: He'd be comic if he weren't tragic. It's strange, but in all his meannesses there's a kind of grandeur. Can't you find one good word to say about him?

ALICE [*sits*]: I could. But not for him to hear. One word to encourage him, and his arrogance exceeds all limits.

KURT: He can't hear anything. I've given him morphine.

ALICE: Well — he was born in a poor home, one of a large family. From an early age he had to support them by giving lessons, because his father was an idler — or worse. It must be hard for a young man to have to give up his youth to slave for a pack of ungrateful brats who weren't even his own. I remember first seeing him when I was a little girl — it was winter, twenty-five below zero, and he hadn't even an overcoat, though they all had. I thought it was noble, and I admired him for it, but his ugliness frightened me. He is unusually ugly, isn't he?

KURT: Yes — sometimes repulsively so. I noticed it particularly every time I quarrelled with him. And then, when he wasn't there, his image grew, took on strange forms and monstrous proportions. He literally began to haunt me.

ALICE: How do you suppose it must be for me, then? Oh, I suppose those first years as an officer must have been a martyrdom for him. He got help now and then, but he'll never admit it, and everything he could get he took as his due without a word of thanks.

KURT: We ought to speak charitably of him.

ALICE: After he's dead! Yes; well, then, I'll say no more.

KURT: Do you think he's evil?

ALICE: Yes. And yet, he can be kind and sensitive. But if he hates you, he's a monster.

KURT: Why didn't he become a major?

ALICE: Does it surprise you? They didn't want to have a man over them who'd already proved himself a tyrant under them! But you must never mention that. *He* says he didn't want to become a major. Did he say anything about the children?

KURT: Yes, he wanted to see Judith.

ALICE: I can imagine! Do you know who Judith is? She's the spit of him, and he's trained her to oppose me. Would you believe it, my own daughter has raised her hand against me.

KURT: Surely not?

ALICE: Hush! He's moving. I wonder if he heard us? He's cunning, too.

KURT: Yes — he's waking up.

ALICE: Doesn't he look like the devil himself! I'm frightened of him.

Silence.

CAPTAIN[stirs, wakes, stands up and looks around]: It's morning. At last!

KURT: How are you feeling?

CAPTAIN: Bad.

KURT: Would you like a doctor?

CAPTAIN: No. I want to see Judith. My child.

KURT: Don't you think you should — make arrangements — before — in case — anything happens?

CAPTAIN: What do you mean? What should happen?

KURT: What can happen to everyone.

CAPTAIN: Oh, rubbish. I won't die that easily, believe me. Don't start celebrating in advance, Alice.

KURT: Think of your children. Make your will, so that at least your wife can be sure of her furniture.

CAPTAIN: You want her to inherit my possessions while I am still alive?

KURT: No. But if anything should happen, you don't want her to be thrown out on the road. Someone who for twenty-five years has cleaned, dusted and polished this furniture should have some right to it. Shall I get a lawyer?

CAPTAIN: No.

KURT: You're a cruel man. Crueller than I thought.

CAPTAIN [*falls helplessly on the bed*]: Ah! There it is again!

KURT: Go, Alice. There's little we can do here.

ALICE *goes.*

CAPTAIN [*comes to*]: Well, Kurt. How are you planning to arrange this quarantine?

KURT: Oh, I shall manage.

CAPTAIN: No, I'm in charge on this island, and you've got to deal with me. Don't forget that.

KURT: Have you ever seen a quarantine?

CAPTAIN: Have I? Yes, before you were born! And I'll give you some advice. Don't put the disinfection ovens too near the shore.

KURT: I thought they ought to be close to the water —

CAPTAIN: That shows how much you know about your job. Water is the natural element of germs. They thrive in it.

KURT: But salt water is necessary to cleanse away the impurities.

CAPTAIN: Imbecile! Well, as soon as you've found somewhere to live, you must bring your children to join you.

KURT: Do you think they'll come?

CAPTAIN: Of course, if you show yourself a man. It'll make a good impression on people here if you make it clear that you know your duties in that field —

KURT: I have always fulfilled my duties in that field.

CAPTAIN [raises his voice]: — In that field where your weakness is most painfully evident.

KURT: Haven't I told you — ?

CAPTAIN [in full spate]: I mean, one doesn't leave one's children like that —

KURT: Oh, carry on!

CAPTAIN: As your kinsman, and as the senior member of the family, I feel a certain duty to tell you the truth, even when it is painful. And you mustn't take offence —

KURT: Are you hungry?

CAPTAIN: Yes, I am!

KURT: Would you like something light?

CAPTAIN: No, something heavy.

KURT: That'd finish you.

CAPTAIN: Isn't it enough to be ill, must one starve too?

KURT: That's the way it is.

CAPTAIN: And no drinking or smoking! Then life's not worth much.

KURT: Death demands sacrifices. Otherwise he comes at once.

ALICE [*enters with some bunches of flowers, telegrams and letters*]: These are for you. [*Throws the flowers on the desk.*]

CAPTAIN [*flattered*]: For me? May I see them?

ALICE: Yes, they're only from the junior officers, the band and the sentries.

CAPTAIN: You're jealous!

ALICE: Oh, no. If they were laurel wreaths, that would be different. But those you'll never get.

CAPTAIN: Hm! Here is a telegram from the Colonel. Read it, Kurt. At least he's a gentleman, though he is a little fool. This one's from — What's this? It's from Judith! Be so good as to telegraph her to come by the next ship. This one —! Well! One isn't without friends after all. It's a comfort that people think without fear or reproach of a sick man who deserves more recognition than he has been granted.

ALICE: I don't understand. Are they congratulating you on being ill?

CAPTAIN: Hyena!

ALICE [*to* KURT]: Yes, we had a doctor here who was so hated that when he left the island they gave a banquet— *after* he'd gone.

CAPTAIN: Put the flowers in vases. I am not a credulous man, and humanity is scum, but this simple homage, by God, it comes from the heart. It cannot but come from the heart.

ALICE: Imbecile!

KURT [*reads one of the telegrams*]: Judith says that she cannot come, because the steamer has been delayed by a storm.

CAPTAIN: Is that all?

KURT: Er — no. There is something more.

CAPTAIN: Out with it!

KURT: Well, she asks you not to drink so much.

CAPTAIN: My God! That's children for you. My only
  beloved daughter — my Judith! My idol!

ALICE: And your spit!

CAPTAIN: This is life. The best life has to offer. Shit!

ALICE: Well, you sowed this harvest yourself. You taught
  her to rebel against her mother, now she turns against her
  father. And you say there is no God!

CAPTAIN [to KURT]: What does the Colonel write?

KURT: He grants you leave from all duties forthwith.

CAPTAIN: Leave! I haven't asked for any leave.

ALICE: No, but I have.

CAPTAIN: I won't accept it!

ALICE: The arrangements have already been made.

CAPTAIN: I don't care!

ALICE: You see, Kurt. For this man no laws exist, no rules
  apply, no human authority matters. He stands above everything and everyone, the universe has been created for his
  private benefit, the sun and the moon are merely his
  messengers to carry his orders to the stars. That's my
  husband! This insignificant captain who couldn't even
  become a major, whose puffed-up pride is a laughing-stock
  to those who he supposes fear him — this coward who is
  afraid of the dark, and believes that all the discoveries of
  science are merely the build-up to his grand finale — a
  barrowload of manure, and that not of the top quality.

CAPTAIN [fans himself with a bunch of flowers compla-
  cently, without listening to her]: Have you invited Kurt
  to lunch?

ALICE: No.

CAPTAIN: Then go at once to the kitchen and grill the two best steaks you can find.

ALICE: Two?

CAPTAIN: I propose to have one too.

ALICE: But we are three.

CAPTAIN: You want one too? Very well, then; three.

ALICE: Where do you expect me to find them? Last night you invited Kurt to supper and there wasn't a crust of bread in the house. Kurt has had to sit up all night with you on an empty stomach and hasn't even had a cup of coffee, because we haven't got any and our credit is finished.

CAPTAIN: She's angry with me because I didn't die yesterday.

ALICE: No, because you didn't die twenty-five years ago. Because you didn't die before I was born.

CAPTAIN [*to* KURT]: Listen to her. That's what happens when you matchmake, my dear Kurt. Our marriage certainly wasn't arranged in heaven!

> ALICE *and* KURT *look at each other meaningfully.*

CAPTAIN [*gets up and walks towards the door*]: However! Say what you may, I am going about my duty. [*Puts on his old artillery helmet with bands. Fastens his sabre about his waist and puts on his greatcoat.* ALICE *and* KURT *try to stop him, but in vain.*]

CAPTAIN: Get away from me! [*Goes.*]

ALICE: Yes, go! That's what you always do, turn your back when things become too much for you, and make your wife cover your retreat. Drunkard, braggart, liar! [*Spits.*]

KURT: Is there no limit to this?

ALICE [*laughs*]: You haven't seen the worst.

KURT: Worse than this?

ALICE: Don't ask me.

KURT: Where's he going now? And where does he find
the strength?

ALICE: You may well ask. Oh, now he'll go down to his
lieutenants to thank them for the flowers. And then he'll
eat and drink with them. And he calls them scum! If you
knew how many times he's been threatened with dismissal!
It's only out of pity for his family that they've spared him.
And he thinks it's because they're scared of him! And these
wretched officers' wives who've tried to help us, he hates
them and calls trash.

KURT: I must confess, I applied for this job in the hope of
finding some peace down here by the sea. I had no idea
how things were with you two —

ALICE: Poor Kurt. What will you do for food?

KURT: Oh, I'll get something at the Doctor's. But what
about you? Can't I arrange something for you?

ALICE: He mustn't know, or he'll kill me.

KURT [looks out through window]: Look. He's standing
on the ramparts. In this wind.

ALICE: One can't but pity him. That he is the way he is.

KURT: I pity both of you. But what is to be done?

ALICE: I don't know. A heap of bills has come too, which
of course he didn't notice.

KURT: It can be a blessing not to be able to see, sometimes.

ALICE [at the window]: Now he's opened his coat and is
letting the wind blow against his chest. He wants to die!

KURT: I don't think he does. Just now, when he felt his
life was slipping away, he clutched on to mine, he began
to smuggle his way into my private affairs, as though he
wanted to worm into me and live my life.

ALICE: That's his way. He's a vampire, he likes to sink his claws into other people's destinies, suck excitement out of other lives, batten on others, because his own life is so totally boring to him. Remember this, Kurt. Never let him into your life, never let him know your friends, or he'll take them from you and make them his. He's a real demon at that. If he ever meets your children, you'll soon find them regarding him as their father, they'll follow his advice, he'll bring them up the way he wants, and above all, he'll oppose every wish of yours.

KURT: Alice! Was it he who took my children from me, when I parted from my wife?

ALICE: Since it's past — yes, it was he.

KURT: I suspected it, but I was never sure. So it was he!

ALICE: When you confided in him and sent him to mediate with your wife, he started a flirtation with her and taught her how she could get custody of the children.

KURT: Oh, God! God in heaven!

ALICE: You didn't know that side of him, did you?

Silence.

KURT: Do you know, last night — when he thought he was going to die — he made me promise that I would remember his children.

ALICE: But surely you don't want to take revenge on my children?

KURT: By keeping my promise? Very well, Alice. I shall remember your children.

ALICE: That would really be the most terrible revenge you could take on him. There's nothing he loathes like magnanimity.

KURT: Then I may find myself revenged by doing nothing.

ALICE: I love revenge as I love justice. It makes me happy to see evil punished.

KURT: You still feel like that?

ALICE: I always shall. The day I forgive or love an enemy, call me a hypocrite.

KURT: Alice! It can be a duty sometimes to leave things unsaid, to turn a blind eye. It's what's called charity, and we all need that.

ALICE: I don't. I've no secrets to hide. I have always played clean.

KURT: That's a big claim.

ALICE: I could claim more. What have I not suffered for this man, whom I never loved — ?

KURT: Why did you marry him?

ALICE: Why did I? Because he took me. Seduced me. I don't know. And then, I wanted to get into society —

KURT: And gave up your work —

ALICE: Because society despised it. But you know, he cheated me. He promised me a good life, a beautiful home, and all I found was debts. The only gold I ever saw was on his uniform, and that wasn't real. He cheated me.

KURT: Alice! When a young man falls in love, he dreams of the future, and one must forgive him if his hopes don't always materialize. I have the same guilt on my conscience, but I don't regard myself as a cheat. What are you looking at out there?

ALICE: I'm looking to see if he has fallen.

KURT: Has he fallen?

ALICE: No such luck. Didn't I say, he always cheats me?

KURT: Well, I'll go and see the Doctor and the Governor.

ALICE [*sits by the window*]: You go, Kurt dear. I'll sit here and wait. I've learned to wait.

ACT TWO

Scene 1

The same. Daylight. The sentry is on duty at the battery as before. ALICE *is seated in the armchair, right. She is grey-haired.*

KURT [*knocks and enters, left*] : Good morning, Alice.

ALICE : Good morning, Kurt. Sit down.

KURT [*sits in the other armchair*] : The steamer's coming in.

ALICE : I know what to expect, if he's on it.

KURT : He is. I saw the glint of his helmet. What has he been doing in town?

ALICE : I can work it out. He put on his parade uniform, which means he was going to see the Colonel, and he took his suede gloves, so he must have been doing the social round.

KURT : Did you notice how quiet he was yesterday? Since he gave up drinking and over-eating he's been a different person. Calm, reserved, considerate —

ALICE : I know. If that man had always been sober, he'd have been a frightful danger to the world. Perhaps it's a good thing he made himself ridiculous and harmless with his whisky.

KURT : The genie in the bottle has tamed him! But have you noticed how since death set its mark on him he has acquired a kind of dignity, an exaltation? Perhaps the prospect of mortality has caused him to rethink his views on life.

ALICE : Don't you deceive yourself. He's plotting some

evil. And don't believe what he says. He's a premeditated liar, and a born intriguer —

KURT [*looks at her*] : Alice! What's this? You've become grey-haired in these two nights!

ALICE: No, Kurt. I've been that for a long time. It's just that I've given up dyeing it since my husband became a dead man. Twenty-five years in this fortress. Do you know it used to be a prison once?

KURT: A prison? Yes, you could guess that from the walls.

ALICE: And from my complexion. Even the children became prison-coloured in here.

KURT: It's difficult to imagine children playing within these walls.

ALICE: They didn't often play. And the two who died withered for lack of light.

KURT: What do you think will happen now?

ALICE: He'll attempt some *coup de grâce* against you and me. I saw a familiar glint in his eye when you read him that telegram from Judith. He'd have liked to take his revenge on her, but she's out of range so his hatred transferred to you.

KURT: What do you suppose he's planning?

ALICE: Hard to say. He has an incredible gift for — or luck at — nosing his way into other people's secrets. You must have noticed how all yesterday he lived himself into your quarantine, sucked vitality out of your children, devoured your children alive. I know him, Kurt. He's a cannibal. His own life is passing from him — or has passed —

KURT: I've got that impression too — that he's already on the other side. His face has a kind of phosphorescence, as though he was in a state of dissolution. And his eyes flame like will-o'-the-wisps over graves or marshes. Here

he is! Tell me — do you think he could possibly be
jealous?

ALICE: No, he's too proud for that. "Show me the man I'd
need to envy!" That's what he said.

KURT: Thank God for that. Even his vices have some merits!
Shall I go out and greet him?

ALICE: No. Be offhand to him, or he'll think you're up to
something. And when he starts lying, pretend to believe
him. I know how to translate his lies, I can always find
the truth from them with my lexicon. I feel something
dreadful's going to happen . . . But Kurt, don't lose control
of yourself. My only advantage in our long war has been
that I've always been sober and had my wits about me.
His whisky was his weakness! Now we'll see.

> *The* CAPTAIN *enters left in parade uniform, helmet,
> cloak and white gloves, calm and grave, but pale and
> hollow-eyed. He stumbles forward and sits in his
> cloak and helmet far from* KURT *and* ALICE *on
> stage right. During the ensuing dialogue he holds his
> sabre between his knees.*

CAPTAIN: Good morning. Forgive my sitting down like
this, but I am a little tired.

ALICE: Good morning.

KURT: Good to see you.

ALICE: How are you?

CAPTAIN: Fine. Just a little tired.

ALICE: What news from town?

CAPTAIN: Little but good. Amongst other people I saw
the Doctor, and he says there's nothing wrong with me,
that I can live for twenty years if I take care of myself.

ALICE [to KURT]: He's lying. [To CAPTAIN.] Well, that
was good news, my dear.

CAPTAIN: Yes, it was.

> Silence. The CAPTAIN looks at ALICE and KURT as though asking them to speak.

ALICE [to KURT]: Say nothing. Make him speak first and show his hand.

CAPTAIN [to ALICE]: Did you say something?

ALICE: No. I said nothing.

CAPTAIN [slowly]: Kurt, old chap —

ALICE [to KURT]: You see, he's off!

CAPTAIN: I — I was in town, as you know.

> KURT nods.

CAPTAIN: I — er — made the acquaintance . . . amongst others . . . of a young cadet . . . [hesitantly] . . . in the artillery. [Pause. KURT looks uneasy.] Since . . . we're short of volunteers on this island, I arranged with the Colonel that he should be allowed to come here . . . This should please you particularly, when I inform you that it . . . was. . . your own son.

ALICE [to KURT]: The vampire! You see!

KURT: Under normal circumstances this news would please a father, but as things are I find it painful.

CAPTAIN: That I don't understand.

KURT: You don't need to. It's enough that I don't want it.

CAPTAIN: I see, that's how you feel! Well, you must know that the young man has been posted here and is now subject to my orders.

KURT: Then I shall make him apply for another regiment.

CAPTAIN: You can't; You have no rights concerning your son.

KURT: I have no — ?

CAPTAIN: No. The court has awarded them to his mother.

KURT: Then I shall contact his mother.

CAPTAIN: There is no need.

KURT: No need?

CAPTAIN: No. I have already done so. Yes!

   KURT *starts to rise, but falls back in his chair.*

ALICE [*to* KURT]: Now he must die!

KURT: He *is* a cannibal.

CAPTAIN: So. That is that. [*Sharply, to* ALICE *and* KURT.] Did you say something?

ALICE: No. Have you become hard of hearing?

CAPTAIN: A little. But if you move closer, I'll tell you a secret. Between us two.

ALICE: There's no need for that. And a witness might be a good thing, for both parties.

CAPTAIN: Quite right! Witnesses are always a good thing. But first, is my will ready?

ALICE [*hands him a paper*]: The lawyer has drafted it.

CAPTAIN: In your favour? Good. [*Reads the will, then tears it carefully into pieces which he scatters on the floor.*] So. That's that. Yes!

ALICE [*to* KURT]: Have you ever seen a human being like him?

KURT: He isn't a human being.

CAPTAIN: Oh, Alice. I wanted to tell you something else —

ALICE [*uneasy*]: Yes?

CAPTAIN [*calmly, as before*]: In view of your oft-expressed wish to terminate the misery of your unhappy marriage, plus the complete lack of affection shown to your husband

and children, plus the negligence with which you have handled our domestic economy, I decided, during my visit to town, to deposit at the courthouse a petition for divorce.

ALICE: Oh? And your reason?

CAPTAIN [*still calmly*]: In addition to the reasons already listed, I have personal ones. Now that it has been established that I may live for another twenty years, I have decided to exchange my present unhappy state of matrimony for one better suited to my position. I intend to unite my destiny with that of a lady able to bring into my home not merely a wifely affection but also youth and — shall we say? — a hint of beauty.

ALICE [*takes off her ring and throws it at the* CAPTAIN]: Go ahead!

CAPTAIN [*picks up the ring and puts it in his waistcoat pocket*]: She throws away her ring. Will the witness be so good as to note this?

ALICE [*rises emotionally*]: And you intend to throw me out and put another woman in my house?

CAPTAIN: Yes.

ALICE: Right, then. Let's have it all out. Kurt — this man has been guilty of the attempted murder of his wife.

KURT: Attempted murder!

ALICE: Yes. He pushed me into the sea.

CAPTAIN: Without witnesses!

ALICE: He's lying. Judith saw it.

CAPTAIN: What's that got to do with it?

ALICE: She can testify.

CAPTAIN: No, she can't. She says she saw nothing.

ALICE: You've taught the child to lie!

CAPTAIN: I didn't need to. You'd taught her already.

ALICE: Have you been seeing Judith?

CAPTAIN: Yes.

ALICE: Oh, God! Oh, God!

CAPTAIN: The fortress has capitulated. The garrison is granted a safe conduct in ten minutes from now. [*Places his watch on the table.*] Ten minutes. By my watch. [*Clutches his heart and remains standing.*]

ALICE [*goes over and takes his arm*]: What is it?

CAPTAIN: I don't know.

ALICE: Do you want something? Would you like a drink?

CAPTAIN: Whisky? No, I don't want to die! Alice! [*Straightens himself.*] Don't touch me! Ten minutes, or the garrison will know what to expect. [*Draws his sabre.*] Ten minutes! [*Goes out upstage.*]

KURT: Who is this man?

ALICE: He's not a man, he's a demon.

KURT: What does he want with my son?

ALICE: He wants to have him as a hostage so that he can have you in his power. He wants to isolate you from the island's authorities. Do you know what this island is called by the people who live here? "The Little Hell."

KURT: I didn't know. Alice, you are the first woman who has ever made me feel sorry for her. All the others have seemed to me to deserve their fate.

ALICE: Don't abandon me now. Don't leave me, or he'll beat me. He has beaten me for twenty-five years — and in front of the children. He has even pushed me into the sea —

KURT: I can't try to be his friend any longer. I came here with no thought of malice. I was willing to forget how he'd humiliated me and blackened my name. I even for-

gave him when you told me it was he who'd taken my
children from me, because I could see he was sick and
dying. But now that he wants to take away my son, he
must die — he, or I.

ALICE: Good! Don't surrender the fortress, blow it to
hell and him with it, even if we have to go with him. I'll
find the gunpowder.

KURT: I wasn't angry with him when I came here. When I
felt your hatred infecting me, I thought of running away.
But now I feel an irresistible duty to hate this man as one
should hate evil. What can we do?

ALICE: I've learned my strategy from him. Get his enemies
together. Look for allies.

KURT: Fancy his managing to track down my wife! Why
didn't those two meet twenty-five years ago? That would
have been a match to make the earth tremble!

ALICE: But now they have met — and they must be parted.
I know his Achilles' heel — I've long suspected it —

KURT: Who is his worst enemy on this island?

ALICE: The Ordnance Officer.

KURT: Could we trust him?

ALICE: Yes. And he knows what I — yes, I know it too! — he
knows what the Sergeant-Major and my husband have been
up to together.

KURT: Up to? What do you mean?

ALICE: Embezzlement.

KURT: It's horrible. Look, I don't want to have anything
to do with this.

ALICE [laughs]: You can't strike an enemy?

KURT: I could once. Not any more.

ALICE: Why?

KURT: Because I have discovered that in the end, justice is always done.

ALICE: And you're prepared to wait? Till they've taken your son from you? Look at my grey hairs — yes, feel how thick they still are. He's planning to re-marry, so I am free to do the same. I am free! And in ten minutes he will be sitting down there, under arrest, down there! [*Stamps on the floor.*] Down there — and I shall dance above his head, I shall dance the *March of the Boyars.* [*Performs a few dance steps, with arms akimbo, and roars with laughter.*] And I'll play the piano, so that he shall hear! [*Hammers on the piano.*] Oh! the fortress will open its gates and the sentry with the drawn sword will no longer stand guard over me, but over him! Titti-tum-tum-ta, titti-tum-tum-tay! Him, him, him — !

KURT [*who has been watching her as though intoxicated*]: Alice! are you a devil like him?

ALICE [*jumps up on a chair and takes down the laurel wreaths*]: I shall wear these as I march out of this place. The laurels of triumph! And their ribbons will flutter — they're a little dusty, but they're evergreen. Like my youth. I'm not old, Kurt.

KURT [*his eyes aflame*]: You are a demon!

ALICE: In my little Hell! Look — I'll make myself ready. [*Loosens her hair.*] Give me two minutes to dress — two minutes to see the Ordnance Officer — and then, up goes the fortress!

KURT [*as before*]: You are a demon!

ALICE: You always used to say that when we were children. Do you remember, when we were children and said we'd marry each other! [*Laughs.*] You were shy, of course —

KURT [*earnestly*]: Alice!

ALICE: Yes, you were. And it suited you. You see — there

are coarse women who like shy men, and there — are said to be shy men who like coarse women. You liked me a little even then. Didn't you?

KURT: I don't know where I am. What are you?

ALICE: An actress who isn't scared by your conventions, and is a woman! And now I am free, free, free! Turn your back and I'll change my dress.

> *She begins to unbutton her dress.* KURT *rushes towards her, seizes her in his arms, lifts her high into the air and bites her on the throat. She screams. Then he throws her from him on to the sofa and runs out left.*

Scene 2

The same. Evening. The sentry can still be seen through the windows upstage. The laurel wreaths hang over the back of a chair. The ceiling lamp is lit. Soft music.

The CAPTAIN, *pale, hollow-eyed and, grizzled, in a worn uniform with riding boots, is seated at the desk playing patience.*

The interval music continues after the rise of the curtain until the other characters enter.

The CAPTAIN *continues with his game but now and then gives a start and looks up and listens anxiously.*

He seems unable to make his game come out; becomes impatient and sweeps the cards together. Then he goes to the window left, opens it and throws the cards out. The window remains open, shaking on its hinges.

He goes to the cupboard, is frightened by the noise the window makes, turns round and looks to see what it is. Takes out three dark, square-sided whisky bottles, looks at them carefully, and throws them out of the window. Then he takes out some boxes of cigars, smells inside one of them, and throws them out through the window.

*He takes off his glasses, dries them and tests them
to see how he sees with them. Then he throws them
out through the window, stumbles among the furniture
as though seeing badly, and lights a candelabra with
six candles that stands on the secretaire. Sees the
laurel wreaths, picks them up and goes towards the
window, but turns. Takes the piano cloth, and carefully
wipes the wreaths, takes some pins from the desk
and re-fixes the corners, then puts them all on a chair.
Goes to the piano, strikes the keys with his fists, shuts
the keyboard and throws the key through the window.
Then he lights the candles on the piano. Goes to the
whatnot, takes his wife's photograph, looks at it, tears
it up and throws the pieces on to the floor. The window
shakes on its hinges and frightens him again. He calms
himself, takes the photographs of his son and daughter,
kisses them lightly and stuffs them in his breast
pocket. The other photographs he sweeps to the floor
with his elbow and kicks into a heap with his boot.*

*Then he sits, tired, at the desk and feels his heart.
He lights the writing candles and sighs. Stares as
though seeing unpleasing visions. Gets up and goes to
the secretaire, opens the flap, takes out a bundle of
letters fastened with blue silk ribbons and throws
them into the stove. Shuts the secretaire. The telegraph taps a single stroke, then falls silent. The
CAPTAIN starts fearfully and stands with his hand on
his heart, listening. But hearing nothing more from
the telegraph, he listens towards the door left. Goes
over and opens it, takes a step inside and comes out
with a cat on his arm which he strokes along its back.
Then he goes out right. The music ceases.*

*ALICE enters upstage, dressed for walking with
her hair black, a hat and gloves. She looks around,
surprised at the many candles. KURT enters left,
nervous.*

ALICE: It looks like Christmas here.

KURT: Well?

ALICE [*holds out her hand for him to kiss*] : Thank me. [*He kisses her hand, unwillingly.*] Six witnesses, four of them irrefutable. The application has been despatched and the reply will come on the telegraph — here, into the heart of the fortress.

KURT: I see.

ALICE: Say "Thank you", not "I see".

KURT: Why has he lit so many candles?

ALICE: Because he's afraid of the dark, of course. Look at the telegraph! Doesn't it look like the handle of a coffee-mill? I grind, I grind, and the beans crunch. Like extracting a tooth —

KURT: What's he been doing in this room?

ALICE: It looks as though he's been making preparations to go. Down into the cells, that's where you'll go!

KURT: Alice, don't talk like that. I think it's horrible. He used to be my friend when we were young, and he was often kind to me when I was in trouble. I feel sorry for him.

ALICE: What about me? I did nothing to anyone and had to sacrifice my career for this monster.

KURT: That career of yours. Was it so brilliant?

ALICE [*furious*] : What the hell do you mean? Do you know who I am, or who I was?

KURT: Now, now. Don't get angry.

ALICE: Are you beginning too, already?

KURT: Already?

> ALICE *throws her arms round his neck and kisses him. He takes her in his arms and bites her on the neck so that she screams.*

ALICE: You're biting me!

KURT [*beside himself*]: Yes, I want to bite your neck and suck your blood like a stoat! You have woken the beast in me. I tried for years to stifle it by denying and tormenting myself. When I came here I thought myself a little better than you two — but now I am the meanest of us all. Since I saw you as you really are, in all your nakedness, since lust distorted my sight, I realize the full power of evil — it makes the ugly seem beautiful, the good seem ugly and weak. I want to strangle you — with a kiss! [*Embraces her.*]

ALICE [*shows her left hand*]: Do you see the mark of the bond from which you liberated me? I was a slave. Now I am free.

KURT: But I shall bind you —

ALICE: You?

KURT: I.

ALICE: I thought for a moment you were —

KURT: Getting religious?

ALICE: Yes. The other day you began to talk about the Fall —

KURT: Did I?

ALICE: And I thought you had come to preach at me —

KURT: You thought that? In an hour we shall be in town. Then you shall see what kind of a man I am —

ALICE: Tonight let us go to the theatre. Let us show ourselves. Don't you see? If I run away, the shame will be his.

KURT: I begin to understand. It isn't enough to put him in prison —

ALICE: No, it isn't enough. I want him shamed too.

KURT: A strange world. You commit the deed of shame, but he must bear it.

ALICE: That's the world's fault.

KURT: These walls! It's as though they'd soaked in all the evil of everyone who's ever been imprisoned here! One needs only to breathe here to be infected. While you have been thinking of the theatre and supper, I have been thinking of my son.

ALICE [*strikes him on the mouth with her glove*]: Fool!

KURT *raises his hand to strike her back.*

ALICE [*shrinks*]: Charming!

KURT: Forgive me.

ALICE: On your knees, then. [*He kneels.*] On your face! [*He presses his forehead to the floor.*] Kiss my foot! [*He kisses her foot.*] And never do that again. Get up!

KURT [*gets up*]: What have I come to? Where am I?

ALICE: You know quite well.

KURT [*looks around in horror*]: I think I'm —

CAPTAIN [*enters right, dejected, supporting himself on a stick*]: May I speak with Kurt? Alone.

ALICE: Is it about the safe-conduct?

CAPTAIN [*sits at the sewing-table*]: Kurt, will you please sit with me for a little? Alice, will you grant us a moment's — peace?

ALICE: What's this? Here's a change. [*To* KURT.] By all means, sit down. [KURT *sits unwillingly.*] And hearken to the voice of age and wisdom. If a telegram comes, leave it to me. [*Goes out left.*]

CAPTAIN [*after a pause, gravely*]: Can you understand the purpose of a life like mine? Like ours?

KURT: No. As little as I understand my own.

CAPTAIN: Then what is the meaning of this chaos?

KURT: In my better moments I have believed that the

meaning of life is just that. That we should not know
the meaning, and yet should bow to it —

CAPTAIN: If I have no fixed point outside myself, how
can I bow to it?

KURT: Correct. But you, as a mathematician, should
surely be able to find that unknown point, given certain
data —

CAPTAIN: I have looked for it — and have not found it.

KURT: Then your calculations have been at fault. You
must start again.

CAPTAIN: I will. Tell me, where did you find such resignation?

KURT: I have none left. Don't overrate me.

CAPTAIN: As you may possibly have noticed, I have
understood the art of living to be a question of blotting
out the past. Forget, and go on living. When I was young
I made a little bag and stuffed into it all my humiliations,
and when it was full I threw it into the sea. I don't
believe any mortal being has suffered as many humiliations
as I have. But when I blotted them out and went on living,
they ceased to exist.

KURT: I've noticed what kind of a life you've created for
yourself. And for those around you.

CAPTAIN: How else could I have lived? How could I have
stood it? [*Clutches at his heart.*]

KURT: How are you feeling?

CAPTAIN: Bad. [*Pause.*] Then there comes a moment
when the ability to create, as you call it, stops. And then
reality stands forth in all its nakedness. It's terrifying.
[*Now he speaks with an old man's tearfulness in his voice,
and drooping lower jaw.*] You see, my dear friend . . .
[*Controls himself and speaks with his normal voice.*] Forgive me. When I was in town just now and spoke with the

Doctor — [*Tearfully again.*] He said I was all to pieces — [*In normal voice.*] And that I couldn't live long.

KURT: Did he say *that*?

CAPTAIN: Yes, he said that.

KURT: Then it wasn't true?

CAPTAIN: What? Oh, yes, that . . . No, it wasn't true.

Pause.

KURT: Was the other thing a lie too?

CAPTAIN: How do you mean, old chap?

KURT: That my son was to be ordered here?

CAPTAIN: I've never heard any mention of that.

KURT: You know, your ability to forget the past is quite unbelievable!

CAPTAIN: Old chap, I don't understand what you mean.

KURT: Then you *are* all to pieces.

CAPTAIN: Yes, there isn't much left.

KURT: Perhaps you haven't petitioned to divorce your wife, either?

CAPTAIN: Divorce? No, never mentioned it.

KURT [*gets up*]: Then you admit you've been lying?

CAPTAIN: Old chap, you use such strong words. We all need a little indulgence.

KURT: You've realized that?

CAPTAIN [*firmly, in a clear voice*]: Yes, I have realized that. Forgive me, Kurt. Forgive me everything.

KURT: Bravely spoken. But I have nothing to forgive you. And I'm not the man you think, any longer. Least of all worthy to accept your confessions.

CAPTAIN [*in a clear voice*]: Life was so strange! So hostile, so cruel — ever since childhood. People were so cruel, so that I became cruel too — [KURT *walks over uneasily and glances at the telegraph.*] What are you looking at?

KURT: Can one shut off a telegraph machine?

CAPTAIN: Not easily.

KURT [*with rising unease*]: Who is Sergeant-Major Östberg?

CAPTAIN: He's an honest chap. Bit of a dealer, of course.

KURT: Who is the Ordnance Officer, then?

CAPTAIN: Oh, he's my enemy, all right. Not a bad fellow really, though.

KURT [*looks out through the window, where a lantern can be seen moving*]: What are they doing with that lantern out there by the guns?

CAPTAIN: Is there a lantern?

KURT: Yes, and people moving.

CAPTAIN: Probably what we call a welcoming committee.

KURT: What's that?

CAPTAIN: A platoon with a corporal. Some poor devil's going to be arrested.

KURT: Oh.

Pause.

CAPTAIN: Well, now that you know Alice, what do you think of her?

KURT: I can't say. I just don't understand people at all. I find her as inexplicable as I find you — and myself! I'm getting to the age when if one's wise one admits one knows nothing, and understands nothing. But when I see something happen, I want to know the reason. Why did you push her into the sea?

CAPTAIN: I don't know. It just seemed to me quite

natural when she stood there on the jetty that she should
go in.

KURT: Have you never regretted it?

CAPTAIN: Never.

KURT: That's strange.

CAPTAIN: Yes, it is. So strange that I can't believe it was I
who could have done such a paltry thing.

KURT: Did it never occur to you that she'd get her revenge?

CAPTAIN: God knows she has. And I find that equally
natural.

KURT: How have you come to be so cynically resigned in
such a short space of time?

CAPTAIN: Since I looked death in the eyes, I have seen
life from a different standpoint. Kurt, if you had to judge
between Alice and me, which would you say was right?

KURT: Neither. I feel infinite pity for you both. Perhaps a
little more for you.

CAPTAIN: Give me your hand, Kurt.

KURT [holds out one hand and puts the other on the
CAPTAIN's shoulder]: Old friend!

ALICE [enters left, carrying a parasol]: Charming! Did I
hear the word friend? Hasn't the telegram come?

KURT [coldly]: No.

ALICE: This delay's making me impatient, and when I get
impatient I hurry things up. Look, Kurt. I'm going to
finish him off now, and this'll settle him. First, I load — I
know the drill, if anyone does, the famous rifle-drill that
didn't sell five thousand copies. Then I take aim, fire!
[She aims the parasol.] How is your new wife? That
young, beautiful, unknown girl? You don't know. But I
know how my lover is. [Puts her arms around KURT's
neck and kisses him. He pushes her away.] He's splendid,

but he's still shy. [*To the* CAPTAIN.] You scum, whom I never loved, you were too vain to be jealous, you never saw how I led you by the snout!

> *The* CAPTAIN *draws his sabre and stumbles at her, hewing, but strikes only the furniture.*

ALICE: Help! Help!

> KURT *stands motionless.*

CAPTAIN [*falls, the sabre in his hand*]: Judith! Avenge me!

ALICE: He's dying. Thank God!

> KURT *moves towards the upstage door.*

CAPTAIN [*gets up*]: Not yet! [*Sheathes his sabre, goes over and sits in the chair by the sewing-table.*] Judith! Judith!

ALICE [*goes towards* KURT]: Now I'm going. With you.

KURT [*pushes her away so that she falls on her knees*]: Go to hell, whence you came! Goodbye. For ever.

CAPTAIN: Don't leave me, Kurt! She'll kill me.

ALICE: Kurt! Don't leave me! Don't leave us!

KURT: Goodbye. [*Goes.*]

ALICE [*changes her tone*]: What a wretch! There's a friend for you!

CAPTAIN [*gently*]: Forgive me, Alice, and come here. Come quickly!

ALICE: That man is the most contemptible and hypocritical wretch I have ever met in my life. At least you're a man.

CAPTAIN: Alice, listen to me. I can't live for long.

ALICE: Oh?

CAPTAIN: The Doctor told me.

ALICE: Then the other thing was untrue too?

CAPTAIN: Yes.

ALICE [*desperate*]: Oh, God! What have I done?

CAPTAIN: Nothing is irreparable.

ALICE: Yes. This is irreparable.

CAPTAIN: Nothing is irreparable, as long as one blots out the past and goes on living.

ALICE: But the telegram! The telegram!

CAPTAIN: What telegram?

ALICE [*on her knees beside him*]: Are we damned? Did this have to happen? I've destroyed myself — I've destroyed both of us! Why did you let yourself be fooled? And why did this man have to come and tempt me? We are lost. Everything could have been all right — you could have forgiven me —

CAPTAIN: What is it that cannot be forgiven? What have I not forgiven you?

ALICE: I know. But this time, there's no help.

CAPTAIN: I know how inventive you are in evil, but I can't guess what you —

ALICE: Oh, if I could undo it! If I could undo it, I would take care of you! Edgar, I would love you!

CAPTAIN: Listen to her! What's going on?

ALICE: Do you think no one can help us? Yes — no mortal can —

CAPTAIN: Who could, then?

ALICE [*looks the* CAPTAIN *in the eyes*]: I don't know. Think — what will become of the children? Their name will be dishonoured —

CAPTAIN: Have you dishonoured our name?

ALICE: No, not I! Not I! But — they'll have to leave school.

And when they go out into the world, they'll be alone like us, and evil like us. . . Then you didn't meet Judith either, I realize now?

CAPTAIN: No. But blot that out too.

The telegraph taps. ALICE *jumps up.*

ALICE [*screams*]: Now it's happening! Don't listen to it!

CAPTAIN [*calmly*]: I won't listen to it, dearest child. Calm yourself —

ALICE [*stands by the telegraph and stands on tiptoe to look out through the window*]: Don't listen! Don't listen!

CAPTAIN [*holds his ears*]: I'm holding my ears, Lisa, my child.

ALICE [*on her knees with outstretched hands*]: God help us! They're coming to arrest you. [*Weeps.*] God in heaven!

She moves her lips as though in silent prayer. The telegraph is still tapping gently, and a long ribbon of paper has crept from it. Then it falls quiet again.

ALICE [*gets up, tears off the strip of paper and reads it silently. Then she glances upwards, goes over and kisses the* CAPTAIN *on the forehead*]: It's all right. It was nothing. [*Sits in the other chair and sobs violently into her handkerchief.*]

CAPTAIN: What secrets have you got there?

ALICE: Don't ask. It's over now.

CAPTAIN: As you wish, my child.

ALICE: You wouldn't have spoken like that three days ago. Why now?

CAPTAIN: Alice. That first time I fell, I was a short while on the other side of the grave. What I saw I have forgotten, but the impression remained.

ALICE: What was it?

CAPTAIN: Hope of a better —

ALICE: A better —?

CAPTAIN: Yes. I have never really believed that this was life. This is death. Or something even worse —

ALICE: And we — ?

CAPTAIN: It was our destiny to torment each other — it seems.

ALICE: Have we tormented each other enough?

CAPTAIN: Yes, I think so. I think so. [*Looks around.*] Shall we tidy up after us? And leave things clean?

ALICE [*gets up*]: If we can.

CAPTAIN [*looks around the room*]: It won't be done in a day. Not in a day.

ALICE: But some time —

CAPTAIN: Let us hope so.

  Pause.

CAPTAIN [*sits again*]: So you didn't escape this time. But you didn't get me put away either. [*She is amazed.*] Yes, I knew you wanted to have me put in prison. But I blot that out. You've done worse things than that. [*She is silent.*] You know, I didn't embezzle that money.

ALICE: And now you propose that I shall be your sick-nurse?

CAPTAIN: If you wish to be.

ALICE: What other choice have I?

CAPTAIN: I don't know.

ALICE [*sits limply, in despair*]: But this is eternal hell. Is there no end, then?

CAPTAIN: Yes, if we are patient. Perhaps when death comes, life begins.

ALICE: If only that could be true!

Pause.

CAPTAIN: You think Kurt was a hypocrite?

ALICE: I'm sure of it.

CAPTAIN: I don't think so. But everyone who comes near us becomes evil, and moves on. Kurt was weak, and evil is strong. [*Pause.*] How banal life is nowadays! In the old days one fought, now one merely threatens. I'm pretty sure that in three months we will celebrate our silver wedding — with Kurt to propose the toast — and the Doctor and Gerda will be there . . . The Ordnance Officer will make a speech, and the Sergeant-Major will lead the cheers. And if I know the Colonel, he'll invite himself. Yes, you laugh. But do you remember Adolf's wedding — that fellow in the Hussars? The bride had to wear her ring on her right hand because the bridegroom, in a fit of tender passion, had chopped off the third finger of her left hand with a jewelled penknife.

> ALICE *holds her handkerchief to her mouth to stifle a laugh.*

CAPTAIN: Are you crying? No, I believe you're laughing! Yes, child, sometimes we cry and sometimes we laugh. Which is the more fitting? Don't ask me, The other day I read in a newspaper that a man had been divorced seven times, *ergo* had married seven times — and in the end ran away at the age of ninety-eight and re-married his first wife. There's love for you! Is life serious or just a hoax? I don't know. When it's a farce it can be a nightmare, when it's serious it can be quite soothing and tolerable. But when you finally decide to play it serious, someone always comes along and treats you like a clown. Kurt for instance. Do you want to celebrate our silver wedding? [ALICE *is silent.*] Say yes, Alice. They'll laugh at us, but what of that? We'll laugh too — or be serious. Whichever way it turns out.

ALICE: Yes. Let us.

CAPTAIN [*earnestly*] : Well, then. Our silver jubilee. [*Gets up.*] Blot out the past and go on living. Well. Let's go on.

PART II

(1900)

CHARACTERS

EDGAR, the CAPTAIN

ALICE

KURT

ALLAN, KURT's son

JUDITH, EDGAR's daughter

THE LIEUTENANT

Scene 1

*An oval drawing-room in white and gold. The rear
wall is broken by glass doors, which stand open to
reveal the garden terrace outside, with a balustrade of
stone pillars and blue-white earthenware pots
containing petunias and geraniums. This terrace is part
of the garden walk. Beyond can be seen the shore
battery with a sentry. In the distance, the open sea.*

*In the room, to the left, stands a gilt sofa, with a
table and chairs. To the right, a grand piano, a desk
and a fireplace. Downstage, an American armchair. By
the desk, a copper standard-lamp, with a table attached.
Various old oil-paintings on the walls.*

ALLAN *is seated at the desk, engaged in mathematical calculations.* JUDITH *enters through the
upstage door in a short summer dress, with a pigtail
down her back, her hat in one hand and a tennis racket
in the other.* ALLAN *gets up, grave and respectful.*

JUDITH [*earnest yet friendly*] : Why won't you come and
play tennis?

ALLAN [*shy, fighting his feelings*] : I'm so busy —

JUDITH: Didn't you see I put my bicycle *facing* the oak,
not away from it?

ALLAN: Yes, I saw that.

JUDITH: Well, what does that mean?

ALLAN: It means — that you want me to come and play
tennis — but my duties — I have these problems to solve,
and your father is a pretty severe taskmaster.

JUDITH: Do you like him?

ALLAN: Yes, I do. He takes an interest in all his pupils —

JUDITH: He takes an interest in everyone and everything. Do you want to come?

ALLAN: You know I want to. But I shouldn't.

JUDITH: I'll ask Daddy to give you permission.

ALLAN: Don't do that. People'll only talk.

JUDITH: You think I can't manage him? He wants what I want.

ALLAN: That's because you're so hard. Yes!

JUDITH: You should be, too.

ALLAN: My family aren't wolves.

JUDITH: Then you'll become a sheep.

ALLAN: I'd rather that.

JUDITH: Tell me, why won't you come and play tennis?

ALLAN: You know.

JUDITH: Tell me, though. The Lieutenant?

ALLAN: Yes. You don't care a bit about me, but you don't enjoy being with the Lieutenant unless I'm around so you can see me suffer.

JUDITH: Am I so cruel? I didn't know.

ALLAN: Now you do know.

JUDITH: Then I'll be good from now on. I don't want to be cruel, I don't want to seem bad — to you.

ALLAN: You only say that to get me back in your power. I'm already your slave, but you aren't content with that, your slave has to be tortured and thrown to the beasts! You've already got *him* in your claws, what do you want with me, then? Let me go my way, and you go yours.

JUDITH: Are you telling me to get out? [ALLAN *does not reply*.] All right, I'll go. We'll have to meet occasionally because we're cousins, but I won't bother you.

ALLAN *sits at the desk and returns to his calculations.*
JUDITH, *instead of going, comes into the room and
gradually approaches the desk where* ALLAN *is
sitting.*

JUDITH: Don't be frightened, I'll go in a minute. I just
wanted to see what kind of a house the Quarantine
Master has. [*Looks around.*] White and gold! A piano,
Bechstein! Mm! We're still in the fortress, now Daddy's
pensioned. The fortress, where Mother has sat for
twenty-five years. And we're there on charity. You're
rich, all you lot —

ALLAN [*quietly*]: We're not rich.

JUDITH: You say that, but you're always so smartly
dressed — and whatever you wear suits you. Are you
listening to me? [*Goes closer.*]

ALLAN [*submissively*]: I'm listening.

JUDITH: How can you listen when you sit doing sums, or
whatever you are doing?

ALLAN: I don't listen with my eyes.

JUDITH: Your eyes, yes. Have you looked at them in a
mirror?

ALLAN: Go away.

JUDITH: You despise me!

ALLAN: My dear girl, I don't think about you.

JUDITH [*comes closer*]; Archimedes, sitting at his sums as
the soldiers break in and cut him down! [*Ruffles his papers
with her racket.*]

ALLAN: Don't touch my papers!

JUDITH: That's what Archimedes said. Now you're getting
ideas, of course. You think I can't live without you.

ALLAN: Why can't you leave me in peace?

JUDITH: Be nice, and I'll help you with your exam —

ALLAN: You?

JUDITH: Yes. I know the examiners —

ALLAN [*sternly*]: What do you mean?

JUDITH: Don't you know that it helps to have the examiners on your side?

ALLAN: Meaning your father and the Lieutenant?

JUDITH: And the Colonel.

ALLAN: You mean that with your help I needn't do any work?

JUDITH: That's a nasty translation.

ALLAN: Of a nasty original.

JUDITH: You're beastly!

ALLAN: I'm doing this for your sake, and mine. I'm ashamed I even listened to you. Why don't you go?

JUDITH: Because I know you like my company. Yes, you always manage to walk past my window! You've always some errand that takes you to town on the same steamer as me, you can't go out in a boat without me to work the sail.

ALLAN [*shyly*]: A young girl shouldn't talk like that.

JUDITH: Do you think I'm a child?

ALLAN: Sometimes you're a delightful child, sometimes a scheming woman. You seem to have chosen me to be your sheep.

JUDITH: You are a sheep, so I shall protect you.

ALLAN [*gets up*]: A wolf is always a bad sheepdog. You want to eat me — that's the real truth. You're willing to stake your beautiful eyes in return for my head.

JUDITH: Oh, you have noticed my eyes? I didn't think you were that bold.

ALLAN *gathers his papers and makes to go out right.*
JUDITH *puts herself between him and the door.*

ALLAN: Get out of my way, or —

JUDITH: Or?

ALLAN: If you were a boy, I'd — ! But you're a girl.

JUDITH: Well?

ALLAN: If you had an atom of pride, you'd have gone. I
as good as kicked you out.

JUDITH [*walks angrily towards the glass doors*]: I'll make
you sorry for this!

ALLAN: I don't doubt it.

JUDITH: I'll — make — you — sorry — for — this. [*Goes.*]

KURT [*enters left*]: Where are you going, Allan?

ALLAN: Is it you?

KURT: Who was that who ran out in such a hurry?

ALLAN: Judith.

KURT: She's a bit explosive. But she's a good girl.

ALLAN: When a girl is hard and ruthless, people always
say she's a good girl.

KURT: You mustn't be such a Puritan, Allan. Aren't you
happy with your new relations?

ALLAN: I like Uncle Edgar —

KURT: Yes, he has many good sides. And your other
teachers? The Lieutenant, for example?

ALLAN: He's so moody. Sometimes he seems to have
some grudge against me.

KURT: Oh, no. You imagine too much. Don't brood so.
Do your work, be polite to people and let them be themselves.

ALLAN: Well, I do, but — they won't leave me in peace. They suck one in — just like those octopuses down by the jetty. They don't bite, but they stir up a whirlpool that pulls one down —

KURT [*gently*]: I think you tend to look on the dark side of things. Aren't you happy here with me? Is there something you miss?

ALLAN: I've never known such kindness, but — there's something here that suffocates me.

KURT: Here by the sea? Don't you like the sea?

ALLAN: The open sea, yes. But the water here's different, it's full of snare-grass, octopuses, jellyfish, nettlefish or whatever they call them.

KURT: You shouldn't sit indoors so much. Go out and play tennis.

ALLAN: I don't want to.

KURT: You're angry with Judith, I can see.

ALLAN: Judith?

KURT: You're so touchy about people. One mustn't be that, or one finds oneself alone.

ALLAN: I'm not touchy, but — I feel as though I was a log at the bottom of the wood-pile, having to wait my turn to get into the fire. Everything's on top of me, and it presses, and presses —

KURT: Wait till your turn comes. The pile will grow smaller —

ALLAN: Yes, but so slowly, so slowly! Ugh! And meanwhile I lie here mouldering.

KURT: It's no fun being young. And yet one envies you —

ALLAN: Does one? Would you like to change places with me?

KURT: No, thank you!

ALLAN: Do you know what the worst thing is? Having to sit and keep quiet while old people talk nonsense! Sometimes I *know* I know more about something than them, but I have to keep my mouth shut. Sorry, I don't think of you as old.

KURT: Why not?

ALLAN: Perhaps because I've really only just got to know you —

KURT: And because — you had a different picture of me before?

ALLAN: Yes.

KURT: I imagine that during those years we were parted you didn't always have the warmest feelings about me?

ALLAN: No.

KURT: Did you ever see a photograph of me?

ALLAN: Only one. And that was very unflattering.

KURT: And old?

ALLAN: Yes.

KURT: Ten years ago I went grey-haired in a single night. Later it returned to its old colour. Of its own accord. Let's talk about something else. Look. Here comes your aunt. My cousin. What do you think of her?

ALLAN: I'd rather not say.

KURT: Then I won't ask.

ALICE [*enters in a very light-coloured summer walking-dress, with a parasol*]: Good morning, Kurt. [*She gives a look signifying that* ALLAN *should leave them.*]

KURT [*to* ALLAN]: Leave us.

> ALLAN *goes out right.* ALICE *sits on a sofa left,* KURT *in a chair beside her.*

ALICE [*irritably*]: He'll be here in a moment, so you needn't feel embarrassed.

KURT: Why should I be?

ALICE: You're such a moralist.

KURT: Only as regards myself.

ALICE: Oh, yes! Once I forgot myself, when I thought I saw you as a liberator, but you kept your head, so we can forget what never happened.

KURT: Forget it, then.

ALICE: Yes, but I don't think *he* has forgotten —

KURT: You mean, that night he had a heart attack? And you thought he was dead and started celebrating prematurely?

ALICE: Yes. And he recovered. But when he gave up drinking he learned to keep silent, and now he's terrifying. He's up to something I don't understand —

KURT: Alice. Your husband is a decent ass, who shows me nothing but kindness —

ALICE: Beware of his kindnesses. I know them.

KURT: Alice, please —

ALICE: So he's fooled you too. Don't you see the danger, can't you sense the traps?

KURT: No.

ALICE: Then you haven't a hope.

KURT: Oh, really!

ALICE: It's extraordinary. I sit here and see disaster creeping up on you like a cat. I point it out to you, but you won't see it.

KURT: Allan can't see it either, and he has no reason to be biased. Though I admit he can only see Judith. But that should be a guarantee of a good relationship.

ALICE: Do you know Judith?

KURT: A little flirt with plaits down her back and skirts that are too short —

ALICE: Exactly! But I saw her dressed up the other day in a long skirt and what I saw then was a young lady — not so young, either, when her hair was up.

KURT: She is a little forward for her age, I admit.

ALICE: And she's playing with Allan.

KURT: That's all right, as long as it's just play.

ALICE: Oh, that's all right, is it? [*Pause.*] Edgar will be here in a moment. He'll sit in that armchair. He's got an obsession about that. You be careful he doesn't steal it.

KURT: He's welcome to it.

ALICE: Let him sit there, then we can stay here. And when he starts talking — he's always garrulous in the morning — when he says things that seem meaningless, I'll translate them for you.

KURT: Oh, Alice, you *worry* too much, you worry *too much*. What have I got to fear as long as I do this quarantine job properly and don't offend anyone?

ALICE: You believe in justice and honour and all that?

KURT: Yes, experience has taught me to. Once I used to believe the opposite. It cost me dearly.

ALICE: Here he is.

KURT: I've never seen you scared before.

ALICE: My courage was only ignorance. Of the danger.

KURT: The danger? You'll start scaring me soon.

ALICE: If only I could. Here he is.

> The CAPTAIN *enters upstage in mufti* — *a black, buttoned morning coat, a military cap, a stick with*

a silver handle. He greets them with a nod and sits in the armchair.

ALICE [*to* KURT]: Let him speak first.

CAPTAIN: This is a superb chair you have, my dear Kurt. Quite superb.

KURT: You can have it if you like. As a gift.

CAPTAIN: I didn't mean that —

KURT: But I do. Think of all you've given me.

CAPTAIN [*garrulously*]: Oh, rubbish . . . And when I sit here, I look out over the whole island, over the promenades, I see all the people on their verandahs, all the ships that sail on the sea, coming in and going out. You've certainly managed to get the best corner of this island, and it isn't exactly a Garden of Eden. No, it's known as Little Hell, and Kurt has built himself a Paradise here — without his Eve, of course, whose coming put an end to Paradise. By the way, do you know this was once a royal hunting-lodge?

KURT: So I have heard.

CAPTAIN: You live like a king yourself. But I do wish people wouldn't say you have me to thank for it.

ALICE [*to* KURT]: You see. Now he's trying to steal you.

KURT: I have much to thank you for.

CAPTAIN: Oh, rubbish. By the way, did you get those cases of wine?

KURT: Yes.

CAPTAIN: And you like them?

KURT: Very much. Please thank your shipper and tell him so.

CAPTAIN: He always sells first-class stuff —

ALICE [*to* KURT]: At second-class prices, and you have to pay the difference.

CAPTAIN: What did you say, Alice?

ALICE: I? Nothing.

CAPTAIN: Well. When this post of Quarantine Master was established, I considered applying for it myself. So I began to study the subject.

ALICE [to KURT]: He's lying.

CAPTAIN [boastfully]: The views held by the authorities regarding the problems of disinfection struck me as obsolete. I preferred those of the Neptunists, so called because they favour the water method —

KURT: Forgive me, but I remember clearly that it was I who advocated the water method, and you who believed in the ovens.

CAPTAIN: I? Nonsense.

ALICE [loudly]: Yes, I remember that too.

CAPTAIN: You?

KURT: I remember it clearly, because —

CAPTAIN [interrupts]: Well, it's just possible, but in any case it's irrelevant. We have now reached the point where a new situation — [To KURT who is about to interrupt.] If you don't mind! — has arisen — and the science of quarantine is about to take a giant step forward.

KURT: Talking of that, do you know who it is who's writing those idiotic articles in the newspaper?

CAPTAIN [reddens]: I don't know, but why do you call them idiotic?

ALICE [to KURT]: Watch out. He wrote them.

KURT [to ALICE]: He? [To the CAPTAIN.] Perhaps I should have said not wholly informed.

CAPTAIN: You are not able to judge.

ALICE: Are you two trying to pick a quarrel?

KURT: No —

CAPTAIN: It's difficult to stay friends with anyone on this island, but we two should set an example —

KURT: Yes, can you explain that to me? When I first came here I soon got friendly with all the authorities, and became particularly intimate with the Judge Advocate — well, as intimate as one can, at our age. But after a while — I remember, it happened soon after you got well — they suddenly all began to act very coldly towards me, and yesterday the Judge Advocate cut me on the promenade. I was very upset. [*The* CAPTAIN *is silent.*] Have you noticed any unfriendliness towards you?

CAPTAIN: No, on the contrary.

ALICE [*to* KURT]: Don't you see, he's stolen your friends.

KURT [*to the* CAPTAIN]: I wondered if it could be that new share issue I refused to come in on?

CAPTAIN: Oh, I'm sure not. But can you tell me why you didn't want to subscribe?

KURT: Because I'd already invested my small savings in a lime works. And also, well, a new issue suggests that the old shares are shaky.

CAPTAIN [*absent-mindedly*]: That's a superb lamp you have. Where did you get it?

KURT: In town, of course.

ALICE [*to* KURT]: Watch out for your lamp, now.

KURT [*to the* CAPTAIN]: You mustn't think I'm ungrateful or disloyal, Edgar.

CAPTAIN: Well, it isn't very loyal of you to edge out of something you helped to start.

KURT: My dear Edgar, common prudence demands that one should try to save oneself and what one has while there is still time.

CAPTAIN: Save oneself? Is there some danger afoot? Is someone planning to rob you?

KURT: Why do you use such words?

CAPTAIN: Weren't you pleased when I helped you to invest your capital at six per cent?

KURT: Yes, I was very grateful.

CAPTAIN: You are not grateful now. Still, you're made that way and you can't help it.

ALICE [to KURT]: Listen to him!

KURT: Doubtless my character is imperfect and doubtless it sometimes gets the better of me, but I never deny my obligations —

CAPTAIN: Show it, then. [*Reaches out a hand and takes a newspaper.*] Hullo! What's this? An announcement — [*Reads.*] The Chief Medical Officer is dead. [*as though to himself.*] This will involve certain changes.

ALICE [to KURT]: He can't even wait till the fellow's buried.

KURT [to the CAPTAIN]: What kind of changes?

CAPTAIN [*gets up*]: No doubt we'll learn.

ALICE: Where are you going?

CAPTAIN: I think I must go into town. [*Catches sight of a letter-card on the desk, registers it mentally, reads the outside of it and puts it back.*] Forgive this digression.

KURT: Not at all.

CAPTAIN: Aren't those Allan's mathematical instruments? Where is the boy?

KURT: He's out playing with the girls.

CAPTAIN: That big lad? I don't like that. And Judith will have to watch herself. You must keep an eye on your young man. And I'll keep one on my young lady. [*Walks past the piano and strikes a few notes.*] Superb tone this instrument has. A Steinbech? Eh?

KURT: Bechstein.

CAPTAIN: You're doing well for yourself, Kurt. You should be grateful to me for bringing you here.

ALICE [*to* KURT]: He's lying. He tried to stop you coming.

CAPTAIN: Well, goodbye, you two. I'll catch the next boat. [*Goes, inspecting the paintings on the walls en route.*]

ALICE: Well?

KURT: Well?

ALICE: I still don't get what he's up to. But tell me one thing. That envelope he was looking at. Who's it from?

KURT: I must confess, that was my one secret.

ALICE: And he sniffed it out. He's a demon, I told you. Is the sender's name on the outside?

KURT: Yes. "Constituency Headquarters".

ALICE: Then he's guessed your secret. You're hoping to stand for Parliament. Now you'll see — he'll go for the candidacy and get it.

KURT: Has he ever had plans in that direction?

ALICE: No, but he has now. I saw it in his face while he was reading the envelope.

KURT: Is that why he's going into town?

ALICE: No. He decided that when he saw the obituary notice.

KURT: What can he gain from the Medical Officer's death?

ALICE: You tell me. Perhaps he was some enemy who stood in his way.

KURT: If he's as dreadful as you say, then one has reason to fear him.

ALICE: Didn't you hear how he wanted to steal you, to tie your hands by making you feel ungrateful without any reason at all? He never got you this job, he tried to stop you getting it. He's a stealer of souls, a parasite, a worm who wants to eat your entrails, so that one day you'll find yourself hollow like a rotten tree. He hates you, even though he's bound to you by the memory of your early friendship —

KURT: How penetrative one becomes when one hates someone.

ALICE: And blind when one loves. Blind and stupid.

KURT: Alice! Don't talk like that.

ALICE: Do you know what is meant by a vampire? It's the soul of a dead person that looks for a living body to dwell in as a parasite. Edgar is dead, ever since that day he fell. He has no interests, no personality, no initiative. But once he gets hold of someone he sinks his teeth into them, drops his roots into their flesh and starts to grow and bloom. Now he has fastened on to you.

KURT: If he comes too close I'll shake him off.

ALICE: Shake off a leech? Just you try. Do you know why he doesn't want Judith and Allan to meet?

KURT: I suppose he's afraid of them getting hurt.

ALICE: It's not that. He wants to marry Judith off — to the Colonel.

KURT [*startled*]: That old widower?

ALICE: Yes.

KURT: How horrible. What does she say?

ALICE: If she could get the General, who's eighty, she'd take him, to spite the Colonel, who's sixty. Spite, Kurt — that's what she lives on. Jackboots and spite — those are the only words that breed understands.

KURT: Judith? That beautiful young girl — so proud,
so full of life?

ALICE: Yes. We know her. May I sit here and write a letter?

KURT [*tidies the desk*]: Of course.

ALICE [*takes off her gloves and sits at the desk*]: Now I'll
try my hand as a tactician. I failed once, when I tried to
kill that monster. But now I've learned the craft.

KURT: You know that one must load before one shoots?

ALICE: Yes. And with real bullets.

> KURT *goes out right.* ALICE *thinks and writes.*
> ALLAN *runs in without noticing her and throws him-*
> *self headlong on the sofa, sobbing into a lace handker-*
> *chief.* ALICE *watches him for a moment, then gets up*
> *and goes over to the sofa.*

ALICE [*gently*]: Allan!

> ALLAN *sits up embarrassed, and hides the handkerchief*
> *behind his back.*

ALICE [*gentle, feminine, earnest*]: You mustn't be afraid
of me, Allan. You have nothing to fear from me. What's
the matter? Are you ill?

ALLAN: Yes.

ALICE: What's wrong with you?

ALLAN: I don't know.

ALICE: Have you a headache?

ALLAN: No.

ALICE [*touches her breast*]: Something here?

ALLAN: Yes.

ALICE: It hurts, so that your heart wants to break? And
it tears, and tears —

ALLAN: How do you know that?

ALICE: And then one wants to die, one wishes one were dead, and everything's so difficult. And one thinks only of one thing — or rather, one person — but if two people think about the same person, then one of those two is doomed. [ALLAN *has forgotten himself and is picking at his handkerchief.*] It's the sickness which no one can cure — one can't eat, one doesn't want to drink, one only wants to weep, and one weeps so bitterly. Preferably out in the forest, so no one can see, because people laugh at that kind of grief. People are cruel! Ugh! What do you want from her? Nothing. You don't want to kiss her mouth, because then you believe you would die. When your thoughts fly to her, you feel as though death had touched you. And it is death, my child. The death that gives life. But you can't understand that yet. There's a smell of violets. It is she! [*Approaches* ALLAN *and slowly takes his handkerchief.*] It is she, she is everywhere, she and only she. [*Laughs loudly.* ALLAN *hides his face in her lap.*] Poor boy! Poor boy! Oh, how it hurts, how it hurts! [*Dries his tears with the handkerchief.*] There, there, there. Cry, cry, yes. It will ease your heart. [*Pause.*] But now, get up, Allan, and be a man, otherwise she won't want to look at you. The cruel one, who is not cruel. Has she tormented you? With the Lieutenant? Listen, my boy. You must be friends with the Lieutenant, then you'll be able to talk about her together. That helps a little too.

ALLAN: I don't want to see the Lieutenant.

ALICE: Listen, little boy. It won't be long before the Lieutenant comes to see you to talk about her. Because — [ALLAN *looks up with a glimmer of hope.*] Well, shall I be nice and tell you? [*He bows his head.*] Because he is as unhappy as you.

ALLAN [*happily*]: No?

ALICE: Of course he is, and he needs someone to open his heart to when Judith hurts him. You seem happy already!

ALLAN: Doesn't she want the Lieutenant?

ALICE: She doesn't want you either, my dear. She wants the Colonel. [*He is downcast again.*] Is it raining again? You can't keep that handkerchief, Judith minds about her belongings and won't like losing it. [*He looks crestfallen.*] Well, Allan, that's how Judith is. Sit there now while I write another letter, then you can go on an errand for me.

She goes to the desk and writes. The LIEUTENANT *enters upstage. He looks melancholy without appearing comic. He does not notice* ALICE *but makes for* ALLAN.

LIEUTENANT: Cadet! [ALLAN *springs to attention.*] Please sit down.

ALICE watches them. The LIEUTENANT *goes over to* ALLAN *and sits beside him. Sighs, takes out a handkerchief like the one we have seen and dries his forehead.* ALLAN *looks at the handkerchief covetously. The* LIEUTENANT *looks at* ALLAN *sadly.* ALICE *coughs. The* LIEUTENANT *springs to attention.*

ALICE: Please sit down.

LIEUTENANT: I beg your pardon, madam.

ALICE: Not at all. Please sit there and keep the cadet company. He feels a little lonely on this island. [*Writes.*]

LIEUTENANT [*softly to* ALLAN, *embarrassed*]: It's terribly hot.

ALLAN: Yes.

LIEUTENANT: Have you finished Book Six yet?

ALLAN: I'm just doing the last problem.

LIEUTENANT: That's a tricky one.

Silence.

LIEUTENANT: Have you — [*searches for words*] — played tennis today?

ALLAN: No, it was too hot in the sun.

LIEUTENANT [*tormented, but not absurdly so*]: Yes, it's tremendously hot today.

ALLAN [*whispers*]: Yes, it is very hot.

   Silence.

LIEUTENANT: Have you — been out sailing today?

ALLAN: No, I couldn't get anyone to crew for me.

LIEUTENANT: Would you — trust me to — crew for you?

ALLAN [*respectfully, as before*]: It would be too great an honour, Lieutenant.

LIEUTENANT: By no means, by no means. Do you think — there'll be a good breeze today, around noon? That's the only time I can be free.

ALLAN [*shrewdly*]: There'll be very little wind at noon, and — that's when Miss Judith has her lesson —

LIEUTENANT [*crestfallen*]: I see, I see. Hm. Do you think that — ?

ALICE: Would one of you two young gentlemen be so kind as to take a letter for me? [*The two men look at each other distrustfully.*] To Miss Judith? [ALLAN *and the* LIEUTENANT *jump up and go over to* ALICE, *but with a certain dignity so as to conceal their feelings.*] Both of you? It'll be all the surer to reach her, then! [*Hands the letter to the* LIEUTENANT.] Oh, Lieutenant, may I have that handkerchief? My daughter gets so worried if she loses any of her clothes. She's rather small-minded about such things. Would you let me have it, please? I don't want to laugh, but you two really mustn't make yourselves ridiculous — unnecessarily. And the Colonel doesn't like to act Othello. [*Takes the handkerchief.*] Be off with you now, the pair of you, and try to hide your feelings as best you can!

   The LIEUTENANT *bows and goes, closely followed by* ALLAN.

ALICE [*calls*] : Allan!

ALLAN [*stops unwillingly in doorway*] : Yes, Aunt Alice?

ALICE: You'd better stay. If you don't want to hurt your-self more than you can bear.

ALLAN: But he's going!

ALICE: Let him burn his fingers. But you take care.

ALLAN: I don't want to take care.

ALICE: You'll cry later. And I'll have to be the one who'll comfort you.

ALLAN: I want to go!

ALICE: Go, then. But come back, you young idiot, so that I have the chance to laugh at you.

> ALLAN *runs after the* LIEUTENANT. ALICE *writes again.*

KURT [*enters*] : Alice, I've received an anonymous letter which bothers me.

ALICE: Have you noticed that ever since Edgar put away that uniform he's been another person? I never thought a coat could do so much.

KURT: You haven't answered my question.

ALICE: It wasn't a question, it was a statement. What are you frightened of?

KURT: Everything.

ALICE: He's going in to town. Those trips always have some unpleasant outcome.

KURT: But I can't take any measures, because I don't know from which point the attack will come.

ALICE [*seals her letter*] : Let's see if I've guessed right.

KURT: Will you help me, then?

ALICE: Yes. But no further than my interests allow. That is to say, my children's.

KURT: I understand. Listen — how quiet it is here, in the fields, on the sea, everywhere!

ALICE: But behind the silence I can hear voices — wailing, screaming.

KURT: Ssh! I hear something too. No, it was only the gulls.

ALICE: I can hear something else. Well, I'll go to the post-office. With this letter.

Scene 2

The same. ALLAN *is working at the desk.* JUDITH *is standing in the doorway in a tennis hat holding the handlebars of a bicycle.*

JUDITH: Can I borrow your screwdriver?

ALLAN [*not looking up*]: No, you can't.

JUDITH: You're being rude now, every time I ask you for something.

ALLAN [*not harshly*]: I'm not being anything, I just want to be left in peace.

JUDITH [*comes forward*]: Allan.

ALLAN: Well, what is it?

JUDITH: You mustn't be angry with me.

ALLAN: I'm not.

JUDITH: Give me your hand on it.

ALLAN [*gently*]: I don't want to take your hand, but I'm not angry. What do you want with me, really?

JUDITH: Oh, you're so stupid!

ALLAN: If you say so.

JUDITH: You think I'm just nasty.

ALLAN: No, I know you're kind too. You *can* be kind.

JUDITH: Well, it's not my fault that you and the Lieutenant go off and cry together. Tell me, why do you cry?
[ALLAN *is embarrassed.*] Tell me. I never cry. And why
are you such good friends now? What do you talk about
as you walk arm in arm? [*He does not answer.*] Allan!
You'll soon see what I really am, and that I can do things
for those I care about. And I'll give you one piece of
advice — though I don't want to tell tales. You watch out —

ALLAN: For what?

JUDITH: Unpleasantnesses.

ALLAN: From whom?

JUDITH: From the direction you least expect.

ALLAN: I'm pretty used to unpleasantnesses. I haven't
had so much fun out of life. What's brewing now?

JUDITH[*thoughtfully*]: You poor boy. Give me your
hand! [*He stretches out his hand.*] Look at me. Daren't
you look at me?

　　　He runs out left to hide his emotion.

LIEUTENANT[*enters upstage*]: Excuse me. I was hoping
to find Cadet —

JUDITH: Tell me, Lieutenant. Do you want to be my friend?
May I confide in you?

LIEUTENANT: If you choose so to honour me —

JUDITH: I do. Just one word. Don't abandon Allan, when
it happens.

LIEUTENANT: When what happens?

JUDITH: You'll soon see — perhaps today. Do you like
Allan?

LIEUTENANT: The young man is my best pupil, and I

admire him also for his strength of character. There are moments in life when one needs — [*stresses the words*] — strength to — in a word, to carry on, to endure, to suffer.

JUDITH: That's more than one word. But — you like Allan?

LIEUTENANT: Yes.

JUDITH: Go and find him, and stay with him —

LIEUTENANT: That was why I came here. I had no other motive —

JUDITH: I wasn't suggesting you had. Of the kind you mean. Allan went out that way. [*Points left.*]

LIEUTENANT [*as he hesitantly exists left*]: I — I will do as you suggest.

JUDITH: Please do.

ALICE [*enters upstage*]: What are you doing here?

JUDITH: I wanted to borrow a screwdriver.

ALICE: Will you listen to me for a moment?

JUDITH: Certainly. [ALICE *sits on the sofa.* JUDITH *remains standing.*] But say what you have to say quickly. I don't like long lectures.

ALICE: Don't you? Right. Put up your hair and wear a long dress.

JUDITH: Why?

ALICE: Because you're not a child any longer. And you're too young to need to act as though you were younger.

JUDITH: What does that mean?

ALICE: That you're old enough for marriage, and that the way you dress now causes offence.

JUDITH: All right. I will.

ALICE: You understand, then?

JUDITH: Oh, yes.

ALICE: And we're agreed?

JUDITH: Completely.

ALICE: On all points?

JUDITH: Every one.

ALICE: Will you also please stop playing — with Allan?

JUDITH: You want me to be serious?

ALICE: Yes.

JUDITH: Then we can start at once.

> She has put down her bicycle handlebars and now
> lets down her cycling-skirt, reshapes her plait into a
> bun, takes a hairpin from her mother's hair and
> fastens her own.

ALICE: One doesn't perform one's toilet in other people's
houses.

JUDITH: Am I all right like this? Right, I'm ready. Now,
come who dares!

ALICE: Well, at least you look respectable now. And leave
Allan in peace.

JUDITH: I don't know what you mean by that.

ALICE: Can't you see he's suffering?

JUDITH: Yes, I think I noticed. But I can't imagine why.
I'm not suffering.

ALICE: That's *your* strength. But you wait. One day — oh,
yes, you'll know. Go home now, and don't forget you have
a long dress on.

JUDITH: Must one walk differently, too?

ALICE: Try.

JUDITH [*tries to walk like a lady*]: Oh! It's like wearing
clogs, my feet are tied, I can't run any more!

ALICE: Yes, child. Now you must learn to walk, the slow road towards the unknown, which one knows about but must pretend to know nothing of. Shorter steps — and slower, much slower! You must throw away your children's shoes and start wearing boots, Judith. You don't remember when you gave up oversocks and started wearing shoes, but I remember.

JUDITH: I shall never be able to stand this!

ALICE: But you must. You must!

JUDITH [*goes to her mother and kisses her lightly on the forehead, then exits gravely like a lady, forgetting her handlebars*]: Goodbye!

KURT [*enters right*]: Are you here already?

ALICE: Yes.

KURT: Has *he* been here again?

ALICE: Yes.

KURT: What was he wearing?

ALICE: The lot. So he must have been to see the Colonel. Two medals on his chest!

KURT: Two? I knew he'd get one when he retired. What's the other?

ALICE: I don't know what it was. A white cross inside a red one.

KURT: Must have been Portuguese, then. Wait a minute. Let me think. Those magazine articles of his, weren't they about quarantine conditions in Portuguese ports.

ALICE: As far as I remember, yes.

KURT: And he has never been in Portugal?

ALICE: Never.

KURT: I have, though.

ALICE: Why tell me this? He can hear, and has a good memory.

KURT: Don't you think Judith must have got him that decoration?

ALICE: Now really! There are limits. [*Gets up.*] And you have overstepped them.

KURT: Are we going to quarrel now?

ALICE: Depends on you. Keep your nose out of my affairs.

KURT: When they touch mine, I can't ignore them. Here he comes.

ALICE: Now it will happen.

KURT: What will happen?

ALICE: We shall see.

KURT: Let's hope he comes into the open. I can't stand this state of siege much longer. I haven't a friend left on the whole island.

ALICE: Wait. Sit here on the sofa. He'll take the armchair. Don't worry, I'll prompt you.

CAPTAIN [*enters upstage in full dress uniform wearing the Order of the Sword and the Portuguese Order of Christ*]: Good morning! So. We meet.

ALICE: You're tired. Sit down. [*The* CAPTAIN *sits unexpectedly on the left side of the sofa.*] Make yourself comfortable.

CAPTAIN: I'm happy here. You are too kind.

ALICE [*to* KURT]: Be careful, he suspects us.

CAPTAIN [*irritably*]: What did you say?

ALICE [*to* KURT]: He must have been drinking.

CAPTAIN [*roughly*]: No, he hasn't been.

Silence.

CAPTAIN: Well. How have you two been amusing yourselves?

ALICE: How have you?

CAPTAIN: Are you looking at my medals?

ALICE: No.

CAPTAIN: I think you are. You're envious. People normally congratulate one on receiving a decoration.

ALICE: Congratulations.

CAPTAIN: We get these things the way actresses get laurel wreaths.

ALICE: If you're referring to the ones on the walls at home —

CAPTIAN: Which you got from your brother —

ALICE: Oh, shut up.

CAPTAIN: And before which I have had to genuflect for twenty-five years. And which took me twenty-five years to learn the truth about.

ALICE: Have you met my brother?

CAPTAIN: Yes.

ALICE *is crushed. Silence.*

CAPTAIN: Well, Kurt. You're saying nothing, old chap.

KURT: I'm waiting.

CAPTAIN: By the way. You've heard the big news?

KURT: No.

CAPTAIN: Well, it's not pleasant for me to have to be the one who tells you —

KURT: What is it?

CAPTAIN: The lime works has gone bust.

KURT: That is bad news. How does it affect you?

CAPTAIN: I'm all right. I sold in time.

KURT: How clever of you.

CAPTAIN: But how does it affect you?

KURT: Badly.

CAPTAIN: It's your own fault. You should either have sold in time or subscribed to those new shares.

KURT: Then I'd have lost them too.

CAPTAIN: No. Then the company would have stayed solvent.

KURT: Not the company, only the board. In my opinion that new issue was just a whip-round for the directors.

CAPTAIN: Will this opinion save you? Ask yourself.

KURT: No. I shall lose everything.

CAPTAIN: Everything.

KURT: Even my house and furniture.

CAPTAIN: How terrible.

KURT: I've known worse.

   Silence.

CAPTAIN: That's what happens when amateurs speculate.

KURT: You surprise me. You know that if I hadn't subscribed, I'd have been boycotted. New opportunities for local industry, unlimited capital, unlimited as the ocean, philanthropy, national asset — that's what you wrote about it, and got printed. And now you call it speculation?

CAPTAIN [*unmoved*]: What do you plan to do now?

KURT: I shall have to auction everything I have.

CAPTAIN: Yes, you'd better.

KURT: What do you mean by that?

CAPTAIN: What I said. [*Slowly.*] Certain changes are going to take place here —

KURT: On this island, you mean?

CAPTAIN: Yes. For example — you will hav ₁o exchange your present abode for a humbler one.

KURT: I see.

CAPTAIN: Yes, the idea is to move the quarantine station to the coast, so that it will be next to the water.

KURT: But that was my original idea!

CAPTAIN [*drily*]: I don't know about that. I am not aware of your views on the subject. However — I think you would be wise to dispose of your furniture now so that it will attract less attention. The scandal, I mean.

KURT: What?

CAPTAIN: The scandal. [*Works himself up.*] For it is a scandal to come to a new place and immediately start speculating in a manner calculated to cause the maximum embarrassment to one's blood relations.

KURT: Surely I shall be the one who will suffer most embarrassment.

CAPTAIN: I must tell you something, my dear Kurt. If you hadn't had me on your side in this crisis, you'd have lost your job.

KURT: That too!

CAPTAIN: You don't always seem able to behave like a gentleman. There have been complaints about you.

KURT: Justifiable complaints?

CAPTAIN: Yes! For you are — despite your other admirable qualities — a slop. Don't interrupt me. You are a dreadful slop.

KURT: You surprise me.

CAPTAIN: However. I think it would be wise for you to move as soon as possible. And I would advise you to arrange that auction immediately, or better still try to sell the stuff privately.

KURT: Privately? Where will I find a purchaser here?

CAPTAIN: Surely you are not implying that I would wish to sit in your chairs? That would be a pretty thing — [*Begins to speak in bursts.*] Hm! Especially if one—remembers what happened — in the past —

KURT: What was that? You mean what *didn't* happen —

CAPTAIN [*changes tack*]: Alice is very quiet. What's the matter, old lady? Have you become a vegetable?

ALICE: I'm thinking.

CAPTAIN: Oh, God! Are you thinking? Well, you must think quickly and sharply, and precisely, if it's to be any use. Right, now, think! One, two, three![*Roars with laughter.*] Can't you? Well then, I'll go. Where is Judith?

ALICE: She's somewhere.

CAPTAIN: Where is Allan? [ALICE *is silent.*] Where is the Lieutenant? [ALICE *is silent.*] Tell me, Kurt. What are you thinking of doing with Allan now?

KURT: Doing with him?

CAPTAIN: Yes, you won't be able to afford to keep him in the Artillery, will you?

KURT: Perhaps not.

CAPTAIN: You must try to get him into some cheap infantry regiment, up in Lapland or somewhere.

KURT: Lapland?

CAPTAIN: Yes. Unless you put him into some trade. If I were you I'd start him in some office — Why not? [KURT *is silent.*] In these enlightened times! Yes. How extraordinarily silent you are, Alice. Well, my children, such is life's seesaw, one moment one's up aloft as cocky as you please, the next moment one's down, and then up one pops again. Etcetera! So much for that. Yes. [*To* ALICE.] Did you say something? [*She shakes her head.*] We can expect company here within the next few days.

ALICE: Did you say something to me?

CAPTAIN: We can expect company within the next few days. Important company.

ALICE: Who?

CAPTAIN: You see. You're interested. Now you can sit down and guess who they'll be, and between guesses you can read this letter once again. [*Hands her an open letter.*]

ALICE: My letter! Opened. Which I sent to the post-office?

CAPTAIN [*gets up*]: Yes. In my capacity as head of the family and your legal guardian I protect the sacred interests of that family and block with an iron hand any attempt to loosen the ties of blood by criminal correspondence! So! [ALICE *is crushed.*] I am not dead, Alice, but you must not get angry at my trying to extricate us all from this unmerited humiliation. Unmerited by me, at any rate.

ALICE: Judith! Judith!

CAPTAIN: Am I to be her Holofernes? Pah! [*Goes out upstage.*]

KURT: Who is this man?

ALICE: Don't ask me.

KURT: We're beaten.

ALICE: Beyond doubt.

KURT: He has gnawed me to pieces, but so cunningly that I can't accuse him of anything.

ALICE: On the contrary. You are in his debt.

KURT: Does he know what he's doing?

ALICE: No, I don't think so. He follows his nature and his instincts. And just now he seems to be in favour with the powers that dispense good and evil.

KURT: I suppose it must be the Colonel he's expecting.

ALICE: Must be. That's why he wants Allan out of the way.

KURT: And you agree with him?

ALICE: Yes.

KURT: Then our ways must part.

ALICE: A little. But we shall meet again.

KURT: Probably.

ALICE: And you know where.

KURT: Here.

ALICE: You feel that?

KURT: It's obvious. He will take my home, and buy my furniture.

ALICE: I think so too. But don't abandon me.

KURT: Not for so little.

ALICE: Goodbye. [*Goes.*]

KURT: Goodbye.

Scene 3

The same. Outside it is overcast and raining. ALICE *and* KURT *enter upstage in raincoats with umbrellas.*

ALICE: Well, I've got you here! Kurt, I won't be so cruel as to say "Welcome" to your old home.

KURT: Oh! Why? I've gone through this three times in my life — and more besides. It doesn't bother me.

ALICE: Did he summon you here?

KURT: It was a formal summons. I don't know on what grounds.

ALICE: He isn't your boss, is he?

KURT: No. But he's established himself as King of this island. And as soon as anyone resists he mentions the Colonel's name and everyone touches their forelock. By the way, is it today that the Colonel's coming?

ALICE: He's expected, but I don't know for sure. Sit down.

KURT [*sits*]: Everything's the same here.

ALICE: Don't think about it. Don't open the wound.

KURT: Wound? I just think it's a little strange. Strange like that man. Do you know, when I first met him as a young man, I ran away from him. But he came after me. Flattered me, offered me his services, and bound me to him. I tried to run away again, but it was useless. Now I am his slave.

ALICE: Yes, why? He's really in your debt, but you're the one who suffers.

KURT: Since I became ruined, he has offered to help Allan through his exam —

ALICE: You'll have to pay dearly for it. That candidature of yours for Parliament — is that still on?

KURT: Yes — as far as I can see, there should be no obstacle.

    Silence.

ALICE: Is Allan really leaving today?

KURT: Yes. If I can't stop him.

ALICE: That was a short happiness for you.

KURT: Short like everything else, except life, which is horribly long.

ALICE: Yes. Won't you go inside and wait in the drawing-room? If this place doesn't upset you it does me.

KURT: If you want me to.

ALICE: I'm ashamed, I'm ashamed to death. But I can't change it.

KURT: Let's go, then. As you wish.

ALICE: Someone's coming, anyway.

They go into the room left. The CAPTAIN *and*
ALLAN *enter upstage, both in uniform with*
military caps.

CAPTAIN: Sit down here, my boy, I want to talk with you. [*Sits in arm chair.* ALLAN *sits in the chair left.*] It's raining today. When it's fine I like to sit here and look at the sea. [*Silence.*] Well? You don't want to go, then?

ALLAN: I don't want to leave my father.

CAPTAIN: Ah, yes, your father. He is a rather unfortunate man. [*Silence.*] And parents seldom understand what is best for their children. That is — naturally there are exceptions. Hm! Tell me, Allan. Have you any contact with your mother?

ALLAN: Yes, she writes sometimes.

CAPTAIN: You know that she is your legal guardian?

ALLAN: Yes.

CAPTAIN: Tell me, Allan. Are you aware that your mother has given me a power of attorney to take decisions on her behalf?

ALLAN: I didn't know that.

CAPTAIN: Well, you know now. So there will be no further discussion of what you will do. You will go to Lapland.

ALLAN: But I haven't the money.

CAPTAIN: I have seen to that.

ALLAN: Then I have nothing left but to thank you, Uncle.

CAPTAIN: You're a grateful lad. Not everyone is. Hm! [*Raises his voice.*] The Colonel — do you know the Colonel?

ALLAN [*embarrassed*]: No, I don't.

CAPTAIN: The Colonel — [*underlines his words*] — is a close personal friend of mine — [*more quickly*] — as perhaps you know. The Colonel has chosen to take an interest in my family, including my wife's relatives. The Colonel has by his personal intervention succeeded in obtaining for you the money required for you to complete your training. Now you know your debt and your father's debt to the Colonel. Have I made myself clear? [ALLAN *bows.*] Go now and pack your things. The money will be handed to you when you go on board. Well, goodbye, my boy.

> *He gets up and goes out right.* ALLAN, *dejected, looks round the room.* JUDITH *enters upstage with an umbrella, wearing a hood. Beneath this she is elegantly dressed, with a long skirt and her hair up.*

JUDITH: Is that Allan?

ALLAN [*turns and looks at her closely*]: Is *that* Judith?

JUDITH: You don't recognize me? But where have you been for so long? What are you looking at? My long dress — and my hair? You haven't seen it like that before?

ALLAN: No.

JUDITH: Do I look like a woman?

> *He turns away.*

JUDITH [*earnestly*]: What are you doing here?

ALLAN: I've resigned my post.

JUDITH: What? Are you going away?

ALLAN: I am being sent to Lapland.

JUDITH [*shocked*]: To Lapland? When will you leave?

ALLAN: Today.

JUDITH: Whose idea is that?

ALLAN: Your father's.

JUDITH: I might have guessed. [*Walks a few paces and stamps her foot.*] I wish you could have stayed today.

ALLAN: To meet the Colonel?

JUDITH: What do you know about the Colonel? Must you go?

ALLAN: I have no choice. And now I want to.

    Silence.

JUDITH: Why do you want to now?

ALLAN: I want to get away from here. Out into the world.

JUDITH: It's too confined here! Yes, I understand you, Allan. It's intolerable here. They speculate. In lime, and in human beings.

    Silence.

JUDITH [*sincerely*]: Allan. You know me. I'm happy, I don't easily suffer. But now I'm beginning to learn.

ALLAN: You?

JUDITH: Yes. Now I'm beginning. [*Presses both hands against her breast.*] Oh, how it hurts! Oh!

ALLAN: What is it?

JUDITH: I don't know. I'm — choking. I think I'm dying.

ALLAN: Judith!

JUDITH [*screams*]: Ah! Is *this* how it feels? Like this? You poor boys!

ALLAN: I ought to laugh, if I were as cruel as you.

JUDITH: I'm not cruel. I just didn't know any better. You mustn't go.

ALLAN: I must.

JUDITH: Go, then. But give me a remembrance.

ALLAN: What have I to give you?

JUDITH [*in genuine agony*]: Allan! No, I won't let this happen! [*Screams and clutches her breast.*] I'm suffering, I'm suffering! What have you done to me? I don't want to live any more. Allan, don't go, not alone. We'll go together, we'll take the little dinghy, the little white one — and we'll sail out together, under full sail — there's a good wind — and we'll sink, out there, far out where there's no snare-grass, no jellyfish — ! Well? Say something! But we should have washed the sails yesterday — they ought to be pure white — I want to see white at that moment — and then you'll swim with me in your arms until you tire — and then we'll sink — ! [*Turns.*] That's beautiful. Much more beautiful than to sit here and grieve, writing secret letters which Father will open and laugh at. Allan! [*Takes his arms and shakes him.*] Are you listening?

ALLAN [*who has been watching her with shining eyes*]: Judith! Judith! Why didn't you say this before?

JUDITH: Because I didn't know how to say it. I didn't know.

ALLAN: And now I have to leave you! But I suppose it's the best way — the only way. I can't compete with a man who —

JUDITH: Don't speak of the Colonel.

ALLAN: Isn't it true?

JUDITH: It is true — and untrue.

ALLAN: Could it become quite untrue?

JUDITH: Yes. Now it shall. Within an hour.

ALLAN: Will you promise me that? I can wait, I can suffer, I can work. Judith!

JUDITH: Don't go yet. How long must I wait?

ALLAN: A year.

JUDITH [*joyfully*]: A year? I shall wait a thousand years, and if you don't come then I shall spin the sky backwards so that the sun will rise in the west! Hush, someone's coming. Allan, we must part! Hush. Hold me tightly! [*They embrace.*] But you mustn't kiss me. [*Turns away her head.*] No — go now! Go now!

> ALLAN *goes upstage and puts on his cloak. Then they run into each other's arms so that* JUDITH *disappears inside the cloak and they kiss for a moment.* ALLAN *runs out.* JUDITH *throws herself on the sofa and sobs.* ALLAN *comes back and falls on his knees by the sofa.*

ALLAN: No, I can't go! I can't leave you now!

JUDITH [*gets up*]: If you knew how beautiful you are now, if you could see yourself!

ALLAN: Ssh! A man can't be beautiful! But you, Judith! You — that *you* — I see now that when you were kind, another Judith appeared. That one is mine. But if you fail me, I shall die.

JUDITH: I think I shall die anyway! Oh, if I could die now, when I am happy!

ALLAN: Someone's coming!

JUDITH: Let them come! I'm not afraid of anything in the whole world now! But I wish you'd take me under your cloak. [*She pretends to hide beneath it.*] And that I could run away with you to Lapland! What shall we do in Lapland? Join that regiment that has plumes in its hats? That's a handsome uniform, it will suit you well. [*Fondles his hair. He kisses her finger-tips, one after the other, then kisses her boot.*] What are you doing, you young lunatic?

Your face'll get black. [*Gets up violently.*] And then I
won't be able to kiss you when you go. Come! I'll go with
you.

ALLAN: No, you mustn't. I'll be arrested.

JUDITH: I'll be arrested with you.

ALLAN: You couldn't. No, we must part.

JUDITH: I'll swim after the steamer — then you'll jump
overboard and save me, and it'll be in the paper, and
we'll get engaged! Shall we do that?

ALLAN: You can still joke about this?

JUDITH: It's always easy to weep. Say goodbye now!

> *They embrace passionately, then* ALLAN *runs out
> through the door upstage. It remains open. They
> embrace again outside in the rain.*

ALLAN: You'll get soaked. Judith!

JUDITH: What do I care?

> *They tear themselves apart.* ALLAN *goes.*
> JUDITH *stands in the rain and wind which blows
> her hair and clothes while she waves her hand-
> kerchief. Then she runs inside and throws herself
> on the sofa, her face in her hands.*

ALICE [*enters and goes over to* JUDITH]: What's the
matter? Are you ill? Stand up and let me look at you.
[JUDITH *gets up.* ALICE *looks at her closely.*] No,
you aren't ill. But I can't comfort you.

> *She goes out right. The* LIEUTENANT *enters upstage.*

JUDITH [*gets up and puts on her hooded cloak*]: Will you
accompany me to the telegraph-office, please, Lieutenant?

LIEUTENANT: Any way in which I can be of service —
but I doubt if it would seem proper —

JUDITH: So much the better! I want you to compromise me.
But don't get any illusions! You go first.

They go out upstage. The CAPTAIN *and* ALICE *enter right, the* CAPTAIN *in undress uniform.*

CAPTAIN [*sits in the armchair*] : Let him in.

> ALICE *goes left and opens the door, then sits on the sofa.* KURT *enters left.*

KURT: You want to speak to me?

CAPTAIN [*amiably but somewhat condescendingly*] : Yes, I have several important pieces of information to impart to you. Sit down.

KURT [*sits on the chair left*] : I'm all ears.

CAPTAIN: Well. [*Oratorically.*] You are aware that the subject of quarantine has been neglected in this country for the best part of a century — hm!

ALICE [*to* KURT] : He's practising for Parliament.

CAPTAIN: But thanks to the unprecedented developments now taking place in —

ALICE [*to* KURT] : Communications, of course.

CAPTAIN: — in every possible field, the Government has decided to encourage further research. To this end the Department of Health has appointed an inspector — and —

ALICE [*to* KURT] : He's dictating.

CAPTAIN: You may as well know now as later. I have been appointed Inspector of Quarantine.

> *Silence.*

KURT: May I congratulate you. And at the same time formally pay my respects.

CAPTAIN: In view of the ties of blood that bind us, our personal relationship will remain unchanged. Now, to turn to other matters. Your son Allan has, at my request, been transferred to an infantry regiment in Lapland.

KURT: But I don't want that.

CAPTAIN: In this matter your wishes take second place to those of the boy's mother. And the mother having granted me full legal authority to decide the boy's future, I have decided!

KURT: I admire you.

CAPTAIN: Is that your only reaction to being parted from your son? Have you no human feelings?

KURT: You mean I ought to be suffering?

CAPTAIN: Yes.

KURT: It would make you happy if I suffered. You want me to suffer?

CAPTAIN: Can you suffer, Kurt? There was a time once when I fell sick. You were present, and I can only recall that your face expressed undisguised joy.

ALICE: That's not true. Kurt sat by your bedside all night and calmed you when your conscience began to torment you. But once you had recovered, you showed him no gratitude —

CAPTAIN [*pretending not to hear her*]: So, Allan must leave us.

KURT: Who will find the money?

CAPTAIN: I have already done that — that is to say, we have. A consortium interested in the young man's future —

KURT: Consortium!

CAPTAIN: Yes. And that you may rest assured that the formalities have been observed, here are the lists. [*Hands him some papers.*]

KURT: Lists? [*Studies them.*] But these are charity lists!

CAPTAIN: You could call them that.

KURT: Have you been begging for my son?

CAPTAIN: Are you being ungrateful again? An ungrateful friend is the worst thing a man can have.

KURT: But this will ruin my credit as a citizen! And will mean the end of my candidature —

CAPTAIN: What candidature?

KURT: For Parliament, of course.

CAPTAIN: Surely you weren't seriously dreaming of that? Especially since I, as you might have guessed, have decided as the senior authority here to stand myself. You seem to have underrated me.

KURT: Well! So that's finished. That too.

CAPTAIN: It doesn't seem to bother you very greatly.

KURT: Now you have taken everything. Do you want anything more?

CAPTAIN: Have you anything more? And have you any grounds with which to reproach me? Think carefully, if you have any grounds with which to reproach me.

   Silence.

KURT: Strictly speaking, none. Everything has been done legally and correctly, like an everyday transaction between honourable fellow-citizens —

CAPTAIN: You speak with a resignation which strikes me as cynical. But your whole nature, my dear Kurt, is inclined towards cynicism, and there are moments when I am tempted to share Alice's opinion of you, that you are a hypocrite, a copper-bottomed hypocrite.

KURT [*calmly*]: Is that Alice's opinion?

ALICE [*to* KURT]: It was once. But not any longer. To endure what you have endured requires pure courage, or — something else.

CAPTAIN: Well, I think we can regard this discussion as closed. Be off now, Kurt, and say goodbye to Allan. He will leave by the next boat.

KURT [*gets up*]: So soon? Well. I have been through worse than this.

CAPTAIN: Yes, you say that so often. I begin to wonder what you got up to in America.

KURT: Got up to? Well, I encountered misfortune. And it's every human being's indisputable right to be smitten by misfortune.

CAPTAIN [*sharply*]: There are misfortunes that one brings upon oneself. Was yours that kind?

KURT: It was a question of conscience.

CAPTAIN [*curtly*]: Have you a conscience?

KURT: There are wolves and there are sheep, and it's no honour to be a sheep. But I'd rather be that than a wolf.

CAPTAIN: Don't you know the old saying, that every man creates his own luck?

KURT: Is *that* a saying?

CAPTAIN: And you should know that a man's strength —

KURT: Yes, I learned that that night when your strength failed you and you lay on the floor.

CAPTAIN [*raises his voice*]: A deserving person such as myself — yes, look at me! — I have fought for fifty years — against the world — and in the end I won, thanks to my steadfastness, my devotion to duty, my energy and — my sense of honour!

ALICE: You should let other people say that.

CAPTAIN: Other people don't say it because they are jealous of me. However! I am expecting a visitor. My daughter, Judith, is today to meet her future . . . Where is Judith?

ALICE: She's out.

CAPTAIN: In this rain? Send for her.

KURT: Perhaps I may go now?

CAPTAIN: No, wait. Is Judith dressed? Properly?

ALICE: Well enough. Did the Colonel definitely say he'd come?

CAPTAIN [*gets up*] : Yes. That is — he wants to pay her a surprise visit, as the saying goes. And I expect his telegram any moment. [*As he goes out right.*] I shall be back shortly.

ALICE: What a man! Is he a man?

KURT: When you asked me that before, I answered no. Now I think him the most typical human being I could ever meet on this earth. Perhaps we're a little like him? Using people and exploiting opportunities?

ALICE: He has eaten you and your son alive. And you defend him?

KURT: I have known worse. This cannibal has left my soul untouched. He couldn't devour that.

ALICE: What "worse" have you known?

KURT: You ask that?

ALICE: Are you being discourteous?

KURT: I don't want to be. So — don't ask me again.

CAPTAIN [*enters right*] : The telegram was here all the time. Please read it to me, Alice, my eyes aren't so good. [*Sits importantly in the armchair.*] Read! Kurt need not leave us.

> ALICE *glances through it quickly and silently, and looks astounded.*

CAPTAIN: Well? Does it displease you?

> *She looks at him silently.*

CAPTAIN [*sarcastically*] : Who is it from?

ALICE: It is from the Colonel.

CAPTAIN [*pleased*] : I thought as much. Well, what does the Colonel say?

ALICE: He says this. "In view of Miss Judith's impertinent telephone message I consider our relationship terminated." [*Looks at the* CAPTAIN.]

CAPTAIN: Once more. If you please.

ALICE: "In view of Miss Judith's impertinent telephone message I consider our relationship terminated."

CAPTAIN [*pales*]: Judith!

ALICE: And Holofernes!

CAPTAIN: What are you, then?

ALICE: You'll soon see.

CAPTAIN: You have done this!

ALICE: No.

CAPTAIN [*wild with rage*]: You have done this!

ALICE: No!

> The CAPTAIN *tries to rise and draw his sabre, but collapses with a stroke.*

ALICE: Now you have your deserts!

CAPTAIN [*with an old man's tearfulness in his voice*]: Don't be angry with me! I'm so ill.

ALICE: Are you? I'm happy to hear it.

KURT: Let us carry him to his bed.

ALICE: No. I don't want to touch him. [*Rings the bell.*]

CAPTAIN [*as before*]: Alice — Kurt — you mustn't be angry with me. [*To* KURT]. Think of my children.

KURT: That's sublime. I'm to feel sorry for his children, when he has stolen mine!

ALICE: How can a man be so blind to himself?

CAPTAIN: Think of my children! [*He continues to slobber unintelligibly: "blu-blu-blu-blu".*]

ALICE: At last this tongue has stopped. It can brag no longer, lie no longer, wound no longer. You, Kurt, who believe in God! Thank Him from me! Thank Him for freeing me from my prison, my wolf, my vampire!

KURT: Alice, don't talk like that.

ALICE [*puts her own face close to the* CAPTAIN's]: Where is your "own strength" now? Well? And your "energy"? [*He speechlessly spits in her face.*] Can you still spit venom, viper? I'll tear the tongue from your mouth! [*Strikes him in the face.*] The head is off but the cheek still flushes, the blood still flows! Oh, Judith, my darling girl, whom I carried like a vengeance beneath my heart — you, you, have liberated us all! Have you more heads, Hydra? We'll take them too! [*Seizes his beard.*] So there *is* justice in the world! I dreamed it sometimes, but never believed it. Kurt, ask God to forgive me for misjudging Him! Oh, there *is* justice! Now I'll be one of His lambs like you. Tell Him that, Kurt! A smile from fortune makes us believers, unbroken adversity makes us wolves.

The LIEUTENANT *enters upstage.*

ALICE: The Captain has had a stroke. Help us, please. Wheel his chair out.

LIEUTENANT: Madam —

ALICE: What is it?

LIEUTENANT: Miss Judith —

ALICE: Help us with this first. You can tell us about her later. [*The* LIEUTENANT *wheels the chair out right.*] Out with the corpse! Out with it, and open the doors! Let's clean the air in here! [*Throws open the upstage doors. The weather is now clear outside.*] Usch!

KURT: Are you going to abandon him?

ALICE: You abandon a wrecked ship, don't you? And the crew save themselves. Why should I lay out the corpse of a rotting beast? Let the scavengers or the anatomists have him! A garden would be too good a resting-place for this barrowload of muck. I'll go and wash myself all over, to cleanse my body of his touch, his filth. If I ever can.

> JUDITH *appears outside by the balustrade, bare-headed, waving her handkerchief towards the sea.*

KURT: Who's there? Judith! [*Shouts.*] Judith!

JUDITH [*enters, cries*] : He's gone!

KURT: Who?

JUDITH: Allan has gone.

KURT: Without saying goodbye?

JUDITH: We said goodbye. And he sends you his love, Uncle.

ALICE: So that was it!

JUDITH [*throws herself into* KURT's *arms*] : He's gone!

KURT: He will come back, dear child.

ALICE: Or we will follow him.

KURT [*with a gesture towards the door left*] : And leave *him*? The world —

ALICE: To hell with the world. Pah! Judith, come here to me. [JUDITH *goes over to her.* ALICE *kisses her on the forehead.*] Do you want to follow him?

JUDITH: Can you ask me?

ALICE: But your father is ill.

JUDITH: What do I care about that?

ALICE: That's my Judith! Oh, I love you! Judith!

JUDITH: Anyway, Father isn't small-minded, he hates sentimentality. He's a real aristocrat, Father, isn't he?

ALICE: In his way.

JUDITH: And I don't think he'll want to see me, after that telephone call I made. Well, why should he try to saddle me with some old man? No, Allan, Allan! [*Throws herself into* KURT's *arms.*] I want to go to Allan! [*Tears herself free and runs outside to wave.* KURT *follows her and waves too.*]

ALICE: Strange how flowers can blossom out of filth.

The LIEUTENANT *enters right.*

ALICE: Yes?

LIEUTENANT: Madam — Miss Judith —

ALICE: Are you so impatient to speak her name that you forget the dying?

LIEUTENANT: But, Madam, she said —

ALICE: She? No, you'd better say Judith. But tell me first — how are things in there?

LIEUTENANT: In there? Yes — it's finished.

ALICE: Finished? Oh, God, I thank Thee, for my sake and all mankind's, that Thou hast freed us from this evil. Give me your arm, Kurt. I want to go outside and breathe. Breathe! [*The* LIEUTENANT *offers her his arm. She pauses.*] Did he say anything before he died?

LIEUTENANT: Miss Judith's father did say a few words.

ALICE: What did he say?

LIEUTENANT: He said: "Forgive them, for they know not what they do."

ALICE: Strange.

LIEUTENANT: Miss Judith's father was a good and noble man.

ALICE: Kurt!

KURT *enters.*

ALICE: It is finished.

KURT: Ah!

ALICE: Do you know what his last words were? No, you don't. "Forgive them for they know not what they do."

KURT: Can you interpret that?

ALICE: I suppose he must have meant that *he* had always acted correctly, and that life had wronged him.

KURT: No doubt there'll be fine words spoken over his grave.

ALICE: And hundreds of wreaths. From his lieutenants.

KURT: Yes.

ALICE: A year ago he said, "It looks as though life is simply a gigantic fraud."

KURT: Do you think he was mocking us even at the moment of death?

ALICE: No. But now he's dead, I feel a curious urge to speak well of him.

KURT: Let us do that.

LIEUTENANT: Miss Judith's father was a good and noble man.

ALICE [*to* KURT]: You hear?

KURT: "They know not what they do." How often haven't I asked you that — if he knew what he was doing. And you didn't think he did. So forgive him.

ALICE: Riddles! Riddles! But listen. There is peace in this house now. The wonderful peace of death. As wonderful as the solemn unrest when a child is born into the world. I hear the silence — and I see the marks in the floor of the chair that carried him away. And I feel — that now my life is finished and I await corruption. You know, it's strange. Those simple words of the Lieutenant — and he is a simple soul — haunt me — but he is right. My husband, the love of my youth — yes, laugh! — he *was*, in spite of everything, a good and noble man.

KURT: In spite of everything? He was brave too. The way he fought, for himself, and for others.

ALICE: What miseries he suffered! And what humiliations! And he blotted them out — so that he could go on living.

KURT: He was a man whom life passed by. That explains much, Alice. Go in to him.

ALICE: No. I can't. Because while we've been speaking here, I suddenly remembered him as he was when he was young. I've been seeing him, I see him now, as he was when he was twenty. I must have loved that man.

KURT: And hated him.

ALICE: And hated him. Peace be with him.

She walks towards the door right, and stops there, with clasped hands.

Introduction to

THE VIRGIN BRIDE

DALECARLIA, the area of central Sweden that surrounds Lake Siljan, is particularly rich in folk lore; with its ancient and cherished traditions, and even its own language, it is to Swedes — how shall one say? — what a combination of Wessex and the Western Isles of Scotland would be to Britons. For Strindberg, as for most Swedes (then and now), it held an especial attraction; and he had recently had occasion to immerse himself in its atmosphere, since in 1899 he had set the first act of GUSTAV VASA there, and had had the Dalecarlian leaders speak the dialect. On 5 August 1900, a week after finishing his play MID-SUMMER, he wrote from Stockholm to the painter Carl Larsson: "A big play about Dalecarlia has just come to me, and I see it bright and fair! But you must tell me: can one have the peasants around Siljan talk ordinary Swedish? I mean, ordinary written Swedish, with a slight accent? That language I used in GUSTAV VASA is tiresome and ugly. . . Would you, for the sake of a big theatre project in Stockholm*, be willing to make some sketches. . . so that for once one could see the Swedish countryside on the stage, with red cottages, white birches and green pine-trees? Do this; not for me but for Sweden and Dalecarlia and the Swedish Theatre. The play has a contemporary setting."

That last half of 1900 was a period of unusual dramatic activity even for Strindberg, and before starting his Dalecarlian play he wrote EASTER, THE DANCE OF DEATH and the short one-act comedy CASPER'S SHROVE TUESDAY. Some time towards the end of the year, possibly before he had finished Part II of THE DANCE OF DEATH, he started work on THE VIRGIN BRIDE, and completed it on 5 January 1901. "Tell me, on a postcard, as brief as this question," he asked a folk-lore expert,

---

*Presumably the theatre that Strindberg was planning to found himself, though it was to be another seven years before he succeeded in doing so.

August Bondeson, on 9 November, "how is the violin tuned
when the fiddler plays the River God song? A friend from
Skania says E. A. C sharp. E., but experts say this is un-
likely, as the strings would break!" According to Gunnar
Ollén, Strindberg ended up by composing the music for
the River God's song himself, the only completed musical
composition of his that is known to have survived.

Instead of giving it a contemporary setting, as at first
intended, he set it, as we can tell from the reprieve at the
end, which is signed by King Carl XV, in the latter's reign
(1859–1872), i.e. during the period of Strindberg's own
childhood and youth. He may have found the idea of the
plot in the antiphonal song which Kersti and Mats sing to
each other in the opening scene, and which he had discovered in an anthology entitled SWEDISH HERDSMEN'S
SONGS AND HORN MELODIES, collected by Richard
Dybeck. Dybeck accompanied this song with a traditional
tale about a peasant boy and girl who have a child together,
conduct their own wedding ceremony in the forest and
(like Ellida and the Stranger in Ibsen's THE LADY FROM
THE SEA) consequently regard themselves as married. In
Dybeck's tale, their affair is discovered and they are legally
wedded by a priest. Strindberg envisaged a less happy
ending, though in his first draft he merely had their marriage
end in divorce. It was only later that he introduced the
murder of the child. This almost certainly stemmed from
his memory of what had happened to his first child, Kerstin,
whom Siri von Essen had borne to him shortly after their
marriage in 1877. They had left her with a midwife, and
she had died when only two days old. The epilogue, too, has
its origin in Dybeck's collection, which includes a tale about
a sunken Dalecarlian church.

Somewhat surprisingly, Strindberg claimed that he had
written THE VIRGIN BRIDE under the influence of
Maurice Maeterlinck. In a letter which he wrote to
Harriet Bosse on 8 February 1901, a month after complet-
ing the play — but which, like several of his letters to her,
he never sent — he explained that in THE VIRGIN BRIDE
he was "trying. . . to enter Maeterlinck's wonderful

world of beauty, abandoning analysis, questions and view-
points, and only seeking beauty in colour and mood".
Strindberg was, at this time, much excited by Maeterlinck,
whose volume of essays, LE TRÉSOR DES HUMBLES, he
was to describe the following April as "the greatest book
I have read". Maeterlinck, like Strindberg during his
INFERNO period and after, believed in the existence of
dark powers who played games with mortals, and in the
existence of a divine guidance whose intentions mortals
might know; and — or so at any rate Strindberg believed —
he was influenced by the same French occultism which
has influenced Strindberg during his stay in Paris. Strindberg
was especially fascinated by Maeterlinck's belief that souls
would soon be able to communicate telepathically, that
invisible links already existed, and that silence was a more
powerful link than words; he translated several passages
from LE TRÉSOR DES HUMBLES, and dedicated the
manuscript to Harriet. "His people exist on another plane
than ours," he declared in one of his OPEN LETTERS TO
THE INTIMATE THEATRE a few years later. "He is in
contact with a higher world." At the same time, it is
difficult to see how so sombre a play as THE VIRGIN
BRIDE could be described as a "wonderful world of beauty",
and if anyone but Strindberg himself had claimed that the
play had been influenced by Maeterlinck one would
dismiss it out of hand; as Martin Lamm has observed, the
claim could far more fittingly be made in respect of
SWANWHITE, the play which Strindberg wrote next and
which is indeed Maeterlinckian. But the problem is ever-
present with Strindberg, that one can never for sure believe
even his simplest-seeming statements about himself.
Unlike Ibsen, who was always reluctant to admit a literary
debt to anyone, Strindberg was over-generously inclined
to claim influences which sometimes seem rather doubtful.

The character of Kersti may partly have been inspired
by Strindberg's daughter Greta, who was then nineteen and
embarking on a career as an actress. Two summers earlier
she had taken part, dressed in rustic costume, in a festival

at Furusund, in the Stockholm archipelago, organized in honour of the eighteenth-century Swedish poet Carl Bellman; she had the very fair hair which is particularly associated with the people of Dalecarlia, and he was keen to write a part specially for her. She played it many times, in both Swedish and Finnish, before her premature death at the age of thirty-one in a railway accident in 1912, the year of Strindberg's own death.

The rustic scene, like anger, tended to bring out the best in Strindberg; one thinks of his novels, THE PEOPLE OF HEMSÖ and IN THE OUTER SKERRIES, and of the fine peasant dialogues in several of his historical plays such as the opening scenes of GUSTAV VASA and THE EARL OF BJÄLBO, and the scenes involving Private Måns in ERIK THE FOURTEENTH. It is a pity he did not write more plays with rural settings; he was at his best when dealing with the kind of primitive emotions that so often swept over him, and must often have regretted the inhibitions forced on him by his urban upbringing. Modern audiences, certainly, find these emotions easier to accept in peasants that in supposedly civilized town-dwellers — though it was of course part of Strindberg's great contribution to the theatre that he showed that these emotions exist, and often force their way to the surface, in town-dwellers too. Judiciously cut — a qualification which one must make in regard to most, if not indeed all of Strindberg's plays — THE VIRGIN BRIDE works marvellously on the stage. The Epilogue of reconciliation is almost always omitted in performance in Sweden (though Ingmar Bergman included it effectively in a famous production of the play at Malmö in 1952); one regrets losing the opening pages of this scene, with its splendid dialogue between the Fisherman and the Midwife, but where anger brought out the best in Strindberg, reconciliation tended to bring out the worst, especially in the final scene of a play (the last act of EASTER is difficult for this reason). The elaborate stage directions, as always in Strindberg (most notably in A DREAM PLAY) need to be ignored; he was fascinated by what were then modern techniques, with back-projection and the like, but which now seem artificial and old-fashioned. (The Midwife's tail, surely, comes into this category.) I have sometimes. thought that the River God and the White Child might be suggested by sound rather than seen; yet, stripped of the more extreme of their stage directions, they, too, can work powerfully.

The Swedish title, KRONBRUDEN, literally means THE CROWN BRIDE: according to an ancient tradition, only a virgin bride might wear the coveted small golden crown on her head during the wedding ceremony and the feast following. The play has usually been called THE BRIDAL CROWN in English, but THE VIRGIN BRIDE seems closer to the full meaning of the original. It was the first Strindberg play I ever read, long before I knew a word of Swedish; even in the terrible old Edwin Björkman translation, it excited me, and for a short while, until I read the better-known plays, I supposed Strindberg to be a primitive rural writer with strong religious undertones, a kind of John Clare of dramatists; which is not far from the truth.

Like THE DANCE OF DEATH and so many of his best plays, THE VIRGIN BRIDE had to wait several years before it was staged. The première took place in Helsinki on 24 April 1906, under bizarre circumstances. Harriet Bosse, from whom Strindberg was now divorced, acted Kersti, with her future husband, Gunnar Wingård, as Mats and, most extraordinary of all, Strindberg's first wife Siri as prompter. Harriet and Wingård played the principal roles at the Swedish première, too, on 14 September 1907 in Stockholm. The play has frequently been revived in Sweden, but has seldom been seen abroad, though in 1950 it was successfully performed in Vienna with a distinguished cast which included Curt Jürgens as Mats, Käthe Gold as Kersti, and Werner Kraus as the Justice. At the time of writing, it has never (at any rate professionally) been staged in England, though it was excitingly performed on sound radio in 1974, with the cast named on p. 472. Derek Parker in the *Listener* praised the director, Martin Jenkins, for "recreating a vividly atmospheric landscape, as it were, of country life in the Dark Ages, in which a subtle and beautiful orchestration of voices told a fearful fairy-story which tore away at the nerves''.

THE VIRGIN BRIDE

(1900—1901)

This translation of THE VIRGIN BRIDE was commissioned by the British Broadcasting Corporation, and was first performed on sound radio on Radio Three on 24 November 1974. The cast was:

MATS	Martin Jarvis
KERSTI	Sarah Badel
KERSTI'S MOTHER	Pauline Letts
THE SOLDIER	John Hollis
THE VERGER	Cyril Luckham
BRITA	Frances Jeater
MATS' GRANDFATHER	Timothy Bateson
MATS' FATHER	Manning Wilson
MATS' MOTHER	Norma Ronald
MATS' GRANDMOTHER	Hilda Schroder
LILL-ANNA	Emily Richard
LILL-MATS	Judy Bennett
THE JUSTICE	Colin Douglas
THE PRIEST	Alan Rowe
THE RIVER GOD	Alan Dudley
THE MIDWIFE	Sheila Grant
THE WHITE CHILD	Judy Bennett
THE FISHERMAN	Sion Probert

Produced by Martin Jenkins

CHARACTERS

MATS

KERSTI

KERSTI'S MOTHER

THE SOLDIER, KERSTI's father

THE VERGER, KERSTI's grandfather

BRITA, MATS' SISTER

MATS' GRANDFATHER

MATS' FATHER

MATS' MOTHER

MATS' GRANDMOTHER

LILL-ANNA
LILL-KAREN } MATS' sisters

LILL-MATS, MATS' brother

THE JUSTICE

THE PRIEST

THE RIVER GOD

THE MIDWIFE

THE WHITE CHILD

THE FISHERMAN

ACTS

1. The summer pasture
2. The family council in the millhouse
3. The night before the wedding, in the SOLDIER's cottage
4. The wedding in the millhouse
5. The penance before the church
6. The ice

ACT ONE

A summer pasture in Dalecarlia, central Sweden. Down-stage, the cowman's hut of red-painted wood; by it, two birch trees, with trunks white to their roots. Right, the edge of a pine forest with a small waterfall, beneath which is a lake with water-lilies. Upstage, a large lake with blue mountains on the far shore. In the distance, a church. By the side of the hut, a grindstone. It is sunset on a Sunday.

KERSTI'S MOTHER is seated on a log outside the hut smoking a pipe. KERSTI enters carrying a cow-horn in her hand. She stops in front of her MOTHER.

MOTHER: Where have you been all this time, daughter?

KERSTI: I've been in the forest, Mother!

MOTHER: Picking wild strawberries, I see from your red lips.

KERSTI: Why did you call me on the horn, Mother?

MOTHER: I heard padding and thumping in the forest, child. Was it the bear?

KERSTI: I don't know.

MOTHER: Did I hear an axe, or did my ears deceive me?

KERSTI: Bears don't have axes, Mother.

MOTHER: Why are you wearing such fine clothes, daughter?

KERSTI: Isn't it Sunday, Mother?

MOTHER: You've milk on your nipple, child. Have you been milking May-Rose and Sea-Star?

KERSTI: If I could milk the stars! And the moon! [*Sighs.*]

MOTHER: In the night! [*Sighs, mocking her.*]

KERSTI: Day and night!

MOTHER: Night and day! I know. You watch out for that bear.

KERSTI: You think he'll attack the calf?

MOTHER: Have you lost her?

KERSTI: I'll ask Anna.

MOTHER: Ask her.

KERSTI [*takes the horn and blows it. Then she sings*]: Coo-ee! Bearhill Anna! Can you see our little calf, or the bell-cow down there?

MATS [*sings back from the distance in a high tenor*]: Yes, come here! Little calf, bell-cow, they're both here!

MOTHER: Strange how harsh Anna's voice sounds.

KERSTI: She's been calling the cows ever since sundown.

MOTHER: What do you hear from the village, child?

KERSTI: Old wives' chattering, goatbells' tinkling—

MOTHER: Is that all?

KERSTI: I hear cock-crow, hound-bark, gun-roar, cart-screech, and oars lapping in rowlocks.

MOTHER: Whose cock, whose hound?

KERSTI: The miller's.

MOTHER: What is the miller's name? [KERSTI *is silent.*] Is it Anna? [KERSTI *is silent, embarrassed.*] What can you see down there in the village?

KERSTI: I see the wheel in the millrace, the smoke from the chimney —

MOTHER: Whose chimney? [KERSTI *is silent.*] The millfolk's?

KERSTI: The sun's going down, Mother.

MOTHER: All right, I'll go; before it gets dark. [*Gets up.*] This has been the longest Sunday I've lived through. What's that smell?

KERSTI: Forest smell, smell of beasts, smell of hay —

MOTHER: No, Kersti. Those were strange berries you plucked. [*Loses herself in her thoughts. Sings.*] How light it was then and how dark it is now! [*Says.*] How light it was then and how dark it is now!

KERSTI: Night's coming, mother.

MOTHER: I see it, daughter mine. The darkness is falling thick as a pelt. I'll be off, down to the village. Yes, down to the village! You stay here and watch the milk curding. I'll be able to tell from the smoke if the fire dies. Trust me!

KERSTI: The fire won't die. Trust me, Mother!

MOTHER: Good night, then. Don't forget to say your evening prayer.

KERSTI: Good night, Mother.

MOTHER: How light it was then, how dark is it now? Don't forget your prayers!

> She goes out left. KERSTI *opens the door of the hut. We see a pot on the fire, at which she glances. Then she comes out and, after making sure that her* MOTHER *has gone, takes the horn. She sounds it.*

MATS [*sings back from the mountains, right*]: Little Kersti, little Kersti! Our little one sleeps in the forest! Far, far off in the forest!

KERSTI [*sings*]: Tullerilull! Does he still live? Does he still live? Far off in the forest?

MATS [*sings*]: Of course he still lives. Of course, he still lives. Our little one lies in his cradle. Far, far off in the forest.

KERSTI [*sings*] : Take off your shoes And milk the cow And give our little one drink. I cannot come. I cannot come. I must help mother with supper.

MATS [*sings*] : The wind blows And the birch rocks And our little one sleeps so sweetly. Kersti, little Kersti!

The wind begins to blow. The scene is in shadow, except in the highest part of the forest right, where the sunshine can still be seen. Then, around and behind, first far off, then nearer, can be heard the shouts and cries of beaters, hounds baying, horses trotting and galloping, shots, beaters' rattles, the crash of falling trees and, increasingly, the rustle of the waterfall. Then ten hunting horns, the first starting and holding while the others successively join in. KERSTI stands frightened, looking about her. As the noise recedes into the distance and ceases, she goes into the hut and brings out bunches of pine-twigs, which she places on the ground and covers with a rug of various colours. Then she sets up two young pines stripped of their bark but still branched on top at either side of the door; goes to the lake and gathers white water-lilies which she binds into a garland for her head. MATS enters left with a baby in a skin bag, with straps. KERSTI runs to him and kisses the baby.

KERSTI: Little one, little one, pretty one! Is he still asleep?

MATS: Of course he is!

KERSTI: Come. Let him rock in the tree.

They tie the cradle between the two birches, which sway in the wind.

KERSTI [*sings softly*] : "And the wind blows, and the birch rocks, and the little one sleeps so softly." Mats, did you hear the hunt?

MATS: No one's hunting as late as this.

KERSTI: But I heard it!

MATS: You couldn't have. What did your mother say?

KERSTI: She goads me, she'll goad the life out of me.

MATS: Well, Kersti. We'll find no peace nor happiness till our union is sanctified and our little one baptized.

KERSTI: As long as our parents stay enemies, there'll be no wedding. But we should ask God to bless our union before we give our little one a name.

MATS: That we've agreed. Now we must do it.

KERSTI: I've made everything ready. You see?

MATS: You've done bravely. Poor us, it'll be a poor wedding.

KERSTI: If God looks into our hearts and souls and sees naught there but the truth, the rest don't matter. Have you the book?

MATS: I have it. But, Kersti, it isn't sinful, this that we're doing?

KERSTI: Far from it. The midwife can baptize him, civil-like.

MATS: Yes, I'd forgotten her.

KERSTI [*puts the garland on her head*]: Shall we begin then?

MATS: In God's name! May we never regret it!

They drop to their knees facing each other on the rug. MATS *hands* KERSTI *a ring, which she holds while* MATS *reads from the prayer book.*

MATS: I, Mats Anders Larsson, take thee Kersti Margreta Hansdotter to be my wedded wife, to love thee for better for worse, as a sign whereof I give thee this ring.

KERSTI: I, Kersti Margreta Hansdotter, take thee Mats Anders Larsson to be my wedded husband, to love thee for better for worse, as a sign whereof I take this ring.

They offer a short, silent prayer, and rise. They take each other's hands but do not kiss.

MATS: Well, Kersti dear, now you are mine, before God. What people may say hereafter we care not.

KERSTI: We care not!

MATS: Well, Kersti dear, what have we for supper?

KERSTI: Nothing, Mats.

Pause.

MATS: Then we must smoke a pipe of tobacco.

They sit on two three-legged stools, strike a light with flint and steel, and smoke.

MATS: What was that you were saying about the hunt, just now, Kersti?

KERSTI: I'll not mind any more, Mats, now I know what kind of people they are. I'll not mind any more.

MATS: Best not to. Do you see how the cradle rocks of itself?

KERSTI: That's the wind, Mats. It's the wind that blows the birches.

MATS: But the wind can't touch those pines.

KERSTI: Why, no, nor it does. Yes, trolls move at night.

MATS: Don't say that!

KERSTI: Do you see how my smoke drifts northwards?

MATS: And mine to the south!

KERSTI: And the midges dance —

MATS: As at a wedding.

KERSTI: Are we happier now, do you think?

MATS: No.

Pause.

KERSTI: Do you hear how the blackcock sings?

MATS: As at a wedding.

KERSTI: But no church-bells —

MATS: They're tired after their Sunday toil. What shall
we call the little one?

KERSTI [*wildly*]: Millstone, cross-luck, driver; crown-thief —

MATS: Why crown-thief?

KERSTI: Because, because, because. . . Because I
couldn't wear a crown, even if they let us have a true
wedding. Because only a virgin bride can wear a crown to
church.* What shall we call him? Bride-shame, mother's
grief, forest brat — !

MATS: Evil be to him who wisheth evil!

KERSTI: I know.

> KERSTI'S MOTHER *appears among the trees in the
> forest, watching* MATS *and* KERSTI.

MATS: Evil eyes reign here.

KERSTI: And evil thoughts. You brew and I drink. You
grind and I bake.

> *The* MOTHER *disappears.*

MATS: Do you know why our parents hated each other
so unheathenly?

KERSTI: Twas some matter of property. Prior rights and
unlawful seizure, a deaf judge and — all evil, evil, evil!

MATS: And their hatred flowered into love, passion,
burning —

KERSTI: But twas all poisoned.

MATS: So dark, when hatred came!

KERSTI [*throws her garland into the lake*]: Ay, so it was!
Cursed by this garland, without a crown!

*This sentence is not in the Swedish, and is added for explanatory
purposes

MATS: Don't say that!

KERSTI: We wed like beggars, like vagabonds, like thieves! Naught to eat, naught to drink; no taste but tobacco! That's our bridal feast! The fire's dying under the pot. Go and fetch wood, Mats. That's our bridal dance!

MATS: If beauty's a guide, you're born to be a queen!

KERSTI: Maybe. Not to milk cows, that's for sure.

MATS: Our little one, our little one! Lord Jesus, life is cruel.

KERSTI: Poor little one. What will become of us all? What awaits us? Go and fetch wood, Mats. The milk will curdle, and then mother'll beat me. Go, Mats!

MATS: Kersti, once you served in my father's house. Now I serve you. He was hard to you. So I'll be gentle with you.

KERSTI: You're good, Mats. I'm not. I wish I were!

MATS: Become good!

KERSTI: Become evil, Mats. You see if you can.

MATS: You don't mean that.

KERSTI: Who knows? Hurry, Mats, hurry — someone's coming! I know her footsteps, it's Mother.

MATS: Is it your mother? But the baby — ?

KERSTI [*picks up the rug and throws it over the cradle, then takes her fur from the wall of the hut and spreads it over it*]: Go, go, go!

MATS: Guard our little one. Guard him. [*Goes out right.*]

KERSTI: Yes — but . . . Yes . . . but . . .

MOTHER [*enters left*]: Was that Anna?

KERSTI: Yes.

MOTHER [*looks at her*]: It was her? With that deep voice?

KERSTI: Yes.

MOTHER: Was it her who chopped those two bridal trees? And these branches?

KERSTI: Why not?

MOTHER [*seizes* KERSTI *by the hair*]: Liar, slut, whore — !

KERSTI [*raises her hand*]: Don't you dare!

MOTHER: Would you lift your hand against me, you loose minx? Did Mats teach you that? Mats' father drove us out of house and home, and you give yourself to him! O-oh!

KERSTI [*mocks her*]: O-oh!

MOTHER [*points to the cradle*]: What have you got there?

KERSTI: I'm airing clothes.

MOTHER: Small clothes!

KERSTI: Not so small.

MOTHER: What's in that cradle?

KERSTI: Small clothes, but not that small.

MOTHER: It's the child!

KERSTI: What child?

MOTHER: Yours!

KERSTI: I haven't one.

MOTHER: Will you swear that!

KERSTI: I swear! May the river troll take me if I lie.

MOTHER: Don't swear by a heathen power!

KERSTI: I'll never swear by any other.

MOTHER [*sits*]: There's a rumour in the village.

KERSTI: Oh?

MOTHER: A strange rumour.

KERSTI: No!

MOTHER: They say Mats is to have the mill.

KERSTI [*gets up*] : Is that the truth?

MOTHER: As true as that impatience brings bad luck.

KERSTI: Is Mats to have the mill? Then he'll be thinking of marriage.

MOTHER: Yes, they're asking that too.

KERSTI: With whom?

MOTHER: Whoever it is, and whoever his fancy lights on, it'll have to be a virgin bride, who can wear a crown.*

KERSTI: Oh!

MOTHER: Oh! [*Pause.*] You've gold on your finger.

KERSTI: Yes.

MOTHER: Are you engaged?

KERSTI: Yes.

MOTHER: But the crown? [KERSTI *is silent.*] Have you lost something?

KERSTI [*has begun to walk uneasily up and down*] : Do you know, it was foretold that I should wear a bridal crown?

MOTHER: Old wives' talk. A virgin's crown is comelier than a queen's. There's few as have the right to wear it.

KERSTI: Oh!

MOTHER: Oh! [*Pause.*] Poor we were; evil came to us, and ruin followed. Ay, ay!

KERSTI: Poor we were, but we'll be rich. Our luck will turn.

MOTHER: Family hatred; fire and water; now it's boiling.

KERSTI: The fire burned, and the water cooled; yes, now it gets hot.

*These last five words are not in the original.

MOTHER [*gets up to go*] : How light it was then, how dark is it now? [*Goes towards exit right.*] There's a garland floating in the lake. But where's the crown?

> *She goes out. The* RIVER GOD *appears in a bright white light up by the waterfall. He wears a silver tunic with a reed-green sash round his waist and a red cap. He plays on a golden fiddle with a silver bow.*

RIVER GOD [*sings as he plays*]: I hope. . . I hope that my Redeemer liveth.

KERSTI [*has been standing buried in thought, She sees the* RIVER GOD *and, when he has sung his song twice, she says scornfully*] : You have no Redeemer!

> *The* RIVER GOD *pauses, looks at her sadly and repeats his song twice more.*

KERSTI: If you keep quiet now you may play at my wedding.

> *The* RIVER GOD *nods assent and the rock swallows him up again. The* MIDWIFE *enters from behind the hut, dressed in a long black cloak with a black broad-brimmed hat. Beneath her cape she carries a bag. She does not show her back.*

MIDWIFE: Good evening, little maid. I hope I don't disturb you?

KERSTI: Aren't you the midwife, Mrs Larsson?

MIDWIFE: Of course I am. It was I who helped you, little maid. When —

KERSTI: Yes, yes. But you promised you'd never speak of it —

MIDWIFE: We won't speak of it, then. But — how fares the little one?

KERSTI [*impatiently*] : All right.

MIDWIFE: Now don't be so impatient, little maid —

KERSTI: Who said I was?

MIDWIFE: Your curt little voice and your light little foot. But there's gold on your finger, I see. Then I can expect to be at a wedding soon?

KERSTI: You?

MIDWIFE: I've often attended a baptism — well, naturally But never a wedding. I think that'd be so nice.

KERSTI: Perhaps it would.

MIDWIFE: Of all the virtues of man and womankind, there's one I value the most —

KERSTI: You don't often find that.

MIDWIFE: What don't exist is beyond price. But gratitude now. That's a thing I prize.

KERSTI: Weren't you paid?

MIDWIFE: There are some services which can't be paid off with money.

KERSTI: And some people who never let themselves be paid off.

MIDWIFE: Quite right, my chick. And I'm one of them.

KERSTI: So I see.

MIDWIFE: Me — and one other.

KERSTI: Who?

MIDWIFE: The justice.

KERSTI [*starts*]: The justice?

MIDWIFE: Yes. The justice. That's a most remarkable man. I don't know anyone who knows the law by heart like he does, from cover to cover. You and I could never get to know it like he does. But — there's one bit that I in my job have had to learn by heart. It's that peculiar Chapter

Fourteen. *Too* peculiar it is, with all those paragraphs it's got. What's the matter?

KERSTI [*shaken*]: Say what you know!

MIDWIFE: I don't know anything. I'm only a poor woman who's come to ask for a night's shelter —

KERSTI: Ask for shelter — here?

MIDWIFE: Yes. Here.

KERSTI: Clear off!

MIDWIFE: I can't walk in the forest on this dark night —

KERSTI [*picks up a stick and threatens her*]: You can't walk? Run, then!

MIDWIFE [*shrinks back slightly, without turning her back*]: Oh, we're there now, we're there, are we? You drop that stick, or else —

KERSTI: Or else?

MIDWIFE: It'll be the justice, not me. And his fourteenth chapter —

KERSTI [*lifts the stick to strike her*]: Go to hell, you damned witch!

Her stick falls to the ground in pieces. The MIDWIFE *roars with laughter.* KERSTI *picks up a flint and steel and strikes fire.*

KERSTI: In the name of Christ's wounds, get thee hence!

The MIDWIFE *turns her back and reveals a fox's back with a hanging tail. She canters out, hissing.*

MIDWIFE: We'll meet at the wedding, invited or uninvited! With the justice! With the justice! Eh? Psst! Eh? Psst! Eh! Psst!

KERSTI is left alone. At first she goes irresolutely to the lake as though wishing to throw herself in; then she paces to and fro in front of the cradle; then takes

off her jacket and puts it on the other clothes in the
cradle. Sits down on the chair by the hut door, her
hands over her face. The grindstone begins to whirl
and hiss; the small tinkling of goatbells is heard,
close by.

The RIVER GOD *appears and begins to sing his*
song: "I hope that my Redeemer liveth." KERSTI
rises to her feet and stands frozen with fear. Then,
from the lake, comes the sound as of a glass harmonica.
A CHILD *clothed in white, invisible to* KERSTI, *rises*
among the water-lilies in the lake and walks over to the
cradle.

Now the stage becomes silent; the grindstone
ceases to spin. The RIVER GOD *disappears, as do*
all the fairy lights except one. The WHITE CHILD,
still invisible to KERSTI, *rocks the cradle slowly, listens,*
and stands there sadly; begins to cry and hides its face
with its arm. Throughout this, the glass harmonica is
heard. Then the WHITE CHILD *picks white water-lilies*
and pulls them to pieces so that the petals fall on the
cradle; kisses the cradle and descends again into the
lake. Then the last light goes out and the glass harmonica
stops playing.

MIDWIFE [*enters with her bag visible*] : Now perhaps I can
come back? Now perhaps the little maid will receive the
midwife?

KERSTI: What have you to give me?

MIDWIFE [*takes a bridal crown from her bag*] : This.

KERSTI: What will you take from me?

MIDWIFE [*points at the cradle*] : You see it, I see it, the
whole world sees it. And yet it don't exist.

KERSTI: Then take it.

MIDWIFE [*goes to the cradle*] : I have it!

She takes something which we cannot see out of the

*cradle and puts it in her bag, which she then hides
under her cloak.*

MIDWIFE: May I come to the wedding now?

KERSTI: Come.

MIDWIFE: Say "welcome".

KERSTI: That'd be lying.

MIDWIFE: Get some practice.

KERSTI: You are welcome. If you go now.

MIDWIFE [*backs out*] :   Four times round and round.
Eight times underground.
Four stand in the sky.
Four where the crossroads lie.

MATS [*offstage, sings joyfully*] : Come, dearest, dearest,
dearest! Come, dearest, dearest, dearest!

> KERSTI *listens, happy, swelling with pride and
> courage.* MATS *enters, happy, with a bundle of
> wood.*

KERSTI [*goes towards him*] : Did you meet anyone?

MATS: Yes, but — there's going to be a wedding! [*Throws
the wood into the hut.*] Let the pot boil over! I'm
boiling too!

KERSTI: You've seen your father?

MATS: Father and Mother! And I'm to have the mill!

KERSTI [*shows him the crown*] : Look what I —

MATS: Where did you get that?

KERSTI: My mother gave it to me.

MATS: Was she here?

KERSTI: Joyful she was.

MATS: But the little one! The little one, the little one.

KERSTI: Sit down, Mats. Sit down. I know what I'm doing.

MATS: Our son, our son.

KERSTI: There, now. Mats! Now that our darkness is ending and life grows light, don't you think if we're patient we may tread a long road together?

MATS: It must be a straight road.

KERSTI: Straight roads are short.

MATS: What do you want?

KERSTI: "For great things to be won may small things be undone."

MATS: Can't you speak plainly?

KERSTI: Wait a little.

MATS: I am waiting.

KERSTI: Your parents have made conditions.

MATS: I know.

KERSTI: They demand a virgin bride. What is a virgin bride? One who can wear the crown.

MATS: With honour!

KERSTI: With or without. What isn't seen, what no one knows, is not.

MATS: Let me think. [*Pause.*] Very well. Go on.

KERSTI: "The great things will be won if small things be undone."

MATS: But not — *that* small one!

KERSTI: Will you fail me now?

MATS: I'll not fail you. Not you, Kersti dear.

KERSTI: Suppose now: the banns are read, the wedding prepared, but the little one sleeps in the forest. Who will milk the cow? Who will dress the little one and give him drink? Who, who, who?

MATS: You may well ask! [*Thinks.*] If one dared — did you say something?

KERSTI: Nothing at all.

MATS: I was thinking — if one dared —

KERSTI: Say it.

MATS: No, you say it.

KERSTI: You must.

MATS: Someone must see to the little one.

KERSTI: Who?

MATS: There's only one person.

KERSTI: Shouldn't be hard to guess, then.

MATS: Then say it.

KERSTI: You must say it.

MATS: There's only one person aside of us who knows about the little one.

KERSTI: Who?

MATS: Since you know, why don't you say?

KERSTI: Because you shall say it.

MATS: It's the midwife. Isn't that what you said?

KERSTI: I said nothing; but now you've said it. And I obey you, Mats, you know that.

MATS: I don't think so.

KERSTI: But I have obeyed you! The little one mustn't lie in the forest, he must be under a roof, the nights will grow cold and if anything happens, then — the justice will come.

MATS: The justice? Yes, he will come.

KERSTI [*jumps up*]: Will he come?

MATS: If anything happens. Well. Where is the midwife?

KERSTI: Will you call her?

MATS: I wish she was here.

KERSTI: What would you want with her?

MATS: That she should take the little one under some roof.

KERSTI: Whose?

MATS: Hers.

KERSTI: For how long?

MATS: Till the wedding's over.

KERSTI: But if the little one should fall sick when he's with her?

MATS: It'd be better than that he should freeze in the forest, freeze to death in the forest. [*Listens to the cradle.*] Ssh! I heard him!

KERSTI: Impossible. He's asleep —

MATS: Ssh! I heard him

KERSTI: You can't hear anything.

MATS [*gets up*]: Quiet. I heard him.

KERSTI [*places herself between him and the cradle*]: Don't wake him. If he cries, someone might hear.

MATS: Oh! Do you think anyone heard him? Your mother — ? We should never have done this, Kersti dear.

KERSTI: Better if we hadn't.

MATS [*gloomily*]: We must take him tonight to the midwife. I must go down to the village.

KERSTI: I'll take him.

MATS [*approaches the cradle*]: Take him!

KERSTI: But don't wake him!

MATS: I must kiss him goodnight.

KERSTI: Don't touch him.

MATS: Think if I never saw him again — our little one.

KERSTI: Then it'd be His will, which we can't alter.

MATS: His will be done!

KERSTI: You said it!

MATS: What did I say, that so pleases you?

KERSTI: That — that you bow to His will, without which nothing happens.

MATS [*simply*]: All that happens is by His will.

KERSTI: Yes.

MATS: Good night then, Kersti dear. And my little one. [*Goes.*]

KERSTI: Good night, Mats.

> *She unfastens the empty cradle and sinks it in the lake. The* WHITE CHILD *rises and threatens her with its finger.* KERSTI *shrinks. The* RIVER GOD *appears again, threateningly, now with a gold harp and bare-headed.*

RIVER GOD [*sings to his harp*]:

The clouds hang low and the water stands still,
The water stands still.
I saw the sun when in the world of time
Blissful I lived.
The sun is down,
The night is nigh,
Sin is heavy,
The river is deep.
Light it was then!
Dark is it now!
My home is sorrow.
My home is sleep.

*During this time, KERSTI has picked up the bridal
crown and carried it into the hut. As she extinguishes
the fire under the pot, smoke rises from the chimney
in the form of curiously shaped and many-coloured
snakes, dragons, birds, etc. When she comes out she
is wearing a jacket and carries a bag and a horn. She
locks the door and walks away, straight-backed, with
proud steps, as the RIVER GOD sings his last words.*

ACT TWO

*The main room in the mill. Everything is white with
flour dust. Upstage right, a large open hatch, through
which can be seen part of the water-wheel. Slightly
to the right of this emerges the drum, to the bottom
of which a flour-sack is fastened. Beside this, the
mill-boom. Upstage centre, large doors. Left of these,
big hatches, as in a barn. Right, a big open stove with
a coal fire and a cauldron. Left, a bed and a hand-
loom, a bobbin, a reel and a spinning-wheel. Right,
a door.*

*In front of the stove in a circle sit MATS'
GRANDFATHER, GRANDMOTHER, MOTHER
and FATHER: his adult sister BRITA, younger
sister ANNA, and small sister and brother, LILL-
KAREN and LILL-MATS. All are smoking iron
pipes and are very grave. BRITA is making something
from a hank of hair. LILL-KAREN and LILL-MATS
each have a doll.*

BRITA [*to* LILL-KAREN]: Where did you get that doll,
Karen?

LILL-KAREN: Kersti gave it to me.

BRITA [*takes the doll from her*]: Give it to me. [*To* LILL-
MATS.] Where did you get yours?

LILL-MATS: Kersti gave it to me.

BRITA [*takes it*]: Give it here.

FATHER: Hush! Hush! Grandfather is thinking!

   Silence.

MOTHER [*to* BRITA]: What are you making there?

BRITA: A watch-cord. But I'm running out of hair.

MOTHER: Where will you get more?

BRITA: I know where there's hair that needs pulling.

MOTHER: It's only horsehair that's pulled.

BRITA: And hens are plucked, sows give brushes and girls use them. Combed hair is good, but cut hair is best!

FATHER: Hush! Hush! Grandfather is thinking!

   Silence.

ANNA [*whispers to* BRITA]: What's he thinking about?

BRITA: You ask him. Then we'll all know.

ANNA: Is it about Mats? [BRITA *is silent.*] And Kersti? Is there going to be a wedding?

FATHER: Hush, hush! Grandfather is thinking!

   Silence.

ANNA [*to* BRITA]: You can have some of my hair.

BRITA: It's the wrong colour.

ANNA: Whose is the right colour? [BRITA *is silent.*] Kersti?

BRITA: Be quiet.

   Silence.

GRANDMOTHER [*to* GRANDFATHER]: Have you thought?

GRANDFATHER [*Bible and prayer book on his knees,*

buried in meditation, awakes] : I have thought! [*Opens
prayer book at random and says to those near him.*]
Number two hundred and seventy-eight, verse four.
Let us read that.

ALL [*read in unison, like children in school*] :

> Death and birth make all as one.
> Only study dead men's bones.
> Who can then tell slave from prince,
> Beggar-man from nobleman?
> Shall the babe that cradled lies
> Slumbering so peacefully
> End in some sweet feather-bed
> Or upon the gallows-tree?

GRANDFATHER: It is spoken. He that hath ears to hear,
let him hear. Is it spoken?

GRANDMOTHER: Not yet.

FATHER: Not clearly.

MOTHER: Lord, Thou seest!

BRITA: What does the Book say?

ANNA: "Thinkest thou that God judgeth unjustly, or that
the Almighty shall pardon the evildoer?"

LILL-KAREN: What must I say?

GRANDFATHER: Yes, my child, you must counsel us,
even though we reject your counsel; for truth may come
from the mouths of babes and sucklings. Shall Kersti
have Mats?

LILL-KAREN: If they want each other.

GRANDFATHER: Well spoken. Lill-Mats?

LILL-MATS [*his fingers in his mouth*]: I want to have my
dolly.

GRANDFATHER: And Mats wants to have his. Should he?

LILL-MATS: If it's Kersti he can, because she gave me my dolly.

BRITA: Listen to him!

GRANDFATHER: Let us consult the scripture. [*Opens the Bible and reads.*] The Book of Genesis, Chapter thirty-four, Verse eight. "And Hamor communed with them, saying, The soul of my son Shechem longeth for your daughter. I pray you give her him to wife." Is it sufficient?

GRANDMOTHER: It is sufficient.

FATHER: Was there anything there about the mill too?

MOTHER: His will be done.

BRITA [*curtly*]: Amen.

ANNA: Yes, yes, let it be so.

LILL-KAREN: I like Kersti because she's nice.

LILL-MATS: Me too.

FATHER: Hush, hush. Grandfather is thinking.

Silence.

GRANDFATHER [*to* FATHER]: Call your brother-in-law.

The FATHER *gets up and goes to the rear door, where he stops. The* GRANDFATHER *goes to the bed, pulls out a drawer from beneath it and takes out a bundle of papers. He turns to the* FATHER.

GRANDFATHER: Let him enter.

FATHER [*opens door*]: Come in, Stig Mattsson, my brother-in-law.

The JUSTICE *enters in uniform.*

JUSTICE: God's peace on this house.

ALL [*rise*]: God's peace on thee.

GRANDFATHER: Stig Mattsson! I have asked you to come here, you know the cause. Kersti Margreta Hansdotter —

[*sighs*] — is to wed Mats Anders Larsson, my grandson.
Our families have fought and feuded a long time, too long.
I have now at long last decided that before I close my
eyes and go to my final rest, an end must be set to this
strife. Look at these papers. [*The* JUSTICE *takes the
bundle of papers and looks at them.*] Court proceedings,
exchanges, receipts, letters of authority. Some concern
settled actions, some unsettled. Have you looked?

JUSTICE: I have looked.

GRANDFATHER[*takes the papers back*]: Good. Then I
shall put them in the fire. There is a time for hatred and
a time for love. The time for hatred must end. I long for
peace. Therefore I beg my family to regard all that has
passed as though it had never been. And I ask you all;
will you forget what has been and, without grudge or
reserve, meet your new kinsmen and greet them as friends?
Answer.

ALL: Yes.

GRANDFATHER: Then I consign the evil of bygone days
to the fire. [*Throws the bundle of papers into the fire,
pulls down the main shutter of the stove and opens the
small shutters.*] Sit!

> *They all sit round the stove, and stare at the red
> glow, which shines through the small shutters.*

ANNA[*whispers to* BRITA]: Hark how it sings!

BRITA: It groans. My heart aches.

> *Silence. The* GRANDFATHER *gets up. The others do
> likewise.*

GRANDFATHER[*to* FATHER]: Bring him in.

> *The* FATHER *goes to the door right and brings in*
> MATS. MATS *goes to the rear door and admits*
> KERSTI, *her* MOTHER, *her* FATHER *(the*
> SOLDIER*), who is dressed in old-fashioned military
> parade uniform, and* KERSTI'S GRANDFATHER,
> *the* VERGER.

MATS' GRANDFATHER [*making no gestures*]: God bless
ye! Be seated.

> *All sit except* MATS, KERSTI *and the* JUSTICE.
> MATS *has taken* KERSTI's *hands. Silence.*

GRANDFATHER: When do you wish to have the wedding?

MATS: In two weeks, on the third banns day.

GRANDFATHER: Is there need for haste?

> KERSTI *makes a movement.*

MATS: Have we not waited long enough?

GRANDFATHER: Perhaps you have.

MATS [*to his kinsmen*]: Will no one say a word to Kersti?
[*Silence.*] No one?

JUSTICE [*comes across to her and takes both her hands
kindly*]: So! Here we have the child! [KERSTI *blenches
and tries to free herself.*] Afraid of me? No! Look me in
the face, Kersti. I have played with you on my knees
when you were a child, and I have held your pretty head
in my hands. You have such a pretty head, with a brow
like a young bull's. That's why you have had your way.
[*Releases her.*]

GRANDFATHER: Go all of ye, and leave the young pair
alone.

> *They all get up and walk past* MATS *and* KERSTI
> *through the rear door.* BRITA, *the last to leave,
> spits as she passes* KERSTI.

BRITA: Fie on you!

MATS [*spits*]: Fie, Brita!

> KERSTI *and* MATS *are left alone.*

MATS: Welcome to my house! Kersti!

KERSTI: To your house? Yes.

MATS: What do the others matter?

KERSTI: You tell me.

MATS: You're not marrying my family.

KERSTI: I'm marrying into it.

MATS: My people are not cruel, you know. But they are not flatterers.

KERSTI: So I see. Is this where we shall live?

MATS: Yes. What do you think of it?

KERSTI: Everything is white.

MATS: That's the flour dust. Don't you like it?

KERSTI: And wet.

MATS: That's the mill-race.

KERSTI: It's cold, too.

MATS: From the bottom of the lake.

KERSTI: Will we have newer furniture than this?

MATS [*laughs*]: No. Nothing new is ever made here. Everything is handed down.

KERSTI: Can we dust away this whiteness, then?

MATS [*laughs*]: No. It's needful in a mill, like the crust in a tobacco pipe. Mustn't be touched.

KERSTI: Is that the wheel there?

MATS: That's the wheel.

> *He walks over and pulls the boom. The water roars and the wheel moves.*

KERSTI: Ugh, no! Can you *hear* it?

MATS: It's ours. And it's a glad sound, for it means flour.

KERSTI: The sun never enters here.

MATS: Never. How could it?

KERSTI: And nothing grows. Only green slime on the wheel.

MATS: We catch eels there. And lampreys.

KERSTI: Ugh, no! It's better on the hill-top, where the wind blows —

MATS: And the birch-trees sway.

KERSTI [*weeps into her apron*]: Must I live here, under the water, on the bottom of the lake?

MATS: I was born here.

KERSTI: And we shall die here.

MATS: Oh!

KERSTI: Stop the wheel, then!

MATS: Don't you like it? Very well —

KERSTI [*lifts a hatch in the floor*]: What's here?

MATS: That's the mill-race.

KERSTI: Stop the wheel!

MATS [*pulls the boom, but the wheel does not stop*]: Listen! Is there evil afoot? It won't stop!

KERSTI: I shall die here!

MATS: Let me climb on the plank and stop it. There *is* evil afoot outside.

KERSTI: And inside.

MATS: Kersti dearest — !

KERSTI: Mew, mew, said the cat.

MATS: What's the matter?

KERSTI: I have what I wanted.

MATS: And when one has that, it's nothing. [*The wheel groans and begins to turn backwards.*]: Help! Jesus Christ! The wheel is turning backwards!

He runs out through the rear door. KERSTI *is left
alone. The hand-loom begins to turn, the reel,
bobbin and distaff spin. The scene is illuminated as
though by bright sunshine. Then it becomes dark and
the stove swings round so that the red light from the
three small openings seems to stare at* KERSTI, *while
the stove follows her like a Fury. The stove returns
to its former place, the mill-wheel peals like thunder
and the* RIVER GOD *appears on it with his gold
fiddle and red cap. He sings and plays as before.*

RIVER GOD [*sings*] : I hope, I hope that my Redeemer
liveth!

He repeats this several times.

KERSTI [*runs out upstage*] : Mats! Mats!

The RIVER GOD *disappears, but his song is heard as
it dies away. The* MIDWIFE *enters, goes over to a
hatch in the floor and opens it. Through it she stuffs
her skin bag.*

MIDWIFE:
If you come back, that's no good.
If you don't come back, that's all right.
There, now, there, yes! Now I can dance at the wedding!

*She dances, but without showing her back. The hand-
loom strikes up in three-four time, the bobbin, reel
and distaff spin. Then she disappears through the
rear door, and when she turns her back she shows her
fox's brush. The loom goes on weaving, the bobbin,
reel and distaff spin.* KERSTI *enters; everything falls
still. The* VERGER *enters.*

KERSTI: Is it you, Grandfather?

VERGER: Yes, child, I forgot something. [*Takes his skin
bag from the bed.*]

KERSTI: What have you got there?

VERGER: Well, I've been with the sacristan, and I must
take the numbers home and clean them.

KERSTI: What numbers?

VERGER: Why, the numbers for the psalms, to put up on the board —

KERSTI: Can I see them?

VERGER [*takes out the board with its brass numbers*] : Here they are, child. What's the matter with you, chick?

KERSTI: I don't know, Grandfather. I don't think I should ever have come here.

VERGER: Child, child, what a way to talk!

KERSTI: There's evil in this house —

VERGER: Oh, no, heaven forbid! Dearest child —

KERSTI: Oh, oh, oh! Something new and strange has entered this place —

VERGER: Little Kersti, what could that be?

KERSTI: Yes, tell me, tell me!

VERGER: I must go now, child. I must go to church and fetch the bridal crown, to take it to the goldsmith to be polished with spirits of wine —

KERSTI: Go, then, grandfather.

VERGER: It's for your sake, you see, the crown's to be polished. Your sake — [*Goes out upstage. The* SOLDIER *enters.*]

KERSTI: Is it you, Father?

SOLDIER: Only me. Forgot my cap. [*Takes down helmet.*]

KERSTI: Father, dear Father, I'm so unhappy —

SOLDIER [*drily*] : What's happened?

KERSTI: Nothing's happened.

SOLDIER: How can you be unhappy, then?

KERSTI: You don't understand me.

SOLDIER [*gruffly, as he buttons his helmet-strap*] : Calm
yourself, child.

KERSTI: Don't go, Father.

SOLDIER: The sadness of love soon passes. Calm yourself,
that's my advice. Calm yourself.

He goes. BRITA *enters.*

KERSTI: What have *you* forgotten?

BRITA: I don't forget, my girl.

KERSTI: What are you looking for?

BRITA: You.

KERSTI: How loving of you.

BRITA: Think so?

KERSTI: You hate me.

BRITA: You are a whore.

KERSTI: You are my sister-in-law.

BRITA: Don't be so sure.

KERSTI: Are you prophesying, witch?

BRITA: Rope!

KERSTI: Don't speak of rope in a hanged man's house.*

BRITA [*goes to the sack hanging from the mill-drum*] : See,
I prophesy! The mill is yours; take care how you grind!
[*Takes a handful of black earth from the sack and makes
a small grave-mound on the floor.*] Whores give their
husbands earth to fill their mouths.

KERSTI: You are a witch!

BRITA: Yes! And I can sniff out people's treasures. Shall
I sniff out your little treasure?

*A Swedish proverb.

KERSTI: Witch! Fie, take care! You sin against Christ, you should burn in fire, you would float on water!

BRITA [*takes a pinch of earth from the sack and scatters it on* KERSTI's *head*]: I consecrate thee with earth, I crown thee with a crown of earth! Shame on thee!

KERSTI: Ah! Shame on *you*, shame on you!

A CHILD'S VOICE [*repeats*]: Shame on you!

KERSTI: Who was that?

CHILD'S VOICE: Who was that?

BRITA: Guess! That was the mocking-bird.

KERSTI: The mocking-bird?

BRITA: Your treasure. Do you know about the Meuling?

KERSTI: Yes.*

BRITA: The ghost of a child that has not received Christian burial.*

KERSTI: What has that to do with me?

CHILD'S VOICE: To do with me?

BRITA: The wages of sin is death!

KERSTI [*cries*]: Mats!

CHILD'S VOICE: Mats!

KERSTI [*despairingly*]: Oh! Oh! [*Unfastens her red garter and ties it round her throat.*] I want to die, I want to die!

BRITA: No one is stopping you.

KERSTI: Hang me in a tree!

CHILD'S VOICE: In a tree!

BRITA: Not I.

*These lines are not in the original, and are added for clarification.

MATS [*outside, sings*] : Kersti dearest, does he sleep still?

BRITA: Far away in the forest! Fie on you!

> *She goes.* MATS *enters, happy.*

MATS: Far, far away in the forest! [*Comes up behind* KERSTI *and puts his hands over her ears.*] Who is it?

KERSTI: Oh, you're hurting me!

MATS [*takes hold of the garter round her neck*] : What a necklace!

KERSTI: Let go!

MATS [*pulls the garter playfully*] : Now I'll lead you, now you're my captive, my dove, my goat, which I shall lead to pasture. [*Leads her by the garter.*] My white goatie, my baby calf! [*Sings.*] Come, dearest, dearest, dearest! Come dearest, dearest!

KERSTI: You are merry, Mats.

MATS: Yes, I am merry. Guess why?

KERSTI: Can't any more.

MATS: I met the midwife. She sends you greetings from the little one.

KERSTI: No?

MATS: Yes. He sleeps, she said, so soundly, so soundly.

KERSTI: Oh!

MATS: Deep in the forest. What's that in your hair?

KERSTI: Mould.

MATS: Grave-mould!

KERSTI: I am already buried.

MATS [*dusts it from her hair*] : Ugh! Who has done this to you?

KERSTI: Guess.

MATS: Brita! She has the evil eye.

KERSTI: Can you blind it?

MATS: Not I. Only the Lord Jesus.

The evening bell chimes.

KERSTI: Pray for me.

MATS: One must pray for oneself.

KERSTI: If one can.

MATS: One can, when one's conscience is clean.

KERSTI: When is it?

MATS: Do you hear the evening bell?

KERSTI: No.

MATS: I hear it. So you must hear it.

KERSTI: Oh! I don't hear it! Ah! Ah!

MATS: That is bad. Do you hear the waterfall?

KERSTI: The waterfall in the forest, the flail in the barn, the rattle of cartwheels. But not the church bell.

MATS: That is bad. I remember — when the old Justice was buried, all the bells were rung, we saw them move, but no man heard them. That is bad.

KERSTI: Brita has bewitched me!

MATS: She will pay for it.

KERSTI: Come with me to the hill pasture. I must see the sun.

MATS: I'll come with you, Kersti dearest.

KERSTI: Oh!

MATS [*embraces her head and presses it to his breast*]: Oh!

ACT THREE

The "maids'-night" in the SOLDIER's *cottage. Over
the door upstage is his scutcheon, with his crest and
number. Left and right of this door are windows with
flowers. The floor is of boards, newly-polished with
knots and nail-heads showing. Left, a large open
stove with a cowl above it. In front of this, a bench
with woven covers. Right, under the window, a
bureau with a standing mirror under a white veil.
Candlesticks, plaster figures and other small objects.
Downstage right, a table with benches. On the wall
above hangs the* SOLDIER's *rifle, an old weapon
with a yellowed birch stock, a red thong and a
percussion lock; also a cartridge-bag and a white band-
olier with a bayonet and spiked helmet. Under this
a lithograph of Carl XV in uniform. Through the open
rear door can be seen an August landscape with
shocks of corn.*

   As the curtain rises a SERVANT GIRL *is
standing at the stove, scouring cups, saucepans, pots
and coffee-pans. At the table right sits the* VERGER,
*cleaning the numbers for the psalmboard, which lies
beside him. On the table is the collection-bag of red
velvet with silver embroidery, and a little bell. The*
SOLDIER, *in undress uniform, with his cap on his
head, is seated at the same table going through papers
and making notes with a lead pencil which he
occasionally sucks. Also at this table, standing with
their heads resting on the edge, are* LILL-KAREN
and LILL-MATS *watching the* VERGER *closely and
excitedly with large eyes and their fingers in their
mouths. The* VERGER *now and then smiles at them
and strokes their hair.* KERSTI'S MOTHER *is standing
at the stove holding two handkerchieves before the
fire to dry.*

Girls can be heard singing outside. But in the hut there is an atmosphere of dull routine. Everyone is occupied with his or her task, regardless of the others.

GIRL'S SONG [*offstage*] :

When I was a little maiden
I took our cows to graze.
But then I lost our bell-cow
And brindled Sea-Star too.
Then I climbed up a little hill
And called for them and cried
Then I heard Sea-Star moo, moo, moo
Far far away in the forest.
"Hush," said the branch.
"You will soon get her back."
The pine-tree told me not to fall,
The willow told me not to cry.
The birch-tree promised me spink-spank-spank
                    for supper!

The song stops.

SOLDIER [*looks up. Slowly, to* KERSTI'S MOTHER] : I say, Mother.

MOTHER: What is it?

SOLDIER: Was it six barrels of wheat we harvested last year?

MOTHER: Yes, it was six.

SOLDIER [*writes*] : Good.

Silence.

VERGER: Are the girls in the bath yet?

MOTHER: Yes. People want this kind of wedding. We should have got the oats in. And it'll soon be cranberry time.

VERGER: The dog-days'll soon be out. You can see that from the flies. They're sluggish. There'll be a fine crop of cranberries this year.

MOTHER: Yes.

Silence.

SOLDIER: Won't the girls be here soon?

MOTHER: I don't know why they're so long.

SOLDIER: It's hot.

VERGER: Can't be much fun on manoeuvres.

SOLDIER: The infantry'll have a rough time.

VERGER: It was lucky you managed to get leave.

SOLDIER: It was that.

MOTHER: Is that them coming now?

SOLDIER: Have you fed them?

MOTHER: They've had that in the bath-house. They've nothing to complain of.

> *Chatter and laughter is heard; then* KERSTI *enters from her bath, pale, white-faced, her hair hanging wet. She is followed by* BRITA *and* ANNA, *with the bridesmaids,* ELSA, RIKEN, GRETA *and* LISA. *These last four carry stone jars and wine-glasses, which they put down by the stove.* KERSTI, BRITA *and* ANNA *carry handkerchieves with coloured borders which they hang up by the door.* KERSTI'S MOTHER *puts a chair in the middle of the room for* KERSTI, *and dries her hair with the handkerchieves, then combs it. The* BRIDESMAIDS *sit on the bench, left; but* BRITA *sits in such a position that she can stare at* KIRSTI. *No one greets anyone or displays any emotion whatever.*

MOTHER: Bring the looking-glass here.

KERSTI: I don't want any glass. Let it be.

BRITA: You ought to look at yourself, since no one else can.

KERSTI: What do you mean by that?

BRITA: You tell me. Beautiful hair. Can I have what falls?

KERSTI: No!

MOTHER [*to* BRITA]: What do you want that for?

BRITA: For Mats' watch-cord.

MOTHER: Mats must have it.

KERSTI: I don't want that!

BRITA [*takes a hank of hair on which she has been working from her pocket*]: Won't I ever get that colour?

KERSTI: When I'm dead you can have it.

BRITA: Keep your word on that!

KERSTI: I'll keep it.

Silence.

SOLDIER: Mother, can you tell me — quiet a moment, children! — is the colour sergeant invited?

MOTHER: Vesterlund? Yes.

SOLDIER: Four o'clock tomorrow at the church, isn't it?

MOTHER: That's right.

SOLDIER [*gathers his papers*]: I'll be off to the priest, then. And afterwards to the sacristan. [*To himself.*] Ye-es. That's that, then. That's that.

He goes out pensively without looking at anyone. Silence.

VERGER [*affectionately, to* LILL-KAREN *and* LILL-MATS]: Now you won't touch anything, my chicks, if I leave them here?

LILL-KARIN: I'll see Lill-Mats doesn't touch anything.

VERGER: You see he doesn't.

MOTHER: Where are you going, Father?

VERGER: I've just got to collect the crown from the carrier. He's coming in from town.

BRITA [*scornfully*]: The crown!

VERGER [*gets up*]: It's been with the goldsmith, you see, to be polished with spirits of wine. You whiten it with spirits of wine, that's what you do with silver.

BRITA *laughs scornfully.*

MOTHER [*to* VERGER]: Wait a minute. I'll come with you.

VERGER: Is it all right to leave them here alone?

BRITA: What could happen?

MOTHER: They're grown people.

BRITA: And Kersti likes to be alone. She can't bear anyone looking at her —

MOTHER: You keep a hold on your tongue.

BRITA: Especially when she goes into the bath, she doesn't want any company. But she's a grown person, so she's not afraid.

KERSTI *twists on her chair to avoid* BRITA's *eyes.*

MOTHER: Sit still!

BRITA: She's not a child any longer, not her. Grown out of her clogs, she has, and other things too. Perhaps the crown won't fit her? Have you tried it?

VERGER [*simply*]: We must go now.

The VERGER *goes out, accompanied by* KERSTI's MOTHER. *Silence.* KERSTI *sits down at the table right and fingers the numbers.*

BRITA [*follows her with her eyes*]: It's fun on the night before the wedding.

KERSTI: Do you want to play games?

BRITA: Play mummy and daddy and children?

KERSTI: Guess riddles?

BRITA: I've already guessed —

KERSTI: Shall we sing?

BRITA: Rock-a-bye baby? No, we'll read the Bible.

KERSTI: The Bible?

BRITA: Yes. Genesis thirty-four, verse eight.

KERSTI: Shechem?

BRITA: Yes, him. And Dinah, whom his heart longed for. Do you know who Dinah was?

KERSTI: The daughter of Jacob and Leah.

BRITA: Right. And do you know what Dinah was?

KERSTI: Is that a riddle?

BRITA: No. Do you know what she was?

KERSTI: No.

BRITA: She was a little — spoiled.

KERSTI: Is that a pun?

BRITA: Certainly. [KERSTI *bows her head to her breast as though wishing to hide it.*] You understand? [*Silence.*] Have you invited any other guests beside Mother Larsson?

KERSTI: Have I invited — ? The midwife?

BRITA: So she said.

KERSTI: Then she was lying.

BRITA: As midwife she is bound by oath; but whether her oath was sacred or profane is not known. She doesn't lie; but she does swear. [KERSTI *bows her head again.*] Lift your head! Can't you look people in the face?

KERSTI [*to the other girls*] : Say something!

Silence.

BRITA: It's not good to say what one hasn't seen. But — one knows what one knows.

The JUSTICE *appears in the doorway.*

JUSTICE: May I come in? An old man can join the girls tonight — though the lads must stay away.

BRITA [*goes over to* KERSTI *and holds her fist under* KERSTI'*s face*]. You'll not wear that crown.

KERSTI: Perhaps.

> BRITA *goes out. The* JUSTICE *comes forward, takes a chair and sits directly facing* KERSTI . *The* GIRLS *tiptoe out, one by one. But* LILL-MATS *stays, clinging to* KERSTI'*s skirt. The* JUSTICE *speaks friendlily, but when he tries to be refined he becomes clumsy, and his words take on another meaning than that intended by him.*

JUSTICE [*takes* KERSTI'*s hand and looks her in the eyes*]: Now listen, my child. Is this a bride, looking so sad when she has got what her heart longs for? What's the matter?

KERSTI [*coldly*] : Don't know what you mean.

JUSTICE [*flips her lightly on the cheek*]: Oh! Is that a way to answer? An old friend, who'll be a kinsman by this time tomorrow? There are plenty of young girls who envy you, and would like to have gone to the bridal chamber before you.

KERSTI: Perhaps.

JUSTICE: Or this new life which awaits you in the mill and the kitchen. There'll be no more shouting and singing in the forest, where the wind blows and the birch-tree sways, or dancing in the barn on Saturday night. You must stand at the stove and sit by the cradle, and have the food on the table when Mats comes. And keep a tight rein on your temper and passions when dark days dawn — for they always come, like rain after sunshine. Are you scared of growing up, little friend? That's nothing to be scared of. It makes life good and less of a game.

KERSTI: Oh!

JUSTICE: Why o-oh? There's something here that don't belong to a young girl's thoughts. There's some secret here. Out with it, little friend, I must know about this! [*Jokingly.*] The justice always ferrets out the truth — from everyone. What's on your heart? Is Mats not good to you?

KERSTI: Oh, yes, yes!

JUSTICE: Are his kinsfolk being grand or sharp with you? Are you having trouble with them — ?

> LILL-MATS *clambers up on to* KERSTI's *knee; puts his arms round her neck; then huddles down in her lap and falls asleep.*

JUSTICE: Look at that little admirer. He likes his sister-in-law, and that bodes well. Children know who their real friends are. Do you like children, Kersti?

KERSTI [*suspiciously*]: Why do you ask?

JUSTICE: Fie, what an answer! Isn't it a rare thing to have a little one like him? In your lap, and feel him trust himself to you? As though he knew there was no perfidy nor deceit in those breasts. I think he's falling asleep; entrusting his defenceless slumbers to a stranger, who wishes harm to no one!

KERSTI: Have you seen Mats?

JUSTICE: He's been out with the lads preparing the mill-room for the dance tomorrow. [*Silence.*] It's a long time since we had a crown bride here.

KERSTI: Is it?

JUSTICE: Yes. Well — new customs have come in, with these people from the towns, and army camps —

KERSTI [*spitefully*]: They used to blame the timber men —

JUSTICE: Ah, yes. But without the timber men you'd not have had the mill —

KERSTI: They're always blaming, blaming —

JUSTICE: You're getting a good man —

KERSTI: Yes, good. Too good for me.

JUSTICE: Don't be bitter. I only meant kindly —

KERSTI: I wasn't bitter. I was speaking the truth —

JUSTICE: We have difficulty in understanding each other. It looks as though we can't be friends —

KERSTI: Why not?

JUSTICE: When I mean good, you see evil. Well — it's often so when something's awry.

KERSTI: What is awry?

JUSTICE [*gets up*]: Don't ask me. I don't know.

KERSTI: Nor do I, but one doesn't say that to a girl.

JUSTICE: Now wait, wait! A clean conscience can be heaped high without spilling, but — but — but —

KERSTI: Are you cross-questioning me?

JUSTICE: I wasn't.

KERSTI: You — don't know how to talk to women.

JUSTICE [*sharply*]: Kersti!

KERSTI: Well, what do you mean?

JUSTICE [*looks at her*]: What do *you* mean?

KERSTI: What do *you* mean?

JUSTICE: Well, now, that's what my women usually ask when they want to know if I know anything.

KERSTI: What should you know?

JUSTICE: Oh. Are we there? Are we there? [*Silence.*] Well. Then I'll go. I'll go.

> *Goes slowly out upstage with his finger on his lips, as though enjoining himself to be silent.* KERSTI, *left alone, kisses the sleeping* LILL-MATS *on the head.* MATS *appears at the window, right. Dusk has begun to fall, though it is still light.*

MATS: Oh!

KERSTI: Mats! Come in!

MATS: No, I mustn't. I've promised.

KERSTI: Oh, come!

MATS: No, no. Is the little one asleep?

KERSTI: He? Yes. Hush, hush!

> *From the distant camp is heard the bugle calling for regimental prayers.*

KERSTI [*frightened*]: Is that the hunt again?

MATS: Why, no. They don't hunt in the evening.

KERSTI: What is it, then?

MATS: A soldier's daughter ought to know that.

KERSTI: Well, say.

MATS: It's the bugle call from the camp. For evening prayers.

KERSTI: Yes, of course. I'm so muddled and confused.

MATS: Come here, Kersti. To the window.

KERSTI: Shall I? Just let me put the little one to bed.

MATS: That little one?

> KERSTI *gets up carefully and tiptoes with* LILL-MATS *to the bench by the stove, where she lays him*

*down and tucks him up. She hums a lullaby. A psalm
is heard distantly from the camp.* KERSTI *kneels
and tries to pray, but twists her hands in despair.
Then she kisses the child's boots, gets up, goes to
the window and stands there.*

MATS: They're a wonderful thing, children.

KERSTI: Yes — yes.

MATS: They left you alone?

KERSTI: Yes, they all went. Everything's — hostile to me
here. Everything.

MATS: Tomorrow's the wedding.

KERSTI: Oh, yes. Think!

MATS: Yes, think! Tomorrow's our wedding!

KERSTI: And then I'll be mistress of the mill.

MATS: Yes. My mill.

KERSTI: Till death do us part.

MATS: That's a long time off.

KERSTI: Oh!

ACT FOUR

*The wedding. The mill-room has been cleared. The
rear doors are raised so that we can see through into
a big storehouse, now laid out like a banquet-room
with a large laid coffee-table. The hatches to the big
rectangular opening left of the rear door have also
been removed, showing a table with candles for the
musicians. Right of the rear door is the opening to
the mill-wheel. The loom etc., and the bed, are gone.
On the floor beneath the musicians' aperture stands
the "Old Men's Table", with pots, mugs, tobacco*

*pipes, packs of cards, etc. In the middle of the room
stand benches and chairs, over which clean white
sheets, pillow-cases and cloths are spread to dry.
SIX SERVANT-GIRLS are grinding the coffee-mills;
the church bells are pealing, and a bridal march is
being played on fiddles. The* GIRLS *sing as they
gather and fold the sheets and other laundry.*

GIRLS [*sing*] :

Kulleri toova,*
Twelve men in the forest!
Twelve men are they.
Twelve swords they carry.
They hanged the black bull.
They flayed the bell-cow.
They tried to seduce me.
Kulleri toova.

The bridal procession approaches. The GIRLS *go out
with the laundry and set the benches and chairs along
the walls to either side. Now the stage is empty, and
silence has fallen outside. Then the* RIVER GOD's
song is heard in the wheel, but he cannot be seen.

RIVER GOD: I hope, I hope, that my Redeemer liveth.

The hatch in the floor opens and the WHITE CHILD
*rises, a chaos of white veils in which can be indistinctly
seen the outlines of a small child in a long baptismal
robe, which hovers above the hatch. Then the bridal
march is heard outside. The* RIVER GOD *falls silent,
the* WHITE CHILD *vanishes.*

*The bridal procession enters the rear room —
first the* FIDDLERS, *then the* BRIDESMAIDS *and*
YOUNG MEN, *then the* BRIDE *and* BRIDEGROOM,
the PRIEST, *the* PARENTS, KINSFOLK, YOUNG
PEOPLE, *etc. The procession marches into the mill-
room, silent and subdued. They seat the* BRIDE *on a
chair in the middle of the room and behind the floor-*

*These two words are meaningless.

*hatch, so that she has to look at it. Now they all begin
to circle and defile past the* BRIDE, *who is pale and
looks down at the floor in front of her. Then one
by one they all go up to her, say a few words to her
and go out into the rear room.*

MATS [*to* KERSTI] : Well, Kersti. Now our troubles are
over. [*Goes.*]

BRITA [*with the* BRIDESMAIDS, *to* KERSTI] : You have
your crown. Guard it well. [*Goes with the* BRIDESMAIDS.]

KERSTI'S MOTHER [*puts the crown straight on* KERSTI's
head] : Straighten your back, child, and keep your head
up. [*Goes.*]

SOLDIER [*to* KERSTI] : God bless you. [*Goes.*]

VERGER [*to* KERSTI] : And keep you! [*Goes.*]

MATS' GRANDFATHER [*to* KERSTI] : You are beautiful
as the day. [*Goes.*]

MATS' MOTHER [*to* KERSTI] : Welcome to our family.
[*Goes.*]

MATS' FATHER [*to* KERSTI] : Henceforth you are my
daughter. What's past is forgotten. [*Goes.*]

JUSTICE [*to* KERSTI] : So pale a cheek! The blood must
have gone to your heart. What weight lies there?

KERSTI [*raises her head and looks spitefully at him*] :
Nothing!

JUSTICE : Nothing *was* something. Nothing *is* — nothing,
now.

KERSTI : Go!

JUSTICE : When you go, I shall walk before you. Whither
you walk, I shall not follow you. When you fall to your
knees, I shall stand. Who casts a stone at you? Not I.

KERSTI : Watch your neck, evil one!

JUSTICE [*places the flat of his hand on her neck*] : Watch yours!

> *He goes. The other* RELATIVES *walk past her, greeting her coldly. The* FIDDLER *has seated himself at the table through the hatch left. The* OLD MEN *have sat down at the Old Men's Table, and are smoking. The* FIDDLER *strikes up a polka. As he does so, the* RIVER GOD's *fiddle is heard in the mill-wheel playing his music (as in Act One), without words but echoed by two other fiddles. As the dance begins, there is a cry from the rear room: "Take the crown from the bride!" From within the mill-room comes the answering cry: "Take the crown from the bride!"* KERSTI *becomes uneasy. The* PRIEST *approaches her.*

FIDDLER [*now notices the* RIVER GOD's *music, and cries*] : Who's playing in there?

ALL [*without looking at the mill-wheel and not knowing whence the music comes*] : Who's playing in there?

> *The music continues; the* RIVER GOD *falls silent. Then the* PRIEST *takes* KERSTI's *hand and walks with her slowly and solemnly round the room. As he puts his hand round her waist to begin the dance, the* RIVER GOD *begins to play again.* KERSTI's *crown falls from her head and rolls down into the conduit leading to the mill-race.*

KERSTI: Jesus Christ!

ALL IN THE MILL-ROOM [*jump to their feet*] : The crown's fallen in the mill-race!

ALL IN THE REAR ROOM: What's happened?

ALL IN THE MILL-ROOM: The crown's fallen in the mill-race!

> *The music stops. Commotion.*

MATS [*at the rear door*] : Come outside and find it!

ALL: Outside and find it!

PRIEST: God in heaven protect us!

ALL: God in heaven protect us!

JUSTICE: Outside and find it!

ALL: Outside and find it!

MATS: Outside and find it!

> *They all rush out upstage except* KERSTI, *who sits down on her chair. Dusk has fallen. The mill-wheel begins to turn and the* RIVER GOD *is seen with his harp. He sings his earlier song: "The clouds hang low . . . " As the song begins, the hatch at* KERSTI's *feet opens and the* WHITE CHILD *rises as before.* KERSTI *at first gazes at it in horror, but then stretches out her arms towards it and takes it to her breast. The* CHILD'S VOICE *is heard from beneath the hatch.*

CHILD'S VOICE: Cold is the mill-stream. Warm is my mother's breast. In life you gave me nothing. In death I take what is mine.

KERSTI[*who has been rocking the baby, now gropes painfully at her breast*]: Oh, help me! Save me!

CHILD'S VOICE: A life for a life! Now I am drinking yours.

KERSTI[*screams*]: Save me, save me!

MIDWIFE[*enters, fussily*]: All right, all right! I'm coming, I'm coming! Calm yourself, little mother. [*Takes the* CHILD *from* KERSTI's *breast and puts it back through the hatch.*] I know how to manage these little ones. I bring them into the world. And I put them into the ground. Well! I've come to the wedding!

> BRITA *has appeared at the* FIDDLER's *hatch and has seen that something has been pushed down the floor hatch.*

MIDWIFE: The river troll was invited too. Did he come?

KERSTI: Leave me! What do you want?

MIDWIFE: What you no longer have.

KERSTI: You mean the crown?

MIDWIFE: Not exactly. Hush, there's someone walking about up there. I'll hide in the stove. You see! I came after all! [*Gets into the stove and closes its shutters.*]

BRITA [*enters and goes over to* KERSTI]: Now it is you or I!

KERSTI: You — !

BRITA: A gift awaits you.

KERSTI: Give it to me.

BRITA: A bracelet it is; but not from me. [*Silence.*] A bracelet of iron. [*Stands on the hatch.*] Now I tread on your head, now I stand on your heart, now I stamp your secret out of the earth, or the water, or the fire. [*Silence.*] Now I shall have your hair, now I shall have my watch-cord which is no watch-cord. Where is the midwife, where is the guest of honour at this virgin's wedding?

> You stole the crown, and the river troll stole him.
> You stole the mill, but he will walk.
> Shechem's Dinah was shamed, not spoiled.
> The little one sleeps in the stream, not in the forest.
> You have shamed my brother, my family, my name.
> You shall die.

KERSTI [*passively*]: I am dead. I have died these days on end. Are you content?

BRITA: You shall die more days on end. You shall die for lying, for perjury, for theft, for slander, for perfidy and for murder. Six times shall you die; and a seventh time, that men may see you die. You shall not lie in consecrated ground, you shall have no black coffin with silver stars, no pine-twigs at your door, no bells at your burial.

KERSTI: I can imagine it.

BRITA: So shall it be. Do you hear those footsteps?
Count them. One, two, three, four, five, six —

> *The* JUSTICE *enters upstage.* BRITA *goes to him
> and whispers. The* JUSTICE *walks over to the
> hatch in the floor.*

JUSTICE: It lies here.

BRITA: Not the crown?

JUSTICE: That, or something else. [*Opens hatch.*] It isn't
the crown. Poor Kersti! Did you put this here?

KERSTI: No.

JUSTICE: No? Tell the truth.

BRITA [*strikes her on the mouth*]: The truth!

KERSTI: I did not put that there.

BRITA [*puts her hand into the* JUSTICE's *pocket and
takes out a pair of handcuffs*]: Put this bracelet on
her.

JUSTICE [*to* BRITA]: Hangman and torturer! [*Covers
his face and weeps.*] Alas for us all! Alas!

PRIEST [*enters upstage*]: Has it been found?

JUSTICE: Not that. But —

PRIEST: Say no more. I know. [*Covers his face and weeps.*]
Alas for us all! Alas!

SOLDIER [*enters upstage*]: Is the crown found?

JUSTICE: Not the crown. But —

SOLDIER: Ssh! I know. [*Covers his face.*]

KERSTI'S MOTHER [*enters upstage*]: Is the crown found?

JUSTICE: Alas, no.

MOTHER: Oh! [*Looks at* KERSTI, *who stretches out her
hands towards the handcuffs which* BRITA *is holding out
to her. Screams.*] Ah!

She takes a pair of scissors and cuts KERSTI's *hair,*
which she throws to BRITA, *who catches it and*
smells it as though it smelt good. The MOTHER
tears the veil and bridal jewels from KERSTI, *and*
throws a scarf over her head. MATS *enters upstage,*
stops before KERSTI *and looks at her amazed.*

MATS: Who is this?

BRITA: Look carefully.

MATS [*looks more closely at her*]: She is like someone —

BRITA: Look carefully.

MATS: I do not know her.

BRITA: Would you had never known her!

MATS: Look, her eyes are gone. But her mouth, that
pretty mouth — and that little chin — no, it is not her!
[*Turns his back on her and sees the open hatch.*] What
is that? You stand as though round a grave.

BRITA: It is a grave.

MATS: What lies there?

BRITA: Everything. Everything that mattered in your life.

MATS: Then it is the little one. Who has done this to me?

BRITA: She, she, she!

MATS: It isn't true!

All the others have now silently gathered in the
background.

BRITA: It is true.

MATS: Liar!

SOLDIER [*to* BRITA]: Liar, like all your kin!

MATS' KINSFOLK [*gather left of* KERSTI]: Liars, thieves!
Kersti lies!

KERSTI'S KINSFOLK [*gather to the right*]: Mats lies! Mats!

PRIEST: Peace! Peace! In God's name!

ALL: Peace!

JUSTICE: Let no man prejudge them.

ALL: Let us hear.

JUSTICE: Who accuses?

ALL: Who accuses?

BRITA: I, Brita Lisa Larsson.

ALL: Brita Lisa Larsson accuses. Who stands accused?

BRITA: Kersti Margreta Hansdotter.

ALL: Kersti Margreta Hansdotter! Speak the charge!

BRITA: The bride is tainted and unfit to wear the crown.

KERSTI'S KINSFOLK: Proof, proof!

BRITA: Two witnesses are sufficient.

MATS' KINSFOLK: Two witnesses are sufficient!

KERSTI'S KINSFOLK: We challenge the charge!

JUSTICE: Do not challenge without cause.

BRITA: The mother farmed out her child. If it has died, the mother is guilty of its death.

MATS' KINSFOLK: Guilty of its death!

KERSTI'S KINSFOLK [*move threateningly towards* MATS' KINSFOLK]: Shame on you! Go home!

MATS' KINSFOLK: Shame on *you*!

KERSTI'S KINSFOLK [*to* MATS]: Wretched and vengeful man, yours is the crime! Mats is the guilty one!

MATS' KINSFOLK: Mats is not guilty!

KERSTI'S KINSFOLK: Mats is guilty! He did the deed!

MATS' KINSFOLK [*with raised hands*]: What deed? Ask Kersti!

KERSTI'S KINFOLK: Ask him!

JUSTICE [*to* KERSTI]: Have you killed the child?

KERSTI: I have.

MATS' KINSFOLK: Hear the murderess! [KERSTI'S KINFOLK *give a deep groan.*] Hear the murderess!

> MATS, *who has been standing by the stove with his back to the others, flings away his bridegroom's apparel on the floor, stands motionless for a moment, then runs frenziedly up on to the Old Men's Table and out through the* FIDDLER's *hatch.*

MATS [*as he goes*]: How light it was then, how dark it is now! Little Kersti! Our little one sleeps in the forest!

PRIEST [*covers his face and weeps, then says over the open hatch*]: O Lord, grant peace to the dead, and comfort to those that live!

> ALL *speak a silent prayer behind their hands, as when the Lord's Prayer is read silently in church or at the graveside.*

PRIEST: God bless ye and keep ye.

ALL [*weeping behind their hands*]: Amen.

> *They go out, silent and grieving. When they have gone, leaving* KERSTI *sitting alone, the* JUSTICE *closes and locks the rear doors, then the* FIDDLER's *hatch. A roar as of thunder is heard in the stove.* KERSTI *jumps up, terrified.*

RIVER GOD [*appears in the mill-wheel and sings to his fiddle*]: I hope, I hope that my Redeemer liveth!

> *He repeats this several times.* KERSTI *drops to her knees, raising her manacled hands. The* WHITE CHILD *appears from behind the stove, carrying a*

basket with pine-twigs and flowers. The RIVER
GOD *ends his song and disappears. The* WHITE
CHILD *strews the pine-twigs in front of him so that
they form a kind of path to the hatch in the floor.
When he reaches this, he scatters flowers down it.
The glass harmonica is heard, like the ringing of
bells. Then the* CHILD *goes behind* KERSTI, *who
does not see him, clasps his hands slowly above her
head and looks upwards as though praying.*
KERSTI's *face which had previously expressed
despair, is now calm and happy.*

ACT FIVE

The Penance.
        *Right, the open porch of a country church. It is
glisteningly whitewashed; the roof is of black shingle.*
KERSTI *is lying in the stocks in prison dress, her
head hooded. In the background is a lake and the landscape of Dalecarlia; downstage of this, a jetty. Upstage
right is a spit of land on which is visible a scaffold,
consisting of a platform with a block.*
        At the entrance to the porch TWO SOLDIERS
*with rifles stand at ease. Organ music can be heard
from the church. Two large church-boats enter, one
from the left, the other from the right. The boats glide
forward, the rowers holding their oars aloft. They
jostle for position at the jetty.* MATS' KINSFOLK
are in the boat to the left, KERSTI's *in that to the
right.*

MATS' KINSFOLK: Keep to your water, Meulings!

KERSTI'S KINSFOLK: Keep to yours, millfolk!

MATS' KINSFOLK [*raise their oars threateningly*] : Keep
  away!

KERSTI'S KINSFOLK [*gesture threateningly with their oars*]: You keep away!

MATS' KINSFOLK: Shall eight pairs of oars be the weapons?

KERSTI'S KINSFOLK: Sixteen if need be! Have at ye!

MATS' KINSFOLK: Have at ye!

The two teams fight with their oars.

PRIEST [*bare-headed, in the prow of the left-hand boat*]: Peace! In the name of Jesus Christ, peace!

KERSTI'S KINSFOLK: Peace!

MATS' KINSFOLK: No! Fight to the death!

PRIEST: Peace!

MATS' KINSFOLK: Death!

> *The* VERGER *comes out of the porch and pulls the bell-rope. At the sound of the bell, the oars fall and the boats glide in to the jetty and make fast side by side. From the left boat step, first the* PRIEST, *then* MATS, *carrying a small white coffin trimmed with cotton-lace. Then all* MATS' KINSFOLK *and* FRIENDS. *From the right boat step, first the* SOLDIER, *then* KERSTI'S MOTHER, *then all* KERSTI'S KINSFOLK *and* FRIENDS. *Both parties put their clothes in order, scowling at the other.* MATS *comes forward with the coffin, followed by the* PRIEST.

MATS [*stops in front of* KERSTI. *He looks crazed*]: The little one lies here. Light he is to carry, light as an evil woman's heel. Now he sleeps. Soon you shall sleep.

KERSTI [*lifts her head so that the cowl falls back*]: Oh!

MATS: Yes, you may say O! O is the end; A is the beginning. Between A and O lie many letters, but O is the last. Say O now for the last time — so that the little one hears it. He shall tell of it to the Lord and to the Saviour, so

that you may find forgiveness. Yes. Kiss the white coffin
then, down there by the little feet, the little, little feet
that were never allowed to tread the sinful earth.

KERSTI *kisses the coffin.*

MATS: So. Now we shall go in to play and sing and ring
the bells for the little one — but the priest may not read
for him — that is your fault. But I shall read for him, when
we come to the pit. We shall lay him in the earth like a
seed of corn, to lie and sprout and grow into a flower
which God will give wings so that later it may fly up to
Him on a breath of wind under the midsummer sun.

PRIEST [*takes him by the arm*]: That's enough now, Mats.
Come with me.

MATS: Yes I'm coming.

*They go into the church, the others gradually
following.*

SOLDIER [*stops for a moment in front of* KERSTI, *shakes
his head sorrowfully and tries to get out a few words*]:
Well . . . Well . . . [*Goes into the church.*]

KERSTI'S MOTHER [*drily, trying to be gentle*]: We'll
meet again. Did they hurt you in the prison? [KERSTI
shakes her head.] Is there anything you want? Food or
drink? You can now. Did you get any tobacco in there?
[KERSTI *shakes her head.*] Hold yourself straight,
Kersti, so the millfolk won't mock us. And don't cry so
much. Your father's a soldier and he can't abide that.
[*Puts a prayer-book by her.*] Take this book — and
read where I've put the marker. Look at that marker. I
got it from someone — from someone who'll be thinking
of you at the last. That'll help you against the shakes. I
won't go with you any further, Kersti, because I can't.
I can't because I'm old —

KERSTI: Do as you will, Mother. I have found peace, for
I know that my Redeemer liveth.

KERSTI'S MOTHER: That's all right then, child. That was all I wanted to know. So you won't want me to go with you — ?

KERSTI: No, Mother. Spare yourself. Haven't you had enough trouble with me?

KERSTI'S MOTHER: I can trust you then to see the mill-folk won't have anything to mock us for. I can trust you, so we'll be able to say: Kersti wanted to have it that way, and her last wish is like the written law; it is [*Goes into the church.*]

BRITA [*points towards the scaffold*]: A queen you were born, a crown you got. There's your throne now, heaven above it and hell beneath. You'd not disdain to milk cows now; now you'd gladly gather firewood, scour the pots, rock your child, grease boots — ay, now that you've shamed my kin, your kin, our parish, our county, our country, so the whole land's full of it. Fie on you! [KERSTI *bows her head over the prayer-book.*] My brother must bear your bastard to the grave — *my* brother! But I shall go with you to the block to see you flogged, and I shall be your bridesmaid at the scarlet altar. "Behold a corpse, that is not yet dead; behold a child that is not yet born; behold a bride that shall have no wedding!"

LILL-MATS: Hush, Brita! Kersti is nice. [BRITA *laughs.*] Yes, she is. But she shouldn't wear that ugly cloak, that's more yours. Dear Kersti! Why are you lying here? Is it communion today? And why did you go away from the wedding? Who was in that white box? Is it all a fairy tale? Do you know, I've lost my dolly that you gave me. Kersti, dear Kersti! Why are you sad?

> *He puts his arm round her neck.* KERSTI *clasps him to her breast and kisses him.*

KERSTI: Lill-Mats, Lill-Mats!

BRITA [*to the* SOLDIERS]: Is this allowed?

> *The* SOLDIERS *stand to attention but do not reply.*

BRITA [*takes* LILL-MATS *from* KERSTI]: Come along.

KERSTI: Go with your sister, Lill-Mats. And stay away from me! [*She reads in a whisper from her prayer-book.*]

BRITA [*to* KERSTI]: Shall I tell him?

KERSTI: For God's sake! Not the child!

BRITA: Very well. For the child's sake.

KERSTI: Thank you, Brita. Thank you. For the child's sake.

> BRITA *goes into the church with* LILL-MATS. KERSTI *is left alone. Upstage right the* EXECUTIONER *enters with a large coffin under his arm.* KERSTI *senses his presence although he does not look at her, nor she at him.*

KERSTI: Jesus Christ, Saviour of the world, who suffered and died for us — help me!

MIDWIFE [*enters left and goes over to* EXECUTIONER]: Excuse me, kind sir. Can I stand beside you — when it happens — for I need a little red, for a sick person, a sick person who's failing?

> *The* EXECUTIONER *goes out left without replying.*

MIDWIFE: I see! One of those ones that won't let you speak to them. [*Goes over to* KERSTI]: Ah, there's my little — !

KERSTI [*with a gesture of repulsion*]: Get away from me!

MIDWIFE [*behind a pillar, unseen by the* SOLDIERS]: Wait a minute, wait a minute! Now listen, little maid. What other people can't do, I can. The clock will soon strike, and the Black Man waits.

KERSTI: Get away from me, in Jesus' name!

MIDWIFE: Listen to me! I can do what others can't. I can help you to get free.

KERSTI: I have found my helper. Jesus Christ.

MIDWIFE: But I can do things to the judge —

KERSTI: He Who judgeth the living and the dead, He Who is the life and the resurrection, has condemned me to temporal death and — eternal life!

MIDWIFE: Look at the soldiers, they're sleeping. Take my cloak and run!

KERSTI: The soldiers sleeping?

MIDWIFE: With closed eyes. Run, run, run!

KERSTI [*lies down again*]: No! Rather fall into the hands of the living God. Get away from me!

She raises her prayer-book with the gold cross on the cover. The MIDWIFE *shrinks.*

MIDWIFE: Shall we meet one Thursday night at the cross-roads?

KERSTI: On the road of the cross I shall meet my Redeemer, but not you! Get away from me!

MIDWIFE [*shrinks*]: There's a boat by the shore and a horse and cart on land. Mats is there; the justice isn't there. Run, run, run!

KERSTI [*fights with herself*]: O God! Lead us not into temptation! But deliver us from evil!

MIDWIFE: Tch, tch, tch, tch! Horse and cart!

KERSTI *seizes the church bellrope and pulls it thrice. At the third peal, the* MIDWIFE *runs out, squeaking and hissing. The* WHITE CHILD *appears from behind a pillar. He is dressed in a Rättvik (Dalecarlian) girl's dress, but everything is white, even his shoes.*

KERSTI [*as though blinded*]: Who are you, little child? who come when the evil one goes? [*The* WHITE CHILD *puts his finger on his lips.*] White as snow, white as flax. Why are you white?

WHITE CHILD [*softly*]: Your faith has saved you. Hope has engendered faith. [*Approaches* KERSTI.]

KERSTI: Oh, my dear, don't tread on that ant!

WHITE CHILD [*bends down and seems to pick up something on a leaf*]: But greatest is love, love of all living things, big and small. Now the ant will go back to the forest and tell the Ant-King, and then the ant people will come and gnaw through your rope and you will be free.

KERSTI: Oh, no! Don't talk like that!

WHITE CHILD: Doubt not, but believe. Believe! Kersti! Believe!

KERSTI: How can I?

WHITE CHILD: Believe!

> *He goes out behind the pillar. It grows dark. The* RIVER GOD *appears on the lake with his harp.*

RIVER GOD [*sings as before*]: I hope, I hope, that my Redeemer liveth.

KERSTI: He sings to me of the Redeemer. He gives me hope! But I gave him none.

> *The* RIVER GOD *sinks into the lake. The* JUSTICE *enters right, reading a document. He comes over to* KERSTI, *a few paces at a time, looking alternately at the ground and at the document.*

JUSTICE: Kersti!

> *She looks up, and at once bows her head.*

JUSTICE [*slowly with pauses*]: Look at the justice! You only fear him. Is it so with all men? Imagine a case when people send for the justice that he may help those who are in need. Is he welcome? But — my goodness! Kersti, have you ever seen so many ants? [*She raises her head and listens.*] Look how they run in groups, in lines! Just look! You know what that means? It means good. You never believe any good of me. You didn't believe me *that* time either — and so you were found out. Look at

the ants! Look at them! Now they are approaching you,
Kersti. Aren't you afraid?

KERSTI: I have been, but am no longer.

JUSTICE: Big forest ants — and I do believe the King
himself is with them. What can the King do, which
other powers cannot? Do you know? Other powers can
judge; all can judge, harshly or gently. But only one can
grant mercy. That is the King. Shall we ask the Ant King
if he will grant mercy? [*Puts his hand to his ear, as though
listening.*] Will the Ant King grant mercy, from the
worst thing of all? Did you hear what he answered? I
think he said yes. But I may have heard wrong. And I
don't trust what I hear, I am a justice and like things
to be in writing. We shall ask the Ant King to write, he
has so many pens in his forest, small sharp steel pens
like nails; and he carries his own ink, that stings and burns!
If only we had some paper [*Pretends to search in his
pocket and takes out the document he had been reading.*]
Why, bless my soul! Look, the King has written this with
his own hand. There it is C-A-R-L, Carl! [*Raises his cap.*]
Such big letters you haven't seen since you were at
school, Kersti. And this red seal that smells so good, like
resin in the forest when the sun shines hot. And these gold
and blue silk ribbons — and this lion, these crowns —
they're the King's too. Read for yourself, Kersti, and I'll
see to the soldiers.

> KERSTI *takes the document. The* JUSTICE *talks
> softly to the* SOLDIERS, *who go.* KERSTI *has read
> the document, and hands it back, calmly and gravely.*

JUSTICE: Are you happy, Kersti?

KERSTI: I am grateful, that my kinsfolk and yours have
been spared the greatest shame. Happy, no, I am not, for
a life in chains is less than the eternal life.

JUSTICE: Regard it as a time of preparation.

KERSTI: I will.

JUSTICE: Are you still afraid of me?

KERSTI: I fear nothing, now that I have looked at death.

JUSTICE: Come with me, then.

KERSTI: Free me, then.

> The JUSTICE *unfastens the rope. Organ music is heard from the church.* KERSTI *lifts her hands towards heaven.*

EPILOGUE

> *A great ice-covered lake, with a distant shore beyond. The ice is covered with snow. The floor of the stage is also ice. On this can be seen the winter road marked out with pine-branches. A big square fishing-hole up-stage centre, lined with spruce-branches. On the fringe of this hole lie long-tailed ducks, singing.* * *Around it small sticks with fishing-lines hanging in the water. In the background can be seen the prison, an ugly old building with towers and battlements. It is dark.*
>
> *The* FISHERMAN *enters right, in a fur coat with sledge and ice-hook. The ducks dive into the water. He begins to examine the fishing-lines. The* MIDWIFE *enters left.*

MIDWIFE: Fishing on Easter morning?

FISHERMAN: I'm not fishing. I'm only seeing if I've caught anything.

MIDWIFE: Clever, eh? Are you clever enough to tell an old woman who's lost her way where she is?

FISHERMAN: Can I borrow a light, then?

MIDWIFE: Give me a flint and steel, then.

---

*Strindberg was interested in an old Swedish legend about ducks that sing.

FISHERMAN [*hands her two pieces of ice*] : Try with these.

MIDWIFE: Ice? Well, water's fire and fire's water. [*Tears a strip from her cloak and strikes the ice-bits against each other. Sets fire to the strip and hands it to the* FISHERMAN, *who lights his pipe with it.*]

FISHERMAN: I know where I ought to be when I see you.

MIDWIFE: But where am I?

FISHERMAN: In the middle of Crookdyke's lake, and that's his castle. Crookdyke was a king in olden times. Like Herod, he had all the little boys murdered, because he was worried about his crown. But now that castle of his holds all the girls who didn't worry enough about *their* crowns.

MIDWIFE: What are they doing there?

FISHERMAN: Spinning flax.

MIDWIFE: It's a spinning-mill, then?

FISHERMAN: You could say that.

MIDWIFE: But this lake?

FISHERMAN: Ah, there's a story! Where you see this lake there used to be land. On this land stood a church. There was a fight about that church. This fight was about seating arrangements. The millfolk who were the grandest around here wanted to sit closest to the altar, but the Meulings were stronger. There was a great battle one Easter Day and blood was spilled. The church was desecrated, and could never be made clean. So it was closed and left desolate, and sank into the earth and fifteen ells of water rose above the cock on the steeple. And now the lake's washed it and washed it for hundreds of years, but as long as the millfolk and the Meulings fight, God's house can never be clean.

MIDWIFE: Why are they called Meulings?

FISHERMAN: Because they're descended from the child-murderer, Crookdyke.

MIDWIFE: And they're still fighting?

FISHERMAN: Still fighting, and still murdering. You remember Kersti, the soldier's daughter?

MIDWIFE: I'll say I do.

FISHERMAN: She's in that prison. But today she must do her yearly penance at the altar.

MIDWIFE: I see.

FISHERMAN: The Meulings will fetch her and the millfolk will come to watch.

MIDWIFE: Do you hear how the ice sings?

FISHERMAN: I'll say I do.

MIDWIFE: Is the thaw coming?

FISHERMAN: Could be.

MIDWIFE: It'll break away from the shores, then?

FISHERMAN: Most of it, yes. But if the water rises it'll run out into the waterfall down there.

MIDWIFE: Is the fall far from here?

FISHERMAN: No. You can hear the kelpie clearly.

MIDWIFE: Kelpie?

FISHERMAN: That's what we call the god of the waterfall. He's about today. He's expecting something.

MIDWIFE: What can he be expecting?

FISHERMAN: You know.

MIDWIFE: I don't. Tell. me.

FISHERMAN: Well, they *say* . . . that every Easter morning, when the Saviour rose out of his grave, Crookdyke's church rises out of the water. And whoever sees it has peace for the year.

The MIDWIFE *gallops out right, squeaking and hissing.*

FISHERMAN: That was ill met. [*Draws up a fish and takes it off the line.*] Aha, my beauty! [*The fish jumps into the water-hole. The* FISHERMAN *gropes for him with his net. Several fish stick their heads out of the water.*] Dumb, but not deaf, are ye? "Who calls higher than the crane? Who is whiter than the swan?"

THE WHITE CHILD [*enters left on skis with a torch, again in a white, Rättvik girl's dress*]: The thunder of heaven calls higher than the crane. Whiter than the swan is he who never doeth evil!

The fishes disappear.

FISHERMAN: Who solved my riddle?

WHITE CHILD: Who loosed the captive's bonds, who loosed the fish's tongue?

FISHERMAN: No one!

WHITE CHILD: No one of human born, but one born of the creator God. He who built the bridge of glass can break it. Take care!

He goes out right. The FISHERMAN *gathers together his things. The* MILLFOLK (MATS' FAMILY) *enter left, on skis with staves.* MATS *carries a torch.*

MATS: Where is the winter path?

FISHERMAN: Did you see the fish's path in the water?

MATS: But the horse's in the snow?

FISHERMAN: Is that the path to the council or the path to church?

MILLFOLK: The path to church!

FISHERMAN: All paths lead to the waterfall for those who stray. [*The ice thunders.*] The ice is breaking!

MILLFOLK: Where is the path to church?

FISHERMAN: You stand on it, you are walking on it. Soon it will be here.

MILLFOLK: Is this Crookdyke's lake?

FISHERMAN: Crookdyke's lake and Crookdyke's pound; Crookdyke's church will soon be drowned!

MILLFOLK: God protect us!

> *They go out right. The* MEULINGS (KERSTI'S FAMILY) *enter left with staves, on skis. The* SOLDIER *carries a torch.*

MEULINGS: Where is the path to church?

FISHERMAN: This is the path to the fall. Turn back.

MEULINGS: The ice is breaking, the water is rising! The ice is parting from the shore!

FISHERMAN: Go eastwards. The sun awaits you.

MEULINGS: Eastwards!

> *They go out right. The* MILLFOLK *re-enter right.*

FISHERMAN: Turn back! The ice has parted from the western shore!

MILLFOLK: And from the eastern! Come north!

FISHERMAN: There lies the river.

MILLFOLK: South, then!

FISHERMAN: There lies the fall!

MILLFOLK [*rest on their staves, beaten*]: God have mercy on us!

MATS: The Meulings laid a false trail!

BRITA: As always.

MATS' FATHER: They took the first place in church!

GRANDFATHER: A grievous matter. But that day I burned the documents — I do not bless that day.

MATS' MOTHER: When shall we find peace?

GRANDFATHER: "The nobly meek live purest, and seldom harbour sorrow."

MILLFOLK [*raise their staves*]: The Meulings!

MEULINGS [*enter right, with raised staves*]: Millfolk! Stand! You have laid a false trail!

MILLFOLK: Liars!

MEULINGS: Ye are liars!

MILLFOLK: Perjurers!

MEULINGS: Ye are the perjurers!

  The ice thunders.

FISHERMAN: Peace in Jesus' name! The water is rising!

ALL [*cry fearfully*]: The water is rising!

MATS' GRANDFATHER: The ice is sinking! Stay where you are!

MATS' GRANDMOTHER: For we must die! And after this, the judgement!

  The MILLFOLK *embrace each other. The women take up their children and clasp them to their breasts. The* MEULINGS *do likewise.*

MATS' MOTHER [*to* MATS]: Because of your mad love, we must die!

KERSTI'S MOTHER: Let no man censure another man's love. "Beauty oft ensnareth the wise man, seldom the fool."

SOLDIER: For this fault let no man censure him. Love is powerful. It turns the sons of men from wise men into fools.

MATS [*stretches out his hand to the* SOLDIER] : Thank you for those words. I once called you Father!

SOLDIER: Death makes us all one —

MATS' FATHER: So say I. Give me your hand.

SOLDIER [*hesitantly stretches out his hand*] : Here it is. We are Christian men, and today is Easter, the day of reconciliation. Let the sun not rise on our wrath.

MEULINGS: Reconciliation!

MILLFOLK: Reconciliation!

> The TWO FAMILIES *approach each other with outstretched hands. The ice thunders, and a great crack splits it, dividing the two parties.*

MATS' GRANDFATHER: Divided in life, divided in death!

MATS' GRANDMOTHER: The bridge broke under the weight of our sins.

MATS' MOTHER: Where is Kersti?

MILLFOLK: Where is Kersti?

MEULINGS: Where is Kersti?

SOLDIER: Behold, it was good that one died for the people.

MATS' GRANDFATHER: Then said they unto him: "What shall we do unto thee, that the sea may be calm unto us?"

KERSTI'S MOTHER: "Take me up and cast me into the sea. For I know that for my sake this great tempest is upon you."

MATS' GRANDMOTHER: Is it spoken?

ALL: It is spoken!

KERSTI'S MOTHER: Behold the fire and the wood; but where is the lamb for a burnt offering?

MEULINGS: Where is Kersti?

MILLFOLK: Where is Kersti?

The PRIEST *enters with the* VERGER.

PRIEST [*to* SOLDIER]: The Lord said: "Lay not thine hand upon the child, for now I know that thou fearest God, seeing thou hast not withheld thine only child from me."

ALL [*to* PRIEST]: Save us!

PRIEST: There is but one God, one Saviour. Pray to Him!

ALL *kneel.*

PRIEST: Out of the deep I cry unto Thee, O God!

ALL: Lord, hear my voice!

PRIEST: Lord, have mercy upon us!

ALL: Christ, have mercy upon us!

PRIEST: Lord, have mercy upon us!

ALL: Christ have mercy upon us!

The JUSTICE *enters upstage, with a torch, accompanied by* FOUR SOLDIERS *carrying* KERSTI's *body.* ALL *rise.*

PRIEST: Who is that that you bear?

JUSTICE: We bear the virgin bride. We bear Kersti.

PRIEST: Is she alive?

JUSTICE: She is dead. The waters took her.

PRIEST: May the Lord receive her soul!

SOLDIERS: O God, look mercifully upon our offering, since Thou didst offer Thyself for our sake.

PRIEST: For God so loved the world that He gave His only son.

BRITA: The water is sinking!

ALL: The water is sinking!

The ice meets across the crack. MATS *and* BRITA *go across to the* MEULINGS, *break pine and spruce-branches and scatter them over* KERSTI's *body.*

PRIEST: Is there peace now?

ALL: Peace! And reconciliation!

PRIEST [*over* KERSTI's *body*]: O Lord, grant the dead peace, and comfort to those that live!

The church rises from the lake in the background; first the golden cock, then the cross and the globe, the steeple and the white semi-circular church with its black shingle roof. The RIVER GOD *is heard far off, but now in D minor.*

RIVER GOD [*sings*]: I hope, I hope, that my Redeemer liveth!

PRIEST: Thank and praise the Lord!

ALL: The Lord be thanked and praised!

MATS *and* BRITA *kneel by* KERSTI's *body.*

ALL [*sing, kneeling*]:
O God, we praise Thee! O God, we thank Thee!
Eternal Father, all things worship Thee!
The angels, heavens and all powers praise Thee!
To Thee cherubim and seraphim continually cry
Holy, Holy, Holy, Lord God of Sabaoth!

Introduction to

A DREAM PLAY

STRINDBERG wrote A DREAM PLAY in 1901, at the
age of fifty-two. It was his favourite among all his
works; in a letter to his publisher, Karl-Otto Bonnier,
on 31 August 1906, he said that he prized it more than any
thing he had written, and on 17 April 1907 he described it
to his German translator, Emil Schering, as "my most
beloved play, child of my greatest pain". The matter and
mood of it stemmed directly from his third, final and vol-
canic marriage, with the Norwegian actress Harriet Bosse.

In 1900, while searching for someone to act the Lady
in TO DAMASCUS, which was shortly to be staged by
the Royal Theatre, he had seen Harriet, then aged twenty-
two*, act Puck in A MIDSUMMER NIGHT'S DREAM. He
at once chose her for the Lady; the same year, he wrote
EASTER for her; and the following May they married. But
the marriage was a failure, as his two earlier ones had been;
he was nearly thirty years older than Harriet, and she was
as domineering a personality as he was. "We are now convinced that our union will be a lasting one, for we are living
in complete harmony," he wrote in his diary on 25 June;
but the following day she left him "without saying goodbye,
without saying where she was going"; returned to him in
August, pregnant, but left again the same month. "I
cannot be trampled in the dirt," she wrote to him on 27
August. "Rather than face a horrible future, full of unjust
insults and pain for us both, I am going now, while I still
have fresh in my memory all you have given me that is
beautiful." Ten days later Strindberg bitterly noted in his
diary:

"E. V. Hartman says that love is a farce invented by
nature to fool men and women into propagating their

*She is sometimes described as having been nineteen when they met,
but she was born on 19 February 1878.

species. Life disgusts me and has always done so. Everything is worthless ! . . . People are not born wicked, but
life makes them wicked. So life cannot be an education,
nor can it be a punishment (which improves); it is simply
an evil! . . . Resignation! Yes, that is what I tried last. But
if you put up with everything, you have in the end to
endure filth and humiliation, and that is what you have
no right to do!"

He meditated suicide much that autumn. "The impulse
to die by my own hand grows stronger," he noted on 25
September. "It will soon be irresistible . . . My blood shall
atone for my past, and with my blood my longing for evil
will be obliterated . . . I have lived as I could, and not as I
should have wished." Yet on 4 October he dined with
Harriet and they made love; and the following day, three
and a half months' pregnant, she returned to live with him.
Such was the background against which, over the next six
and a half weeks, he composed A DREAM PLAY.

He based it on a straightforward realistic play which
he had drafted earlier in the year, entitled THE CORRIDOR
DRAMA. In this, a composer has been waiting seven years
for his opera to be performed, and seven years for a wife.
Now his opera has been accepted, he has become engaged,
and is waiting at the theatre for his fiancée, a singer who
has achieved success in his opera; as a sequel to their mutual
triumph, they are to marry and go to the south. But she
does not come; the summer passes, the roses wither, and at
last he hears that she has gone abroad alone. The composer
dies, and the stage-door keeper scatters roses over him.
Strindberg stopped work on this when Harriet first left
him that June, took it up again, according to his diary, on
22 August a few hours before he received a letter from
Harriet telling him that she had left him for good, and
finally, after their reunion in October, re-worked it as
A DREAM PLAY (though when he completed it on 18
November he called it THE RISING CASTLE).

In a short preface to the play, he explained his
intention:

"In this dream play, the author has, as in his former

dream play, TO DAMASCUS, attempted to imitate the
inconsequent yet transparently logical shape of a dream.
Everything can happen, everything is possible and
probable. Time and place do not exist; on an insignificant
basis of reality, the imagination spins, weaving new
patterns; a mixture of memories, experiences, free fancies,
incongruities and improvisations. The characters split,
double, multiply, evaporate, condense, disperse, assemble.
But one consciousness rules over them all, that of the
dreamer; for him there are no secrets, no illogicalities,
no scruples, no laws. He neither acquits nor condemns, but
merely relates; and, as a dream is more often painful than
happy, so an undertone of melancholy and of pity for all
mortal beings accompanies this flickering tale."

   Strindberg had long been preoccupied with dreams,
He had studied with fascination Edgar Allan Poe's treatment
of them (Poe was, with Dickens, one of his favourite authors)
and, in 1899 he had been greatly impressed by Rudyard
Kipling's story IN THE LAND OF DREAMS, in which two
people have the same dream in which they meet. This pre-
occupation had been intensified since his meeting with
Harriet; he had felt that he was moving in a dream world.
A week after their engagement, on 13 March 1901, he
wrote: "In what land of dreams I am living I know not,
but I dread descending again to reality." And on 2
November 1901, a fortnight before he finished A DREAM
PLAY, he wrote to the painter Carl Larsson: "Life becomes
more and more dreamlike and inexplicable to me.
Perhaps death really is the awakening." His diary during
this year is full of details of his own dreams; and on 18
November, the day he finished A DREAM PLAY he noted:

   Am reading about Indian religions.

   The whole world is but a semblance (= Humbug or
relative emptiness). The primary Divine Power (Maham-
Atma, Tad, Aum, Brama), allowed itself to be seduced by
Maya, or the impulse of procreation.

   Thus the Divine Primary Element sinned against

itself. (Love is sin, therefore the pangs of love are the greatest of all hells.)

The world has come into existence only through Sin — if in fact it exists at all — for it is really only a dream picture (consequently my DREAM PLAY is a picture of life), a phantom, and the ascetic's allotted task is to destroy it. But this task conflicts with the love impulse, and the sum total of it all is a ceaseless wavering between sensual orgies and the anguish of repentance.

This would seem to be the riddle of the world.

I turned up the above in [Arvid Ahnfelt's] History of Literature, just as I was about to finish my Dream Play, THE GROWING CASTLE, on the morning of the 18th. On this same morning I saw the Castle (= Horseguards' Barracks) illuminated, as it were, by the rising sun.

Indian religion, therefore, showed me the meaning of my DREAM PLAY, and the significance of Indra's Daughter, and the Secret of the Door = Nothingness.

Read Buddhism all day.

The dream technique, with its swift and apparently irrelevant cutting from one scene to another, was, as Strindberg stated in his preface to A DREAM PLAY, something that he had practised in TO DAMASCUS, where likewise we can never be sure what is real and what is imagined. For years he had been fascinated by magic lanterns, with their similar capacity to provide seemingly disconnected yet suggestively relevant images. On 14 September 1904 he referred to them to describe his own idyllic memories of that summer. "Those were only magic lantern pictures I gave you from Furusund. *Förvandlingsbilder,* dissolving views.* But that's what life is."

As with every play that Strindberg wrote (including

*Thus in the Swedish original; Strindberg added the English words "dissolving views" as a translation of *förvandlingsbilder,* which literally means "transformation pictures".

some twenty historical ones), A DREAM PLAY includes
much that is identifiable as direct personal experience. The
"Rising Castle" in which the Officer is imprisoned was, as
his diary implies, the new cavalry barracks with its gilded
onion-shaped dome ("the most beautiful building in
Stockholm", he called it in an essay), which he could see
from his windows in Karlavägen. Like the Officer, he had
waited in the corridor of the Royal Theatre, first for Siri
more than twenty years before, and more recently for
Harriet. There was a door there with a clover-shaped
hole, and he had often wondered where it led to.
Fairhaven, to which the Officer flees with Agnes, was
the coastal resort of Fagervik (literally "Fair Bay"), just
outside Stockholm. Strindberg used to stay there with his
brother-in-law, Hugo Philp, who on gaining his doctorate
in 1896 had become a schoolmaster and had had to re-
learn his early and forgotten knowledge in order to teach
beginners. Strindberg himself had a recurrent nightmare of
finding himself a schoolboy again, threatened by the cane;
hence the classroom scene, where the Officer sits at a small
desk, unable to multiply two by two. At Fagervik he
had met a jeweller and art collector named Christian Hammer,
who owned the island, and had lost his sight. He too was
to appear in the play, as the Blind Man. In 1899, Strindberg
had seen the Baths Doctor there, Elias Nordström, go to a
ball wearing a Moorish mask; hence the Quarantine Master,
Ordström, with his blackened face and sulphur ovens
(there had been a cholera outbreak at Fagervik some years
before). Opposite Fagervik lay Skarmsund, which Strindberg, by the removal of a single letter, altered to Skamsund
(literally Shame-Sound = Foulstrand). The incident of the
degree ceremony probably stemmed from a rumour which
had reached Strindberg's ears the previous year that he was
to be given a doctorate at the University of Lund. The
childhood scene with the Officer's parents is directly autobiographical; so are the marriage scenes between the
Advocate and Agnes. Strindberg once stated that a carefree
lieutenant named Jean Lundin, whom he had known
twenty years earlier when he was writing THE RED ROOM,

was the original of the Officer; but Strindberg himself was the principal original of that character, and of the Advocate and the Poet (as of most of his leading male characters, in everything he wrote).

Like PEER GYNT, the last act of which is also a dream play, Strindberg's A DREAM PLAY was regarded, on publication, as unstageable, and it was not until more than five years later, on 17 April 1907, that it received its first performance, with Harriet Bosse in the dual role of Indra's Daughter and Agnes. Strindberg, following his usual custom, did not attend (he seldom saw any of his plays after the dress rehearsal); but he noted in his diary: "At 11 o'clock this evening Harriet, Castengren [the director] and Ranft [the theatre owner] telephoned to say that A DREAM PLAY had been a success. T.b.t.g. [Thanks be to God]!" There had been problems; Castengren had planned to use magic lantern slides to provide the various scenic effects, but the German apparatus gave trouble in rehearsal, and they had to resort to ordinary décor which, Strindberg recorded in his OPEN LETTERS TO THE INTIMATE THEATRE, "disturbed the actors' mood and caused interminable intervals; moreover, the whole thing became materialized, instead of the intended opposite, i.e. dematerialization". Yet the audience admired it, and at first refused to leave until the author had taken his call, so that Albert Ranft had to come forward and promise to telephone their approbation to him.

In 1921 Max Reinhardt, whose productions of THE DANCE OF DEATH, THE PELICAN and THE GHOST SONATA had established him as a Strindberg pioneer, directed A DREAM PLAY in Stockholm; but it had a mixed reception, and the first really successful perform- ance was in 1935 when Olof Molander, a great Strind- berg director, staged it in the Swedish capital, underlin- ing the realism of the play by using immediately recognizable Stockholm locations against a background of darkness pierced only by the occasional spotlight, with an imaginative use of the forestage so that the characters sometimes seemed to move out of their surroundings into

the audience. Molander directed four further productions
of the play during the next twenty years, in each instance
using the full technical resources of the theatre, so that
A DREAM PLAY came to be thought of as a "spectacular".
I saw Molander's final production, in 1955, and remember
its huge and varied visual effects. It was a very impressive,
very long evening; one watched the spectacle with
admiration but no sense of involvement; the play seemed
remote and dated. Nor was the effect different when
Ingmar Bergman directed it for Swedish television in 1963,
with Ingrid Thulin as Indra's Daughter and Agnes — a
production which the director himself regarded as a failure.

In 1970 Bergman directed the play again, on stage at
the Royal Theatre of Stockholm, and this time he treated
it very differently. He presented it in the small studio
auditorium of the Royal Theatre, which seats only three
hundred and fifty people, judiciously cut and without an
interval, so that the performance lasted under two hours,
and virtually without décor. In other words, laying his
usual emphasis on close personal contact between actors
and audience, he offered it not as a spectacular but as a
chamber play like THE GHOST SONATA, and the
difference was extraordinary. What had previously seemed
verbose and antiquated now sprang to life. For décor, he
used only a black backdrop with the minimum of
properties, varied by a white backdrop for the scenes at
Fairhaven, the inhabitants of which were likewise dressed
in white. He dispensed totally with Strindberg's elaborate
stage directions, such as "the flower bud on the roof
blossoms forth into a huge chrysanthemum", which made
the play seem particularly old-fashioned when I saw the
Molander production in 1955, and considerably shortened
the final third of the play. Bergman's adaptation has been
published in English (Secker & Warburg, London, The
Dial Press, New York and P. A. Norstedt, Stockholm,
1973), and to my mind works far better on the stage than
the full version as printed here; some great plays (BRAND
is another) need bold cutting and transposition for their
stageability (as opposed to their literary worth) to become

apparent, and students may find it instructive to compare
that imaginative and poetically faithful adaptation with
Strindberg's full original — remembering Strindberg's
advice to August Falck when the latter was about to direct
the first Swedish production of THE FATHER in 1887:
"Cut more if you wish! You'll hear at rehearsal what doesn't
work."

At the time of writing, A DREAM PLAY has never
received a full-scale production in London, though Pax
Robertson bravely presented it at her Chelsea Arts Theatre
in 1930, and G. R. Schjelderup directed a single performance at the Grafton Theatre (off the Tottenham Court
Road) in 1933, with Donald Wolfit as the Officer. It was
performed on English sound radio in 1948 and 1957.
Ingmar Bergman's Swedish production visited the Aldwych
Theatre during the World Theatre Season of 1971, and
created a memorable impression, and on 2 May 1974 Michael
Ockrent directed it excitingly at the Traverse Theatre, Edinburgh, using only nine players to portray the more-than-
forty characters — a production that was successfully revived
later in the year for the Edinburgh Festival. Ockrent
employed the unusual device of having three actresses play
Agnes simultaneously on three different physical levels and
in different characterizations, to suggest her various aspects.
Cordelia Oliver in the *Guardian* described the performance
as "gripping the imagination from the first moment when,
one by one, on different levels like hallucinations, the
intense faces of the women float, disembodied, in the black-
ness", and Irving Wardle in the *Times* praised its "violently
abrupt changes of rhythm, particularly where it erupts into
Parisian gallops and blazing organ sonorities", and its
"startling expressionistic imagery". Completely different in
conception from the Bergman production, it did not suffer
by comparison.

AUTHOR'S NOTE

In this dream play the author has, as in his former
dream play, TO DAMASCUS, attempted to imitate the
inconsequent yet transparently logical shape of a dream.
Everything can happen, everything is possible and probable.
Time and place do not exist; on an insignificant basis of
reality the imagination spins, weaving new patterns; a mixture of memories, experiences, free fancies, incongruities
and improvisations. The characters split, double, multiply,
evaporate, condense, disperse, assemble. But one consciousness rules over them all, that of the dreamer; for him
there are no secrets, no illogicalities, no scruples, no laws.
He neither acquits nor condemns, but merely relates; and,
just as a dream is more often painful than happy, so an
undertone of melancholy and of pity for all mortal beings
accompanies this flickering tale. Sleep, the liberator,
often seems a tormentor, but when the agony is harshest
comes the awakening and reconciles the sufferer with
reality — which, however painful, is yet a mercy, compared
with the agony of the dream.

A DREAM PLAY

(1901)

This translation of A DREAM PLAY was first
performed, in an adaptation by Ingmar Bergman, at the
Lyric Players Theatre, Belfast, on 28 February 1973. The
cast was:

THE POET	Hamish Roughead
AGNES	Kathleen McClay
GLAZIER	Michael Duffy
OFFICER	Pitt Wilkinson
FATHER	Louis Rolston
MOTHER	Trudy Kelly
LINA	Maureen Dow
INDRA	Peter Templar
INDRA'S DAUGHTER	Linda Wray
STAGE-DOOR KEEPER	Maureen Dow
BILL-POSTER	Peter Templar
VICTORIA	Pat Smylie
DANCER	Pat Smylie
SINGER	Trudy Kelly
PROMPTER	Clem Davies
POLICEMAN	William Walker
ADVOCATE	John Franklyn
KRISTIN	Trudy Kelly
QUARANTINE MASTER	John Keenan
FIRST SICK MAN	Alan Bryce
SECOND SICK MAN	Peter Templar
DON JUAN	Maurice O'Callaghan
COQUETTE	Maureen Dow
HE	Clem Davies
PENSIONER	Michael Duffy
FIRST COAL-CARRIER	William Hamilton
SECOND COAL-CARRIER	William Walker
GENTLEMAN	Alan Bryce
HIS WIFE	Maureen Dow
EDITH	Pat Smylie
HER MOTHER	Trudy Kelly
NAVAL OFFICER	John Pine

ALICE	Alison Kelly
BLIND MAN	Louis Rolston
SCHOOLMASTER	Maurice O'Callaghan
BOYS	Andrew Kennedy, John O'Reilly, John O'Rourke
CHANCELLOR	Alex McClay
DEAN OF THEOLOGY	Pat Brannigan
DEAN OF PHILOSOPHY	William Hamilton
DEAN OF MEDICINE	Maurice O'Callaghan
DEAN OF LAW	John Pine

Designed by John L. Stark
Directed by Donald Bodley

On 2 May 1974 it was performed at the Traverse Theatre, Edinburgh. The cast was:

POET	Roger Kemp
AGNES	Maggie Jordan, Janet Amsden, Susan Carpenter
GLAZIER, QUARANTINE MASTER, SCHOOLMASTER, A COAL-CARRIER	Simon Callow
OFFICER	James Snell
FATHER, ADVOCATE, A GENTLEMAN	Roy Marsden
BILL-POSTER, A COAL-CARRIER, BLIND MAN	Richard Vanstone
LINA, KRISTIN, EDITH	Lyndy Lawson

Designed by Poppy Mitchell
Directed by Michael Ockrent

CHARACTERS

INDRA
*INDRA'S DAUGHTER
*AGNES
THE GLAZIER
THE OFFICER
HIS FATHER
HIS MOTHER
LINA
THE STAGE-DOOR KEEPER
THE BILL-POSTER
A BALLET DANCER
A SINGER
A PROMPTER
A POLICEMAN
THE ADVOCATE
KRISTIN
THE QUARANTINE MASTER
A DANDY
A COQUETTE
HER "FRIEND"
THE POET
HE
SHE
A PENSIONER
EDITH
EDITH'S MOTHER
A NAVAL OFFICER
ALICE
THE SCHOOLMASTER
A NEWLY-MARRIED HUSBAND
A NEWLY-MARRIED WIFE
THE BLIND MAN

*The parts of Indra's Daughter and Agnes are sometimes doubled, sometimes played by separate actresses. (Translator's note)

FIRST COAL-CARRIER
SECOND COAL-CARRIER
A GENTLEMAN
HIS WIFE
THE CHANCELLOR
DEAN OF THEOLOGY
DEAN OF PHILOSOPHY
DEAN OF MEDICINE
DEAN OF LAW

DANCERS, SINGERS, CLERKS, CHILDREN,
SCHOOLBOYS, SAILORS, ETC.

PRELUDE

[*A background of banks of cloud like crumbling slate mountains, with ruined castles and fortresses. The constellations of Leo, Virgo and Libra are visible. Between them shining brightly, is the planet Jupiter.* INDRA'S DAUGHTER *is standing on the topmost cloud.*] *

INDRA'S VOICE [*from above*] :
   Where are you, daughter, where?

INDRA'S DAUGHTER:
   Here, Father, here!

INDRA'S VOICE:
   You have lost your way, child. Take care, you are falling.
   How did you come here?

INDRA'S DAUGHTER:
   I followed the lightning flash from furthest space,
   And rode upon a cloud.
   But the cloud began to fall, and I fall with it.
   Say, mighty father, Indra, what strange regions
   Are these? The air is sparse and hard to breathe.

INDRA'S VOICE:
   You have left the second world and entered the third.
   Beyond Cukra, the morning star,
   You have passed far, and enter now
   The vaporous realm of earth. [Mark there
   The seventh house of the sun, that men call Libra.
   The day-star stands at the balance-point of autumn,
   When day and night weigh equal.]

   *The passages enclosed in bold brackets, [ ], are those cut by Ingmar Bergman in his adaptation of the play (see p. 551). He also made numerous transpositions which it has been impracticable to indicate here.

INDRA'S DAUGHTER:
> You said the earth. Is that this dark
> And gloomy world illumined by the moon?

INDRA'S VOICE:
> It is the densest and the heaviest
> Of the spheres that roam in space.

[INDRA'S DAUGHTER:
> Does the sun never shine there?

INDRA'S VOICE:
> The sun shines there indeed, but not perpetually.

INDRA'S DAUGHTER:
> The cloud is parting, and I see down there —

INDRA'S VOICE:
> What do you see, child?

INDRA'S DAUGHTER:
> I see . . . that there is beauty. Green forests,
> Blue waters, white mountains and yellow fields —

INDRA'S VOICE:
> Yes. It is fair, like all that Brahma made.
> But it was once yet fairer there,
> In the morn of time. Then something happened.
> A shaking of the orbit; perhaps more.
> Revolt followed by crime, that had to be quelled.]

INDRA'S DAUGHTER:
> Now I hear sounds from down there.
> What race dwells there?

INDRA'S VOICE:
> Descend and see.
> I speak no ill of the Creator's children.
> But what you hear rise upwards is their speech.

INDRA'S DAUGHTER:
> It sounds like . . . It has not a joyful sound.

[INDRA'S VOICE:
> You do not surprise me. Their mother tongue

Is named complaint. The people of the earth
Are a discontented and ungrateful race.

INDRA'S DAUGHTER:

Do not say so. Now I hear cries of joy,
And shots, and boomings. I see lightnings flash.
Bells ring, and fires are lit, and many thousand
Thousand voices sing praise and thanks to heaven.
[*Pause.*]
You judge them harshly, Father.]

INDRA'S VOICE:

Descend and see, and hear, and then return,
And tell me, child, if their complaints
And wailings are well-founded.

[INDRA'S DAUGHTER:

I shall obey and go. But come with me, Father.

INDRA'S VOICE:

No, I cannot breathe there.]

INDRA'S DAUGHTER:

The cloud is falling, the air grows close, I choke.
I breathe no air, but only smoke and water,
So heavy, that it drags me down, and down,
And now I can discern its heeling mass.
Ah, this third world is not the best —

INDRA'S VOICE:

It is not the best, for sure, but not the worst.
[It is called dust, it wheels like all the rest,
And so its people are sometimes seized with dizziness,
And hover between imbalance and madness.
Have courage, child. It is but a trial.

INDRA'S DAUGHTER [*on her knees, as the cloud sinks*]:
I'm falling!

[*The backcloth now shows a forest of gigantic holly-
hocks in bloom — white, pink, purple, sulphur-yellow,*

*violet. Above them can be seen the gilded roof of a
castle, topped by a flower-bud shaped like a crown.
Beneath the walls of the castle piles of straw are
spread, covering the manure removed from the stables.
The wings, which remain the same throughout the
play, are stylized wall-paintings which simultaneously
represent interiors, exteriors and landscape.*]

The GLAZIER *and* INDRA'S DAUGHTER *enter.*

DAUGHTER: The castle is still rising from the earth.
Father, do you see how much it has grown since last
year?

GLAZIER [*to himself*] : I've never seen that castle before
. . . never heard of a castle rising . . . but — [*to the*
DAUGHTER *with conviction.*] Yes, it has grown eight
feet, but that's because they've manured it. And if you
look carefully, you'll see that a wing has grown on the
side facing the sun.

DAUGHTER: Won't it flower soon? We're past midsummer.

GLAZIER: Don't you see the flower up there?

DAUGHTER: Yes, I see it! [*Claps her hands.*] Father, why
do flowers grow out of dirt?

GLAZIER [*piously*] : Because they don't like the dirt, so
they run up into the light as fast as they can, to blossom
and die.

DAUGHTER: Do you know who lives in the castle?

GLAZIER: I did once, but I've forgotten.

DAUGHTER: I think there's a prisoner inside. I'm sure
he's waiting for me to free him.

GLAZIER: But at what price?

DAUGHTER: One doesn't bargain about one's duty. Let's
go into the castle.

GLAZIER: Yes, let's go.

They go towards the rear of the stage, which gradually opens out towards the wings, revealing a simple, bare room with a table and a few chairs. On one of the chairs sits an OFFICER *in a highly unusual modern uniform. He is rocking in his chair and striking the table with his sabre.*

DAUGHTER [*goes to the* OFFICER *and gently takes the sabre from his hand*] : You mustn't, you mustn't.

OFFICER: Please, Agnes, let me keep my sword.

DAUGHTER: No, you'll break the table. [*To her* FATHER.] Go down to the harness-room and put the window in, and we'll meet later. [*The* GLAZIER *goes.*] You are a prisoner in your room. I have come to free you.

OFFICER: I suppose I've been waiting for that. But I wasn't sure you'd want to.

DAUGHTER: The castle is strong, it has seven walls, but — we'll manage. Do you want to or not?

OFFICER: To be honest, I don't know. Either way I'll suffer. Every joy in life must be paid for with a double portion of sorrow. Sitting here is hard, but if I buy my freedom I'll have to suffer threefold. Agnes, I'd rather stay here, if only I can see you.

DAUGHTER: What do you see in me?

OFFICER:[The beauty which is the harmony of the universe. There are lines in your figure which I find only in the orbits of the solar system, in the sound of a violin, in the vibrations of light.] You are a child of God —

DAUGHTER: So are you.

OFFICER: Then why must I guard horses? Clean stables, and shovel manure?

DAUGHTER: So that you shall long to get away.

OFFICER: I do long, but it's so hard to break the habit.

DAUGHTER: But it's a duty to seek freedom in the light.

OFFICER: Duty? Life has never shown any sense of duty towards me.

DAUGHTER: You feel life has been unjust to you?

OFFICER: Yes! It has been unjust.

[*Voices are now heard behind the screen dividing off the rest of the stage. It is drawn aside, and the* OFFICER *and the* DAUGHTER *look at what it reveals and stand frozen, their expressions also frozen.*

At a table sits the MOTHER, *ill. Before her burns a tallow candle, which she now and then trims with a pair of candle-scissors. On the table lie piles of newly-sewn shirts, which she is marking with marking-ink and a goose quill. Left stands a brown clothes-cupboard.*]

FATHER [*offers her a silk cloak, gently*]: You don't want it?

MOTHER: A silk cloak for me, my dear? What's the use? I shall die soon.

FATHER: You believe what the doctor says?

MOTHER [*touches her breast*]: I believe the voice that speaks in here.

FATHER [*sadly*]: And you think of your children, first and always.

MOTHER: They've been my life, my justification, my joy and my grief.

FATHER: Kristina, forgive me — for everything.

MOTHER: Oh, my dear. Forgive me, dearest. We have tormented each other. Why? We don't know. We couldn't do otherwise. But here are the children's new clothes. See they change twice a week, on Wednesday and

Sunday, and that Louisa washes them — all over. Are you going out?

FATHER: I must go up to the college. It's eleven o'clock.

MOTHER: Ask Alfred to come in before you go.

FATHER [*points at the* OFFICER]: Here he is, the little dear.

MOTHER: My eyes are starting to go, too. Yes, it's getting dark. [*Trims the candle.*] Alfred. Come here.

> The FATHER *goes out through the middle of the wall, nodding goodbye. The* OFFICER *goes over to the* MOTHER.

MOTHER: Who is that girl?

OFFICER [*whispers*]: It is Agnes.

MOTHER: Oh, is it Agnes? Do you know what they say? That she's the God Indra's daughter, who asked to be allowed to come down to earth to see what human life is really like. But don't say anything.

OFFICER: She is a god's child!

MOTHER [*aloud*]: Alfred dear, I shall soon be leaving you and your brothers and sisters. Let me give you some advice.

OFFICER [*sadly*]: Yes, Mother.

[MOTHER: It's just this. Never strive with God.

OFFICER: What do you mean, Mother?]

MOTHER: You mustn't go round feeling life has been unjust to you.

OFFICER: But when people do treat me unjustly?

MOTHER: You're thinking of the time you were unjustly punished for stealing a penny that was later found?

OFFICER: Yes. And that injustice warped my whole life.

MOTHER: I know. But now go to that cupboard —

OFFICER [*embarrassed*]: You know, then? It's —

MOTHER: *The Swiss Family Robinson.* Which —

OFFICER: Don't go on.

MOTHER: Which your brother got punished for — and which you'd torn up and hidden.

OFFICER: Fancy that cupboard still standing there after twenty years. We've moved so often, and my mother died ten years ago.

MOTHER: Well, what of it? You always have to ask questions about everything. That way you'll ruin the best life has to offer. Ah, here's Lina.

LINA [*enters*]: Please, madam. It's very kind of you, but I can't go to the christening —

MOTHER: Why not, child?

LINA: I've nothing to wear.

MOTHER: You can borrow this cloak of mine.

LINA: Oh, madam, I can't do that.

MOTHER: I don't understand. I shall never go to any more parties —

OFFICER: What will Father say? It's a gift from him —

[MOTHER: He wouldn't be so small -minded.]

FATHER [*puts his head in*]: Are you lending my gift to the servant?

MOTHER: Don't speak like that. Remember I was once a servant too. Why must you hurt someone who is innocent?

FATHER: Why must you hurt me, your husband?

MOTHER: Oh, this life! When one does a good deed, there's always someone for whom it's ugly. Help one person, you hurt another. Ah, this life!

[*She trims the candle so that it goes out. The stage is darkened and the screen is drawn again.*]

DAUGHTER: Alas for mankind!

OFFICER: You think so?

DAUGHTER: Yes. Life is hard — but love conquers all! Come and see.

[*The backcloth is raised, revealing a shabby wall. In the middle of it is a gate opening onto a green area bathed in light, and containing an enormous blue monk's-hood or aconite. To the left of the gate sits a female* STAGE-DOOR KEEPER, *with a shawl over head and shoulders, knitting another and more elaborate shawl. On the right is a cylindrical bill-hoarding, which the* BILL-POSTER *is cleaning. Beside him stands a fishing-net with a green handle. Further to the right is a door with air-holes in the form of a four-leaved clover. Left of the gate stands a slender lime-tree with a pitch-black trunk and a few light-green leaves. Next to it is a manhole.*]

DAUGHTER [*walks over to the* STAGE-DOOR KEEPER]: Isn't that shawl ready yet?

STAGE-DOOR KEEPER: Why, no, my dear. Twenty-six years is no time for such a task.

DAUGHTER: And your lover never came back?

STAGE-DOOR KEEPER: No, but it wasn't his fault. He *had* to go away, poor man. That was thirty years ago.

DAUGHTER [*to the* BILL-POSTER]: Wasn't she a dancer? Up there, in the opera?

BILL-POSTER: She was the star. But when he went, he seemed to take her dancing with him. And she never got any more parts.

DAUGHTER: Everyone complains. With their eyes, if not their tongues.

BILL-POSTER: I don't complain. Not now, since I got a fish-chest and a green fishing-net.

DAUGHTER: And that makes you happy?

BILL-POSTER: Oh, yes, so happy! It was the dream of my youth. And now it's come true. Of course, I'm — fifty now—

DAUGHTER: Fifty years for a fish-chest and a fishing net —

BILL-POSTER: A green fishing-net, a green one.

DAUGHTER [to the STAGE-DOOR KEEPER]: Give me the shawl, then I can sit here and watch the people. But you must stand behind and tell me about them. [Takes the shawl and seats herself beside the gate.]

STAGE-DOOR KEEPER: Today's the last day before the theatre closes. Now they learn whether they're being kept on or not —

DAUGHTER: What happens to those who aren't?

STAGE-DOOR KEEPER: Blessed Jesus, you'll see. [I'll put the shawl over your head.]

DAUGHTER: Poor people.

STAGE-DOOR KEEPER: Look, here comes one. She's not one of the chosen. See how she's crying.

> The SINGER runs in from the right and out through the door with her handkerchief to her eyes. She stops a moment in the passage outside the door and leans her head against the wall, then hurries out.

DAUGHTER: Alas for mankind!

STAGE-DOOR KEEPER: But look at this one. There's a happy man.

> The OFFICER enters through the door, in frock-coat and top-hat, carrying a bouquet of roses, radiant and happy.

STAGE-DOOR KEEPER: He is to marry Miss Victoria.

OFFICER [*downstage, looks up and sings*]: Victoria!

STAGE-DOOR KEEPER: She'll be right down.

OFFICER: Good, good. The carriage is waiting, the table laid, the champagne on ice. May I embrace you, ladies? [*Embraces the* DAUGHTER *and the* STAGE-DOOR KEEPER. *Sings.*] Victoria!

A GIRL'S VOICE [*from above, sings*]: I am here!

OFFICER [*begins to stroll around*]: Ah, well. I'll wait.

DAUGHTER: Do you know me?

OFFICER: No, I know only one woman. Victoria! For seven years I have walked here and waited for her — at noon, when the sun stood above the chimneys, and at evening, when the gloom of night began to fall. Look at the floor here, you can see the footprints of the faithful lover. Hurrah! She is mine! [*Sings.*] Victoria! [*He gets no reply.*] Well, she's getting dressed. [*To the* BILL-POSTER.] You've a fishing-net, I see. Everyone at the opera house is crazy about fishing-nets — or rather fish! They like dumb fish, because they can't sing. What does a thing like that cost?

BILL-POSTER: It's quite expensive.

OFFICER [*sings*]: Victoria! [[*Shakes the lime-tree.*] Look — it's coming into leaf again. For the eighth time.] Victoria! Now she's combing her fringe. [*To the* DAUGHTER.] Come, madam, let me go up and fetch my bride.

STAGE-DOOR KEEPER: No one's allowed on to the stage.

OFFICER: Seven years I have been walking here. Seven times three hundred and sixty-five makes two thousand five hundred and fifty-five! [*Stops and points at the door with the clover-shaped holes.*] And that door I've stared at two thousand five hundred and fifty-five times, without discovering where it leads to. And that clover-leaf to let in light. For whom does it let in light? Is there some-one inside? Does someone live there?

STAGE-DOOR KEEPER: I don't know. I've never seen it opened.

OFFICER: It looks like a pantry door I saw when I was four and went away one Sunday afternoon with the maid. Away, to [other families and] other maids, but I never got beyond the kitchens, and I sat between the water-cask and the salt-barrel. I've seen so many kitchens in my time, and the pantries were always in the porch, with bored round holes and a clover-leaf. But the opera house has no pantry, for they have no kitchen. [*Sings.*] Victoria! Tell me, she can't go out any other way but this, can she?

STAGE-DOOR KEEPER: No there's no other way.

OFFICER: Good, then I shan't miss her. [DANCERS, *etc., hurry out and are quizzed by the* OFFICER.] Now she must be here soon. I say! That flower out there, that blue monk's-hood. I haven't seen that since I was a child. Is it the same one? I remember in a parsonage, when I was seven — two doves, on it, blue doves under that hood — but once a bee came and crept into the hood. Then I thought, "Now I have you!", so I pinched the flower shut; but the bee stung through it and I cried. But then the parson's wife came and put wet earth on it — and we had wild strawberries and milk for supper. I think it's getting dark already. [*To the* BILL-POSTER.] Where are you going?

BILL-POSTER: Home for supper.

OFFICER [*feels his eyes*]: Supper? At this time of day? Look — may I go in for a moment and telephone to the rising castle?

DAUGHTER: What do you want there?

OFFICER: I must tell the glazier to put in double windows, for it'll soon be winter and I'm so terribly cold. [*Goes to the* STAGE-DOOR KEEPER'S *lodge.*]

DAUGHTER: Who is Miss Victoria?

STAGE-DOOR KEEPER: The girl he loves.

DAUGHTER: Well answered. What she may be to us and others, he doesn't care. All she is, is what she is to him.

[*It grows rapidly dark.*]

STAGE-DOOR KEEPER [*lights lamp*]: It's getting dark quickly today.

[DAUGHTER: To the gods a year is as a minute.

STAGE-DOOR KEEPER: And to humans a minute can be as a year.]

The OFFICER *returns. He looks dusty, the roses are withered.*

OFFICER: She hasn't come yet?

STAGE-DOOR KEEPER: No.

OFFICER: She'll *come. She'll* come. [*Wanders about.*] But perhaps I'd better cancel the lunch. As it's already evening. Yes, I'll do that. [*Goes in and telephones.*]

STAGE-DOOR KEEPER [*to the* DAUGHTER]: May I have my shawl now?

DAUGHTER: No, [take a little time off,] I'll do your job. I want to learn to know people and life, to find out if it's as hard as they say.

STAGE-DOOR KEEPER: But you mustn't sleep at your post here. Never sleep, night or day —

DAUGHTER: Not sleep at night?

STAGE-DOOR KEEPER: Yes, if you can, with the bell-rope round your wrist — there are night-watchmen on the stage and they're relieved every three hours.

DAUGHTER: But that's inhuman —

STAGE-DOOR KEEPER: You may think so, but folk like

me are glad of such a job, and if you knew how envied I am —

DAUGHTER: Envied? [For doing this?]

STAGE-DOOR KEEPER: Yes. But, you know, what's worse than the hours and the drudgery and the draughts and the cold and the damp is being everybody's confidante. They come to me — why? [Perhaps they read in the lines of my face the runes of suffering that invite confidences.] That shawl hides thirty years of sorrows, mine and others'.

DAUGHTER: It's heavy too, and it burns like nettles.

STAGE-DOOR KEEPER: Wear it if you wish. When it gets too heavy, give me a shout and I'll come and relieve you.

DAUGHTER: [Goodbye.] What you can bear, I surely can.

STAGE-DOOR KEEPER: We'll see. But be kind to my little friends, and don't yawn at their sorrows.

She disappears down the passage. [The stage is darkened and the scene changes so that the lime-tree is bare of leaves and the monk's-hood almost withered. When the lights go up, the foliage outside is autumn-brown.] The OFFICER *enters. Now he has grey hair and a grey beard. His clothes are dilapidated, his shirt-collar black and limp, the bouquet of roses so withered that only the branches remain. He wanders around.*

OFFICER: From all the evidence, summer is past and autumn near. [I see that from that lime-tree and that monk's-hood.] [*Wanders.*] But the autumn is my spring. Then the theatre will open again! And then she must come. Kind lady, may I sit on this chair for a little while?

DAUGHTER: Sit, my friend. I can stand.

OFFICER [*sits*] : If only I could sleep a little, things would be better. [*Sleeps for a second, then jumps up and starts wandering again. Stops before the door with the clover-leaf and points.*] This door, that gives me no peace. What is behind it? There must be something. [*Soft music is heard from above, in dance rhythm.*] Ah! Now the re-hearsals have begun. [[*The stage is spasmodically illum-inated as by a lighthouse.*] What is this? [*Follows the changing light.*] Light and darkness — light and darkness?

DAUGHTER [*similarly*] : Day and night. Day and night. A merciful Providence wishes to shorten your waiting; so the days flee the pursuing nights.

> *The stage remains illuminated.*] *The* BILL-POSTER *enters with his fishing-net and bill-posting equipment.*

OFFICER: There's the bill-poster with his fishing-net. Had good fishing?

BILL-POSTER: Oh, yes. The summer was hot and a little long. The net was very good, but not quite as I'd imagined —

OFFICER [*stresses the words*] : Not quite as I'd imagined. Excellently said. Nothing is as I had imagined. Because the thought is more than the deed — bigger than the fact. [*Wanders round and slaps the bouquet against the walls so that the last leaves fall.*]

BILL-POSTER: Hasn't she come down yet?

OFFICER: No, not yet, but she'll come soon. Do you know what's behind that door?

BILL-POSTER: No, I've never seen that door open.

OFFICER: I'll telephone for a locksmith to come and open it. [*Goes to the telephone. The* BILL-POSTER *sticks up a poster.*]

DAUGHTER: What was wrong with your net?

BILL-POSTER: Wrong? Well, there wasn't anything actually wrong — but it wasn't as I'd imagined it, so I didn't get so much pleasure from it.

DAUGHTER: How had you imagined the net?

BILL-POSTER: How? That I can't say —

DAUGHTER: Let me tell you. You had imagined it
as it wasn't. Green, yes, but not *that* green.

BILL-POSTER: You know, madam! You know everything
— that's why everyone comes to you with their worries.
If you'd listen to me just once too —

DAUGHTER: Yes, gladly. Come in here, [and tell me
everything].

> She goes into her lodge. The BILL-POSTER *stands
> outside the window and speaks to her.* [The stage is
> darkened. When it becomes light, the lime-tree is green
> again, the monk's-hood in flower and the sun is
> shining on the green foliage outside.] *The* OFFICER
> *enters. Now he is old, white-haired and shabby, with
> worn-out shoes, and carries the twigs of his rose
> bouquet. He wanders up and down, slowly, like an
> old man. He reads the poster. A* BALLET DANCER
> *enters, right.*

OFFICER: Has Miss Victoria gone?

BALLET DANCER: No, not yet.

OFFICER: Then I'll wait. She'll come soon, won't she?

BALLET DANCER [*earnestly*]: Oh, yes, certainly.

OFFICER: Don't go now, you'll be able to see what's
behind this door, for I've sent for the locksmith.

BALLET DANCER: It'll be really interesting to see that
door opened. That door and the rising castle. Do you
know the rising castle?

OFFICER: Do I know it? I've been a prisoner there.

BALLET DANCER: No, was that you? But why did they
have so many horses there?

OFFICER: It was a cavalry barracks, of course.

BALLET DANCER [*annoyed with herself*] : How stupid I am. Fancy my not realizing that!

A SINGER *enters right.*

OFFICER: Has Miss Victoria left?

SINGER [*earnestly*] : No, she hasn't left. She never leaves.

OFFICER: That is because she loves me. You mustn't go before the locksmith comes to open this door.

SINGER: Oh, is the door to be opened? What fun! I must just ask the stage-door keeper something —

PROMPTER *enters right.*

OFFICER: Has Miss Victoria left?

PROMPTER: Not as far as I know.

OFFICER: You see! Didn't I say she was waiting for me? You mustn't go before the door is opened.

PROMPTER: Which door?

OFFICER: Is there more than one door?

PROMPTER: Oh, I know. The one with the clover-leaf. Yes, I'll certainly stay. I must just have a word with the stage-door keeper.

The BALLET DANCER, SINGER *and* PROMPTER *group themselves beside the* BILL-POSTER *outside the* STAGE-DOOR KEEPER's *window, where in turn they speak to the* DAUGHTER. *The* GLAZIER *enters through the gate.*

OFFICER: Is that the locksmith?

GLAZIER: No, the locksmith was busy. But it can be done as well by a glazier.

OFFICER: Yes, yes, I'm sure. But have you got a diamond?

GLAZIER: Of course. Who ever heard of a glazier without a diamond?

OFFICER: That's true. Then let us get to work! [*He claps his hands. They all gather in a circle around the door.* [SINGERS *dressed as the Mastersingers and* GIRL DANCERS *dressed for Aida run in right.*] Locksmith — or glazier — do your duty! [*The* GLAZIER *comes forward with a diamond.*] A moment such as this does not often recur in a person's life, so, my good friends, I beg you, consider carefully —

POLICEMAN [*enters*] : In the name of the law I forbid the opening of this door!

OFFICER: Oh, God, the trouble whenever one wants to do anything new and big! We'll take it to court. To the advocate! Then we'll see how the law stands. To the advocate!

[*The scene is changed to an* ADVOCATE's *office. This is done in full view of the audience, thus. The gate remains, serving as part of an entry barrier like a counter which extends the full width of the stage. The* STAGE-DOOR KEEPER's *hatch remains as the* ADVOCATE's *nook containing his desk, opening downstage. The lime-tree, leafless, is now a coat and hat stand. The poster hoarding is hung with notices and court papers. The door with the clover-leaf becomes part of a filing cupboard.*

The ADVOCATE, *in morning-coat and white cravat, is seated on the left inside the gate at a desk covered with papers. His face reflects extreme suffering; it is chalk-white and lined, with purple shadows; he is ugly, a mirror of every kind of crime and vice which his profession forces him to experience vicariously. One of his two* CLERKS *is one-armed, the other one-eyed. The characters who have gathered in the preceding scene to see the door opened are still on stage, now as though awaiting admission to the* ADVOCATE, *with the appearance of having been*

there for ever. The DAUGHTER *(in her shawl) and
the* OFFICER *stand downstage.*]

ADVOCATE [*comes over to the* DAUGHTER]: Please may
I have the shawl? I'll hang it in here till I light the stove.
Then I'll burn it with all its griefs and sorrows.

DAUGHTER: Not yet, I want to finish it first. And I want
to gather up all *your* griefs, the confidences you've
received about crimes and vices, unjust imprisonments,
slanders, calumnies —

ADVOCATE: My little friend, your shawl would not
suffice. Look at these walls. Isn't it as though all these
sins had soiled the paper? Look at these documents on
which I write accounts of injustices. Look at me. No one
ever comes here who laughs. Only hard glances, bared
teeth, clenched fists. And they all spray their malice,
their envy, their suspicions, over me. Look, my hands
are black, and can never be cleansed, do you see how
they are cracked and bloody? I can never wear clothes
for more than one or two days, because they stink of
other men's crimes. Sometimes I have sulphur burned
here, but it doesn't help. I sleep in here and dream only
of crimes. I've a murder case right now; that I can bear,
but do you know what's the worst of all? To part a
husband and wife; that makes the earth cry out to heaven,
cry treachery against creation, against goodness, against
love. And when these briefs are filled with their mutual
accusations and at length a humane fellow creature
receives one of the two in private, takes him or her by
the ear and, smiling, asks the simple question, "What is
your real complaint against your husband — or wife?"
— then he or she stands there, speechless, unable to
answer. Once, yes, it was a question of a green salad,
another time a single word, most often it's nothing. But
the pain, the suffering! These *I* must endure. Look at me!
Do you think I could win a woman's love with this
criminal's visage? And do you think anyone wants to be
friends with a man who must collect all the city's debts?
It is dreadful to be part of mankind.

DAUGHTER: Alas for mankind!

ADVOCATE: Alas indeed. And what people live on is to me a riddle. [They marry on an income of a hundred pounds, when they need two hundred.] They borrow, of course, everyone borrows. They live from day to day and muddle through to death. And they always leave debts behind them. Who will pay in the end, tell me that?

DAUGHTER: He Who feeds the birds.

ADVOCATE: Yes. But if He Who feeds the birds were to step down to His earth and see how His poor children fare, He might perhaps be moved to pity —

DAUGHTER: Alas for mankind!

ADVOCATE: Alas indeed. [*To the* OFFICER.] What do you want?

OFFICER: I only wanted to ask if Miss Victoria has left.

ADVOCATE: No, she hasn't, you may rest assured. Why are you pointing at my cupboard?

OFFICER: I thought that door was so like —

ADVOCATE: Oh, no! No, no!

The church bells ring.

OFFICER: Is there a funeral?

ADVOCATE: No, they're conferring degrees, doctors' degrees. And I must go and be made a Doctor of Law. Perhaps you'd like to become a Doctor and get a laurel crown?

OFFICER: Yes, why not? It'd make a change —

ADVOCATE: Shall we go at once to the great ceremony? Just go and get dressed.

[*The* OFFICER *goes. The stage is darkened, and the scene is changed thus. The barrier remains but now*

*serves as the chancel rail. The poster-hoarding becomes
the number-board for the psalms; the lime-tree/coat-
stand is a candelabra; the* ADVOCATE's *desk serves
for the handing-out of degrees; the clover-leaf door
now leads to the sacristy. The* MASTERSINGERS
become heralds with sceptres, the GIRL DANCERS
are holding laurel wreaths; the OTHERS *stand around
as spectators. The curtain rises revealing a mighty
church organ with a keyboard beneath and a mirror
above.] Music. At the side, the four faculties of
philosophy, theology, medicine and law.*

[After a moment the HERALDS *enter right
followed by the* DANCERS *holding their laurel
wreaths before them at arm's length.] Three*
RECIPIENTS OF DEGREES *enter left, one after the
other, and are crowned with wreaths by the* DANCERS;
then they go out right. The ADVOCATE *goes up to
be crowned, but the* DANCERS *turn away, refusing to
crown him, and go out. The* ADVOCATE, *crushed,
leans against a pillar. Everyone goes out, leaving the*
ADVOCATE *alone.*

[DAUGHTER [*enters with a white shawl over her head and
shoulders*] : Look, now I've washed the shawl. But why
are you standing here? Didn't you get the wreath?]

ADVOCATE: [No.] I was unworthy.

DAUGHTER: Why? Because you embraced the cause of
the poor, said a good word for the criminal, lightened the
burden of the guilty, won reprieves for the condemned.
[Alas for mankind. They are not angels; but they are much
to be pitied.]

ADVOCATE: Speak no evil of mankind. I shall plead its
cause.

DAUGHTER: Why do they strike their friends in the face?

ADVOCATE: They know no better.

[DAUGHTER: Let us enlighten them. Will you? With me?

ADVOCATE: They will not accept enlightenment. Oh, if only our complaints could reach the gods in heaven!

DAUGHTER: They shall. [*At the organ.*] Do you know what I see in this mirror? The world set to rights. It is twisted out of true.

ADVOCATE: How did it become so?

DAUGHTER: When the copy was made.

ADVOCATE: Yes. The copy. I always felt that it was a false copy. And when I began to think of the prototype, I realized its inadequacy. People called it human insatiability, the glass splinter that Satan sets in human eyes, and so forth —

DAUGHTER: Their vision is certainly distorted. Look at these university faculties! The government, in order to keep society stable, pays lip service to all four of them. Theology, the teaching of God, which is always attacked and ridiculed by philosophy, which claims to be wisdom itself! And medicine, which challenges philosophy and says that theology is no science but a superstition. And they sit in the same senate, which is supposed to teach the young respect — for the university! It's a madhouse. And alas for him who first sees the truth!

ADVOCATE: The first to see it are the theologians. As part of their preliminary studies they read philosophy, which teaches them that theology is nonsense. Then they read in their theology that philosophy is nonsense. Madmen, eh?

DAUGHTER: And law — the servant of all, except the servants.

ADVOCATE: Justice which, seeking to be just, slays itself. Right, that so often causes wrong.

DAUGHTER: Thus have you arranged your world, child of man. Come — I will give you a wreath which will suit

you better. [*Places a crown of thorns on his head.*] Now
I will play for you.

> *She sits at the organ and plays a Kyrie, but instead
> of the music, human voices are heard.*

CHILDREN'S VOICES: Eternal One! Eternal One! [*The
last note is prolonged.*]

WOMEN'S VOICES: Have mercy! [*The last note is prolonged.*]

MEN'S VOICES(TENORS): Save us, for Thy mercy's sake!
[*The last note is prolonged.*]

MEN'S VOICES (BASSES): Spare Thy children, O lord,
and be not wrathful with us!

ALL: Have mercy! Hear us! Pity us mortals! Eternal One,
why hast Thou forsaken us? From the deep we beseech
Thee: mercy, O Eternal One! Place not too heavy a
burden on Thy children. Hear us! Hear us!

> *The stage is darkened. The* DAUGHTER *rises and
> goes towards the* ADVOCATE. *The organ is trans-
> formed by a change of lighting into Fingal's Cave.
> The sea rolls in beneath the basalt columns. We
> hear the sound of wind and waves.*

ADVOCATE: What do you hear, sister?

DAUGHTER: What do you hear?

ADVOCATE: I hear raindrops falling.

DAUGHTER: They are the tears of humans weeping.
What else do you hear?

ADVOCATE: Sighing — wailing — mourning.]

DAUGHTER[: Mankind's complaints have reached here.
They reach no further.] But why this eternal lamentation?
Has life no cause for joy?

ADVOCATE: Yes, the fairest of things, which is the bitterest: love. A wife and a home; the best thing, and the worst.

DAUGHTER: I shall try it.

ADVOCATE: With me?

DAUGHTER: With you. You know the rocks, the reefs. We shall avoid them.

ADVOCATE: I am poor.

DAUGHTER: What of that, if we love each other? And a little beauty costs nothing.

ADVOCATE: I hate things which you may love.

DAUGHTER: Then we must compromise.

ADVOCATE: If we tire of each other?

DAUGHTER: Then a child will come and give us a happiness which will never fade.

ADVOCATE: You want me, poor and ugly, despised, an outcast?

AGNES: Yes. [Let us unite our faults.]

ADVOCATE: So be it, then.

A very simple room in the ADVOCATE's *office. Right, a large double bed beneath a canopy and curtains. By it, a window. Left, an iron stove with saucepans, etc.* KRISTIN *is pasting the inside window-joints.* [*Upstage, an open door to the office, where poor people can be seen waiting for an audience.*]

KRISTIN: I'm pasting, I'm pasting.

DAUGHTER [*pale and haggard, sits by the stove*]: You're shutting out the air. I'm suffocating.

KRISTIN: Now there's only one little crack left.

DAUGHTER: [Air, air!] I can't breathe!

KRISTIN: I'm pasting, I'm pasting!

ADVOCATE: That's right, Kristin. Heat costs money.

DAUGHTER: Oh, it's as though you were pasting my lips together!

ADVOCATE [*in the doorway with a document in his hand*]: Is the child asleep?

DAUGHTER: Yes, at last.

ADVOCATE [*gently*]: His cries scare away my clients.

DAUGHTER [*gently*]: What can we do about it?

ADVOCATE: Nothing.

DAUGHTER: We must find a bigger apartment.

ADVOCATE: We have no money.

DAUGHTER: May I open the window? This air is stifling me.

ADVOCATE: Then the heat will go and we shall freeze.

DAUGHTER: It's horrible. May we scrub the floor out there, then?

ADVOCATE: You haven't the strength, nor have I, and Kristin — Kristin must paste. She must paste the whole house tight, every crack in the ceilings, the floors, the walls.

DAUGHTER: Poverty I was prepared for, but not dirt.

ADVOCATE: Poverty is always more or less dirty.

DAUGHTER: This is worse than I had dreamed.

ADVOCATE: We're not too badly off. There's still food in the pot.

DAUGHTER: But what food!

ADVOCATE: Cabbage is cheap, nourishing and good.

DAUGHTER: If you like cabbage. It revolts me.

ADVOCATE: Why didn't you say so?

DAUGHTER: Because I loved you. I wanted to make a sacrifice for you.

ADVOCATE: Then I must sacrifice for you my love of cabbage. The sacrifice must be mutual.

DAUGHTER: Then what shall we eat? Fish? But you hate fish.

ADVOCATE: And it's dear.

DAUGHTER: This is harder than I had dreamed.

ADVOCATE [*gently*]: You see how hard it is! And the child, that was to have been our bond and our blessing, is becoming our ruin.

DAUGHTER: My dearest! I am dying in this air, in this room with its window on the yard, the child's ceaseless crying so that I can never sleep, the people out there with their complainings, strifes and accusations. I must die if I stay here.

ADVOCATE: Poor little flower. No light, no air —

DAUGHTER: And you say there are some who are worse off.

ADVOCATE: Many of the neighbours envy me.

DAUGHTER: I could bear it if only I could have a little beauty in my home.

ADVOCATE: I know you mean a flower, if possible a heliotrope, but that costs a shilling, and that's twelve pints of milk or four pounds of potatoes.

DAUGHTER: I'll gladly do without food if I may have my flower.

ADVOCATE: There is a kind of beauty which costs nothing,

and whose absence from a home is the worst torment for a man who loves beauty.

DAUGHTER: What is that?

ADVOCATE: If I say, you will be angry.

DAUGHTER: We have agreed not to be angry.

ADVOCATE: We have agreed. Everything will be all right, Agnes, as long as we don't speak sharply. You know what I mean. Not yet!

DAUGHTER: We shall never do that.

ADVOCATE: I never shall.

DAUGHTER: Tell me, now.

ADVOCATE: Well. When I enter a home I first look to see how the curtain sits on its rail. [*Goes over to the window and adjusts the curtain.*] If it hangs like a rope or a rag, I leave. Then I glance at the chairs. If they stand straight, I stay. [*Adjusts a chair against the wall.*] Then I look at the candles in their sticks. If they are crooked, the whole house is awry. [*Corrects a candle on the desk.*] This is the beauty, you see, my dear, that costs nothing.

DAUGHTER [*drops her head*]: Don't speak so sharply, Axel.

ADVOCATE: I was not speaking sharply.

DAUGHTER: Yes, you were.

ADVOCATE: Look, for God's sake — !

DAUGHTER: What kind of language is that?

ADVOCATE: Forgive me, Agnes. But I have suffered from your untidiness as much as you suffer from dirt. And I haven't dared to tidy things up myself, because then you get angry as though I had reproached you. Ugh! Shall we stop now?

[DAUGHTER: It is horribly difficult to be married. The most difficult thing of all. I think one has to be an angel.

ADVOCATE: Yes. I agree.]

DAUGHTER: I think I shall begin to hate you after this.

ADVOCATE: No, Agnes. Let us beware of hatred. I promise I shall never remark on your untidiness again — though it tortures me.

DAUGHTER: And I shall eat cabbage, though it tortures me.

ADVOCATE: We must torture each other, then. What makes one happy, torments the other.

DAUGHTER: Alas for mankind!

ADVOCATE: You see it now?

DAUGHTER: Yes. But let us in God's name avoid these reefs, now we know them so well.

ADVOCATE: Let us do that. We are humane and enlightened people. We can forgive and forget.

DAUGHTER: We can smile at such trifles.

ADVOCATE: We can — *we* can! Do you know, I read in the paper this morning — by the way, where is the paper?

DAUGHTER [*embarrassed*]: Which paper?

ADVOCATE [*harshly*]: Do I take more than one paper?

DAUGHTER: Smile now, and don't reproach me. I used your paper to make the fire.

ADVOCATE [*angrily*]: For God's sake!

DAUGHTER: Smile, now. I burned it because he mocked what is sacred to me —

ADVOCATE: And what is not sacred to me. Well! [*Clasps his hands, furious.*] I shall smile, I shall smile so that my back teeth show. I shall be humane, and sweep my opinions under the carpet, and say yes to everything and act the hypocrite. So, you've burned my newspaper. I see. [*Adjusts the curtain by the bedpost.*] Now I'm tidying things again, and you'll be angry. Agnes, this is impossible.

DAUGHTER: Yes, yes.

ADVOCATE: But we must go on, not because of our vows, but for the child.

DAUGHTER: That's right. For the child. Oh — oh — we must go on.

ADVOCATE: And now I must go out to my clients. Listen, they're buzzing with impatience to get at each other's throats, have each other fined and imprisoned. Lost souls — !

DAUGHTER: Unhappy people. And this pasting! [*Bows her head in silent despair.*]

KRISTIN: I'm pasting, I'm pasting!

The ADVOCATE *stands at the door and fingers the latch nervously.*

DAUGHTER: Oh, how that latch squeaks! It's as though you were squeezing my heart's springs —

ADVOCATE: I'm squeezing, I'm squeezing —

DAUGHTER: Don't do it!

ADVOCATE: I'm squeezing!

DAUGHTER: No!

ADVOCATE: I'm — !

OFFICER [*enters from the office, puts his hand on the latch*]: Allow me.

ADVOCATE [*lets go of the latch*]: Certainly. Since you are now a Doctor.

OFFICER: Now life lies before me! All paths stand open to me, my feet are on Parnassus, I have won my laurels, immortality, honour. [Everything is mine.]

ADVOCATE: What will you live on?

OFFICER: Live on?

ADVOCATE: You must have a home, clothes, food?

OFFICER: That always works out, if only one has someone who loves one.

ADVOCATE: Perhaps. Perhaps. Paste, Kristin! Paste! Till they can't breathe. [*Goes out backwards, nodding.*]

KRISTIN: I'm pasting, I'm pasting! Till they can't breathe.

OFFICER [*to* DAUGHTER]: Will you come with me now?

DAUGHTER: At once. But where?

OFFICER: To Fairhaven! There it is summer, there the sun shines, there are young people, children and flowers, singing and dancing, feasting and joy!

DAUGHTER: Then I want to go there.

OFFICER: Come, come!

ADVOCATE [*enters again*]: Now I am returning to my first hell. This was the second — and the worst. The greatest happiness is the greatest hell. Now she's dropped hairpins on the floor again. [*Picks around on the floor.*]

OFFICER: Fancy, now he's found the hairpins too.

ADVOCATE: Too? Look at this one. Here are two prongs, but one pin. It is two, but it is one. If I straighten it out it is a single entity. If I bend it, it is two without ceasing to be one. That means: these two are one. But if I break it — so! Now they are two, two! [*Breaks the hairpin and throws the pieces away.*]

OFFICER: All this he has seen. But before one can break it, the prongs must diverge. If they converge, then it will hold.

ADVOCATE: And if they are parallel, then they never meet. They will neither hold nor break.

OFFICER: The hairpin is the most complete of all created things. A straight line which is identical with two parallels.

ADVOCATE: A lock which fastens when it is open.

OFFICER: Clasping a plait of hair, whose ends stay open when it is clasped shut.

ADVOCATE: Like this door. When I shut it, I open, the way out, for you, Agnes. [*Goes out and shuts the door.*]

OFFICER: Shall we go, then?

[*The scene changes. The bed with its canopy and curtains becomes a tent. The iron stove remains; the backcloth is raised, and we see, in the right foreground, scorched mountains with red heather and black and white stumps of trees left by a forest fire. Red pigsties and outhouses. Below stands an open gymnasium for the sick, with people exercising on machines resembling instruments of torture. Downstage left are some open sheds of the quarantine building, with ovens, furnace rooms and pipes. Centre stage, a broad sea channel. Upstage, a beautiful beach with trees, and jetties decked with flags. White boats are moored to them, some with sails set, some not. Small Italian villas, pavilions, kiosks and marble statues can be seen through the trees.*] The QUARANTINE MASTER *is walking on the beach dressed as a blackamoor.*

OFFICER [*enters and shakes the* QUARANTINE MASTER's *hand*]: Why, Ordström! Have you landed here?

QUARANTINE MASTER: Yes, I'm here.

OFFICER: Is this Fairhaven?

QUARANTINE MASTER: No, that's on the other side. This is Foulstrand.

OFFICER: Then we've come wrong.

QUARANTINE MASTER: We? Won't you introduce me?

OFFICER: No, that wouldn't be proper. [*Whispers.*] This is Indra's own daughter!

QUARANTINE MASTER: Indra's? I thought it was Waruna herself. Well, aren't you surprised I'm black in the face?

OFFICER: My son, I am fifty years old, and then one is no longer surprised. I assumed immediately that you were going to a masked ball this evening.

QUARANTINE MASTER: Quite right. And I hope you will join me?

OFFICER: By all means. This place — doesn't look tempting. What kind of people live here?

QUARANTINE MASTER: The sick ones live here, the healthy over there.

OFFICER: There are only poor people here, then?

QUARANTINE MASTER: No, my lad, these are the rich ones. Look at that fellow [on the rack there]. He's eaten too much *foie gras* with truffles and drunk so much Burgundy that his feet have become like briar-wood.

OFFICER: Briar-wood?

QUARANTINE MASTER: Yes. He's got briar-wood feet. And that fellow [lying on the guillotine]. He's drunk so much brandy they had to run his spine through the mangle.

OFFICER: That's not good either.

QUARANTINE MASTER: Everyone lives here who has some grief to hide. Look at him, for instance.

An OLD DANDY *is wheeled in in a wheel-chair, accompanied by a sixty-year-old scrawny ugly* COQUETTE, *dressed in the latest mode, and herself accompanied by a* MALE "FRIEND" *of forty.*

OFFICER: It's the Major! Our old schoolfellow!

QUARANTINE MASTER: Don Juan! You see, he's still in love with that spook at his side. He doesn't see that she's grown old, that she's ugly, faithless, cruel.

OFFICER: There's love for you. I'd never have believed that lecher could love so deeply and sincerely.

QUARANTINE MASTER: You're very charitable.

OFFICER: I myself have loved Victoria. Yes, I still walk the corridor and wait for her —

QUARANTINE MASTER: Is it you who walks in the corridor?

OFFICER: It is I.

QUARANTINE MASTER: Well, have you opened the door yet?

OFFICER: No, it's still *sub judice*. The bill-poster is out with his fishing-net, of course, so they're held up for evidence. Meanwhile the glazier has put the windows in at the castle, which has risen half a storey. It's been an uncommonly fine year this year. Warm and damp.

QUARANTINE MASTER: But you've never been as warm as it is where I work.

OFFICER: How hot is it in the ovens, then?

QUARANTINE MASTER: When we disinfect cholera suspects, we bring it up to a hundred and thirty.

OFFICER: Is the cholera loose again now?

QUARANTINE MASTER: Don't you know?

OFFICER: Yes, of course I know, but I so often forget what I know.

QUARANTINE MASTER: I often wish I could forget, especially myself. That's why I go to masquerades, fancy-dress balls and social occasions.

OFFICER: Why, what have you done?

QUARANTINE MASTER: If I talk about it they say I'm boasting, if I keep quiet they call me a hypocrite.

OFFICER: Is that why you've blacked your face?

QUARANTINE MASTER: Yes. A little blacker than I really am.

OFFICER: Who is that coming now?

QUARANTINE MASTER: Oh, some poet who needs a mud-bath.

> The POET *enters, glancing at the sky, with a bucket of mud in his hand.*

OFFICER: Mud? Surely he needs light and air!

QUARANTINE MASTER: No, he always lives miles up in space, so he gets nostalgic for mud. It makes your skin hard like a pig's to roll in mud. Then he doesn't feel the gadfly's sting.

[OFFICER: This curious world of contradictions!]

POET [*ecstatically*]: Out of clay the god Ptah created man on a potter's wheel, a lathe. [*Sceptically.*] Or some other damned thing! [*Ecstatically.*] From clay the sculptor creates his more or less immortal masterpieces. [*Sceptically.*] Which are usually just crap! [*Ecstatically.*] From clay are created those indispensable kitchen utensils which men call by the common names of pots and plates. [*Sceptically.*] What the hell do I care what they're called? [*Ecstatically.*] Such is clay! When clay is liquid they call it mud. *C'est mon affaire!* [*Shouts.*] Lina!

> LINA *enters with a bucket.*

POET: Lina, show yourself to Miss Agnes. She knew you ten years ago when you were a young, happy and we may say beautiful girl. See how she is now! Five children, drudgery, squalling, starvation, ironing! See how her beauty has gone, how her joy has vanished, through the performance of those duties which should have given her that inner happiness which expresses itself in the harmony of the facial lines and the still glow of the eyes —

QUARANTINE MASTER [*puts his hand over the* POET's *mouth*]: Stuff it, stuff it.

POET: That's what they all say. And if one is silent, then they say: "Speak!" Impossible creatures.

DAUGHTER [*goes over to* LINA]: Let me hear your complaint.

LINA: No, I daren't. Or he'll make things worse.

DAUGHTER: Who is so cruel?

LINA: I daren't say, or I'll get beaten.

POET: That's the way it is. [But I'll tell you, even if this blackamoor knocks my teeth out. Let me inform you that injustices sometimes occur. Agnes, daughter of God! Do you hear music and dancing from the hillside up there? Well, that is Lina's sister, who has come home from the city, where she — went astray, if you understand me? Now they are killing the fatted calf, but Lina who stayed at home has to carry the swill and feed the pigs.

DAUGHTER: They rejoice because the prodigal has ceased from her straying, not simply because she has come home. Remember that.

POET: Very well. But then put on a dance and a supper each evening for this irreproachable working-girl who has never strayed! Do that. But they won't do it. When Lina isn't working she has to go to church to be reproached for not being perfect. Is this justice?

DAUGHTER: Your questions are so difficult to answer, because — there are so many things one can't foresee —

POET: That was also the opinion of the Caliph, Haroun the Just. He sat still on his throne and never saw from up there what went on down below. In the end their complaints reached his lofty ear. Then one fine day he stepped down, disguised himself and walked unobserved among his people to see what had gone wrong with his justice.

DAUGHTER: Surely you don't think I am Haroun the Just?

OFFICER: Let's talk about something else. Look, we've got visitors.

A white boat shaped like a dragon with a sail of light-blue silk on a golden yard, and a gilded mast with a rose-red pennant, glides across the water from the left. At the rudder, closely entwined, sit HE *and* SHE.

OFFICER: Look at that. Perfect happiness, unqualified bliss. The joy of young love.]

HE [*stands up in the boat and sings*]:
Hail to thee, Fairhaven,
Where once I saw the spring.
Where I dreamed my first, fair dreams.
Here I am again!
Not alone as then.
Groves and bays,
Sky and sea,
Greet her, my love, my bride,
My sun, my life!

[*The flags on the jetties of Fairhaven greet them. White handkerchieves wave from the villas and the beaches, and a harmony of harps and violins rings out across the water.*

POET: See what a light shines from them! Hear how the sea resounds with music! Such is Love.]

OFFICER: It is Victoria!

QUARANTINE MASTER: Well?

OFFICER: It is his Victoria. I have mine. And mine, no one may see. [Raise the quarantine flag now, and I'll pull in the net.]

The QUARANTINE MASTER *waves a yellow flag.*
[*The* OFFICER *pulls a rope so that the boat swings
towards Foulstrand.*] HE *and* SHE *become aware of
the horrible landscape and grimace with disgust.*

QUARANTINE MASTER: Yes, yes! It isn't nice. But
everyone must come here, everyone who has been contaminated.

[POET: Imagine being able to talk like that, to do such
things, when one sees two people in love! Don't touch
them! Don't touch Love! It's *lèse-majesté*! Alas, alas!
Now all that is beautiful must be debased, hauled down
into the mud!

HE *and* SHE *step ashore, downcast and ashamed.*]

HE: What have we done?

QUARANTINE MASTER: You don't need to have done
anything to be contaminated by the petty dirt of life.

[SHE: So short is happiness and joy!]

HE: How long must we stay here?

QUARANTINE MASTER: Forty days and nights.

[SHE: Then we'd rather go back.]

HE: Live here, among scorched hills and pigsties?

POET: Love conquers all, even sulphur and carbolic.

QUARANTINE MASTER [*lights the oven. Blue sulphur
fumes arise*] : Now I'm lighting the sulphur. Please step
inside.

SHE: Oh! My blue dress will lose its colour.

QUARANTINE MASTER: And turn white. Your red
roses shall also turn white.

HE: And your cheeks. Forty days!

SHE [*to the* OFFICER] That will please you.

OFFICER: No, it will not. Your joy was the cause of my grief, but — it doesn't matter — I am now a Doctor and have a standing over there [on the mainland.] Ho, ho, yes, yes. And in the autumn I shall get a place in a school — to read with schoolboys the lessons I learned in my childhood and youth, and must learn now, the same lessons, throughout my manhood and my old age, the same lessons . . . How much is two times two? How many times does two go into four? Till they retire me and I can go — jobless, waiting for mealtimes and newspapers, — until at last they carry me out to the crematorium and burn me up. Have you no pensioners out here? That must be the worst thing after twice two is four: to start school again, when you've got your Doctorate; to ask the same questions until you die. [*An* OLD MAN *walks by with his hands behind his back.*] Look, there goes a pensioner, waiting for death; doubtless a captain who never became a major, or a high-court clerk who never rose to be judge. Many are called, but few are chosen. He's waiting for his lunch —

PENSIONER: No, for my paper! My morning paper!

OFFICER: And he's only fifty-four. He may live twenty-five more years waiting for his meals and his paper. Isn't it horrible?

PENSIONER: What isn't horrible? Answer me, answer!

OFFICER: Yes, answer who can. Now I must study with schoolboys; twice two is four! How many times does two go into four? [*Clasps his head desperately.*] Oh, Victoria, whom I loved, and therefore wished all happiness on earth — now she has happiness, the best she can imagine, and I suffer — suffer —suffer!

SHE: Do you think I can be happy, when I see you suffer? How can you think that? Perhaps it soothes your pain that I must sit imprisoned here for forty days and nights? Tell me, does that soothe your pain?

OFFICER: Yes and no. I cannot be happy while you suffer. Ah!

[HE: And do you think my happiness can be built on your suffering?

OFFICER: Alas for us all!

ALL [*stretch their hands towards heaven and emit a discordant cry of pain*]: Ah!]

DAUGHTER:[Eternal One, hear them! Life is cruel!] Alas for mankind!

[ALL[*as before*]: Ah!

> For a moment the stage is darkened. Everyone either goes out, or moves to another position. When it becomes light again, we see the shore of Foulstrand, upstage but in shadow. The water still occupies the centre stage; downstage is Fairhaven; both are fully illuminated. Right, the corner of a casino, with windows open, through which can be seen couples dancing. On an empty packing-case outside stand THREE GIRLS, their arms round each others' waists, watching the dancing. On the steps of the casino is a bench on which UGLY EDITH sits, bare-headed and sad, her hair a dishevelled mass. Before her stands a piano, its keyboard open. Left, a yellow wooden house. TWO CHILDREN in summer dress are throwing a ball outside.
>   At the rear of the foreground is a jetty, with white boats and flagpoles with flags. Out in the water is a white man-of-war, rigged brig-fashion, with cannon portholes. But the whole landscape is in winter dress, with snow on the ground and on the leafless trees.
>
>   The DAUGHTER and the OFFICER enter.]

DAUGHTER: Here is the peace and joy of holiday. Work has stopped. They have parties every day. The people walk in holiday clothes. They play and dance even in the mornings. [[*To the* CHILDREN.] Why don't you go inside and dance, children?

CHILDREN: Us?

OFFICER: But they are servants.

DAUGHTER: Oh, yes.] But why is Edith sitting there instead of inside?

> EDITH *hides her face in her hands.*

OFFICER: Don't ask her. She has been sitting there for three hours and no one has asked her to dance. [[*He goes into the yellow house, left.*]]

DAUGHTER: What a cruel pastime!

MOTHER [*enters, bare-necked, goes over to* EDITH]: Why don't you go inside as I told you?

EDITH: Because — I can't offer myself. I'm ugly, I know that, so no one will dance with me, but I don't need to be reminded of it by you.

> *She begins to play the piano:* [*Bach's Toccata and Fugue, opus 10. The waltz from inside the casino is heard, at first softly, then louder, as though competing with the Bach. But* EDITH *plays louder and silences the dance music.* GUESTS *appear in the doorway and listen to her playing. Everyone on stage stands devoutly listening.*]

A NAVAL OFFICER [*takes* ALICE, *one of the guests at the ball, round the waist and leads her down to the jetty*]: Come, quickly!

> EDITH *stops playing, gets up and looks at them in despair. She remains standing like a statue.* [*The wall of the yellow house is removed and*] *we see three school benches, with* SCHOOLBOYS *sitting on them. Amongst them is the* OFFICER, *looking ill-at-ease and worried. The* SCHOOLMASTER, *with spectacles, chalk and a cane, stands facing them.*

SCHOOLMASTER [*to the* OFFICER]: Well, my boy, can you tell me what two times two is? [*The* OFFICER *remains seated, searching his memory painfully without finding the answer.*] Stand up when you're asked a question.

OFFICER [*gets up miserably*] : Two times two. Let me see. It is two two!

SCHOOLMASTER: I see. You haven't done your homework.

OFFICER [*ashamed*] : Yes, I have, but — I don't know why, but I can't say it.

SCHOOLMASTER: You're making excuses! You know, but you can't say it? Perhaps I can help you. [*Pulls the* OFFICER's *hair.*]

OFFICER: Oh, this is dreadful, it's dreadful.

SCHOOLMASTER: Yes, it's dreadful that such a big boy has no ambition —

OFFICER [*in torment*] : A big boy, yes, I am big, much bigger than them. I'm a Doctor. Why am I sitting here? Aren't I a Doctor?

SCHOOLMASTER: You are, but you must sit and mature, you see. You must mature. Isn't that right?

OFFICER [*clutches his forehead*] : Yes, that's right, one must mature. Two times two — is two, and I can prove that by analogy, the highest of all forms of proof. Listen now. One times one is one, so two times two must be two. For what applies to one must apply to the other.

SCHOOLMASTER: Your proof obeys the law of logic, but your answer is incorrect.

OFFICER: What obeys the law of logic cannot be incorrect. Let us try. One into one goes once, so two into two goes twice.

SCHOOLMASTER: Quite correct, according to your analogy. But then, how much is one times three?

OFFICER: It is three!

SCHOOLMASTER: Then two times three must also be three.

OFFICER [*reflectively*] : No, that can't be right. It can't. Unless — ! [*Sits down in despair.*] No, I'm not mature yet.

SCHOOLMASTER: No, not by a long way.

OFFICER: But how long must I sit here, then?

SCHOOLMASTER: How long here? Do you think that time and space exist? Suppose that time exists, then you must be able to say what time is. What is time?

OFFICER: Time. [*Thinks.*] That I can't say, but I know what it is; therefore I can know how much two times two is without being able to say it. Can you tell me what time is?

SCHOOLMASTER: Of course I can.

OFFICER [*and all the class*] : Say, then.

SCHOOLMASTER: Time? Let me see. [*Stands motionless with his finger to his nose.*] While we talk, time runs. So, time is something that runs while I talk.

A BOY [*gets up*] : You're talking now, and while you talk I run; so I am time. [*Runs out.*]

SCHOOLMASTER: That is perfectly correct, according to the laws of logic.

OFFICER: But then the laws of logic are insane, for Nils who ran away cannot be time.

SCHOOLMASTER: That is also perfectly correct according to the laws of logic, although it is insane.

OFFICER: Then logic is insane.

SCHOOLMASTER: It certainly seems so. But if logic is insane the whole world is insane, and why should I sit here and teach you insanities? Let's find a bottle and have a drink and a swim.

OFFICER: This is *posterius prius,* time reversed. People swim first and drink afterwards. You old duffer!

SCHOOLMASTER: Now, Doctor, don't be impertinent.

OFFICER: Lieutenant, if you don't mind. I am an officer, and I don't understand why I'm sitting here being scolded among schoolboys —

SCHOOLMASTER [*raises a finger*] : We must mature!

QUARANTINE MASTER [*enters*] : The quarantine's starting! The quarantine's starting!

OFFICER: Oh, there you are. Can you imagine, this fellow makes me sit on a school bench, although I'm a Doctor.

QUARANTINE MASTER: Well, why don't you get up and go?

OFFICER: What? Go? I can't do that.

SCHOOLMASTER: I should think not. Just you try.

OFFICER [*to* QUARANTINE MASTER] : Save me! Save me from his eyes!

QUARANTINE MASTER: Come along. Come and help us dance. We must dance before the plague breaks out. We must!

[OFFICER: Will the warship sail then?

QUARANTINE MASTER: It will sail first. And then there'll be tears.

OFFICER: Always tears. When he comes, and when he goes. Let us go.

> They go. The SCHOOLMASTER *silently continues with his lesson.*

> The YOUNG GIRLS, *who were standing at the window of the ballroom, go sadly down to the jetty.*

EDITH, *who has been standing as though petrified at the piano, follows them.*

DAUGHTER: Is no one happy in this Paradise?

OFFICER: Yes, there are two who are newly wed. Listen to them!

A NEWLY MARRIED COUPLE *enter.*

THE HUSBAND [*to his* WIFE] : I am so happy that I should like to die.

WIFE: Why die?

HUSBAND: Because in the midst of my happiness there grows a seed of sadness. It consumes itself like fire. It cannot burn eternally, but must die. This foreboding of the end destroys my happiness at its peak.

WIFE: Let us die together, now.

HUSBAND: Die? Yes! I am frightened of happiness. The betrayer!

They go towards the sea.

DAUGHTER: Life is cruel. Alas for mankind!]

OFFICER: Look at this man! He is the most envied of all who live here. [*The* BLIND MAN *is led in.*] He owns these hundred Italian villas; he owns all these bays, inlets beaches, forests, the fish in the water, the birds in the air and the game in the woods. These thousand people are his tenants and the sun rises over his seas and sinks over his lands —

DAUGHTER: Does he complain too?

OFFICER: Yes, and with reason, for he cannot see.

QUARANTINE MASTER: He is blind.

DAUGHTER: The most envied of all!

OFFICER: Now he wants to see the ship sail out, with his son on board.

BLIND MAN: I do not see, but I hear. I hear how the
anchor claws the sea-bed as when one draws the hook
from a fish and the heart follows up through the
throat. My son, my only child, is going abroad across the
wide sea. I can accompany him only in my thoughts. Now
I hear the cable screech, and — something flutters and
swishes like clothes drying on a line — wet handkerchieves,
perhaps — and I hear how it snuffles and sobs, like
people crying — perhaps the small waves lapping against
the nets, or is it the girls on the shore, the abandoned, the
comfortless? Once I asked a child why the sea was salt,
and the child who had a father at sea replied at once:
"The sea is salt because sailors cry so much." "Why do
sailors cry so much?" "Oh," said the child, "because
they are always having to go away. That's why they
always dry their handkerchieves up on the masts." "Why
do people cry when they are sad?" I asked him. "Oh,"
said the child, "because their eyes have to be washed
sometimes so that they can see more clearly."

[*The ship has set sail and glides away. The* GIRLS *on
the shore wave their handkerchieves and dab away
their tears. On the foremast the signal "Yes" is raised,
a red ball on a white background.* ALICE *waves
joyfully in reply.*]

DAUGHTER [*to* OFFICER]: What does that flag mean?

OFFICER: It means yes. That is the lieutenant's "Yes"
in red, like the red heart's blood drawn on the blue cloth
of heaven.

DAUGHTER: How does "No" look, then?

OFFICER: It is blue, like the spoiled blood in his veins.
But see how happy Alice is!

DAUGHTER: And how Edith is crying.

THE BLIND MAN: Meeting and parting. Parting and
meeting. That is life. I met his mother. And then she
went away. I kept our son. Now he is going.

DAUGHTER: He will surely come back.

BLIND MAN: Who is that? I have heard that voice before, in my dreams, in my youth, when the summer holidays began, in the first year of marriage when my child was born. Every time life smiled, I heard that voice.[like the whisper of a breeze from the south, like the music of harps from above, as I imagine the angels to have welcomed Christ on Christmas night.]

> The ADVOCATE *enters, goes over to the* BLIND MAN *and whispers.*

BLIND MAN: I see.

ADVOCATE: Yes, that's what they've done. [*Goes over to* DAUGHTER.] Now you have seen almost everything, but you haven't experienced the worst thing.

DAUGHTER: What can that be?

ADVOCATE: Repetition. Repeating the pattern. Go back! Learn your lesson again. Come.

DAUGHTER: Where?

ADVOCATE: To your duties.

DAUGHTER: What is duty?

ADVOCATE: It is everything you shrink from. Everything you don't want to do and must. It is to abstain, to renounce, to go without, to leave behind. Everything unpleasant, repulsive, tedious —

DAUGHTER: Are there no pleasant duties?

ADVOCATE: They become pleasant when you have performed them —

DAUGHTER: When they no longer exist. So duty is always unpleasant. What is pleasant?

ADVOCATE: Sin is pleasant.

DAUGHTER: Sin?

ADVOCATE: Which must be punished, yes. If I have had a pleasant day and evening, I suffer the pangs of hell and a sick conscience the next day.

[DAUGHTER: How strange!]

ADVOCATE: Yes, I wake up in the morning with a headache; and then the repetition begins, but a perverse repetition. In such a way that everything that the previous evening was beautiful, pleasant, witty, appears this morning in my memory as ugly, repulsive, stupid. The pleasure rots, and the joy crumbles. What people call success is always the prelude to one's next setback. My successes became my defeat. People have an instinctive fear of other men's successes; they think it unjust that fate should favour one man, so they try to restore the balance by setting rocks in their path. To have talent is dangerous. [One can easily starve to death.] However, go back to your duties, or I shall sue you, and we shall go through all the three courts, one, two, three.

DAUGHTER: Go back? To the iron stove with the pot of cabbage, the child's nappies — ?

ADVOCATE: Yes. Today is washing day. We must wash all the handkerchieves —

DAUGHTER: Oh, must I do all that again?

ADVOCATE: Life consists of doing things again. Look at the schoolmaster in there. Yesterday he got his Doctorate, was crowned with laurel to the sound of cannon, ascended Parnassus and was embraced by the King. And today he starts school again, asks what is two times two, and so he must continue until he dies. [But come back, to your home.

DAUGHTER: I would rather die.

ADVOCATE: Die? One may not. Firstly, because it is dishonourable, so much so that even one's dead body is condemned to insult, and secondly — because it disqualifies us from grace. It is a mortal sin.

DAUGHTER: It is not easy to be a human being.

ALL: True!

DAUGHTER: I shall not return to that dirt and degradation with you. I want to return whence I came, but — first I must open the door that I may know the secret. I want the door to be opened!

ADVOCATE: Then you must retrace your steps, return by the same path, and endure all the horrors of trial, the repetitions, the repetitions, the repetitions —

DAUGHTER: So be it. But first I must go alone into the desert to rediscover myself. We shall meet again. [*To the* POET.] Come with me.

> *From the rear of the stage are heard distant cries of anguish.*

DAUGHTER: What was that?

ADVOCATE: The unhappy people of Foulstrand.

DAUGHTER: Why do they cry so much more piteously today?

ADVOCATE: Because the sun is shining here, because here there is music, dancing and youth. It enhances their suffering.

DAUGHTER: We must free them.

ADVOCATE: Try. Someone tried once, and they hanged Him on a cross.

DAUGHTER: Who did?

ADVOCATE: All right-thinking people.

DAUGHTER: Who are they?

ADVOCATE: Don't you know all right-thinking people? Well, you must meet some.

DAUGHTER: Was it they who refused you your laurel wreath?

ADVOCATE: Yes.

DAUGHTER: Then I do know them.

A shore by the Mediterranean. Downstage left is a white wall, with orange trees in fruit visible over the top of it. Upstage, villas and a terraced casino. Right, a big pile of coal with two wheelbarrows. Upstage right, a glimpse of the blue sea.]
    Two COAL-CARRIERS, *stripped to the waist, their faces, hands and the naked parts of their bodies all black, sit on their wheelbarrows in despair. The* DAUGHTER *and* ADVOCATE *watch them from upstage.*

DAUGHTER: This is Paradise!

FIRST COAL-CARRIER: This is hell!

SECOND COAL-CARRIER: Ninety in the shade.

[FIRST COAL-CARRIER: Shall we have a swim?

SECOND COAL-CARRIER: They'd arrest us. We're not allowed to bathe here.

FIRST COAL-CARRIER: Couldn't we pick some of those oranges?

SECOND COAL-CARRIER: They'd arrest us.]

FIRST COAL-CARRIER: I can't work in this heat. I'm giving it up.

SECOND COAL-CARRIER: Then [they'll arrest you. [*Pause.*] And] you'll have no food.

FIRST COAL-CARRIER: No food? We who work most must eat least; and the rich who do nothing, they get most. [Don't it seem a bit unjust? What do you think, Daughter of God?]

DAUGHTER: Tell me. What have you done that you are so black and your lot so hard?

FIRST COAL-CARRIER: What have we done? We were born of poor and not very good parents. Maybe got punished once or twice.

DAUGHTER: Punished?

FIRST COAL-CARRIER: Yes. The unpunished sit up there in the casino and eat eight courses with wine.

[DAUGHTER [to ADVOCATE]: Can this be true?

ADVOCATE: Broadly speaking, yes.

DAUGHTER: You mean that every human being has at some time done something deserving of imprisonment?

ADVOCATE: Yes.

DAUGHTER: You too?

ADVOCATE: Yes.

DAUGHTER: Is it true that these poor men are not allowed to bathe here?

ADVOCATE: Not even with their clothes on. Only those who have tried to drown themselves escape a fine. And they get a thrashing in the police station.

DAUGHTER: Couldn't they go outside the town and bathe somewhere in the countryside?

ADVOCATE: There isn't any countryside, it's all enclosed.

DAUGHTER: I mean in the common land.

ADVOCATE: There isn't any common land. It's all privately owned.

DAUGHTER: Even the sea?

ADVOCATE: Everything. You can't take a boat out or step ashore without paying for it. Pretty, eh?

DAUGHTER: This is not Paradise.

ADVOCATE: I assure you it isn't.]

DAUGHTER: But why do people do nothing to improve their lot?

ADVOCATE: Oh, some do. But all the improvers end in prison or the madhouse.

DAUGHTER: Who puts them in prison?

ADVOCATE: All right-thinking men, all honourable —

DAUGHTER: Who puts them in the madhouse?

ADVOCATE: Their own despair at the hopelessness of endeavour.

DAUGHTER: Does no one suspect that there may be some secret reason why things must be as they are?

ADVOCATE: Yes, the ones who are well off always think that.

DAUGHTER: That life is good as it is — ?

FIRST COAL-CARRIER: And yet we are society's corner-stone. If you didn't get any coal carried, the stove would go out in the kitchen, the fire in the living-room, the machine would stop in the factory; then the lights would go out in the streets, in the shops, in the home; darkness and cold would descend on you. And so we sweat in hell. What do *you* give us?

[ADVOCATE [*to* DAUGHTER]: Help them. [*Pause.*] I know everyone can't be totally equal, but need they be so unequal?]

    A GENTLEMAN *and his* WIFE *pass across the stage.*

WIFE: Do you feel like playing cards?

GENTLEMAN: No, I must take a walk to be able to eat lunch.

FIRST COAL-CARRIER: To be *able* to eat lunch?

[SECOND COAL-CARRIER: To be *able* — ?

    CHILDREN *enter and scream at the sight of the blackened workers.*

FIRST COAL-CARRIER: They scream at the sight of us. They scream.]

SECOND COAL-CARRIER: God damn it! It's time to bring out the knives and operate on this rotten body.

[FIRST COAL-CARRIER: God damn them! [*Spits.*]

ADVOCATE [*to* DAUGHTER]: Mad, isn't it? People aren't so bad. It's just —

DAUGHTER: Just?

ADVOCATE: The way things are run.]

DAUGHTER [*hides her face as she goes.*]: This is not Paradise.

[COAL-CARRIERS: No. It is hell.]

Fingal's Cave. Long green waves lap slowly in. [*Downstage, a red bell-buoy rocks on the water, though it is not heard except when indicated.*] *Music of the winds. Music of the waves. The* DAUGHTER *and the* POET *enter.*

POET: Where have you led me?

DAUGHTER:
Far from the hum and wailing of mankind,
To the limit of the world, this grotto which
We call the Ear of Indra, since the Lord
Of heaven hearkens here to man's complaints.

[POET: Here? How?

DAUGHTER:
Do you not see this cave is built like a shell?
Do you not know your ear is shaped like a shell?
You do, but have not considered it.
    [*Picks up a shell from the shore.*]
When you were a child, did you never hold
A shell to your ear and hear your heart's blood sigh,

Your thoughts whisper in your brain,
A thousand worn knots snap in the web of your body?
You hear that in this tiny shell. Imagine
How it must sound in this far greater one!]

POET [*listens*] : I hear nothing but the sighing of the winds.

DAUGHTER:
Let me interpret. Listen! The winds' complaint.
 [[*Soft music.*]]
Born in the broad abyss of heaven
We were sent by Indra's lightning
Down to dusty earth.
[The field-mud soiled our feet. We had to endure
The highway's dust, the city smoke, foul breaths,
The stink of food, the fumes of wine. We soared
Over the broad sea to cleanse our lungs,
Shake our wings, wash our feet.] O Indra, Lord
Of Heaven, hear us! Hear us when we sigh!
The earth is not clean. Life is not good.
Men are not evil. Nor are they good.
They live as they can, a day at a time. The sons
Of dust in dust must wander. Born of dust
To dust they return. They were given feet to plod,
Not wings. They grow dusty. Is the fault theirs or
yours?

[POET: I heard this once —

DAUGHTER:
Hush! The winds sing still —
 [*Soft music.*]]
We are winds, the air's children.
We carry the complaints of men.
Did you hear us
In the chimney on autumn evenings,
In the cracks of the stove, the gap in the window
When the rain wept outside on the tiles,
Or on winter evenings in snowy forests?
On the gale-swept sea, did you hear our wails and
weeping

In the sails and in the rigging?
We are the winds, the air's children.
The human breasts through which we passed
Taught us these notes of sorrow.
In sickrooms, battlefields and, especially,
Nurseries where new-born babies wail and cry
At the pain of being born, that is us, us,
The winds that whistle and lament.
[Alas! Alas! Alas!

POET: I seem to have heard this once —

DAUGHTER:
Hush! The waves sing.
  [*Soft music.*]
It is we, we, the waves,
That rock the winds to rest. Green cradles are we.
Wet and salt, we are like tongues of fire
Quenching, burning, cleansing, bathing, begetting,
Conceiving. We, we, the waves,
That rock the winds to rest.]
False waves and faithless, all that is not burned
On earth is drowned — in the waves. See here.
  [[*Points to a heap of flotsam.*]]
See what the sea has plundered and destroyed.
[Only the figureheads of the sunk ships remain,
And their names — *Justice, Friendship, The Golden
Peace, Hope.* That is all that remains of Hope.
Treacherous Hope. Rockweed, rowlocks, bailers —
And see! The lifebuoy. He saved himself but let
The mariners perish.]

POET [*gropes among the flotsam*]:
Here is the name-board of the good ship *Justice,*
That left Fairhaven with the Blind Man's son.
So it has sunk. And there on board
Was Alice's lover, Edith's hopeless love.

DAUGHTER: The Blind Man? Fairhaven? I must have
dreamed that. And Alice's lover and ugly Edith. Foulstrand and the quarantine, sulphur and carbolic, the

ceremony in the church, the Advocate's office, the corridor
and Victoria, the rising castle and the Officer — I
dreamed it all.

POET: I wrote it.

DAUGHTER: Then you know what poetry is —

POET: Then I know what dreaming is. What is poetry?

DAUGHTER: Not reality, but greater than reality. No
dream, but waking dreams.

[POET:
      And mortals think we poets only play,
      Invent and fabricate.

DAUGHTER:
      It is better so, my friend. Else would the earth
      Lie waste for lack of encouragement.
      Men would lie on their backs and look at heaven.
      No man would take his turn with plough or spade,
      Plane or pickaxe.

POET:
      You say that, Indra's Daughter,
      You who are of the gods?

DAUGHTER:
      You are right to reproach me.
      I have been down here too long, bathing like you
      In mud. My thoughts can no longer fly.
      Clay on my wings; earth on my feet; and I — ! [*Raises
        her arms.*]
      I sink, sink. Help me, Father, O God of Heaven!
        [*Silence.*]
      I can no longer hear him. The ether
      No longer bears his speech to my ear's shell.
      The silver thread has snapped. Ah! I am earthbound!

POET: Will you leave us soon?

DAUGHTER: As soon as I have burned this flesh. The
ocean cannot cleanse me. Why do you ask?

POET: Because I have a boon to ask. A petition —

DAUGHTER: What kind of petition?

POET: A petition from mankind to the Master of the world, written by a dreamer.

DAUGHTER: To be presented to him by — ?

POET: By Indra's daughter.

DAUGHTER: Can you speak your poem?

POET: I can.

DAUGHTER: Speak it, then.

POET: Better that you should.

DAUGHTER: Where shall I read it?

POET: In my thoughts. Or here. [*Hands her a scroll of paper.*]

DAUGHTER: Very well. I shall speak it. [*Takes the paper, but speaks the words without looking at it.*]
    "Why were you born in pain?
    Why do you torment your mother,
    Child of man, when you should give her
    The joy of motherhood, the greatest of all joys?
    Why do you awake to life?
    Why do you greet the light
    With a cry of hostility and pain?
    Why don't you smile at life,
    Child of man, since the gift of life
    Is meant to be joy itself?
    Why are we born like the beasts,
    We children of the gods and men?
    Our spirit craved another dress
    Than this of blood and dirt.
    Will God's image change its form?"
    Hush! A creation should not censure its maker.
    No one has yet solved the riddle of life.
    "And so begins our pilgrimage

Over thistles, thorns and stones.
Wherever the track is beaten, it is forbidden.
If you pluck a flower, it belongs to someone else.
If the road is blocked by a field and you must go on,
You tread on others' crops.
Then others tread on yours to even matters.
Every joy that you have brings grief to others,
But your grief brings joy to none.
So grief follows grief,
So goes the journey until your death,
Which other men will harvest."
Son of dust, is it thus you would approach the Highest?

POET:

How shall the son of dust find words
Light, clean and simple enough to rise from earth?
Child of God, will you translate our complaint
Into words more fitting for the ears of the Eternal One?

DAUGHTER: I will.

POET [*indicates the buoy*]: What is that floating there? A buoy?

DAUGHTER: Yes

POET: It is like a lung with a windpipe.

DAUGHTER: It is the watchman of the sea. When danger is near, it sings.

POET: The sea seems to be rising. The waves thunder.

DAUGHTER: It is so.

POET: Ah! What is that? A ship — on the reef!

DAUGHTER: What ship can it be?

POET: I think it is the ghost ship.

DAUGHTER: What is that?

POET: The Flying Dutchman.

DAUGHTER: Him? Why is he punished so cruelly, and why does he never come ashore?

POET: Because he has seven faithless wives.

DAUGHTER: Must he be punished for that?

POET: Yes. All right-thinking people condemned him.

DAUGHTER: Strange world! How can he be freed from his curse, then?

POET: Freed? One bewares of freeing —

DAUGHTER: Why?

POET: Because — no, it isn't the Dutchman! It's an ordinary ship, in distress. Why does the buoy make no sound? Look — the sea is rising, the waves run high. Soon we shall be imprisoned in this cave. Now the ship's bell is ringing. Soon we shall have another figurehead. Cry, buoy, do your work, watchman! [*The buoy sings a quadruple chord in fifths and sixths, like foghorns.*] The crew are waving to us. But we shall perish.

DAUGHTER: Do you not want to be liberated from the flesh?

POET: Of course I do. But not now. And not by water.

THE CREW [*sing, four-part*]: Christ! Have mercy on us!

POET: Now they are crying, and the sea is crying. But no one hears.

CREW [*as before*]: Christ! Have mercy!

DAUGHTER: Who is that going to them out there?

POET: Walking on the water? There is only One Who walks on water. It cannot be Peter, the rock, for he sank like a rock.

A white light is visible out at sea.

CREW: Christ have mercy!

DAUGHTER: Is this He?

POET: It is He, the crucified —

DAUGHTER: Why — tell me, why was He crucified?

POET: Because He wished to liberate mankind.

DAUGHTER: Who — I have forgotten — Who crucified Him?

POET: All right-thinking people.

DAUGHTER: What a strange world!

POET: The sea is rising. Darkness is falling on us. The storm is rising. [*The* CREW *scream.*] The crew is crying with fear, now they see their Saviour. And now — they are jumping overboard, in fear of the Saviour. [*They scream again.*] Now they are crying because they have to die. They cry when they are born and they cry when they die.

>   *The rising waves threaten to drown them in the cave.*

DAUGHTER: If I were sure that it was a ship —

POET: In truth — I do not think it is a ship. It is a two-storeyed house, with trees outside. And a telephone tower — a tower that reaches into the clouds. It is a modern Tower of Babel, sending wires into the sky to communicate with the higher powers —

DAUGHTER: Child of man, human thought needs no metal threads to transmit it. The prayers of the godly instantly penetrate the ether. It is no Tower of Babel. If you would storm heaven, storm it with your prayers.

POET: No. It is no house, no telephone tower. Do you see?

DAUGHTER: What do you see?

POET: I see a snow-covered heath, a training-ground. The winter sun shines behind a church on the hill, and its spire casts its long shadow on the snow. Now a troop of soldiers comes marching. They march on the church, they climb the spire. Now they have reached the cross, but I sense that the first man to tread on the weathercock must die. Now they are nearing it — the corporal at their head — [*Laughs.*] A cloud passes over the heath, it blots out the sun — now everything is gone. The cloud's water quenched the sun's fire. The sun's light created the silhouette of the spire, but the silhouette of the cloud blotted out that of the tower.]

During this time, the scene has changed to the theatre corridor.

DAUGHTER [*to* STAGE-DOOR KEEPER]: Has the Lord Chancellor come yet?

STAGE-DOOR KEEPER: No.

DAUGHTER: Or the Deans?

STAGE-DOOR KEEPER: No.

DAUGHTER: Then call them at once, the door is to be opened.

STAGE-DOOR KEEPER: Is that so important?

DAUGHTER: Yes, it is. People feel that the solution to the riddle of existence lies hidden there. So call the Lord Chancellor and the Deans of the four faculties. [*The* STAGE-DOOR KEEPER *blows a whistle.*] And don't forget the glazier with the diamond, or we can't open it.

The theatre personnel enter left, as at the beginning of the play. Also, upstage, the OFFICER *in morning-coat and top-hat, with a bouquet of roses in his hand radiantly happy.*

OFFICER: Victoria!

STAGE-DOOR KEEPER: She'll be down in a moment.

OFFICER: That is good. The carriage is waiting, the table is laid, the champagne on ice. May I embrace you, madam? [*Embraces the* STAGE-DOOR KEEPER.] Victoria!

A WOMAN'S VOICE [*sings from above*]: I am here!

OFFICER [*begins to wander around*]: Good. I'll wait.

POET: I think I have seen this before.

DAUGHTER: I too.

POET: Perhaps I dreamed it?

DAUGHTER: Or wrote it, perhaps?

POET: Or wrote it.

DAUGHTER: Then you know what poetry is.

POET: Then I know what dreaming is.

DAUGHTER: I feel we stood somewhere else and spoke these words.

POET: Then you can soon work out what reality is.

DAUGHTER: Or dreaming.

POET: Or poetry.

> The LORD CHANCELLOR and the DEANS of the faculties of Theology, Philosophy, Medicine and Law enter.

CHANCELLOR: It's this question of the door, of course. What do you think, Dean of Theology?

[DEAN OF THEOLOGY: I do not think, I believe.

DEAN OF PHILOSOPHY: I rationalize —

DEAN OF MEDICINE: I *know* —

DEAN OF LAW: I doubt, until I have proof, with witnessess.

CHANCELLOR: Now they're going to quarrel again. Dean of Theology, what is your opinion?]

DEAN OF THEOLOGY: I believe that this door should not be opened. It conceals dangerous truths.

DEAN OF MEDICINE: Truth is never dangerous.

DEAN OF PHILOSOPHY: What is truth?

DEAN OF LAW: That which can be proved by two witnesses.

DEAN OF THEOLOGY: Anything can be proved with
two witnesses by a law-twister.

DEAN OF PHILOSOPHY:[Truth is wisdom, and wisdom,
which is knowledge, is philosophy.] Philosophy is the
science of sciences, the knowing of knowledge, and all
other sciences are philosophy's servants.

DEAN OF MEDICINE: [The only science is natural science.]
Philosophy is not a science. It is merely barren speculation.

DEAN OF THEOLOGY: Bravo!

DEAN OF PHILOSOPHY [to DEAN OF THEOLOGY]:
You say bravo. [What are you?] Your sort have always
been the enemies of knowledge. [You are the contradiction
of science, you are ignorance and darkness —]

DEAN OF MEDICINE: Bravo!

DEAN OF THEOLOGY [to DEAN OF MEDICINE]: You
say bravo, you, who can't see further than your magnifying
glass. [You only believe in your treacherous senses, your
eyes which may be long-sighted, short-sighted, blind, dim,
squinting, one-eyed, colour-blind, red-blind, green-blind —]

DEAN OF MEDICINE: Idiot!

DEAN OF THEOLOGY: Donkey! [*They start fighting.*]

[CHANCELLOR: Quiet! No need for the pot to call the
kettle black!

DEAN OF PHILOSOPHY: If I had to choose between
these two, Theology and Medicine, I'd choose — neither
of them.]

DEAN OF LAW: [And if I had to judge between you three,
I'd condemn you all. You can't agree on a single issue,
and have never been able to. But to the point.] My Lord
Chancellor, what is your opinion regarding this door and
whether it should be opened?

CHANCELLOR: Opinion? [I have no opinions. I am merely appointed by the government to see that you don't break each other's arms and legs during your deliberations as how best to educate the young.] No, I beware of opinions. I had some once, but they were immediately refuted. Opinions are always immediately refuted — by one's opponent, of course. Perhaps we may open the door now, even at the risk that it may conceal dangerous truths?

DEAN OF LAW: What is truth? [Where is truth?]

DEAN OF THEOLOGY: I am the truth and the life —

DEAN OF PHILOSOPHY: I am the knowing of knowledge—

DEAN OF MEDICINE: I am the exact science.

[DEAN OF LAW: I doubt —

They start fighting.

DAUGHTER: Teachers of the young, you should be ashamed!

DEAN OF LAW: My Lord Chancellor, representative of the government, supremo of all teachers, punish this woman's presumption! She told you to be ashamed, which is an insult, and in a sneering and ironic tone she called you the teacher of the young, which is a slander.

DAUGHTER: Alas for the young!

DEAN OF LAW: She pities the young; that is the same as accusing us. My Lord Chancellor, punish her presumption.

DAUGHTER: Yes, I accuse you, all of you, of sowing doubt and discord in the minds of the young.

DEAN OF LAW: Listen to her! She arouses doubt of our authority in the minds of the young, and accuses us of sowing it! Is not this a criminal offence? I appeal to all right-minded people.

ALL RIGHT-MINDED PEOPLE: Yes, it is criminal.

DEAN OF LAW: All right-minded people have condemned you. Go in peace with your winnings. Otherwise —

DAUGHTER: My winnings? Otherwise — ? Otherwise what?

DEAN OF LAW: Otherwise you will be stoned.

POET: Or crucified.

DAUGHTER: I will go. Come with me, and you will learn the answer to the riddle.

POET: What riddle?

DAUGHTER: What does he mean by "my winnings"?

POET: Probably nothing. It's what we call talk. He was just talking.

DAUGHTER: But he hurt me deeply by saying it.

POET: That's why he said it. Such are mortals.]

ALL RIGHT-MINDED PEOPLE: Hurrah! The door is opened!

CHANCELLOR: What is hidden behind the door?

GLAZIER: I can't see anything.

CHANCELLOR: He can't see anything, no, very likely! Deans! What is hidden behind the door?

DEAN OF THEOLOGY: Nothing! That is the solution of the riddle of existence. Out of nothing in the beginning God created heaven and earth.

DEAN OF PHILOSOPHY: Nothing will come of nothing.

DEAN OF LAW: I doubt that. A fraud has been committed here. I appeal to all right-thinking persons!

DAUGHTER [to POET]: Who are right-thinking persons?

POET: Yes, answer who can! All right-thinking persons usually means just one person. Today it is I and mine, tomorrow you and yours. One gets nominated, or rather one nominates oneself.

ALL RIGHT-THINKING PEOPLE: We have been betrayed!

CHANCELLOR: Who has betrayed you?

ALL RIGHT-THINKING PEOPLE: Indra's daughter!

CHANCELLOR [to DAUGHTER]: Will you kindly tell us what you meant by opening this door?

[DAUGHTER: No, my good friends. If I told you, you wouldn't believe me.

DEAN OF MEDICINE: But there is nothing there.

DAUGHTER: Exactly. But you don't understand.

DEAN OF MEDICINE: She is talking bosh.

ALL: Bosh!]

DAUGHTER [to POET]: Poor people!

[POET: You are serious?

DAUGHTER: Always serious.]

POET: Even the right-thinkers?

DAUGHTER: They most of all.

[POET: And the four faculties too?

DAUGHTER: Them too, and not least. Four heads, four senses, one body! Who created that monster?]

ALL: She doesn't answer!

CHANCELLOR: Beat her, then.

DAUGHTER: I have answered.

CHANCELLOR: Listen, she is answering.

ALL: Beat her! She's answering!

[DAUGHTER: Whether she answers or does not answer — beat her! Come, seer, and far from here I will explain the riddle to you — but out in the wilderness, where no one will hear us, no one will see us. For —]

ADVOCATE [comes to her and takes her by the arm]: Have you forgotten your duties?

DAUGHTER: Oh, God, no! [But I have higher duties.

ADVOCATE: And your child?

DAUGHTER: My child? What more?]

ADVOCATE: Your child is crying for you.

DAUGHTER: My child! [Alas, I am earthbound.] This barb in my breast. This pain — what is it?

ADVOCATE: Don't you know?

DAUGHTER: No.

ADVOCATE: It is the pangs of conscience.

DAUGHTER: Is this the pangs of conscience?

ADVOCATE: Yes. And they come after [every neglected duty, every joy, even the most innocent. If there are any innocent joys, which is doubtful. And after] every suffering one inflicts on the person one loves.

DAUGHTER: And there is no cure?

ADVOCATE: Yes, but only one. It is, immediately to perform one's duty —

DAUGHTER: You look like a demon when you say that word "duty". [But when one has two duties to fulfil, as I have?

ADVOCATE: Then you must fulfil first one, then the other.

DAUGHTER: The highest first. Then, my dearest, look after my child, and I shall fulfil my duty.]

ADVOCATE: Your child misses you. Can you understand that a human being is suffering for you?

DAUGHTER: Now I feel discord in my soul. I have broken in two. I am tearing apart!

ADVOCATE: That is life's small disharmonies — you see?

DAUGHTER: Ah, how it tears me!

[POET: If you could guess how I have spread grief and destruction through fulfilling my calling — yes, my calling! — which is one's highest duty — would you not be willing to grasp my hand?

DAUGHTER: How do you mean?

POET: I had a father who built his hopes on me as his only son who would carry on his business. I ran away from business school. My father grieved himself to death. My mother wanted me to become a priest. I couldn't. So she rejected me. I had a friend who supported me when things were hardest. This friend then emerged as a tyrant against those for whom I spoke and sang. I had to reject this friend and benefactor to save my soul. Since then I have had no peace. People call me infamous, scum; it doesn't help that my conscience says; "You have done right", because in the next instant that same conscience tells me; "You have done wrong". Such is life.

DAUGHTER: Come with me into the wilderness.

ADVOCATE: Your child!

DAUGHTER [indicating everyone present] : These are my children. Each of them is good when alone, but once they meet they fight and become demons. Goodbye.

Outside the castle. The decor is as at the beginning of the play. But the earth at the foot of the castle is now covered with flowers — blue monk's-hoods. On the top of the castle roof, on the glass lantern, can be seen a chrysanthemum bud ready to open. The castle windows are illuminated by candles. The DAUGHTER *and the* POET.]

DAUGHTER: The moment is nigh when, consumed with fire, I shall rise again into the ether. That is what you call death and which you approach with fear.

POET: Fear of the unknown.

DAUGHTER: Which you know.

POET: Who knows it?

DAUGHTER: Everyone. Why don't you believe your prophets?

[POET: Prophets have always been mistrusted. Why is that? And "if God has spoken, why do people not believe?" His word should be irresistible.

DAUGHTER: Have you always doubted?

POET: No. I have often felt certain. But after a while, my certainty always departed, like a dream when one awakes.

DAUGHTER: It is not easy to be a mortal.

POET: You see it, and admit it?

DAUGHTER: Yes.

POET: Tell me. Was it not Indra who once sent his son to earth to listen to man's complaints?

DAUGHTER: It was. How was he received?

POET: How did he perform his mission — to answer with a question?

DAUGHTER: To answer with another — was not man's condition bettered after his visit? Answer truthfully.

POET: Bettered? Yes, a little. Very little. But instead of asking, will you answer me the riddle?

DAUGHTER: Yes, but to what purpose? You will not believe me.

POET: I will believe you, for I know who you are.

DAUGHTER: Well, I will tell you. In the morning of time, before the sun shone, Brahma, the divine primal force, allowed Maja, the world mother, to induce him to multiply himself. This contact between the divine element and the earthly element was heaven's sin. Thus it is that the world, life, and mankind are but a phantom, an illusion, a dream vision —

POET: My dream!

DAUGHTER: A true dream. But to be liberated from the earthly element, Brahma's descendants crave privation and suffering. So, suffering is the liberator. But this need for suffering conflicts with the human desire for pleasure, and with love. Do you yet understand what love, is, with its sharpest joys inseparable from sharpest suffering, happiest when it is most bitter? Do you yet understand what woman is? Woman, through whom sin and death entered into life?

POET: I understand. And the end?

DAUGHTER: That you know. The strife between the agony of ecstasy and the ecstasy of agony. The pangs of the penitent and the joys of voluptuousness.

POET: Strife, then?

DAUGHTER: Strife between opposites generates power, just as fire and water generate steam.

POET: But peace? Rest?

DAUGHTER: Hush! You must ask no more and I may not reply.] The altar is already decked for the sacrifice. The flowers stand guard — the candles are lit — the white sheets cover the windows — the fir-twigs lie in the porch —

[POET: You say this as calmly as though suffering did not exist for you.

DAUGHTER: Not exist? I have suffered all your torments a hundredfold, for my perceptions were finer —

POET: Tell me your sorrows.

DAUGHTER: Poet, if you could tell me yours, and there was a word for every grief, could your words ever match the truth?

POET: No, you are right. To myself, I always seemed like a deaf-mute, and when the mob listened in wonder to my

song it sounded to me like discord. That is why I was
always ashamed when men praised me.

DAUGHTER: And you want *me* to? Look me in the eyes.

POET: I cannot endure your glance.

DAUGHTER: Then how could you endure my words, if I
spoke my tongue?]

POET: Tell me before you go. What did you suffer from
most down here?

DAUGHTER: From — being human. From feeling my sight
weakened by eyes, my hearing muffled by ears, and my
thought, my light, airy thought, cabined by the windings
of a brain. [You have seen a brain — what twistings, what
rat-holes!

POET: Yes. And that is why all right-thinking people
think twistedly.

DAUGHTER: Cruel, always cruel. But you all are.

POET: How can one be otherwise?]

DAUGHTER: Now at last I shake the dust from my feet —
the earth, the clay. [*Takes off her shoes and puts them in
the fire.*]

STAGE-DOOR KEEPER [*enters and puts her shawl in the
fire*]: Perhaps I may burn up my shawl too? [[*Goes.*]]

OFFICER [*enters*]: And I my roses, which have nothing
left but thorns. [[*Goes.*]]

BILL-POSTER [*enters*]: My posters can go, but my fishing-
net, never. [[*Goes.*]]

GLAZIER [*enters*]: My diamond, that opened the door.
Farewell. [[*Goes.*]]

ADVOCATE [*enters*]: The great lawsuit of the Pope's
beard, or the depletion of the sources of the Ganges.
[[*Goes.*]]

QUARANTINE MASTER [*enters*] : A mite, the black mask which made me a blackamoor against my will. [[*Goes.*]]

VICTORIA [*enters*] : My beauty, my sorrow. [[*Goes.*]]

EDITH [*enters*] : My ugliness, my sorrow. [[*Goes.*]]

> Enter the DANDY *in his wheelchair, with the* COQUETTE *and her* "FRIEND".

THE DANDY: Hurry, hurry, life is short! [[*Goes out with the others.*]]

POET: I have read that when life approaches its end, everything and everyone rushes past in a single stream. Is this the end?

DAUGHTER: Yes, it is mine. Goodbye.

POET: Say something to us.

DAUGHTER: No, I can't. Do you think your words could express our thoughts?

[DEAN OF THEOLOGY [*enters, in a rage*] : I am rejected by God, I am persecuted by men, rejected by the government and mocked by my fellows. How can I believe, when no one else believes? How shall I defend a God who will not defend His own? It's all bosh! [*Throws a book on the fire and goes.*]

POET [*takes the book from the fire*] : Do you know what this is? A book of martyrs, a calendar with a martyr for every day in the year.

DAUGHTER: Martyr?

POET: Yes, one who has been tortured and killed for his beliefs. Tell me why! Do you believe that all who are tortured suffer, that all who are killed feel pain? Suffering is the release, and death the liberator.]

KRISTIN [*enters with strips of paper*] : I'm pasting, I'm pasting, till there's nothing left to paste.

POET: And if heaven itself cracked, you would try to paste that together. Go!

KRISTIN: Have you no double windows in your castle then?

POET: No, Kristin, not there.

KRISTIN [*goes*] : Then I'll go, then.

DAUGHTER:
>Our parting is at hand, the end approaches.
>Farewell, you child of man, you dreamer,
>You poet who best knowest how to live.
>Hovering on wings above the earth
>You plunge occasionally into the mire
>To shake it from your feet, not to stick fast.
>[Now I am going —] In the moment of goodbye,
>When one must be parted from a friend, a place,
>How suddenly great the loss of what one loved,
>Regret for what one shattered.
>[Oh, now I feel the agony of existence!
>So this is to be mortal.]
>One even misses what one did not value.
>One even regrets crimes one did not commit.
>One wants to go, and one wants to stay.
>The twin halves of the heart are wrenched asunder
>And one is torn as between raging horses
>Of contradictions, irresolution, discord .
>[Farewell. Tell your brothers and sisters I shall
>   remember them
>In the place to which I return, and in your name
>Shall set their griefs before the throne of God.
>Farewell!

She goes into the castle. Music. The backcloth is illuminated by the burning castle, showing a wall of human faces, enquiring, grieving, despairing. As the castle burns, the bud on the roof bursts open into a giant chrysanthemum.]

APPENDIX

THE following professional productions of the plays in this volume have taken place in London.

TO DAMASCUS

Westminster Theatre, 2 May 1937 (Stage Society)

(Part I only)

STRANGER	Francis James
LADY	Wanda Rotha
BEGGAR	Alexander Sarner
FIRST MOURNER	George Cormack
SECOND MOURNER	Kenneth Bell
THIRD MOURNER	Peter Bennett
FOURTH MOURNER	Bryan Sears
FIFTH MOURNER	Michael Boyle
SIXTH MOURNER	Stephen Patrick
LANDLORD	Stephen Jack
DOCTOR	Neil Porter
HIS SISTER	Olga Martin
CAESAR	Peter Land
A WAITER	Peter Bennett
AN OLD MAN	A. Corney Grain
A MOTHER	Frances Waring
THE SMITH	Norman Thomas
MILLER'S WIFE	Julia Sandham
ABBESS	Natalie Moya
CONFESSOR	Tristan Rawson

Directed by *Carl H. Jaffé*

B.B.C. Third Programme, 14, 15 and 19 December 1953
(Sound radio)

THE UNKNOWN MAN	Valentine Dyall
LADY	Catherine Salkeld
CONFESSOR	Howieson Cuff
LANDLORD	Cyril Shaps
DOCTOR	John Glen
HIS SISTER	Molly Lumley
CAESAR	Anthony Jacobs
MOTHER	Ella Milne
OLD MAN	Stephen Jack
ABBESS	Molly Rankin
FIRST WOMAN	Mary Wimbush
SECOND WOMAN	Betty Baskcomb
WAITRESS	Sulwen Morgan
MAID	Elizabeth London
POLICEMAN	Michael O'Halloran
MIDWIFE	Hester Paton Brown
SYLVIA	Jacqueline Lacey
HOSTESS	Natalie Kent
ERIK	John Scott
TEMPTER	Malcolm Hayes
SHERIFF	T. St John Barry
A FATHER	John Turnbull
MAJA	Nancy Nevinson
THE WIFE	Catherine Nangle
PRIOR	Dennis Arundell
FATHER ISIDOR	John Glen
FATHER CLEMENT	John Gwillim
FATHER MELCHIOR	Arthur Lawrence
EVE	Monica Grey
BAILIFF	Michael O'Halloran

Other parts were played by Evelyn Moore, Alan Reid, Brian Hayes, Reginald Hearne, Catherine Fleming and Janet Burnell.

Directed by *Peter Watts*

B.B.C. Radio Three, 4 and 11 July 1971 (Sound radio)

NARRATOR	Martin Friend
STRANGER	Stephen Murray
LADY	Zena Walker
BEGGAR	Edward Kelsey
A MOURNER	Patrick Tull
LANDLORD	Antony Higginson
DOCTOR	John Rye
CAESAR	Brian Hewlett
HOTEL PORTER	Patrick Tull
MOTHER	Eva Stuart
GRANDFATHER	John Ruddock
ABBESS	Sheila Grant
CONFESSOR	Edward Kelsey
NURSE	Katherine Parr
PROFESSOR	John Ruddock
WHORE	Olwen Griffiths
BARMAID	Katherine Parr
POLICEMAN	Trevor Martin
SYLVIA	Elizabeth Proud
TEMPTER	John Gabriel
EVE	Elizabeth Proud
PRIOR	Trevor Martin
FATHER MELCHIOR	John Ruddock

Directed by *Charles Lefeaux*

EASTER

Bedford Hall, Chelsea, 19 March 1922

MRS HEYST	Catherine Lewis
ELIS	Cyril Stanislaw
ELEONORA	Pax Robertson
CHRISTINA	Catherine Robertson

BENJAMIN   Bruce Moir
LINDKVIST   Gerald Jerome

Directed by *Pax Robertson*

Arts Theatre, 10 October 1928

MRS HEYST   Marie Wright
ELIS   Colin Keith-Johnston
ELEONORA   Gwen Ffragcon-Davies
CHRISTINA   Peggy Ashcroft
BENJAMIN   Charles Hickman
LINDKVIST   George Bealby

Directed by *Allan Wade*

Grafton Theatre, 28 May 1933 (The Scandinavian Theatre)

MRS HEYST   Gertrud Sterroll
ELIS   G. R. Schjelderup
ELEONORA   Natalie Moya
CHRISTINA   Wendla Bang
BENJAMIN   Frederick Peisley
LINDKVIST   Alexander Sarner

Directed by *G. R. Schjelderup*

B.B.C. National Regional Service, 27 March 1938 (Sound radio)

MRS HEYST   Marda Vanne
ELIS   Marius Goring
ELEONORA   Gwen Ffragcon-Davies

CHRISTINA	Lila Maravan
BENJAMIN	Noel Dryden
LINDKVIST	Robert Farquharson

Directed by *Peter Cresswell*

Gateway Theatre, 30 March 1945

MRS HEYST	Nellie Robson
ELIS	Richmond Nairne
ELEONORA	Josephine Stuart
CHRISTINA	Mavis Walker
BENJAMIN	Kenneth Morgan
LINDKVIST	Esmé Percy

Directed by *Basil Ashmore*

B.B.C. Home Service, 29 March 1948 (Sound radio)

MRS HEYST	Louise Hampton
ELIS	Valentine Dyall
ELEONORA	Cherry Cottrell
CHRISTINA	Molly Rankin
BENJAMIN	David Spenser
LINDKVIST	Allan Jeayes

Directed by *Peter Watts*

B.B.C. Third Programme, 23 May 1954 (Sound radio)

MRS HEYST	Betty Hardy
ELIS	Anthony Jacobs
ELEONORA	Elizabeth Henson

CHRISTINA	Margaret Ward
BENJAMIN	Henry Davies
LINDKVIST	Edgar Norfolk

Directed by *Wilfred Grantham*

B.B.C. Third Programme, 27 May 1960 (Sound radio)

MRS HEYST	Dorothy Holmes-Gore
ELIS	Valentine Dyall
ELEONORA	Beryl Calder
CHRISTINA	Molly Rankin
BENJAMIN	Nicholas Edmett
LINDKVIST	Eric Anderson
VOICE	Freda Dowie

Directed by *Peter Watts*

Hampstead Theatre Club, 18 October 1965

MRS HEYST	Hazel Hughes
ELIS	Victor Henry
ELEONORA	Meg Wynn Owen
CHRISTINA	Pauline Wynn
BENJAMIN	Gareth Forwood
LINDKVIST	Sydney Bromley

Directed by *Desmond O'Donovan*

THE DANCE OF DEATH

*St George's Hall, 23 November 1924 (Part I) and 21
December 1924 (Part II) (Sunday Players)*

EDGAR	George Merritt
ALICE	Sybil Arundale
KURT	Paul Smythe
OLD WOMAN	Leila Verney
JENNY	Sylvia Willoughby
SENTRY	Hugh Johnson
JUDITH	Sylvia Willoughby
ALLAN	Colin Keith-Johnston
LIEUTENANT	Keith Pyott

Directed by *George Merritt*, assisted by *Bror Centerwall*

Gate Theatre, 30 November 1925

(Part I only)

EDGAR	George Merritt
ALICE	Molly Veness
KURT	Peter Godfrey

Directed by *Peter Godfrey*

This production was revived with the same cast on 10 May 1926

Apollo Theatre, 16 January 1928

(Part I only)

EDGAR	Robert Loraine
ALICE	Miriam Lewes
KURT	Edmund Gwenn
JENNY	Edith Martyn
OLD WOMAN	Wilfred Fletcher
SENTRY	G. E. Puttergill

Directed by *Robert Loraine*

B.B.C. Third Programme, 12 April 1953 (Sound radio)

EDGAR	Michael Hordern
ALICE	Beatrix Lehmann
KURT	Cyril Luckham
JENNY	Rosamund Greenwood
OLD WOMAN	Hester Paton Brown
JUDITH	Marcia Ashton
ALLAN	Michael Bates
LIEUTENANT	Raymond Mason

Directed by *Donald McWhinnie*

B.B.C. Home Service, 30 January 1961 (Sound radio)

EDGAR	Donald Wolfit
ALICE	Margaret Leighton
KURT	Sebastian Shaw
JUDITH	Catherine Dolan
ALLAN	Nicholas Edmett
LIEUTENANT	John Bryning

Directed by *H. B. Fortuin*

Associated Television, 7 March 1966

EDGAR	Paul Scofield
ALICE	Mai Zetterling
KURT	Alan Dobie
JUDITH	Judy Geeson
ALLAN	Barry Justice
LIEUTENANT	Gary Hope
DOCTOR	Colin Cunningham
COLONEL	Harry R. Fripp
HIS WIFE	Ann Tirard

Directed by *John Moxey*

National Theatre at the Old Vic, 21 February 1967

EDGAR	Laurence Olivier
ALICE	Geraldine McEwan
KURT	Robert Stephens
JENNY	Carolyn Jones
OLD WOMAN	Jeanne Watts
JUDITH	Janina Faye
ALLAN	Malcolm Reynolds
LIEUTENANT	Peter Penry-Jones
CORPORAL	Lewis Jones
SENTRIES	Anthony Hopkins, William Hoyland, Frederick Pyne, Richard Warwick.

Directed by *Glen Byam Shaw*

B.B.C. Radio Four, 5 June 1972 (Sound radio)

(Part I only)

EDGAR	John Moffatt
ALICE	Jill Bennett
KURT	Alan Rowe
JENNY	Helen Worth

Directed by *Christopher Venning*

THE VIRGIN BRIDE

For cast, see p. 472.
B.B.C. Radio Three, 24 November 1974 (Sound radio)

A DREAM PLAY

Grafton Theatre, 2 April 1933 (The Scandinavian Theatre)

(For a single performance)

INDRA	G. R. Schjelderup
INDRA'S DAUGHTER	Natalie Moya
GLAZIER	Frederick Piper
OFFICER	Donald Wolfit
FATHER	Don Gemmel
MOTHER	Gertrud Sterroll
LINA	Celia Clement
PORTRESS	Lilian Mowbrey
BILL-STRIKER (*sic*)	Richard Goolden
SINGER	Stella Wyngate
BALLET GIRL	Celia Clement
CHORUS SINGER	Taylor Reed
PROMPTER	John Fay Smith
POLICEMAN	Donald Mickerson
LAWYER	George Merritt
DEAN OF PHILOSOPHY	Roy Graham
DEAN OF THEOLOGY	Ross Jefferson
DEAN OF MEDICINE	John Fay Smith
DEAN OF JURISPRUDENCE	Don Gemmel
KRISTIN	Celia Clement
MASTER OF QUARANTINE	Henry Wolston
DON JUAN	John Fay Smith
COQUETTE OF 60	Lilian Mowbrey
POET	Wilfred Grantham
HE	Taylor Reed
SHE	Joy Farjeon
PENSIONER	Richard Goolden
SERVANT GIRL	Zena Harcourt
EDITH	Barbara Allen
SCHOOLMASTER	Frederick Piper
A BOY	Bobby Reith
THE HUSBAND	Geoffrey Brigten

THE WIFE	Stella Wyngate
BLIND MAN	Roy Graham

Directed by *G. R. Schjelderup*

B.B.C. Home Service, 22 November 1948 (Sound radio)

DREAMER	David Reed
INDRA	Raf de la Torre
INDRA'S DAUGHTER	Molly Rankin
GLAZIER	Eric Lugg
OFFICER	
LAWYER	Valentine Dyall
POET	
FATHER	Hugh Fawkus
MOTHER	Nell Ballantyne
STAGE-DOOR KEEPER	Elsa Palmer
BILL-POSTER	Charles Leno
KRISTIN	Beryl Calder
QUARANTINE MASTER	Tom Clarkson
SCHOOLMASTER	Franklyn Bellamy
BLIND MAN	John Turnbull
CHANCELLOR	Peter Cresswell
DEAN OF PHILOSOPHY	Arthur Ridley
DEAN OF THEOLOGY	Stephen Jack
DEAN OF MEDICINE	Malcolm Hayes
DEAN OF JURISPRUDENCE	Cyril Gardiner

Other parts were played by Frank Atkinson, Joan Clement Scott, David Enders, Joan Hart, Anthony Jacobs, Molly Lumley, Julian Orde, Lydia Sherwood, Gwen Vaughan and Ella Milne.

Directed by *Peter Watts*

London has also seen two foreign productions of A DREAM PLAY; by the Theater am Kurfurstendamm of Berlin (directed by Oscar Fritz Schuh) at Sadlers Wells Theatre on 21 June 1957, and by the Royal Theatre of Stockholm (directed by Ingmar Bergman) at the Aldwych Theatre on 19 April 1971.